TRIBE of MENTORS

TRIBE of MENTORS

SHORT LIFE ADVICE
FROM THE BEST IN THE WORLD

TIMOTHY FERRISS

Vermilion
LONDON

1 3 5 7 9 10 8 6 4 2

Vermilion, an imprint of Ebury Publishing,
20 Vauxhall Bridge Road,
London SW1V 2SA

Vermilion is part of the Penguin Random House group of companies
whose addresses can be found at global.penguinrandomhouse.com

Penguin
Random House
UK

First published in the United Kingdom by Vermilion in 2017
Published by special arrangement with Houghton Mifflin
Harcourt Publishing Company

www.penguin.co.uk

A CIP catalogue record for this book is available from the British Library

ISBN 9781785041853

Printed and bound in Great Britain by Clays Ltd, St Ives PLC

MIX
Paper from
responsible sources
FSC
www.fsc.org
FSC® C018179

Penguin Random House is committed to a sustainable future
for our business, our readers and our planet. This book is made
from Forest Stewardship Council® certified paper.

PUBLISHER'S LEGAL DISCLAIMER

This book presents a wide range of opinions about a variety of topics related to health and well-being, including certain ideas, treatments, and procedures that may be hazardous or illegal if undertaken without proper medical supervision. These opinions reflect the research and ideas of the author or those whose ideas the author presents, but are not intended to substitute for the services of a trained health care practitioner. Consult with your health care practitioner before engaging in any diet, drug, or exercise regimen. The author and the publisher disclaim responsibility for any adverse effects resulting directly or indirectly from information contained in this book.

TIM'S DISCLAIMER

Please don't do anything stupid and kill yourself. It would make us both quite unhappy. Consult a doctor, lawyer, and common-sense specialist before doing anything in this book.

To all of my "companions on the path," may you be a force for good in this world and see the same in yourselves.

And remember:

"What you seek is seeking you."

— RUMI

CONTENTS

INTRODUCTION

"The only true voyage would be not to travel through a hundred different lands with the same pair of eyes, but to see the same land through a hundred different pairs of eyes."

— MARCEL PROUST

"Albert grunted. 'Do you know what happens to lads who ask too many questions?'

Mort thought for a moment.

'No,' he said eventually, 'what?'

There was silence.

Then Albert straightened up and said, 'Damned if I know. Probably they get answers, and serve 'em right.'"

—TERRY PRATCHETT, *MORT*

To explain *why* I wrote this book, I really need to start with *when*.

Two thousand seventeen was an unusual year for me. The first six months were a slow simmer, and then, within a matter of weeks, I turned 40, my first book (*The 4-Hour Workweek*) had its tenth anniversary, several people in my circle of friends died, and I stepped onstage to explain how I narrowly avoided committing suicide in college.*

Truth be told, I never thought I'd make it to 40. My first book was rejected 27 times by publishers. The things that worked out weren't *supposed* to work, so I realized on my birthday: I had no plan for after 40.

As often happens at forks in the path—college graduation, quarter-life crisis, midlife crisis, kids leaving home, retirement—questions started to bubble to the surface.

Were my goals my own, or simply what I thought I should want?

How much of life had I missed from underplanning or overplanning?

How could I be kinder to myself?

How could I better say no to the noise to better say yes to the adventures I craved?

How could I best reassess my life, my priorities, my view of the world, my place in the world, and my trajectory through the world?

So many things! All the things!

One morning, I wrote down the questions as they came, hoping for a glimmer of clarity. Instead, I felt a wave of anxiety. The list was overwhelming. Noticing that I was holding my breath, I paused and took my eyes off the paper. Then, I did what I often do—whether considering a business decision, personal relationship, or otherwise—I asked myself the one question that helps answer many others . . .

What would this look like if it were easy?

"This" could be anything. That morning, it was answering a laundry list of big questions.

What would this look like if it were easy? is such a lovely and deceptively leveraged question. It's easy to convince yourself that things need to be hard, that if you're not redlining, you're not trying hard enough. This

* tim.blog/ted

leads us to look for paths of most resistance, often creating unnecessary hardship in the process.

But what happens if we frame things in terms of elegance instead of strain? Sometimes, we find incredible results with ease instead of stress. Sometimes, we "solve" the problem by completely reframing it.

And that morning, by journaling on this question—*What would this look like if it were easy?*—in longhand, an idea presented itself. Ninety-nine percent of the page was useless, but there was one seed of a possibility ...

What if I assembled a tribe of mentors to help me?

More specifically, what if I asked 100+ brilliant people the very questions I want to answer for myself? Or somehow got them to guide me in the right direction?

Would it work? I had no idea, but I did know one thing: If the easy approach failed, the unending-labor-in-the-salt-mines approach was always waiting in the wings. Pain is never out of season if you go shopping for it.

So, why not spend a week test-driving the path of least resistance?

And so it began. First, I scribbled down a list of dream interviewees, which started as one page and quickly became ten. It had to be a list with no limitations: no one too big, too out-of-reach, or too hard to find. Could I get the Dalai Lama? The incredible Temple Grandin? My personal white whale, author Neil Gaiman? Or Ayaan Hirsi Ali? I wrote out the most ambitious, eclectic, unusual list possible. Next, I needed to create an incentive to encourage people to respond, so I worked on a book deal. "Be in my book" might work. From the outset, I told the publisher that it also might *not* work, and that I'd return the advance if so.

Then, I started pitching my little heart out.

I sent an identical set of 11 questions to some of the most successful, wildly varied, and well-known people on the planet with "Answer your favorite 3 to 5 questions ... or more, if the spirit moves you."

After hitting "send" dozens of times, I clasped my hands to my excited writer's chest with bated breath, to which the universe replied with ... silence. Crickets.

For 12 to 24 hours, nothing. Not a creature was stirring, not even a mouse. And then, there was a faint trickle through the ether. A whisper of curiosity and a handful of clarifying questions. Some polite declines followed, and then came the torrent.

Nearly all of the people I reached out to are busy beyond belief, and I expected I would get short, rushed responses from a few of them at best. What I got back instead were some of the most thoughtful answers I'd ever received, whether on paper, in person, or otherwise. In the end, there were more than 100 respondents.

Granted, the "easy" path took thousands of back-and-forth emails and Twitter direct messages, hundreds of phone calls, many marathons at a treadmill desk, and more than a few bottles of wine during late-night writing sessions, but . . . it worked. Did it *always* work? No. I didn't get the Dalai Lama (this time), and at least half of the people on my list didn't respond or declined the invitation. But it worked *enough* to matter, and that's what matters.

In cases where the outreach worked, the questions did the heavy lifting.

Eight of the questions were fine-tuned "rapid-fire" questions from my podcast, *The Tim Ferriss Show,* the first business-interview podcast to pass 200 million downloads. These questions have been refined over more than 300 interviews with guests such as actor/musician Jamie Foxx, General Stanley McChrystal, and writer Maria Popova. I knew that these questions worked, that interviewees generally liked them, and that they could help me in my own life.

The remaining three questions were new additions that I hoped would solve my most chronic problems. Before taking them into the wild, I tested, vetted, and wordsmithed them with friends who are world-class performers in their own right.

The older I get, the more time I spend—as a percentage of each day—on crafting better questions. In my experience, going from 1x to 10x, from 10x to 100x, and from 100x to (when Lady Luck really smiles) 1000x returns in various areas has been a product of better questions. John Dewey's dictum that "a problem well put is half-solved" applies.

Life punishes the vague wish and rewards the specific ask. After all, conscious thinking is largely asking and answering questions in your own head. If you want confusion and heartache, ask vague questions. If you want uncommon clarity and results, ask uncommonly clear questions.

Fortunately, this is a skill you can develop. No book can give you all of the answers, but this book can train you to ask better questions. Milan Kundera, author of *The Unbearable Lightness of Being,* has said that "The stupidity of people comes from having an answer for everything. The wisdom of the novel comes from having a question for everything." Substitute "master learner" for "novel," and you have my philosophy of life. Often, all that stands between you and what you want is a better set of questions.

The 11 questions I chose for this book are listed below. It's important to read the full questions and explanations, as I shorten them throughout the rest of the book. Special thanks to Brian Koppelman, Amelia Boone, Chase Jarvis, Naval Ravikant, and others for their hugely helpful feedback.

First, let us take a quick pass of the 11 questions. Some of them might seem trite or useless at first glance. . . . But lo! Things are not always what they appear.

1. What is the book (or books) you've given most as a gift, and why? Or what are one to three books that have greatly influenced your life?

2. What purchase of $100 or less has most positively impacted your life in the last six months (or in recent memory)? My readers love specifics like brand and model, where you found it, etc.

3. How has a failure, or apparent failure, set you up for later success? Do you have a "favorite failure" of yours?

4. If you could have a gigantic billboard anywhere with anything on it—metaphorically speaking, getting a message out to millions or billions—what would it say and why? It could be a few words or a paragraph. (If helpful, it can be someone else's quote: Are there any quotes you think of often or live your life by?)

5. What is one of the best or most worthwhile investments you've ever made? (Could be an investment of money, time, energy, etc.)

6. What is an unusual habit or an absurd thing that you love?

7. In the last five years, what new belief, behavior, or habit has most improved your life?

8. What advice would you give to a smart, driven college student about to enter the "real world"? What advice should they ignore?

9. What are bad recommendations you hear in your profession or area of expertise?

10. In the last five years, what have you become better at saying no to (distractions, invitations, etc.)? What new realizations and/or approaches helped? Any other tips?

11. When you feel overwhelmed or unfocused, or have lost your focus temporarily, what do you do? (If helpful: What questions do you ask yourself?)

Now, let's take a look at each, and I'll explain why they appear to work. You might ask, "Why should I care? I'm not an interviewer." To that, my response is simple: If you want to build (or foster) a world-class network, you need to interact in a way that earns it. All of these points will help.

For instance, I spent weeks testing the order of questions for optimal responses. To me, proper sequencing is the secret sauce, whether you're trying to learn a new language in 8 to 12 weeks,* overcome a lifelong fear of swimming,† or pick the brain of a potential mentor over coffee. Good questions in the wrong order get bad responses. Conversely, you can punch well above your weight class by thinking about sequencing, as most people don't.

Example: the "billboard" question is one of my podcast listener and guest favorites, but it's heavy. It stumps or intimidates a lot of people. I didn't want to scare busy people off, who might opt out with a quick, "Sorry, Tim. I just don't have bandwidth for this right now." So, what to do? Easy: let them warm up with lightweight questions (e.g., Most gifted books, purchase of <$100), which are less abstract and more concrete.

* See *The 4-Hour Chef*
† tim.blog/swimming

My explanations get shorter toward the end, as many of the points carry over or apply to all questions.

1. What is the book (or books) you've given most as a gift, and why? Or what are one to three books that have greatly influenced your life?

"What's your favorite book?" seems like a good question. So innocent, so simple. In practice, it's terrible. The people I interview have read hundreds or thousands of books, so it's a labor-intensive question for them, and they rightly worry about picking a "favorite," which then gets quoted and put in articles, Wikipedia, etc. "Most gifted" is lower risk, an easier search query (easier to recall), and implies benefits for a broader spectrum of people, which the idiosyncratic "favorite" does not.

For the curious and impatient among you, here are a few books (of many) that came up a lot:

> *Man's Search for Meaning* by Viktor E. Frankl
> *The Rational Optimist* by Matt Ridley
> *The Better Angels of Our Nature* by Steven Pinker
> *Sapiens* by Yuval Noah Harari
> *Poor Charlie's Almanack* by Charlie Munger

If you'd like to see *all* of the recommended books in one place, including a list of the top 20 most recommended from this book and *Tools of Titans*, you can find all the goodies at tim.blog/booklist

2. What purchase of $100 or less has most positively impacted your life in the last six months (or in recent memory)? My fans love specifics like brand and model, where you found it, etc.

This might seem like a throwaway, but it isn't. It provides an easy entry point for busy interviewees while providing readers with something immediately actionable. The deeper questions elicit more profound answers, but profundity is the fiber of knowledge—it requires intensive digestion. To keep marching forward in the meanwhile, humans (yours truly included) need short-term rewards. In this book, I accomplish that with questions that provide tangible, easy, and often fun answers—Scooby snacks for your hard-working soul. To get the heavier lifting done, these breathers are important.

3. How has a failure, or apparent failure, set you up for later success? Do you have a "favorite failure" of yours?

This one is particularly important to me. As I wrote in *Tools of Titans*:

> The superheroes you have in your mind (idols, icons, elite athletes, billionaires, etc.) are nearly all walking flaws who've maximized one or two strengths. Humans are imperfect creatures. You don't "succeed" because you have no weaknesses; you succeed because you find your unique strengths and focus on developing habits around them. . . . Everyone is fighting a battle [and has fought battles] you know nothing about. The heroes in this book are no different. Everyone struggles.

4. If you could have one gigantic billboard anywhere with anything on it — metaphorically speaking, getting a message out to millions or billions — what would it say and why? It could be a few words or a paragraph. (If helpful, it can be someone else's quote: Are there any quotes you think of often or live your life by?)

Self-explanatory, so I'll skip the commentary. For would-be interviewers, though, the "If helpful . . ." portion is often critical for getting good answers.

5. What is one of the best or most worthwhile investments you've ever made? (Could be an investment of money, time, energy, etc.)

This is also self-explanatory . . . or so it seems. With questions like this and the next, I've found it productive to give interviewees a real-world answer. In a live interview, it buys them time to think, and in text, it gives them a template. For this question, for instance, I gave everyone the following:

> SAMPLE ANSWER from Amelia Boone, one of the world's top endurance athletes, sponsored by big brands and 4x world champion in obstacle course racing (OCR):
> "In 2011, I shelled out $450 to participate in the first World's Toughest Mudder, a brand new 24-hour obstacle race. Saddled

with law school debt, it was a big expenditure for me, and I had no business thinking I could even complete the race, let alone compete in it. But I ended up being one of 11 finishers (out of 1,000 participants) of that race, and it altered the course of my life, leading to my career in obstacle racing and multiple world championships. Had I not plunked down the cash for that entry fee, none of that would have happened."

6. What is an unusual habit or an absurd thing that you love?

I was first asked this when interviewed by my friend Chris Young, scientist, co-author of *Modernist Cuisine,* and CEO of ChefSteps (search "Joule sous vide"). Before responding, and while sitting onstage at the Town Hall in Seattle, I said, "Oooooh . . . that's a good question. I'm going to steal that." And I did. This question has deeper implications than you might expect. Answers prove a number of helpful things: 1) Everyone is crazy, so you're not alone. 2) If you want more OCD-like behaviors, my interviewees are happy to help, and 3) Corollary to #1: "normal" people are just crazy people you don't know well enough. If you think you're uniquely neurotic, I hate to deliver the news, but every human is Woody Allen in some part of life. Here's the sample answer I gave for this question, taken from a live interview and slightly edited for text:

> SAMPLE ANSWER from Cheryl Strayed, best-selling author of *Wild* (made into a feature film with Reese Witherspoon): "Here's my whole theory of the sandwich . . . every bite should be as much like the previous bite as possible. Do you follow? [If] there's a clump of tomatoes here, but then there's hummus — everything has to be as uniform as possible. So any sandwich I'm ever given, I open it up and I immediately completely rearrange the sandwich."

7. In the last five years, what new belief, behavior, or habit has most improved your life?

This is short, effective, and not particularly nuanced. It has particular application to my midlife reassessment. I'm surprised I don't hear questions like this more often.

8. What advice would you give to a smart, driven college student about to enter the "real world"? What advice should they ignore?

The second "ignore" sub-question is essential. We're prone to asking "What should I do?" but less prone to asking "What shouldn't I do?" Since what we *don't* do determines what we *can* do, I like asking about not-to-do lists.

9. What are bad recommendations you hear in your profession or area of expertise?

A close cousin of the previous question. Many problems of "focusing" are best solved by defining what to ignore.

10. In the last five years, what have you become better at saying no to (distractions, invitations, etc.)? What new realizations and/or approaches helped? Any other tips?

Saying yes is easy. Saying no is hard. I wanted help with the latter, as did many people in the book, and some answers really delivered the goods.

11. When you feel overwhelmed or unfocused or have lost your focus temporarily, what do you do? (If helpful: What questions do you ask yourself?)

If your mind is "beach balling" (nerdy Mac reference to when a computer freezes), nothing else matters much until that is resolved. Once again, the secondary "if helpful" question is often critical.

Since any greatness in this book is from other people, I feel comfortable saying that, no matter where you are in life, you will love some of what's here. In the same breath, no matter how much I cry and pout, you will find some of what's inside boring, useless, or seemingly stupid. Out of roughly 140 profiles, I expect you to like 70, love 35, and have your life changed by perhaps 17. Amusingly, the 70 you dislike will be precisely the 70 someone else needs.

Life would be boring if we all followed exactly the same rules, and you will want to pick and choose.

The more surprising part of all of this is ... *Tribe of Mentors* changes *with* you. As time passes and life unfolds, things you initially swatted away like a distraction can reveal depth and become unimaginably important.

That cliché you ignored like a throwaway fortune cookie? Suddenly it makes sense and moves mountains. Conversely, things you initially found enlightening might run their course, like a wonderful high school coach who needs to hand you off to a college coach for you to reach the next level.

There's no expiration date on the advice in this book, as there's no uniformity. In the following pages, you'll find advice from 30-something wunderkinds and seasoned veterans in their 60s and 70s. The hope is that, each time you pick up this book, not unlike with the *I Ching* or *Tao Te Ching*, something new will grab you, shake your perception of reality, illuminate your follies, confirm your intuitions, or correct your course that all-important one degree.

The entire spectrum of human emotion and experience can be found in this book, from hilarious to heart-wrenching, from failure to success, and from life to death. May you welcome it all.

On my coffee table at home, I have a piece of driftwood. Its sole purpose is to display a quote by Anaïs Nin, which I see every day:

"Life shrinks or expands in proportion to one's courage."

It's a short reminder that success can usually be measured by the number of uncomfortable conversations we are willing to have, and by the number of uncomfortable actions we are willing to take.

The most fulfilled and effective people I know — world-famous creatives, billionaires, thought leaders, and more — look at their life's journey as perhaps 25 percent *finding* themselves and 75 percent *creating* themselves.

This book is not intended to be a passive experience. It's intended to be a call to action.

You are the author of your own life, and it's never too late to replace the stories you tell yourself and the world. It's never too late to begin a new chapter, add a surprise twist, or change genres entirely.

What would it look like if it were easy?

Here's to picking up the pen with a smile. Big things are coming. . . .

Pura vida,

Tim Ferriss
Austin, Texas
August 2017

Some Housekeeping Notes That Might Help

- "Quotes I'm Pondering" are spread throughout this book. These are quotes that have changed my thinking and behavior in the past two years or so. Since publishing *Tools of Titans* roughly 12 months ago, I've had the most productive year of my life, and my selection of books played a large role. The "quotes I'm pondering" (usually from the aforementioned books) were shared on a weekly basis with subscribers of my 5-Bullet Friday newsletter (tim.blog/friday), a free newsletter in which I share the five coolest or most useful things (books, articles, gadgets, foods, supplements, apps, quotes, etc.) I've discovered that week. I hope you find them as thought-provoking as I did.

- Remember those rejection letters I mentioned receiving for this book? Some of the polite declines were so good that I included them! There are three "How to Say No" interludes that feature actual emails.

- We shortened nearly every profile and subjectively selected the "best" answers. Best answers sometimes meant eliminating repetition, or focusing on answers detailed enough to be both actionable and non-obvious.

- In nearly every guest's profile, I indicate where you can best interact with them on social media: TW=Twitter, FB=Facebook, IG=Instagram, LI=LinkedIn, SC=Snapchat, and YT=YouTube.

- During outreach to guests, I always asked the same questions in the same order, but in the following pages, I frequently reordered the answers for optimal flow, readability, and impact.

- I've included some non-responses (e.g., "I'm terrible at saying no!") to make you feel better about having the same challenges. No one is perfect, and we're all works in progress.

"Endings don't have to be failures, especially when you choose to end a project or shut down a business. . . . Even the best gigs don't last forever. Nor should they."

SAMIN NOSRAT
IG: @ciaosamin
FB: /samin.nosrat
saltfatacidheat.com

SAMIN NOSRAT is a writer, teacher, and chef. Called "a go-to resource for matching the correct techniques with the best ingredients" by *The New York Times*, and "the next Julia Child" by NPR's *All Things Considered*, she's been cooking professionally since 2000, when she first stumbled into the kitchen at Chez Panisse. Samin is one of five food columnists for *The New York Times Magazine*. She lives, cooks, surfs, and gardens in Berkeley, California. She is the author of the *New York Times* bestseller *Salt, Fat, Acid, Heat: Mastering the Elements of Good Cooking*.

What purchase of $100 or less has most positively impacted your life in the last six months (or in recent memory)?
Paul Stamets' Host Defense MyCommunity mushroom complex is the most incredible immunity supplement I have ever taken (and I have taken a lot of them!). No matter how much I travel, how many hands I shake, or how exhausted I am, I don't get sick as long as I take the supplement diligently.

How has a failure, or apparent failure, set you up for later success? Do you have a "favorite failure" of yours?

I have had so many spectacular failures, but looking back, I can see how each of them led me a little closer to doing what I actually wanted to do. Years before I was ready to write a book of my own, I bungled two opportunities to co-write cookbooks with other people. These mistakes haunted me, and I was sure I'd never get to write another book. But I waited, and I persisted, and after 17 years I wrote the book I'd always dreamt of.

In 2002 I was a finalist for a Fulbright grant, but didn't receive it and felt like I'd never get to study traditional foodmaking methods in Italy. Instead, I found my way back to Italy and cooked and worked there for a year and a half, and now, 15 years later, I'm working on a documentary that will take me there to study traditional foodmaking methods!

I worked at, and eventually ran, a restaurant that was failing financially for its entire five-year existence. It was grueling, especially because I cared about it as if it were my own. I knew chances of our success were slim about three years in, and was ready to leave then, but the owner, who was also my mentor, just wasn't ready to give up. So we dragged things out for two long years beyond that, and it was really challenging. Unbearable at times, even. By the time things were done, I was exhausted and depressed and just really, really unhappy. We all were. But it didn't have to be that way.

That experience taught me to take agency in my own professional narratives, and that endings don't have to be failures, especially when you choose to end a project or shut down a business. Shortly after the restaurant closed, I started a food market as a small side project, and it ended up being wildly successful. I had more press and customers than I could handle. I had investors clamoring to get in on the action. But all I wanted to do was write. I didn't want to run a food market, and since my name was all over it, I didn't want to hand it off to anyone else, either. So I chose to close the market on my own terms, and I made sure that everyone knew it. It was such a positive contrast to the harsh experience of closing the restaurant. I've learned to envision the ideal end to any project before I begin it now—even the best gigs don't last forever. Nor should they.

On a much, much smaller scale, while cooking, I have ruined more dishes than I can recall. But the wonderful thing about cooking is that it's a pretty quick process, really, and it doesn't allow for much time to get attached to the results. So whether a dish stinks or turns out beautifully, you have to start over from scratch again the next day. You don't get a chance to sit around and wallow (or toot your own horn). The important thing is to learn from each failure and try not to repeat it.

What is one of the best or most worthwhile investments you've ever made?

Ten years ago, while running a restaurant, I made the time to audit a class at the Graduate School of Journalism at UC Berkeley with Michael Pollan. It seemed crazy at the time to leave the restaurant for three hours once a week to go sit in a classroom, to get home after 15-hour days and read the books and articles on the syllabus. But some little voice inside me told me I had to find a way to do it, and I am so glad that I did. That class changed my life —it brought me into an incredible community of writers, journalists, and documentarians who have inspired and supported me along this crazy path. I got to know Michael, who encouraged me to write. He also hired me to teach him how to cook, and over the course of those lessons he encouraged me to formalize my unique cooking philosophy into a proper curriculum, go out into the world and teach it, and turn it into a book. That became *Salt, Fat, Acid, Heat*, which is now a *New York Times* bestseller and is on its way to becoming a documentary series. Total insanity.

What is an unusual habit or an absurd thing that you love?

American cheese. I don't eat it often, but I find the way it melts on a burger to be entirely irresistible.

In the last five years, what new belief, behavior, or habit has most improved your life?

I have to be *on* a lot of the time, whether to be able to think and write clearly, or to be out in the world teaching and talking about cooking. Both parts of my job require extraordinary amounts of energy.

Over the last five years, I've started to become more attuned to the various ways I need to take care of myself. And at the top of that list is sleep. I need eight to nine hours of sleep to function properly, and I've started guarding my sleep time mercilessly. I spend a lot more quiet nights at home, and when I do go out to dinner, I'll insist on an early-bird reservation or cut out early.

I've even been known to go to bed while my guests are still partying. They're happy, I'm happy, it's all good. My obsession with sleep has improved my life immeasurably.

What advice would you give to a smart, driven college student about to enter the "real world"?

When in doubt, let kindness and compassion guide you. And don't be afraid to fail.

In the last five years, what have you become better at saying no to?

Truth be told, I'm still working on getting better at saying no. But I will say this: the more clear I am about what my goals are, the more easily I can say no. I have a notebook into which I've recorded all sorts of goals, both big and small, over the last ten or so years. When I take the time to articulate what it is that I hope to achieve, it's simple to refer to the list and see whether saying yes to an opportunity will take me toward or away from achieving that goal. It's when I'm fuzzy about where I'm headed that I start to say yes to things willy-nilly. And I've been burned enough times by FOMO-based and ego-based decision-making to know that I'll always regret choosing to do something for the wrong reason.

When you feel overwhelmed or unfocused, what do you do?

I try to get out of my head and into my body. On writing days, this usually amounts to getting up and going for a walk around Downtown Oakland. Sometimes I throw in the towel completely and go for a swim. Other times, I decide to go to the farmers' market to look at, touch, smell, and taste the produce and let my senses guide me in the decision of what to cook for dinner.

When I'm cooking or doing other physical work and I get overwhelmed, it's usually because I'm not taking care of myself, so I'll take a break. I'll make a snack or a cup of tea. Or I'll just drink a glass of water and sit down outside for a few minutes. It's usually enough to get me calm and clear.

But the thing that will always get me unstuck is jumping into the ocean. It's been that way ever since I was a kid. I've always loved the ocean, and now, whenever I can, I'll go to the beach to swim or surf or just float. Nothing else resets me like the ocean.

> # "The disease of our times is that we live on the surface. We're like the Platte River, a mile wide and an inch deep."

STEVEN PRESSFIELD
TW: @spressfield
stevenpressfield.com

STEVEN PRESSFIELD has made a professional life in five different writing arenas—advertising, screenwriting, fiction, narrative nonfiction, and self-help. He is the best-selling author of *The Legend of Bagger Vance, Gates of Fire, The Afghan Campaign*, and *The Lion's Gate*, as well as the cult classics on creativity, *The War of Art, Turning Pro*, and *Do the Work*. His Wednesday column on stevenpressfield.com is one of the most popular series about writing on the web.

What is an unusual habit or an absurd thing that you love?

This'll sound crazy, but I have certain places that I go to, usually alone, that summon up for me earlier eras in my life. Time is a weird thing. Sometimes you can appreciate a moment that's gone more in the present than you did when it was actually happening. The places that I go to are different all the time and they're usually mundane, ridiculously mundane. A gas station. A bench on a street. Sometimes I'll fly across the country just to go to one of these spots. Sometimes it's on a vacation or a business trip when I'm with family or other people. I might not ever tell them. Or I might. Sometimes I'll take somebody along, though it usually doesn't work (how could it?).

What advice would you give to a smart, driven college student about to enter the "real world"? What advice should they ignore?

I'm probably hopelessly out of date but my advice is get real-world experience: Be a cowboy. Drive a truck. Join the Marine Corps. Get out of the hypercompetitive "life hack" frame of mind. I'm 74. Believe me, you've got all the time in the world. You've got ten lifetimes ahead of you. Don't worry about your friends "beating" you or "getting somewhere" ahead of you. Get out into the real dirt world and start failing. Why do I say that? Because the goal is to connect with your own self, your own soul. Adversity. Everybody spends their life trying to avoid it. Me too. But the best things that ever happened to me came during the times when the shit hit the fan and I had nothing and nobody to help me. Who are you really? What do you *really* want? Get out there and fail and find out.

What is the book (or books) you've given most as a gift, and why? Or what are one to three books that have greatly influenced your life?

The single book that has influenced me most is probably the last book in the world that anybody is gonna want to read: Thucydides' *History of the Peloponnesian War*. This book is dense, difficult, long, full of blood and guts. It wasn't written, as Thucydides himself attests at the start, to be easy or fun. But it is loaded with hardcore, timeless truths and the story it tells ought to be required reading for every citizen in a democracy.

Thucydides was an Athenian general who was beaten and disgraced in a battle early in the 27-year conflagration that came to be called the Peloponnesian War. He decided to drop out of the fighting and dedicate himself to recording, in all the detail he could manage, this conflict, which, he felt certain, would turn out to be the greatest and most significant war ever fought up to that time. He did just that.

Have you heard of Pericles' Funeral Oration? Thucydides was there for it. He transcribed it.

He was there for the debates in the Athenian assembly over the treatment of the island of Melos, the famous Melian Dialogue. If he wasn't there for the defeat of the Athenian fleet at Syracuse or the betrayal of Athens by Alcibiades, he knew people who were there and he went to extremes to record what they told him. Thucydides, like all the Greeks of his era, was unencumbered by Christian theology, or Marxist dogma, or Freudian psychology, or any of the other "isms" that attempt to convince us that man is basically good, or perhaps perfectible. He saw things as they were, in my opinion. It's a dark vision but tremendously bracing and empowering because it's true. On the island of Corcyra, a great naval power in its day, one faction of citizens trapped their neighbors and fellow Corcyreans in a temple. They slaughtered the prisoners' children outside before their eyes and when the captives gave themselves up based on pledges of clemency and oaths sworn before the gods, the captors massacred them as well. This was not a war of nation versus nation, this was brother against brother in the most civilized cities on earth. To read Thucydides is to see our own world in microcosm. It's the study of how democracies destroy themselves by breaking down into warring factions, the Few versus the Many. *Hoi polloi* in Greek means "the many." *Oligoi* means "the few."

I can't recommend Thucydides for fun, but if you want to expose yourself to a towering intellect writing on the deepest stuff imaginable, give it a try.

What purchase of $100 or less has most positively impacted your life in the last six months (or in recent memory)?

This cost a lot more than a hundred bucks, but I bought an electric car, a Kia Soul, and got some solar panels for my roof. Driving on sun power is a major giggle, trust me.

How has a failure, or apparent failure, set you up for later success? Do you have a "favorite failure" of yours?

I just wrote a book called *The Knowledge* about my favorite failure and guess what? It failed too. In all truth, when my third novel (which, like the first two, never got published) crashed ignominiously, I was driving a cab in New York City. I'd been trying to get published for about 15 years at that point. I decided to give up and move to Hollywood, to see if I could find work writing for the movies. Don't ask me what movies I wrote. I will never tell. And if you find out by other means, BE WARNED! Don't see 'em. But working in "the industry" made me a pro and paved the way for whatever successes finally did come.

If you could have a gigantic billboard anywhere with anything on it, what would it say and why?

I would not have a billboard, and I would take down every billboard that everybody else has put up.

What is one of the best or most worthwhile investments you've ever made?

I've never invested in the stock market or taken a risk on anything outside myself. I decided a long time ago that I would only bet on myself. I will risk two years on a book that'll probably fall flat on its face. I don't mind. I tried. It didn't work. I believe in investing in your heart. That's all I do, really. I'm a servant of the Muse. All my money is on her.

In the last five years, what new belief, behavior, or habit has most improved your life?

I've always been a gym person and an early morning person. But a few years ago I got invited to train with T. R. Goodman at a place called Pro Camp. There's a "system," yeah, but basically what we do (and it's definitely a *group* thing, with three or four of us training together) is just work hard. I hate it but it's great. T. R. says, as we're leaving after working out, "Nothing you face today will be harder than what you just did."

In the last five years, what have you become better at saying no to? What new realizations and/or approaches helped?

I got a chance a couple of years ago to visit a security firm, one of those places that guard celebrities and protect their privacy—in other words, a business whose total job was to say no. The person who was giving me the tour told me that the business screens every incoming letter, solicitation, email, etc., and decides which ones get through to the client. "How many get through?" I asked. "Virtually none," my friend said. I decided that I would look at incoming mail the same way that firm does. If I were the security professional tasked with protecting me from bogus, sociopathic, and clueless asks, which ones would I screen and dump into the trash? That has helped a lot.

When you feel overwhelmed or unfocused, what do you do?

I have a friend at the gym who knew Jack LaLanne (Google him if the name is unfamiliar). Jack used to say it's okay to take a day off from working out. But on that day, you're not allowed to eat. That's the short way of saying you're not really allowed to get unfocused. Take a vacation. Gather yourself. But know that the only reason you're here on this planet is to follow your star and do what the Muse tells you. It's amazing how a good day's work will get you right back to feeling like yourself.

What are bad recommendations you hear in your profession or area of expertise?

Great, great question. In the world of writing, everyone wants to succeed *immediately* and without pain or effort. Really? Or they love to write books about how to write books, rather than actually writing ... a book that might actually be about something. Bad advice is everywhere. Build a following. Establish a platform. Learn how to scam the system. In other words, do all the surface stuff and none of the real work it takes to actually produce something of value. The disease of our times is that we live on the surface. We're like the Platte River, a mile wide and an inch deep. I always say, "If you want to become a billionaire, invent something that will allow people to indulge their own Resistance." Somebody *did* invent it. It's called the Internet. Social media. That wonderland where we can flit from one superficial, jerkoff distraction to another, always remaining on the surface, never going deeper than an inch. Real work and real satisfaction come from the opposite of what the web provides. They come from going *deep* into something—the book you're writing, the album, the movie—and staying there for a long, long time.

"It all happened so suddenly and cinematically that it might defy belief—I remembered that actually I had always wanted to be a writer. So I started writing that very evening."

SUSAN CAIN
TW: @susancain
FB: /authorsusancain
quietrev.com

SUSAN CAIN is the co-founder of Quiet Revolution and the author of the bestsellers *Quiet Power: The Secret Strengths of Introverted Kids*, and *Quiet: The Power of Introverts in a World That Can't Stop Talking*, which has been translated into 40 languages and been on the *New York Times* bestseller list for more than four years. *Quiet* was named the best book of the year by *Fast Company* magazine, which also named Susan one of its "Most Creative People in Business." Susan is the co-founder of the Quiet Schools Network and the Quiet Leadership Institute, and her writing has appeared in *The New York Times*, *The Atlantic*, *The Wall Street Journal*, and other publications. Her TED Talk has been viewed more than 17 million times and was named by Bill Gates as one of his all-time favorite talks.

How has a failure, or apparent failure, set you up for later success? Do you have a "favorite failure" of yours?

Many, many moons ago, I used to be a corporate lawyer. I was an ambivalent corporate lawyer at best, and anyone could have told you that I was in the wrong profession, but still: I'd dedicated tons of time (three years of law school, one year of clerking for a federal judge, and six and a half years at a Wall Street firm, to be exact) and had lots of deep and treasured relationships with fellow attorneys. But the day came, when I was well along on partnership track, that the senior partner in my firm came to my office and told me that I wouldn't be put up for partner on schedule. To this day, I don't know whether he meant that I would never be put up for partner or just delayed for a good long while. All I know is that I embarrassingly burst into tears right in front of him—and then asked for a leave of absence. I left work that very afternoon and bicycled round and round Central Park in NYC, having no idea what to do next. I thought I'd travel. I thought I'd stare at the walls for a while.

Instead—and it all happened so suddenly and cinematically that it might defy belief—I remembered that actually I had always wanted to be a writer. So I started writing that very evening. The next day I signed up for a class at NYU in creative nonfiction writing. And the next week, I attended the first session of class and knew that I was finally home. I had no expectation of ever making a living through writing, but it was crystal clear to me that from then on, writing would be my center, and that I would look for freelance work that would give me lots of free time to pursue it.

If I had "succeeded" at making partner, right on schedule, I might still be miserably negotiating corporate transactions 16 hours a day. It's not that I'd never thought about what else I might like to do other than law, but until I had the time and space to think about life outside the hermetic culture of a law practice, I couldn't figure out what I really wanted to do.

What is one of the best or most worthwhile investments you've ever made?

Seven years of time to write *Quiet*. I didn't care how long it took and, though I wanted the book to succeed, I felt good about the investment of time regardless of the outcome—because I felt so certain that writing in general, and writing that book in particular, was the right thing to do.

I handed in a first draft after the first two years, which my editor (correctly) pronounced crappy. She put it only slightly more delicately. She said, "Take all the time you need, start from scratch, and get it right." I left her office elated—because I agreed with her. I knew that I needed years to get it right (after all, I'd never published a thing before *Quiet*, so I was learning how to write a book from scratch), and I was thrilled that she was giving me the time. Most publishing houses rush books to market long before they're fully baked. If she'd done that, there would be no quiet revolution.

What is an unusual habit or an absurd thing that you love?

I love sad/minor key music. I find it elevating and transcendent, and not really sad at all. I think that's because this kind of music is really about the fragility, and therefore the preciousness, of life and love.

Leonard Cohen is my patron saint. Try "Dance Me to the End of Love" or "Famous Blue Raincoat," or pretty much anything else he's ever written, including, of course, "Hallelujah," his best-known song but really only the tip of the Leonard iceberg! Also: "Hinach Yafah (You Are Beautiful)" by Idan Raichel. It's a gorgeous song of longing for the beloved, but really it's about longing in general.

My favorite word in any language is *saudade*—the Portuguese word that's at the heart of Brazilian and Portuguese culture and music. It means, roughly, a sweet longing for a beloved thing or person that will likely never return. Try the music of Madredeus or Cesária Évora. My next book is (sort of) on this topic!

What advice would you give to a smart, driven college student about to enter the "real world"? What advice should they ignore?

You will hear so many stories of people who risked everything in order to achieve this or that goal, especially creative goals. But I do not believe that your best creative work is done when you're stressed out because you're teetering on the edge of bankruptcy or other personal disasters. Just the opposite. You should set up your life so that it is as comfortable and happy as possible—*and* so that it accommodates your creative work.

I often ask myself whether all those years of Wall Street law were a waste, given that what I was really meant to do, the whole time, was to explore human psychology and to tell the truth (in writing) about what it's like to be alive. And the answer is no, it wasn't a waste, for many reasons. First, because I learned so much about the so-called "real world" that would have otherwise remained a permanent mystery; second, because a front-row seat at a Wall Street negotiation is as good a place as any to study the occasional ridiculousness of humans; but finally because it gave me a financial cushion, when I was ready, to try a creative life. It wasn't a huge cushion, as I hadn't saved that much. But it made a huge difference. Even once I started my writing life, I spent tons of time setting up a modest freelance business (teaching people negotiation skills) that I could use to support myself for as long as it took. I told myself that my writing goal was to get something published by the time I was 75 years old. I wanted writing to be a permanent source of pleasure, and never to be associated with financial stress or, more generally, the pressure to achieve.

Of course, I'm not saying that the smart, driven college student in your question should spend ten years in finance before striking out creatively! But they should be planning how they're going to make ends meet. That way, the time that they do spend with their creative projects—whether it's 30 minutes or ten hours a day—can be all about focus, flow, and occasional glimpses of joy.

When you feel overwhelmed or unfocused, what do you do?

I love espresso and would happily consume it all day. But I only allow myself one latte a day, and I save it for when I'm doing my creative work—partly because it jump-starts my mind almost magically, and partly because this has trained me, Pavlovian style, to associate writing with the pleasure of coffee.

"Thinking of what makes me *happy* doesn't give me the same clarity as thinking about what gives me *bliss.*"

KYLE MAYNARD
IG: @kylemaynard
FB: /kylemaynard.fanpage
kyle-maynard.com

KYLE MAYNARD is a best-selling author, entrepreneur, and ESPY award-winning mixed martial arts athlete, known for becoming the first quadruple amputee to reach the summits of Mount Kilimanjaro and Mount Aconcagua without the aid of prosthetics. Oprah Winfrey called Kyle "one of the most inspiring young men you will ever hear about." Arnold Schwarzenegger described him as "a champion human," and even Wayne Gretzky has spoken of Kyle's "greatness." Kyle was born with a rare condition that resulted in arms that end at the elbows and legs that end near his knees. Despite this, and with the support of his family, Kyle learned as a child to live life independently without prosthetics. Kyle has become a champion wrestler (inducted into the National Wrestling Hall of Fame), CrossFit Certified Instructor, owner of the No Excuses gym, world record-setting weightlifter, and skilled mountaineer.

What is the book (or books) you've given most as a gift, and why? Or what are one to three books that have greatly influenced your life?

Dune by Frank Herbert
The Stranger by Albert Camus
The Hero with a Thousand Faces by Joseph Campbell

How has a failure, or apparent failure, set you up for later success? Do you have a "favorite failure" of yours?

It's almost more difficult to think of a time when an apparent failure *didn't* set me up for later success. Failure is inextricably connected to any major success I've ever had.

My favorite failure was my earliest. My Grandma Betty had this dark green jar she used to ask me to get sugar out of, except the catch was, as an amputee, I used both arms to grip things, and I could only fit one arm inside the jar. I'd sit there for hours, repeatedly failing to balance the scoop on my one arm. I'd get it right to the edge then lose it. After 50 more tries, I'd get it back near the top before I'd lose it again. Eventually, and sometimes to my surprise, I'd succeed. It not only helped with my dexterity and focus, but it also helped build my will. The best way I can describe the feeling is a Finnish word, *"sisu"*—the mental strength to continue to try even after you feel you've reached the limits of your abilities. I don't think failure is sometimes part of the process—it *always* is. When you feel you can't go on, know that you're just getting started.

If you could have a gigantic billboard anywhere with anything on it, what would it say and why? Are there any quotes you think of often or live your life by?

The quote I'd put on that billboard belongs to my friend and former Navy SEAL, Richard Machowicz: "Not Dead, Can't Quit." A few people said it was borderline child abuse that my parents had me continue wrestling after I lost my first 35 matches. Less than a decade later, [those same people] were saying I was unfairly advantaged. My sisters cried after reading comments about how it would take 20 seconds for me to become the first televised death in MMA. Spoiler alert—didn't die. Some said I'd get my team killed on Mount Kilimanjaro and Mount Aconcagua. I'm willing to bet most of those critics haven't stood on top of those mountains like my friends and I have. It's for this reason that I love that quote. It's my mantra during the toughest moments. Richard lost a battle with cancer this year, but he experienced more in this life than most men could in ten, and he lived this quote until his last breath.

What is an unusual habit or an absurd thing that you love?

I think suffering is probably the most absurd thing that I love. Suffering is the greatest teacher I've ever had. Feeling different than other kids because I was born without arms and legs, being pancaked by bigger kids in football, having my nose broken through the states and nationals in wrestling, feeling freezing cold and physically broken on the side of a mountain, being nervous and wondering if I could make payroll at my gym—they weren't always fun at the time, but they're some of my favorite moments. And I love people who love suffering. It took three times for my best friend Jeff Gum to make it through BUD/S, going through "Hell Week" with viral gastroenteritis and rhabdomyolysis. The day he finished ten years as a Navy SEAL, I asked him what the best moment was, and he said it was having everything go wrong and watching the instructors try everything they could to make him quit.

What advice would you give to a smart, driven college student about to enter the "real world"? What advice should they ignore?

Since I read Joseph Campbell's line "follow your bliss," it has become my true north. It helps me in those moments when I'm staring off in the shower for hours looking like someone put me under hypnosis. Thinking of what makes me *happy* doesn't give me the same clarity as thinking about what gives me *bliss*. For me, it's the freedom I feel on top of a mountain or the breeze I feel laying on a catamaran net halfway around the world. Bliss is the highest peak of what brings you joy. If happiness is just above the status quo, bliss is what makes you feel most alive. Expect it will take courage to follow your bliss, and expect it will suck at times. Expect you're going to have to take risks for it. Expect others won't necessarily understand. And also expect that what gives you bliss today may not be what does tomorrow. Just follow it all over again.

What are bad recommendations you hear in your profession or area of expertise?

The worst advice I've ever been given was to not increase the fee I charged to give a keynote speech. I was told I would price myself out of the market, I didn't have enough recent media coverage to compete against well-known speakers, blah, blah, blah. I decided to raise my price anyway—incrementally at first, then I doubled it. Now I have twice as many inquiries, and people even negotiate with me less. I wish I'd done it earlier. It's given me much more freedom. As I write this, I'm spending a week on a yacht in Croatia and the rest of the summer traveling through Europe. Time is the only thing we can't get back. Hopefully by the time you read this, I will be on my way to doubling it again.

In the last five years, what have you become better at saying no to?

My biggest shift came after listening to a successful CEO talk about his philosophy for hiring people. When his company grew and he ran out of time to interview people himself, he had his employees rate new candidates on a 1–10 scale. The only stipulation was they couldn't choose 7. It immediately dawned on me how many invitations I was receiving that I would rate as a 7—speeches, weddings, coffees, even dates. If I thought something was a 7, there was a good chance I felt obligated to do it. But if I have to decide between a 6 or an 8, it's a lot easier to quickly determine whether or not I should even consider it.

QUOTES I'M PONDERING

(Tim Ferriss: Sept. 18–Oct. 2, 2015)

"People think focus means saying yes to the thing you've got to focus on. But that's not what it means at all. It means saying no to the hundred other good ideas that there are. You have to pick carefully. I'm actually as proud of the things we haven't done as the things I have done. Innovation is saying no to 1,000 things."

—STEVE JOBS
Co-founder and former CEO of Apple

"What you seek is seeking you."

—RUMI
13th-century Persian poet and Sufi master

"Anyone who lives within their means suffers from a lack of imagination."

—OSCAR WILDE
Irish writer, author of *The Picture of Dorian Gray*

"In order to 'have' you must 'do,' and in order to 'do' you must 'be.'"

TERRY CREWS
TW/IG: @terrycrews
FB: /realterrycrews
terrycrews.com

TERRY CREWS is an actor and former NFL player (Los Angeles Rams, San Diego Chargers, Washington Redskins, and Philadelphia Eagles). His wide-ranging credits include the original viral Old Spice commercials, television series such as *The Newsroom*, *Arrested Development*, and *Everybody Hates Chris*, and films including *White Chicks*, the *Expendables* franchise, *Bridesmaids*, and *The Longest Yard*. He now stars on the Golden Globe Award–winning Fox sitcom *Brooklyn Nine-Nine*. In 2014, Terry released his autobiography, *Manhood: How to Be a Better Man—or Just Live with One*.

What is the book (or books) you've given most as a gift, and why? Or what are one to three books that have greatly influenced your life?
The Master Key System by Charles F. Haanel. I have read hundreds of personal development books, but this is the one that clearly showed me how to visualize, contemplate, and focus on what it was I truly wanted.

It revealed to me that we only get what we desire most, and to apply myself with a laserlike focus upon a goal, task, or project. That in order to "have" you must "do," and in order to "do" you must "be" — and this process is immediate. Although it takes time for these desires to manifest in our material world, you *must* see the thing you desire as completed, finished, and real, *now*. The better you can do this, the more you can accomplish. I have bought several copies of this book and distributed it to family and friends. I also reread it probably once a month to keep my vision clear.

Two more are Viktor E. Frankl's incredible *Man's Search for Meaning* and David McRaney's *You Are Not So Smart*. Both books are absolutely essential to me in order to keep my perspectives correct in a changing world.

How has a failure, or apparent failure, set you up for later success? Do you have a "favorite failure" of yours?

1986. It was my senior year in high school at Flint Academy in Flint, Michigan. I was the starting center for our class C basketball team. We had a great team that year, and we were expected to go very far, if not all the way, in the state playoffs. We faced Burton Atherton in the district final, and we were expected to trounce them, but they tried something we'd never seen before. They didn't play. They would bring the ball down the court and just pass it back and forth at the top of the key. There was no shot clock, so they did this forever. The only time we scored was when we managed to steal the ball. But our coach, for some reason, decided we were going to let them do it. I remember standing there, with my hands raised in zone defense, watching them hold the ball without even attempting to shoot. I was frustrated, and every attempt I made to step out of the zone was rebuffed by our coach. This method was working for them, because with only five seconds left on the game clock, they were up 47-45.

One of their players made a mistake and tried a long pass cross court and I stole the ball. I desperately dribbled the entire length of the court . . . 5, 4, 3, 2, 1 . . . for our only chance to win. I missed. Their fans go crazy, as it was the biggest upset of the year, and I collapse in a heap, thinking my life is over. The coach afterward told the whole team that I had no business taking that shot and I should have passed it to our star player. It was in the paper the next day that I failed, and I was ridiculed by students and teachers alike. I was beyond crushed. A dark cloud covered me everywhere I went as I internalized the loss.

A few days later, as the fog of failure began to lift, I remember having a rare time alone in my room (I usually shared it with my brother). As I sat in the silence, another thought pierced through my sadness. "I took the shot." It was invigorating, even exciting. "Hey, when all the chips were on the line, you didn't leave your future up to others, YOU TOOK YOUR SHOT." Instantly I felt free and in control. I knew from then on that I could have the courage to fail on my own terms. From that moment, I decided that if I was going to succeed or fail, it was going to be up to me. I was changed forever.

If you could have a gigantic billboard anywhere with anything on it, what would it say and why?

"God will not have his work made manifest by cowards."—Ralph Waldo Emerson

I love this quote because it is all about defeating fear. Every great and extraordinary accomplishment in this world was done through courage. Hell, you don't even get to be born unless your mother has the courage to have you. I repeat this phrase when I'm anxious or nervous about something. I ask myself, what's the worst that can happen. Usually, the answer is, "You can die." Then I answer back, "I'd rather die doing something I feel is great and amazing rather than be safe and comfortable living a life I hate." I talk to myself a lot, and this quote helps me sort out my fears and deal with them. The more you run from your fears, the bigger they get, but the more you go into them, the more they tend to vanish like a mirage.

What advice would you give to a smart, driven college student about to enter the "real world"? What advice should they ignore?

There is a big difference between intelligence and wisdom. Many are fooled into thinking they are the same thing, but they are not. I have seen intelligent serial killers, but I've never seen a wise one. Intelligent human beings have been given this trumped-up position in society where, just because they're intelligent, they are to be listened to, and I have found this is extremely dangerous. I was in a Christian cult along with other very intelligent people but, looking back, if I had heeded wisdom, I would have seen we were all on the wrong path. Intelligence is like following a GPS route right into a body of water until you drown. Wisdom looks at the route but, when it takes a turn into the ocean, decides not to follow it, then finds a new, better way. Wisdom reigns supreme.

Ignore any advice that tells you you are going to miss something. Every mistake I have ever made in business, marriage, and personal conduct was because I thought if I didn't do or get *this* now, it was never going to happen. It's like most clubs in LA. The trick is to keep the line long at the door, while the club itself is empty. The "aura of exclusivity" is really code for "bad atmosphere." To do what you desire to do, you have all you need.

What are bad recommendations you hear in your profession or area of expertise?

"Work hard to beat the competition." The truth is that competition is *the opposite* of creativity. If I am working hard to beat the competition, it actually prevents me from thinking creatively to make all concepts of competition obsolete. As a football player, I was told to work hard to compete against the other team, some perceived future threat (new draftees, age, or injury), and even my current teammates. As an actor, you are told to look a certain way or do things you don't agree with in order to "compete." This competitive mindset *destroys* people. It's the scorched-earth way of thinking, and everyone is burned.

The truth is that you need the success of everyone in your field in order to achieve your own success. Creativity operates differently. You work hard because you're *inspired* to, not because you have to. Work becomes fun, and you have energy for days because this life is not a "young man's game." It is an *"inspired person's game."* The keys belong to whoever is inspired, and no specific age, sex, gender, or cultural background has a monopoly on inspiration. When you're creative, you render competition obsolete, because there is only one you, and *no one* can do things exactly the way you do. Never worry about the competition. When you're creative, you can, in fact, cheer others on with the full knowledge that their success will undoubtedly be your own.

In the last five years, what have you become better at saying no to? What new realizations and/or approaches helped?

I realized that I had to let people leave my life, never to return. Every relationship I have in my life, from family and friends to business partners, must be a voluntary relationship. My wife can leave at any time. Family members can call me or not. Business partners can decide to move on, and it's all okay. But the same is true on my end. If I say I'm ready to move on and someone doesn't accept that, now we have a problem. I remember trying to move on from a very close friend because he was displaying behaviors I wasn't comfortable with. Soon after, I received a letter by certified mail, threatening me with a lawsuit for over a million dollars because of the demise of our "friendship." It was ridiculous and it still is, so I actually framed the letter as a reminder of the necessity of letting people go and moving on. One approach I use is imaginary great-grandchildren. I talk to them all the time. I ask them about decisions and relationships and whether or not to continue them. They tend to speak loud and clear. "Grandpa, you shouldn't do this, or you need to leave these people alone because we will be affected negatively, or worse, we won't exist." Those moments show me that this whole thing is bigger than me. It's the realization that there is a "will to pleasure," a "will to power" and, in the words of Viktor Frankl, a "will to meaning." You won't take a bullet for pleasure or power, but you will for meaning. So you sometimes have to do what I call a "crowd-thinner." One wrong person in your circle can destroy your whole future. It's that important.

"Busy is a decision."

DEBBIE MILLMAN
TW/IG: @debbiemillman
debbiemillman.com

DEBBIE MILLMAN has been called "one of the most influential designers working today" by Graphic Design USA. She is the founder and host of *Design Matters*, the world's first and longest-running podcast about design, where she's interviewed nearly 300 design luminaries and cultural commentators including Massimo Vignelli and Milton Glaser. Her artwork has been exhibited around the world. She's designed everything from wrapping paper to beach towels, greeting cards to playing cards, notebooks to T-shirts, and Star Wars merchandise to global Burger King rebrands. Debbie is the President Emeritus of AIGA (one of only five women to hold the position in the organization's 100-year history), the editorial and creative director of *Print* magazine, and the author of six books. In 2009, Debbie co-founded (with Steven Heller) the world's first master's program in branding at the School of Visual Arts in New York City, which has received international acclaim.

What is the book (or books) you've given most as a gift, and why? Or what are one to three books that have greatly influenced your life?

A book that has influenced my life and one that I keep going back to over and over is the anthology *The Voice That Is Great Within Us: American Poetry of the 20th Century*. Gorgeously, thoughtfully, and carefully edited by Hayden Carruth, it was required reading in a summer college class I attended back in the early 1980s. This funny-looking book introduced me to my most treasured, deeply felt poem, "Maximus to Himself," by Charles Olson, which has since become the blueprint of my life, as well as the poetry of Denise Levertov, Adrienne Rich, Ezra Pound, Wallace Stevens, and so many more. I still have my original copy and though the cover has come off and the spine is cracked in numerous places, I will never replace it.

What purchase of $100 or less has most positively impacted your life in the last six months (or in recent memory)?

The purchase that has influenced me over the last six months is the Apple Pencil. I do soooo much of my artwork by hand, and now there is a device that draws and feels like a "real" pencil that I can use electronically. It has changed the way I work.

How has a failure, or apparent failure, set you up for later success? Do you have a "favorite failure" of yours?

In early 2003, a good friend sent me an email with a subject line that read: "Begin drinking heavily before opening." The email contained a link leading to a blog titled *Speak Up,* the first-ever online forum about graphic design and branding in the world. Suddenly, sprawled before my eyes, I found myself reading an article that disparaged my entire career. This incident, in tandem with a number of historical rejections and setbacks, sent me into a deep depression, and I seriously considered leaving the design profession altogether. However, in the 14 years since this occurred —this takedown of everything I'd done to date (and everything I thought was a complete and total failure for a long time)—transformed into the foundation of everything I've done since. *Everything* I am doing now contains seeds of origin from that time. Turns out, the worst professional experience I've faced became the most important, defining experience of my life.

If you could have a gigantic billboard anywhere with anything on it, what would it say and why?

My billboard would say this: "Busy is a decision." Here's why: Of the many, many excuses people use to rationalize why they can't do something, the excuse "I am too busy" is not only the most inauthentic, it is also the laziest. I don't believe in "too busy." Like I said, busy is a decision. We do the things we want to do, period. If we say we are too busy, it is shorthand for "not important enough." It means you would rather be doing something else that you consider more important. That "thing" could be sleep, it could be sex, or it could be watching *Game of Thrones*. If we use busy as an excuse for not doing something what we are really, really saying is that it's not a priority.

Simply put: You don't *find* the time to do something; you *make* the time to do things.

We are now living in a society that sees busy as a badge. It has become cultural cachet to use the excuse "I am too busy," as a reason for not doing anything we don't feel like doing. The problem is this: if you let yourself off the hook for not doing something for *any* reason, you won't ever do it. If you want to do something, you can't let being busy stand in the way, even if you are busy. Make the time to do the things you want to do and then do them.

What is one of the best or most worthwhile investments you've ever made?

The best investment I've ever made was in psychotherapy. When I first started, I was in my early 30s, and the bills practically killed me. But I knew I needed to deeply understand all the destructive things I was doing in order to try to live a remarkable life, and I wanted this more than anything. Over the years I still sometimes smart at the monthly invoices, but I've never doubted that this investment has profoundly shaped who I have become. Although I still think I have work to do, it changed and then saved my life in every imaginable way.

I'm in psychoanalytic psychotherapy (put another way: psychoanalysis with an emphasis on "Self-Psychology"). For me, talk therapy is the only thing that I've really ever felt drawn to. Things like EMDR and behavior modification seem too voodoo for me.

Some things that I think are important to consider, strictly from my perspective:

- Once-a-week therapy does not work well. Twice or more gives you continuity and an opportunity to germinate in a way that once a week doesn't. Also, once a week almost feels like "catch-up."

- Therapy takes time. It takes dedication, stamina, resilience, persistence, and courage. It's not a quick fix, but it saved my life.

- Tell your therapist everything. If you edit who you are or pretend to be something you are not, or project who or how you want to be seen, it will take that much longer. Just be yourself. If you are afraid your therapist will judge you, tell them. All of these things are important to talk about.

- There is no shame in feeling shame. Almost everyone does, and therapy will help you understand it. There is nothing like understanding your motivations and insecurities to help you integrate those feelings into your psyche in the most healthy and authentic way.

- I would not recommend going to a therapist that one of your friends also goes to. (Most good therapists abide by this rule now.) Things get very blurry and boundaries get weird.

- Yes, it will be expensive. But what is more valuable than better understanding who you are, breaking intrinsic bad habits, getting over much of your shit (or at least understanding why you do it in the first place), and generally living a happier, more contented, more peaceful life?

- My advice to anyone looking for a therapist is to make sure they are "trained" (PhD or MD, plus post-doctoral training).

What is an unusual habit or an absurd thing that you love?

I have been told that because I like to make up silly songs and then sing them in all sorts of absurd situations and occurrences, I am trying to turn my life into a Hollywood musical. I probably wouldn't disagree.

In the last five years, what new belief, behavior, or habit has most improved your life?

After a *Design Matters* interview with the great writer Dani Shapiro, we started to talk about the role of confidence in success. She went on to state that she felt that confidence was highly overrated. I was instantly intrigued. She explained that she felt that most overly confident people were really annoying. And the most confident people were usually arrogant. She felt that overexuding that amount of confidence was a sure sign that a person was compensating for some type of internal psychological deficit.

Instead, Dani declared that courage was more important than confidence. When you are operating out of courage, you are saying that no matter how you feel about yourself or your opportunities or the outcome, you are going to take a risk and take a step toward what you want. You are not waiting for the confidence to mysteriously arrive. I now believe that confidence is achieved through repeated success at any endeavor. The more you practice doing something, the better you will get at it, and your confidence will grow over time.

What advice would you give to a smart, driven college student about to enter the "real world"? What advice should they ignore?

Since I teach, I have a lot of opinions on what advice to give college students. I think one of the most important is about job hunting. Like everything else meaningful in life, it takes training to get good at job hunting. You don't just find and *get* a great job. You find and *win* a great job against a pool of very competitive candidates who may want that job as much, if not more, than you do. Finding and winning a great job is a competitive sport that requires as much career athleticism and perseverance as making it to the Olympics. You must be in the finest career shape possible in order to win.

There is very little luck involved. Winning your great job is about hard work, stamina, grit, ingenuity, and timing. What might look like luck to you is simply hard work paying off. These are questions I tell my students to ask themselves as they set out on their path in the "real" world:

- Am I spending enough time on looking for, finding, and working toward winning a great job?

- Am I constantly refining and improving my skills? What can I continue to get better and more competitive at?

- Do I believe that I am working harder than everyone else? If not, what else can I be doing?

- What are the people who are competing with me doing that I am not doing?

- Am I doing everything I can—every single day—to stay in "career shape"? If not, what else should I be doing?

One piece of advice I think they should ignore is the value of being a "people person." *No one cares if you are a people person.* Have a point of view, and share it meaningfully, thoughtfully, and with conviction.

What are bad recommendations you hear in your profession or area of expertise?

I do not believe in work-life balance. I believe that if you view your work as a calling, it is a labor of love rather than laborious. When your work is a calling, you are not approaching the amount of hours you are working with a sense of dread or counting the minutes until the weekend. Your calling can become a life-affirming engagement that can provide its own balance and spiritual nourishment. Ironically, it takes hard work to achieve this.

When you are in your 20s and 30s and want to have a remarkable, fulfilling career, you must work hard. If you don't work harder than everyone else, you will not get ahead. Further, if you are looking for work-life balance in your 20s or 30s, you are likely in the wrong career. If you are doing something you love, you don't want work-life balance.

When you feel overwhelmed or unfocused, what do you do?

As a loudmouthed native New Yorker, I have often regretted acting impulsively when I am feeling angry or frustrated. Now, when I feel that familiar urge to respond defensively or say things I don't really mean or bang out a wounded response via email or text, I *wait*. I force myself to breathe, take a step back, and *wait* to respond. Just an hour or two or an overnight retreat makes a world of difference. And if all else fails, I try to obey this message I got in a Chinese fortune cookie (which I have since taped to my laptop): "Avoid compulsively making things worse."

"Self-esteem is just the reputation that you have with yourself. You'll always know."

NAVAL RAVIKANT
TW: @naval
startupboy.com

NAVAL RAVIKANT is the CEO and co-founder of AngelList. He previously co-founded Vast.com and Epinions.com, which went public as part of Shopping.com. He is an active angel investor and has invested in more than 100 companies, including many "unicorn" mega-successes. His deals include Twitter, Uber, Yammer, Postmates, Wish, Thumbtack, and OpenDNS. In recent years, he is the person I call most for startup-related advice.

What is the book (or books) you've given most as a gift, and why? Or what are one to three books that have greatly influenced your life?

Total Freedom by Jiddu Krishnamurti. A rationalist's guide to the perils of the human mind. The "spiritual" book that I keep returning to.

Sapiens by Yuval Noah Harari (page 554). A history of the human species, with observations, frameworks, and mental models that will have you looking at history and your fellow humans differently.

Everything by Matt Ridley (page 35). Matt is a scientist, optimist, and forward thinker. *Genome*, *The Red Queen*, *The Origins of Virtue*, *The Rational Optimist*—they're all great.

How has a failure, or apparent failure, set you up for later success? Do you have a "favorite failure" of yours?

Suffering is a moment of clarity, when you can no longer deny the truth of a situation and are forced into uncomfortable change. I'm lucky that I didn't get everything I wanted in my life, or I'd be happy with my first good job, my college sweetheart, my college town. Being poor when young led to making money when old. Losing faith in my bosses and elders made me independent and an adult. Almost getting into the wrong marriage helped me recognize and enter the right one. Falling sick made me focus on my health. It goes on and on. Inside suffering is the seed of change.

If you could have a gigantic billboard anywhere with anything on it, what would it say and why?

"Desire is a contract that you make with yourself to be unhappy until you get what you want."

Desire is a driver, a motivator. In fact, a sincere and uncompromising desire, placed above everything else, is nearly always fulfilled. But every judgment, every preference, every setback spawns its own desire and soon we drown in them. Each one a problem to be solved, and we suffer until it's fulfilled.

Happiness, or at least peace, is the sense that nothing is missing in this moment. No desires running amok. It's okay to have a desire. But pick a big one and pick it carefully. Drop the small ones.

What is one of the best or most worthwhile investments you've ever made?

Every book I read that wasn't assigned to me or that I didn't read with a purpose in mind.

The genuine love for reading itself, when cultivated, is a superpower.

We live in the age of Alexandria, when every book and every piece of knowledge ever written down is a fingertip away. The means of learning are abundant—it's the desire to learn that's scarce. Cultivate that desire by reading what you want, not what you're "supposed to."

In the last five years, what new belief, behavior, or habit has most improved your life?

Happiness is a choice you make and a skill you develop.

The mind is just as malleable as the body. We spend so much time and effort trying to change the external world, other people, and our own bodies, all the while accepting ourselves the way we were programmed in our youths. We accept the voice that talks to us in our head all the time as the source of all truth. But all of it is malleable, every day is new, and memory and identity are burdens from the past that prevent us from living freely in the present.

What advice would you give to a smart, driven college student about to enter the "real world"? What advice should they ignore?

Advice: Follow your intellectual curiosity over whatever is "hot" right now. If your curiosity ever leads you to a place where society eventually wants to go, you'll get paid extremely well.

Do everything you were going to do, but with less angst, less suffering, less emotion. Everything takes time.

Ignore: The news. Complainers, angry people, high-conflict people. Anyone trying to scare you about a danger that isn't clear and present.

Don't do things that you know are morally wrong. Not because someone is watching, but because you are. Self-esteem is just the reputation that you have with yourself. You'll always know.

Ignore the unfairness—there is no fair. Play the hand that you're dealt to the best of your ability. People are highly consistent, so you will eventually get what you deserve and so will they. In the end, everyone gets the same judgment: death.

What are bad recommendations you hear in your profession or area of expertise?

"You're too young." Most of history was built by young people. They just got credit when they were older. The only way to truly learn something is by doing it. Yes, listen to guidance. But don't wait.

In the last five years, what have you become better at saying no to?

I say no to nearly everything. I make a lot fewer short-term compromises. I aspire to only work with people who I can work with forever, to invest my time in activities that are a joy unto themselves, and to focus on the extremely long term.

So I have no time for short-term things: dinners with people I won't see again, tedious ceremonies to please tedious people, traveling to places that I wouldn't go to on vacation.

When you feel overwhelmed or unfocused, what do you do?

Memento mori—"remember that you have to die." All of this will go to nothing. Remember before you were born? Just like that.

"Self-sufficiency is another word for poverty."

MATT RIDLEY
TW: @mattwridley
mattridley.co.uk

MATT RIDLEY is a prominent author whose books have sold more than a million copies, been translated into 31 languages, and won several awards. They include *The Red Queen*, *The Origins of Virtue*, *Genome*, *Nature via Nurture*, *Francis Crick*, *The Rational Optimist* (one of the most recommended books by others in this book), and *The Evolution of Everything*. His TED Talk "When Ideas Have Sex" has been viewed more than two million times. He writes a weekly column in *The Times* (London) and writes regularly for *The Wall Street Journal*. As Viscount Ridley, he was elected to England's House of Lords in February 2013.

What is the book (or books) you've given most as a gift, and why? Or what are one to three books that have greatly influenced your life?

Two books that have greatly influenced my life are *The Double Helix* by James D. Watson and *The Selfish Gene* by Richard Dawkins. What fascinates me about these books is how they revolutionized the telling of scientific stories while themselves breaking new scientific ground in the elucidation of the secret of life. Read these two books and you will get a great answer to a question that has baffled mankind for millions of years: What is life? Watson's "nonfiction novel" was an astonishing literary achievement, and it was about the greatest scientific discovery of the 20th century. Dawkins' "stranger-than-fiction" argument turned evolutionary biology on its head and was written like a great detective story.

What purchase of $100 or less has most positively impacted your life in the last six months (or in recent memory)?

SleepPhones. It's a headband that goes over your eyes and ears and that has inside two ultraflat earphones so you can listen to books as you fall asleep.

In the last five years, what new belief, behavior, or habit has most improved your life?

The habit of listening to books as I fall asleep. This has cured my sometimes-serious insomnia without mood-altering drugs or futile and expensive psychotherapy and given me a chance to "read" even more books. By setting the timer carefully and rewinding a little every time I wake, I can miss almost none of a book.

What advice would you give to a smart, driven college student about to enter the "real world"?

Don't be intimidated by anything. In the vast majority of the professions and vocations, the people who succeed are not any cleverer than you. The adult world is not full of gods, just people who have acquired skills and habits that work for them. And specialize—the great human achievement is to specialize as a producer of goods or services so that you can diversify as a consumer. Self-sufficiency is another word for poverty.

"We spend far too much time complaining about the way things are, and forget that we have the power to change anything and everything."

BOZOMA SAINT JOHN
TW/IG: @badassboz

BOZOMA SAINT JOHN is the chief brand officer at Uber. Until June 2017, she was a marketing executive at Apple Music after joining the company through its acquisition of Beats Music, where she was the head of global marketing. In 2016, *Billboard* named her "Executive of the Year" and *Fortune* included her in their "40 under 40" list. *Fast Company* has included Bozoma on its list of "100 Most Creative People." Bozoma was born in Ghana, and she left the country at 14 with her family to immigrate to Colorado Springs.

What are one to three books that have greatly influenced your life?
I love Toni Morrison's *Song of Solomon*. Her writing style is incredibly poetic and complex. She doesn't "allow" any laziness in reading her work;

so beyond the incredible story, I learned to take my time to absorb the characters, and to reread passages when there was so much to unpack. It was also the book I asked my late husband to read when he dropped his pickup line to get to know me better. Our first date was a book review —and clearly he passed with flying colors. Two months later, he presented me with a painting of his interpretation of the book as a birthday gift. I knew then that I wanted to marry him. Anyone who could take his time to read, comprehend, and interpret Toni Morrison's work, based on my recommendation, was someone I wanted to spend significant time with. That experience taught me that when people care, they'll go beyond the extra mile to understand you. So Toni Morrison helped me set a high bar.

What is an unusual habit or an absurd thing that you love?

I love to people watch. I can literally do that all day long. It's fascinating to watch people go by. There's so much you can learn about a culture by just watching its people walk with each other. Great places to people watch are food courts in American malls, street-corner cafes in Paris, the market in Accra . . . fashion, etiquette, PDA . . . all of it can be learned and make the observer a more respectful participant in that culture.

When you feel overwhelmed or unfocused, what do you do?

I sleep. Or rather, I nap. There's no conundrum that a 20-minute nap can't help me unpack. It's like a refresh button for my mind. I wake up clearer and more able to make the "gut" decision because I've stopped thinking. Whatever I'm feeling when I wake up is the feeling I go forward with.

If you could have a gigantic billboard anywhere with anything on it, what would it say and why? Are there any quotes you think of often or live your life by?

Hands down, it would be "Be the change you want to see in the world." We spend far too much time complaining about the way things are, and forget that we have the power to change anything and everything. I'd have a secondary quote too: "I'm starting with the man in the mirror"—Michael Jackson. Same message; different delivery.

QUOTES I'M PONDERING

(Tim Ferriss: Oct. 9–Oct. 30, 2015)

"An expert is a person who has made all the mistakes that can be made in a very narrow field."

–NIELS BOHR
Danish physicist and Nobel Prize winner

"What we usually consider as impossible are simply engineering problems . . . there's no law of physics preventing them."

–MICHIO KAKU
Physicist and co-founder of string field theory

"These individuals have riches just as we say that we 'have a fever,' when really the fever has us."

–SENECA
Roman Stoic philosopher, famed playwright

"I also have in mind that seemingly wealthy, but most terribly impoverished class of all, who have accumulated dross, but know not how to use it, or get rid of it, and thus have forged their own golden or silver fetters."

–HENRY DAVID THOREAU
American essayist and philosopher, author of *Walden*

"I started out basically imagining I was writing for a stadium full of replicas of myself—which made things easy because I already knew exactly what topics interested them, what writing style they liked, what their sense of humor was, etc."

TIM URBAN
TW/FB: @waitbutwhy
waitbutwhy.com

TIM URBAN is the author of the blog *Wait But Why* and has become one of the Internet's most popular writers. Tim, according to *Fast Company*, has "captured a level of reader engagement that even the new-media giants would be envious of." Today, *Wait But Why* receives more than 1.5 million unique visitors per month and has over 550,000 email subscribers. Tim has gained a number of prominent readers as well, like authors Sam Harris (page 365) and Susan Cain (page 10), Twitter co-founder Evan Williams (page 401), TED curator Chris Anderson (page 407), and *Brain Pickings'* Maria Popova. Tim's series of posts after interviewing Elon Musk have been called by *Vox*'s David Roberts "the meatiest, most fascinating, most satisfying posts I've read in ages." You can start with the first one, "Elon Musk: The World's Raddest Man." Tim's TED Talk, "Inside the Mind of a Master Procrastinator," has received more than 21 million views.

What is the book (or books) you've given most as a gift, and why? Or what are one to three books that have greatly influenced your life?

The Fountainhead, by Ayn Rand, because of the two main characters in the book—Howard Roark and Peter Keating. Neither of the characters is like a real person—they're both too one-dimensional and extreme. But to me, if you put them together, you get each of us. Roark is a totally independent reasoner. He reasons from first principles—the base facts at the core of life like the limits of physics and the limits of his own biology—and uses that information only as the building blocks of his reasoning to construct his conclusions, his decisions, and his life path. Keating is the opposite—he is a totally dependent reasoner. He looks outward and sees contemporary values, social acceptance, and conventional wisdom as the core facts, and then does his best to win the game within those rules. His values are society's values and they dictate his goals. We're all like Roark sometimes and Keating other times. I think the key to life is to figure out when it makes sense to save mental energy and be like Keating (I'm super conforming in my clothing choices because it's not something that's important to me) and when in life it really matters to be like Roark and reason independently (choosing your career path, picking your life partner, deciding how to raise your kids, etc.).

The Fountainhead was a major influence when I wrote a long blog post about why I think Elon Musk is so successful. To me, he's like Roark—he's tremendous at reasoning from first principles. In the post, I call this being a "chef" (someone who experiments with ingredients and comes up with a new recipe). Musk is unusually cheflike. Most of us spend most of our lives being like Keating, or what I call a "cook" (someone who follows someone else's recipe). We'd all be happier and more successful if we could learn to be chefs more often—which just takes some self-awareness of the times we're being a cook and an epiphany that it's not actually as scary as it seems to reason independently and act on it.

Note from Tim Ferriss: I asked Tim to share a fun piece of related background. Here it is.

In early 2015, Elon reached out to schedule a call. He said he had read some *Wait But Why* posts and was wondering if I might be interested in writing about some of the industries he's involved in. I flew out to California to meet with him, tour the Tesla and SpaceX factories, and spend some time with the executives at both companies to learn the full story about what they were doing and why. Over the next six months, I wrote four very long posts about Tesla and SpaceX and the history of the industries surrounding them (during which I had regular conversations with Elon in order to really get to the bottom of the questions I had). In the first three posts, I tried to answer the question, "Why is Elon doing what he's doing?" In the fourth and final post of the series, I examined Elon himself and tried to answer the question, "Why is Elon able to do what he's doing?" That's what led me to explore all these ideas around reasoning from first principles (being a "chef" who comes up with a recipe) versus reasoning by analogy (being a "cook" who follows someone else's recipe).

What purchase of $100 or less has most positively impacted your life in the last six months (or in recent memory)?

The NYTimes crossword puzzle app. I've always liked crossword puzzles but I kind of sucked at them. Since getting the app I've gotten much better (started off mostly doing Monday through Wednesday puzzles and now I do every day of the week) and doing the puzzle is a delightful part of my day every day. I love waking up and working on the day's puzzle in the morning—in bed, while eating breakfast, on the subway, while standing in line at a coffee place, etc. But I have to be careful—the later it gets in the week, the longer the puzzle takes me, and I often don't have the discipline to put down a hard puzzle until I finish it, which can bleed badly into my planned workday and make me hate myself. Or sometimes I'll open the app when I'm taking a five-minute work break, and then that turns it into an 82-minute work break and I again hate myself. So I now try to keep my puzzling to nighttime.

How has a failure, or apparent failure, set you up for later success? Do you have a "favorite failure" of yours?

My senior year of college, I decided to apply to write the music for an annual student-written musical called *The Hasty Pudding*. When I went to the orientation for people applying to be the composer, the session was run by the head of the program and a fellow student who worked at the program and who was assisting the head in the audition process. The head talked us through how applying worked, and the student assistant got on the piano to give some examples of what kind of music they'd be looking for. I left super excited about this—I wanted to compose music for a living after college and was dying to get the gig.

Later that day, they emailed all of the applicants the schedule for when we'd be coming in to play our sample songs for the program head as our audition. On the schedule, I noticed the names of both the person who had written the music for the show the previous year (and I knew the same composer often wrote the music multiple years in a row) *and* the student assistant himself—the one who had given us advice about what they were looking for! Totally deflated, I decided not to apply. Clearly either last year's composer (who already had a relationship with the program head) or the student assistant would end up with the job.

A few months later I saw the show being advertised around campus, and the composer was . . . neither of them. Some other guy got it. I had massive regret and self-loathing for not applying. But a cheap lesson—don't get daunted out of shooting for something you want, especially by potentially unfounded assumptions.

If you could have a gigantic billboard anywhere with anything on it, what would it say and why?

It would be a magical billboard that would display something unique for each person who looked at it. The billboard would be able to mind-read, figuring out which group of people the viewer was most one-dimensionalizing, demonizing, and dehumanizing in their heads. For one viewer today, that might be Trump voters. For another, it might be Muslims. For another, it might be black people, or wealthy white people, or sex offenders. Whichever the group, the viewer would see an image of a member of that group doing something that reminded the viewer of that type or person's full, three-dimensional humanity. Maybe it would be that person sitting by the deathbed of their parent, or helping their child with their homework, or doing some silly hobby that the viewer also happened to like.

I think humans can only feel real hatred of people they're able to dehumanize in their heads. As soon as someone is exposed to reality and reminded of the full humanness of someone they hate, the hatred usually fades away and empathy pours in.

What is one of the best or most worthwhile investments you've ever made?

My first year out of college, I started a small test prep company (tutoring for SAT, ACT, etc.). Over the next nine years, I put a large portion of my time into growing that company. Early on, my co-founder and I realized it was an advantage to be two single dudes in our 20s with no real financial obligations, so we decided to keep our lifestyles at the same level even as the company grew. After a good year, instead of giving ourselves a $25,000 raise each, we'd keep our salaries in the same place and hire a $50,000 employee. After a great year, we'd keep our salaries where they were and hire three or four new employees.

I can credit my co-founder mostly for this, as he's the more disciplined one of the two of us, but it turned out to be a good strategy. By the time I turned 30, the company had 20 employees and was generating probably ten times the revenue it would have been generating had we kept upping our salaries each year. We traded the fun of having fancy lifestyles in our 20s for being far more free people at the age of 30. This freedom is what led me to start *Wait But Why* and become a full-time writer.

What is an unusual habit or an absurd thing that you love?

I have a toy box at home. Well, I actually just have a lot of toys, but my fiancée finally got fucking sick of my shit being everywhere and brought home a box where she insisted I keep all my toys. The toys are all mechanical, tactile, fidgety things—the same toys I liked when I was five. I have a bunch of different kinds of magnets, a wide array of silly putties, fidget spinners, fidget cubes, bouncy balls, etc. This isn't just because I'm a child —it actually helps me focus. I'm a kinetic thinker—the kind of person who paces constantly when on a phone call. And when I'm working—brainstorming, researching, outlining, or writing—I do a lot better with a toy in my hand. If I don't have one, I'll end up biting my nails down until they bleed. I have problems.

In the last five years, what new belief, behavior, or habit has most improved your life?

Working as a writer on your own hours, it's tempting to get into the romantic notion that you don't play by society's rules—you work from home in your underwear, you do your most inspired writing at 3 A.M., you never set an alarm, etc. I've always prided myself on doing things unconventionally, and I'm very physically lazy, so I was definitely a believer in the unconventional work schedule/environment.

The only problem is that it doesn't actually work well for me at all. I'd get stuff done when I had a deadline, but when I didn't, I'd be horribly unproductive. I also found myself in a permanent state of *kind of* working. I was rarely in a long period of full work focus, and I was rarely just carefree off work.

I realized at some point recently that there's something to the "go to an office from nine to five" thing. I stopped writing from home and started putting clothes on and writing from a coffee shop. I started going to bed at a normal human hour and setting an alarm. And I'd try to compartmentalize, being dead serious about work until the late afternoon or early evening and then stopping entirely until the next day. I've even tried taking weekends (or at least one weekend day) off work. I'm not perfectly on this schedule and sometimes fall off the wagon, but when I can manage to pull it off, it's better for me for a few reasons:

- Most people do their best work in the morning, and I'm no exception.

- Working later in the day kills your social life, since most social life happens between 7 P.M. and 11 P.M. on weekdays and on weekends. If you're working in that time you suddenly become that friend who's never available, which is horribly shortsighted and unwise.

- As I detailed in my TED Talk, I think we all have two main characters in our heads: a rational decision-maker (the adult in your head) and an instant gratification monkey (the child in your head who doesn't care about consequences and just wants to maximize the ease and pleasure of the current moment). For me, these two are in a constant battle, and the monkey usually wins. But I've found that if I turn life into a yin-yang situation—e.g., "work till 6 today, then no work till tomorrow"—it's much easier to control the monkey in the work period. Knowing he has something fun to look forward to later makes him much more likely to cooperate. In my old system, the monkey was in a constant state of rebellion against a system that never really gave him any dedicated time.

What advice would you give to a smart, driven college student about to enter the "real world"? What advice should they ignore?

You can kind of group all careers into two major buckets—careers where you're the CEO and careers where you work for a CEO.

Careers where you're the CEO include anything where you're trying to start your own company, anything where you're trying to make your name in the arts and win fans, anything where you're doing freelance work —paths where you're driving the ship of your own career and making the big decisions.

Careers where someone else is the CEO are where you're on an existing ship that's being driven by someone else, and you're doing a job on that ship. This includes obvious situations where you're an employee at a company, but also a situation where the career itself is a predefined ship, like being a doctor or a lawyer.

Society loves to glorify the "you-as-CEO" paths and make people who don't want to be the CEO of their own career feel inferior about their path, but neither of these paths is inherently better or worse than the other—it just depends on your personality, your goals, and what you want from a lifestyle. There are some super smart, talented, special people whose gifts are best expressed as CEO and others whose are best expressed when someone else is worrying about keeping the lights on and you can just put your head down and focus on your work. Likewise, there are some people who need to be CEO to find their work fulfilling and others for whom being CEO and having their work bleed into everything is a recipe for misery.

For some people, they want one thing specifically—like someone who *needs* to be a singer-songwriter to be happy—but most of us leave college pretty torn about the kind of work we want to do most. For those people, I'd recommend thinking hard about the CEO question and experimenting in your 20s to see what it feels like on both sides.

What are bad recommendations you hear in your profession or area of expertise?

I'm a writer, and I find that a lot of advice to young writers—especially those trying to make a name for themselves online—centers around trying to win readers over. If you think of your potential readers as pegs, this advice is about trying to mold yourself into the right-shaped hole—a hole that will fit a lot of readers or draw in a bunch of readers quickly, or some other means of getting a writing career going.

I think the opposite advice is better. Obsess over figuring out the funnest, most exciting, most natural shape of yourself as a writer and start doing that. There are a *lot* of people on the Internet, and they can all access your work with one tap on the phone in their pocket. So even if only one in every thousand of them—0.1 percent—happens to be a reader peg that perfectly matches the shape of your writing hole, that amounts to over a million people who will absolutely love what you're doing.

I started out basically imagining I was writing for a stadium full of replicas of myself—which made things easy because I already knew exactly what topics interested them, what writing style they liked, what their sense of humor was, etc. I ignored the conventional wisdom that online articles should be short, frequent, posted consistently—because I knew the Tims in that stadium didn't care about those things—and instead focused on a single type of topic. And it worked. Four years later, many of those people who happen to like my type of writing have found me.

By focusing inward on yourself as a writer instead of outward on what you think readers will want to read, you'll end up creating the best and most original work, and that one-in-a-thousand person who happens to love it will end up finding their way to you.

In the last five years, what have you become better at saying no to? What new realizations and/or approaches helped?

I've learned to make my "no" list by starting with my "yes" list. The "yes" list should be centered around what's important—but how do you define a vague concept like "important"? I use a couple of simple litmus tests:

When it comes to my work "yes" list, I think about what I might call the Epitaph Test. When I find myself with an opportunity, I ask myself whether I'd be happy if my epitaph had something to do with this project. If the answer is a clear no, it probably means it's not actually very important to me. Thinking about your epitaph, as morbid as it is, is a nice way to cut through all the noise and force yourself to look at your work from a super zoomed-out perspective, where you can see what really matters to you. So I try to make my "yes" list by thinking about the Epitaph Test, and potential time commitments outside of that definition fall on my "no" list. For me, the Epitaph Test is usually a reminder to focus my time and effort on doing the highest-quality and most original creative work I can.

For my social life "yes" list, a similar test could be called the Deathbed Test. We all hear about these studies where people on their deathbed reflect on what they regret most, and the cliché is that nobody ever says they regret spending more time in the office. That's because a deathbed offers people a level of zoomed-out clarity that's hard to get to in our normal lives, and it's only when we're lacking that clarity in the fog of our day-to-day rush that we'd think it makes sense to neglect our most important personal relationships. The Deathbed Test pushes me to do two things:

- Make sure I'm dedicating my time to the right people with the question, "Is this someone I might be thinking about when I'm on my deathbed?"

- Make sure I'm spending enough high-quality time with the people I care about most with the question, "If I were on my deathbed today, would I be happy with the amount of time I spent with this person?" An alternative is thinking about other people's deathbeds—"If X person were on their deathbed today, how would I feel about the amount of quality time I've spent with them?"

The people who matter most are always in competition for your time with both your work and with other people, and the Deathbed Test can be a good reminder that the only way to dedicate the proper amount of time to your key people is by saying no to a lot of other stuff and a lot of other people.

The point of both the Epitaph Test and the Deathbed Test is that by the time you're on your deathbed and your epitaph is being drafted, it's too late to change anything—so we want to do whatever we can to access that magical end-of-life clarity before the end of life actually happens.

Of course, actually saying no to your "no" list is a struggle of its own, and I'm still working on that—but having good mechanisms for defining what's important has helped a lot.

"I used to resent obstacles along the path, thinking, 'If only that hadn't happened life would be so good.' Then I suddenly realized, life *is* the obstacles. There is no underlying path."

JANNA LEVIN
TW/IG: @jannalevin
jannalevin.com

JANNA LEVIN is the Tow Professor of physics and astronomy at Barnard College of Columbia University, and has contributed to an understanding of black holes, the cosmology of extra dimensions, and gravitational waves in the shape of spacetime. She is also director of sciences at Pioneer Works, a cultural center dedicated to experimentation, education, and production across disciplines. Her books include *How the Universe Got Its Spots* and a novel, *A Madman Dreams of Turing Machines*, which won the PEN/Bingham Prize. She was recently named a Guggenheim Fellow, a grant awarded to those "who have demonstrated exceptional capacity for productive scholarship." Her latest book, *Black Hole Blues and Other Songs from Outer Space*, is the inside story on the discovery of the century: the sound of spacetime ringing from the collision of two black holes over a billion years ago.

How has a failure, or apparent failure, set you up for later success? Do you have a "favorite failure" of yours?

Failure is highly underrated. There's an anecdote about Einstein I only came across very recently. In 1915 he thought gravitational waves—ripples in the shape of spacetime—were the most important consequence of his general theory of relativity. He reversed himself a couple of years later, claiming they did not exist. He goes back and forth like this for a bit. Several years on, he submits a paper for publication asserting they do not exist. Somewhere between acceptance and going to press, he slips in an entirely new manuscript that says they do. A friend warns, "Einstein, you have be careful. Your famous name will be on these papers." Einstein laughs. "My name is on plenty of wrong papers," he says. In the 1930s he declares he does not know if gravitational waves exist but it is a most important question. In 2015, 100 years after Einstein first proposes their existence, a massive billion-dollar experimental undertaking records gravitational waves from the collision of two black holes over a billion years ago, waves emitted long before humans emerged on the Earth. We discourage failure and by doing so we subtly discourage success.

My favorite personal failure is my first cosmological theory. When I learned the Earth was round, I believed we lived inside the sphere. I was knocked back and simultaneously thrilled to see another possibility come into focus. We live *on* the sphere. Incredible. Science isn't about being right preemptively or knowing the answer. Science is motivated by the human drive to struggle to discover.

What is one of the best or most worthwhile investments you've ever made?

I recently renovated about 3,000 square feet in Pioneer Works, a spectacular cultural center for art, music, film, and now science. The facility is housed in a former ironworks factory on the water in Red Hook, Brooklyn. We had no architect for the renovation, no plans, no drawings, no measurements. I stood with the founder, Dustin Yellin, and the director, Gabriel Florenz, mostly yelling and laughing and yelling and arguing. Someone would declare: I want a room there. I want all glass. I want no glass. I want walls. I want no walls. A door here. And each of us would occasionally concede to the others while the incredibly talented builder, Willie Vantapool, listened and integrated our ideas and implemented what emerged as a surprisingly coherent design. As a very theoretically leaning physicist, this was the most physical expression of any creative project I've undertaken and was one of the riskiest investments I've considered. I'm now here in the new Science Studios as I write these replies, and I marvel at the outcome. The space is stunning and inviting and inspiring. We're building the world we want to inhabit and, by doing so, we've constructed a remarkable, unusual space for the sciences in an unconventional setting. Science belongs in the bigger world because, as I've gotten into the habit of saying, science is part of culture.

In the last five years, what new belief, behavior, or habit has most improved your life?

I used to resent obstacles along the path, thinking, "If only that hadn't happened life would be so good." Then I suddenly realized, life *is* the obstacles. There is no underlying path. Our role here is to get better at navigating those obstacles. I strive to find calm, measured responses and to see hindrances as a chance to problem-solve. Often I fall back into old frustrations, but if I remind myself, this is a chance to step up, I can reframe conflicts as a chance to experiment with solutions.

In the last five years, what have you become better at saying no to?

I am terrible at saying no. Truly terrible. I'll be reading the other responses for advice here.

"We need a new diversity — not one based on biological characteristics and identity politics but a diversity of opinion and worldviews."

AYAAN HIRSI ALI
TW: @Ayaan
theahafoundation.org

AYAAN HIRSI ALI is a women's rights activist, champion of free speech, and best-selling author. As a young girl in Somalia, she was subjected to female genital mutilation (FGM). When forced by her father to marry a distant cousin, she fled to Holland and claimed political asylum, working her way up from being a janitor to serving as an elected member of the Dutch parliament. As a member, she campaigned to raise awareness of violence against women, including honor killings and FGM, practices that had followed her fellow immigrants into Holland. In 2004, Ayaan gained international attention following the murder of Theo van Gogh, who had directed her short film *Submission*, a film about the oppression of women under Islam. The assassin left a death threat for her pinned to van Gogh's chest. This tragic event is chronicled in her best-selling book, *Infidel*. She is also the author of *Caged Virgin*, *Nomad*, and most recently the bestseller *Heretic: Why Islam Needs a Reformation Now*.

What is the book (or books) you've given most as a gift, and why? Or what are one to three books that have greatly influenced your life?

Karl Popper's *The Open Society and Its Enemies*, first published in 1945. I'd often give this to my politician friends when I was in politics, and now I give it to students. One of the biggest lessons for me from this book is that so many bad ideas that lead to authoritarian consequences begin with good intentions. This is timeless wisdom.

When I was in politics in the Netherlands, I was surrounded by politicians with wonderful intentions. They wanted to do good and involve the government in every aspect of life by expanding programs, yet these good intentions would lead to controlling more and more of people's lives. One example was childcare. We debated whether the government should provide free childcare. It sounds great and came from good intentions to support parents continuing their careers. But in practice it would mean the government replaces the spouse or partner. It would require parents to divulge personal information to the state, it would dictate how people's money was spent and how children should be raised. The price of ceding the authority of parents to government was simply too high. That's just one small example but it illustrates how government loves control. Popper would not have liked that idea.

If you could have a gigantic billboard anywhere with anything on it, what would it say and why?

"We need a new diversity—not one based on biological characteristics and identity politics but a diversity of opinion and worldviews."

What advice would you give to a smart, driven college student about to enter the "real world"? What advice should they ignore?

Students should go to college with an open mind. I advise them to ignore all the absolutism around them, both in terms of ideas and people. When they're told that some people or ideas are wrong, hateful, or offensive, a light bulb should go off in their heads. That is the moment their curiosity should be piqued to find out for themselves whether it is indeed a "bad" thing. Adopting an attitude of critical thinking is most crucial in learning anything.

Many students come to me full of wonderful intentions hoping to change the world; they plan to spend their time helping the poor and disadvantaged. I tell them to first graduate and make a lot of money, and only then figure out how best to help those in need. Too often students can't meaningfully help the disadvantaged now, even if it makes them feel good for trying to. I have seen so many former students in their late 30s and 40s struggling to make ends meet. They spent their time in college doing good rather than building their careers and futures. I warn students today to be careful how they use their precious time and to think carefully about when is the right time to help. It's a well-worn cliché, but you have to help yourself before you help others. This is too often lost on idealistic students.

I am often asked whether one should work in the private or public sector. I always advise working in the private sector, and wish I did this before entering politics and the public sector. The private sector teaches important skills like entrepreneurship that can then be applied to any area of work later on.

"Buddhists observe that we're all on fire. It's so beautiful to sometimes tune in and see the flickering."

GRAHAM DUNCAN
eastrockcap.com

GRAHAM DUNCAN is the co-founder of East Rock Capital, an investment firm that manages $2 billion for a small number of families and their charitable foundations. Before starting East Rock 12 years ago, Graham worked at two other investment firms. He started his career by co-founding the independent Wall Street research firm Medley Global Advisors. Graham graduated from Yale with a BA in ethics, politics, and economics. He is a member of the Council on Foreign Relations and serves as co-chair of the Sohn Conference Foundation, which funds pediatric cancer research. Josh Waitzkin (page 195) calls Graham "the tip of the spear in the realms of talent tracking and judgment of human potential in high-stakes mental arenas."

What is an unusual habit or an absurd thing that you love?

I wear a SubPac M2 Wearable Physical Sound System while I commute on the subway to my office, and sometimes while I work at my desk. The system lets you feel the vibration of music through your body. Music producers, gamers, and deaf people are the primary users. I find the full-body experience of music makes listening to music or even a podcast more of an immersive somatic experience rather than just a conceptual head thing.

If you could have a gigantic billboard anywhere with anything on it, what would it say and why? Are there any quotes you think of often or live your life by?

I have two candidates:

First, "It's not how well you play the game, it's deciding what game you want to play."—Kwame Appiah. This quote separates striving from strategy and reminds me to take a macro view of what I'm doing, like in a video game where you can zoom out and you suddenly see you've been running around in one corner of the maze. It loosens someone's relationship to the game, too, helping to separate having ambition from being ambitious, or accessing hustle without becoming a hustler.

Second, the Buddhist novelist George Saunders said in an interview that he has an image of people's "nectar in decaying containers." That image haunts me. When I think of it on a given morning, it allows me to see the Buddha nature flowing through all these lovely, flawed, living, and slowly dying creatures we encounter every day. My three-year-old daughter's three-year-old self is so temporary. Buddhists observe that we're all on fire. It's so beautiful to sometimes tune in and see the flickering.

What is the book (or books) you've given most as a gift, and why? Or what are one to three books that have greatly influenced your life?

Sam Barondes' book *Making Sense of People* has had a big impact on my thinking, and I sometimes give a copy to people in the midst of hiring someone or even deciding whether to get engaged. As part of my role as an investor, I interview 400 to 500 people a year to decide whether to hire them or invest in their various startups or investment funds, and the most useful mental model I have found to help understand what makes people tick is the one Barondes describes in his book. The model is called the "Big Five" or OCEAN: open-minded, conscientious, extroverted, agreeable, neurotic. The academics who developed the model clumped every English adjective that could be used to describe someone into categories and reduced them to as small a set of factors as they could. The Big Five is considered the equivalent of gravity in the academic literature on personality. There have been thousands of studies using it, and it's considered much more statistically accurate than alternatives such as Myers-Briggs. The killer combination is high open-minded, high conscientious, low neurotic.

There are two other mental models that greatly influence my thinking about people and teams. The first is Harvard professor Robert Kegan's model of adult development. Kegan argues adults develop—and make sense of reality—in five discrete phases. He lays out his theory in the 1994 book *In Over Our Heads*. The title is a reference to how the vast majority of adult Americans are at the "socialized" stage of development. They have difficulty taking other people's perspectives and tend to follow assumptions given to them by society (as opposed to assumptions they freely choose). For people interested in learning more about the model, I recommend Kegan's graduate student Jennifer Garvey Berger's more recent and less academic book *Changing on the Job*.

The third mental model I find myself recommending lately is found not in a book, but on a slightly obscure website: workwithsource.com. This work is based on a European management consultant who studied hundreds of startups and realized that even when there are multiple "co-founders," there is always a single "source": the person who took the first risk on a new initiative. That source maintains a unique relationship with the gestalt of the original idea and has an intuitive knowledge of what the right next step for the initiative is, whereas others who join later to help with the execution often lack that intuitive connection to the founder's original insight. Many organizational tensions and power struggles often revolve around lack of explicit acknowledgment of who the source of the initiative is. A prominent angel investor observed to me recently that many founders seem to hire friends as co-founders more to quell their own anxiety during the early, highly ambiguous days of a new company than to fulfill a specific role. This can work fine as long as everyone is clear on who the source is.

The responsibility to fully own the role of source rests in large part with the source themselves.

Handing off the source role of an initiative to another person is possible but extremely difficult, and is most often mishandled. One key to a successful transition is for the original source to actually move on and allow the new leader room to move. One investment manager told me about a study he did of stock performance following founder CEOs departing their businesses: any subsequent positive stock performance was correlated with the founder completely leaving the board rather than hanging around to mentor the next CEO. Gates remaining on the Microsoft board during Ballmer's tenure may have contributed to the subsequent lackluster stock performance, whereas Ballmer's recent departure from the board allows Satya Nadella to fully assert his own creative vision. I encounter this dynamic in my work managing the wealth of Forbes 500 families, where second and third generations sometimes struggle with how to relate to the original patriarch and "source" of their wealth. Often the responsibility to make the room for a real transition is in the hands of the source. It's the lesson from the George Washington song in the *Hamilton* musical, as Washington declines Hamilton's plea to run for a third term and sings, "We're going to teach them how to say good-bye."

What purchase of $100 or less has most positively impacted your life in the last six months (or in recent memory)?

I recently bought the FINIS swim paddles (under $20; hat tip Ben Greenfield blog). They magically lengthen out my freestyle stroke, and combined with Cressi fins ($29) it feels like I'm flying through water.

How has a failure, or apparent failure, set you up for later success? Do you have a "favorite failure" of yours?

In my role investing in and seeding investment firms, I conduct extensive reference checks on people in order to try to accelerate the process of building trust. In early 2008, I was about to back a firm and conducted a final reference check with the investment manager's former boss, who was quite negative and skeptical of his former analyst. It was enough to make me pause on proceeding with the investment, which then proceeded to work out quite well as the financial crisis unfolded. I had a lot of regret about the size of the profits I missed. Later it emerged that the reference source may have had an agenda to sabotage his former protégé's new firm.

Five years later, I was evaluating another investment manager to partner with, and toward the end of our diligence process I got a reference that was mixed. By this point I was better able to hold multiple perspectives simultaneously without experiencing cognitive dissonance, the state of "negative capability" that Keats referred to as useful to writers. This time, the mixed data points only made me do more work, and I gained even more conviction in the character and competence of the investment manager. This investment has been one of our most profitable, and absent my earlier failure, I suspect I would have not had the ability to see the reality of the situation. Today when I speak with anyone about anything, I try to hold their perspective with a "light grip": the knowledge that they, and I, have very incomplete maps of reality.

What are bad recommendations you hear in your profession or area of expertise?

I think people overuse the term "hedge fund." I think we should throw the term out, perhaps start using "H Structure" instead to capture the concept of incentive compensation. I don't think it's useful to see a "fund" or a "product." These are just temporary collections of flawed, brilliant people, who in any given year decide to make a sequel to the movie they made the prior year. The only product is the set of future decisions the portfolio manager makes. If they get divorced or depressed, if their second in command leaves, the "product" completely changes. Calling it a product ignores the reality that the only source of stability is whether the mindset of the team leader is resilient or even antifragile (Nassim Taleb's notion of actually getting stronger with volatility).

What is one of the best or most worthwhile investments you've ever made?

I invest a disproportionate amount of my income in paying for an ever-growing collection of trainers and coaches. There are two coaches who have had enormous impact on me in the last five years: Carolyn Coughlin at Cultivating Leadership and Jim Dethmer at Conscious Leadership. Carolyn is the most gifted listener I have ever encountered. She surfaces my hidden assumptions—the ones that hold me rather than me holding them—and teaches me to ask better and better questions. Jim Dethmer may be one of the few living bodhisattvas. Jim has helped me refine my communication skills and helped me develop more conscious relationships at work and with my family. I picture masterful coaches like Jim and Carolyn playing the same role as the wizards from *Lord of the Rings*—they exude supportive, loving energy that creates the conditions for life feeling like an adventure from a secure base, an endless unfolding of possibility.

In the last five years, what have you become better at saying no to?

I have my assistant Google pictures of people I'm considering meeting or calling in the next two weeks and put them in Trello cards. I see meeting new people as the opportunity to open a new door to a new world that could change my or their life in some way. Seeing someone's picture allows me to visualize their intentionality and unleashes more creative ideas about what we can discuss and how I may be able to help them. It also lets me access whether I have a "full-body yes" to actually seeing them and opening this new door, and if I don't then I take my hand off the door handle.

When you feel overwhelmed or unfocused, what do you do? What questions do you ask yourself?

I ask myself "what would be the worst thing" about that outcome not going the way I want? I had started using it out loud with my kids, and recently my eight-year-old daughter started asking it back to me. I really like to be punctual. We were late to drop her at school and I was impatient, so she asked me, "Dad, what exactly would be the worst thing about being late?" It completely shifted my mindset in the moment. I like the question because it often surfaces a hidden assumption.

In the last five years, what new belief, behavior, or habit has most improved your life?

I've begun swimming most mornings, and I find it often shifts my mindset for the rest of the day. Swimmers talk about the concept of "water feel," which is getting a grip in the water and pulling your body past that point instead of ripping your hand through the water, which moves you forward but is much less efficient, much less graceful. As David Foster Wallace points out in his speech, "This Is Water," much of life is water to us—we are swimming in it and can't see it because we're either in a hurry or not awake to our context. When I stop to really feel the water before I pull, it shifts my way of being from thrashing toward the other end of the pool to a more effortless flow of working with the reality of where I am.

What advice would you give to a smart, driven college student about to enter the "real world"?

I like to think about careers through Dan Siegel's model of a river flowing between two banks, where one side is chaos and the other side is rigidity. Dan points out that all mental illnesses reside on one bank or the other: schizophrenia is chaos, OCD is rigidity, and healthy integration is swimming in the middle of the river. Most college students have started life closer to the rigidity bank and over the course of their careers will experiment with swimming toward the middle. I have come to think of the lane next to rigidity as an appropriately conventional one for your 20s that requires the skill of "refining reality," a place to swim where it's important to learn the jargon of an industry and apprentice under someone, to develop judgment and discover your zone of genius.

I think swimming in the middle lane happens most often in people's 30s or 40s, a stage where you begin crafting your own language for what you do as an increasingly "strong poet"—you make your craft your own and view your life as more self-expression than simply playing out other people's roles for you. And then some small percentage of people will paddle over to the lane next to chaos, the place where you find novelists Robert Pirsig and David Foster Wallace, investors like Mike Burry or Eddie Lampert, or entrepreneurs like Steve Jobs and Elon Musk. I experience them as consistently "asserting reality" through their powerful storytelling, while always bearing the risk that their egos grow too big and their creative narcissism becomes too well defended. They can lose their feedback loop with reality and flop onto the bank of chaos.

Through this lens, Pirsig's wrestling with his sanity toward the end of his life, Steve Jobs' magical thinking about his illness, and Eddie Lampert's Ayn Randian framing of his investment in Sears may all have been examples of strong poets losing their feel for where they can mythologize to the point of bending our collective reality and where they suddenly appear crazy. I think Musk drives hedge fund managers crazy as half of them are short his shares because he exudes so much promotional hucksterism, and half of them are long because he is actually thinking on a 100-year time scale. It's very confusing.

In retrospect, I would tell my 21-year-old self to have a little more patience in swimming along the rigidity bank rather than constantly seeking the entrepreneurial and chaotic side of the river. In one scary moment, I managed to resign only a minute before my boss was going to fire me for working on my own agenda instead of his. But you also don't want get stuck too close to rigidity and risk living someone else's life instead of your own. Either way, it's critical to remember you can always choose to course-correct and swim toward structure or chaos, apprenticeship or freedom, depending on what you need at that moment, what tempo and phase of your career you want to be in, which riverbank you're coming from and where you want to go. I highly recommend the poem "For Julia, in the Deep Water" [by John N. Morris] to parents who, like me, are navigating the question of when and whether to let their kids swim away.

"Ego is about who's right. Truth is about what's right."

MIKE MAPLES JR.
TW: @m2jr
floodgate.com

MIKE MAPLES JR. is a partner at Floodgate, a venture capital firm that specializes in micro-cap investments in startups. He has been on the *Forbes* Midas List since 2010 and named one of *Fortune* magazine's "8 Rising Stars." Before becoming a full-time investor, Mike was involved as a founder and operating executive at back-to-back startup IPOs, including Tivoli Systems (IPO TIVS, acquired by IBM) and Motive (IPO MOTV, acquired by Alcatel-Lucent). Some of Mike's investments include Twitter, Twitch.tv, ngmoco, Weebly, Chegg, Bazaarvoice, Spiceworks, Okta, and Demandforce.

What is the book (or books) you've given most as a gift, and why? Or what are books that have greatly influenced your life?

The Top Five Regrets of the Dying by Bronnie Ware
Jonathan Livingston Seagull by Richard Bach
Hope for the Flowers by Trina Paulus

Living Forward by Michael Hyatt and Daniel Harkavy
How Will You Measure Your Life? by Clayton M. Christensen

How has a failure, or apparent failure, set you up for later success? Do you have a "favorite failure" of yours?

When I was in college, I was rejected by the fraternities that I was interested in, so I ended up helping to start one. The fraternities that said no are no longer on campus, and the one I helped start turned out to be among the absolute best.

When I came back to Silicon Valley, I didn't get a general partner offer from the venture firms I cared most about, so I ended up starting one called Floodgate. Floodgate is doing awesome, and I am thankful every day that I didn't get what I "wanted."

I love that Bill Campbell's [called "the coach," a famous mentor to tech icons like Steve Jobs, Jeff Bezos, and Larry Page] favorite song was "You Can't Always Get What You Want" by the Rolling Stones. There is so much wisdom in that song. Sometimes . . . not getting what you want opens the door to getting what you need.

If you could have a gigantic billboard anywhere with anything on it, what would it say?

"Integrity is the only path where you will never get lost."

What are some of the best or most worthwhile investments you've ever made?

- Believing in my kids.
- Moving to California to be a VC [venture capitalist] when everyone said it was a stupid idea.
- A dog named Stella (if you can believe it).
- Learning how to slow down and take pictures with a manual focus lens.
- A few startup investments that worked out.

In the last five years, what new belief, behavior, or habit has most improved your life?

Understanding that even though great scientists never believe they can state "this is the truth," they still seek the truth more passionately than all others.

What advice would you give to a smart, driven college student about to enter the "real world"?

Life will go faster than you know. It will be tempting to live a life that impresses others. But this is the wrong path. The right path is to know that life is short, every day is a gift, and *you* have certain gifts.

Happiness is about understanding that the gift of life should be honored every day by offering *your* gifts to the world.

Don't let yourself define what matters by the dogma of other people's thoughts. And even more important, don't let the thoughts of self-doubt and chattering self-criticism in your own mind slow you down. You will likely be your own worst critic. Be kind to yourself in your own mind. Let your mind show you the same kindness that you aspire to show others.

What are bad recommendations you hear in your profession or area of expertise?

"This worked for me in my career, so do it my way."

The best advice I have seen comes from people who don't try to tell me the answer . . . instead they give me a new approach to thinking about the question so that I can solve it better on my own. Most "bad" recommendations I could reduce to "I have been successful, so do it my way." The best advice is more like, "I can't answer your question, but this might be a good way for you to think about it."

Everyone has their own journey. People who offer great advice understand that their goal is to help someone on their unique journey. People who offer bad advice are trying to relive their old glories.

In the last five years, what have you become better at saying no to?

People who are powerful but are not honest or good.

I've realized that accommodating such people is a waste of time. Your time is limited, so it's best to spend it with people who will make you feel like you made the most of your gift of today.

When you feel overwhelmed or unfocused, what do you do? What questions do you ask yourself?

I step back . . . and slow down . . . and ask the five whys. And when I am done, I also ask if I am afraid of something but too afraid to admit it.

We are drawn to the simplicity of jumping to conclusions. We are all ignorant in some way all of the time. So, I have come to learn that what we need are methods to counteract our ignorance.

The five whys is a good way of slowing down and improving decision quality. The most important thing is that it lets me get into a mental space about "what" is going right or wrong rather than "who" is right or wrong.

Let's take an example: Say we miss the sales target for a quarter. It can often become tempting to figure out "whose" fault it was: Did Sales fail to execute? Do we have a marketing problem? Is the product not differentiated enough? If you are not very, very careful, you can contribute to an environment where people will point fingers at each other and lose their ability to truly learn from the problem.

So, instead, I find it helpful to slow down. If I am by myself, I write the five whys on paper. If I am in a group, I write the questions down one at a time on a whiteboard:

Q: Why did we miss our \$1M sales target this quarter?
A: We made fewer sales calls than planned.
Q: Why did we make fewer sales calls than planned?
A: We had fewer leads to work this month.
Q: Why did we have fewer leads this month?
A: We sent fewer email outreaches than planned.
Q: Why did we send fewer outreach emails than planned?
A: We were short-staffed.
Q: Why were we short-staffed?
A: We didn't plan around the fact that two people were on vacation.

In this example, it would be very tempting to answer at the "surface" level and try to figure out if it's a "sales problem" or a "marketing problem" or a "product problem." But before that happens, I find it is better to be focused on honoring the discovery of the truth rather than determining who is to blame.

Going very slow in this exercise is helpful, because it can cause people to turn off their "lizard brains" and fight-or-flight instincts and shift their thinking to their rational brains and problem-solving.

In general, whenever I feel things are moving too quickly, I find the right instinct is almost always to slow down and get my thoughts back in order. It ends up speeding things up because we get better decisions and more alignment of everyone on the team. If someone on the team needs to be replaced because they don't have the right skill set, we should face that problem too, but only after we have done our best to seek the truth of the situation.

Ego is about who's right. Truth is about what's right.

QUOTES I'M PONDERING

(Tim Ferriss: Nov. 6–Dec. 4, 2015)

"Diversity in counsel, unity in command."

—CYRUS THE GREAT
Founder of the Achaemenid Empire, known as the "king of Persia"

"I can't give you a surefire formula for success, but I can give you a formula for failure: try to please everybody all the time."

—HERBERT BAYARD SWOPE
American editor and journalist, first recipient of the Pulitzer Prize

"One should use common words to say uncommon things."

—ARTHUR SCHOPENHAUER
Renowned 19th-century German philosopher

"If you are distressed by anything external, the pain is not due to the thing itself, but to your estimate of it; and this you have the power to revoke at any moment."

—MARCUS AURELIUS
Emperor of Rome and Stoic philosopher, author of *Meditations*

"Just one [trapeze] class made me realize that underneath my mind's chatter, my body has everything under control if I'm willing to take the plunge and fly."

SOMAN CHAINANI
TW: @SomanChainani
IG: @somanc
somanchainani.net

SOMAN CHAINANI is a detailed planner, filmmaker, and *New York Times* best-selling author. Soman's debut fiction series, *The School for Good and Evil*, has sold more than a million copies, has been translated into more than 20 languages across six continents, and will soon be a film from Universal Pictures. A graduate of Harvard University and Columbia University's MFA Film Program, Soman began his career as a screenwriter and director, with his films playing at more than 150 film festivals around the world. He was recently named to the Out100 and has received the $100,000 Shasha Grant and Sun Valley Writers' Fellowship, both for debut writers.

What is the book (or books) you've given most as a gift, and why? Or what are one to three books that have greatly influenced your life?

The War of Art by Steven Pressfield (page 5). I read this slim little book before any new creative project and it lights a torchfire inside me. The crisis with all creative work is that it requires us to trust that generative voice inside us while also silencing the negative ones. It's so easy to mix them all up and end up quietly abandoning our ambitions. (It's why I became a pharmaceutical consultant at 21 years old, selling Viagra instead of writing fantasy like I do now.) Half drill sergeant, half Zen voodoo master, Pressfield shot me out of my stupor and taught me the meaning of creative discipline.

A Little Life by Hanya Yanagihara. The greatest work of fiction I've ever read, with the simplest theme: All of us come with baggage and wounds and pain; all of us. But recognizing that common, human bond is what helps us transcend that pain.

Peter Pan by J. M. Barrie. I think the greatest exercise a person can do when they're stuck is to remember what their favorite children's book was. A book that you read over and over and over again. Somewhere in that book is the clue to not only what makes you tick, but also to your life's purpose. Mine was *Peter Pan*, which featured a title character who was at once charming and also a complete narcissistic, pathological demon. It was that ambiguous space between good and evil that I sparked to as a kid . . . and am now writing stories about as an adult.

How has a failure, or apparent failure, set you up for later success? Do you have a "favorite failure" of yours?

The biggest failure I ever had was with my thesis film at Columbia's graduate film school—a movie I'd poured all of my savings into (nearly $25,000) and worked on for eight months. A day before my final showing to the faculty, I previewed it to a professor who recommended I slash it to pieces and completely recut it. Panicked, I followed his advice and presented the hacked-up version to the faculty the next day, who absolutely despised it. All credibility I'd earned among my professors over the past three years went up in smoke.

A few weeks later, I ran into one of these disappointed faculty members—one who'd been a huge supporter of my work before this and now could barely look at me. I told him the story of the last-minute recutting. He asked to see the original version. When I showed it to him, his eyes lit up: "Ah. Now I see you."

It was the most valuable lesson I ever received. Don't let someone knock you off course before you reach your destination. Trust the work. Always trust the work.

In the last five years, what new belief, behavior, or habit has most improved your life?

There's this dazzling short story by Ted Chiang called "Liking What You See" that did a number on me. The story asserts that beauty has become a modern-day superdrug, that with filtered and face-tuned social media, retouched models on advertisements, and rampant pornography, we've overloaded the senses so that our natural instincts can no longer recognize or react to real beauty anymore. And it's making us confused and miserable, both in how we judge ourselves and how we judge others. That crystal clear warning—beauty is literally ruining our lives—has improved my life tenfold just by making me consciously aware of it (and by making me ignore 90 percent of what's on Instagram).

If you could have a gigantic billboard anywhere with anything on it, what would it say and why?

If I'm in Hollywood, it would say, "They're lying." If I'm anywhere else, it would say, "If you can conceive of it, it's probably wrong." Meditation has taught me that most of the ideas, opinions, rules, and fixed systems I have in my mind aren't the real truth. They're the residues of past experiences that I haven't let go of. What I've learned is that my soul doesn't speak in thoughts at all—it speaks in feelings, images, and clues.

What purchase of $100 or less has most positively impacted your life in the last six months (or in recent memory)?

Mother Dirt: It cured my acne and skin problems permanently. It's a $49 spray with oxidizing bacteria that you use in place of soap, and it restores your skin to its natural balance. If I could buy this for every teenager in America, I would.

What is an unusual habit or an absurd thing that you love?

I don't think I've ever told anyone this, but I read old issues of Archie comics before I go to bed. It's not a new habit: I used to read Archie as a kid, before I tucked in for the night. Riverdale in the comics always seemed so crisp and bright and welcoming (the opposite of the way I felt about my school growing up). It continues to give me a warm, soothing feeling before I drift off to sleep. But more important, closing the day by reading the same thing that I did when I was young gives my life a semblance of beautiful sense and order.

What is one of the best or most worthwhile investments you've ever made?

Flying trapeze lessons. It's like shock therapy for the soul. Once you're 50 feet high, soaring on a trapeze, it's just you, your fear, and your instincts. It's the most intimate experience I've had with myself. Just one class made me realize that underneath my mind's chatter, my body has everything under control if I'm willing to take the plunge and fly.

What advice would you give to a smart, driven college student about to enter the "real world"? What advice should they ignore?

Advice I'd give: Make sure you have something every day you're looking forward to. Maybe it's your job, maybe it's a basketball game after work or a voice lesson or your writing group, maybe it's a date. But have something every day that lights you up. It'll keep your soul hungry to create more of these moments.

Advice to ignore: A little part of me dies every time someone tells me they've taken a job as a "steppingstone" to something else, when they clearly aren't invested in it. You have one life to live. Time is valuable. If you're using steppingstones, you're also likely relying on someone else's path or definition of success. Make your own.

What are bad recommendations you hear in your profession or area of expertise?

Too often, aspiring artists put pressure on themselves to make their creative work their only source of income. In my experience, it's a road to misery. If art is your sole source of income, then there's unrelenting pressure on that art, and mercenary pressure is the enemy of the creative elves inside you trying to get the work done. Having another stream of income drains the pressure on your creative engine. If nothing comes of your art, you still have an ironclad plan to support yourself. As a result, your creative soul feels lighter and free to do its best work.

I'm a personal practitioner of this: Even after three books and a hefty movie deal, I still tutor kids and help them with their college applications. My friends can't understand it, but it's the only way I know how to write without feeling like it's a matter of life and death.

In the last five years, what have you become better at saying no to?

I'm convinced that the reason Hollywood movies are often so terrible is because everyone is working on a thousand projects at once. No one is giving anything their full focus. Working on *The School for Good and Evil* has taught me to be patient. When I'm writing the book, that's all I'm working on and I say no to everything else, no matter how lucrative. Do I miss opportunities? Sure. But it means that when the books hit shelves, I know that I've left everything on the page and that they're the absolute best I could have done, which gives them the greatest chance to survive through time. And, inevitably, because I'm committing to maximum quality, better opportunities arise to replace the ones I've passed up.

When you feel overwhelmed or unfocused, what do you do?

Feeling overwhelmed usually means one of two things: either my blood's trapped in my head and I need to go exercise, or, more likely, I've overcommitted myself and my brain knows there's no way I can reasonably get done everything I've set out to do. Usually the solution is to take a deep breath, look at the calendar, and start canceling things or moving deadlines until the paralysis evaporates.

Feeling unfocused, on the other hand, usually means I haven't quite locked into whatever I'm working on yet—that a part of me still thinks I can pull the ripcord and bail. It usually happens in the first three months of writing a new book. In the end, a lack of focus is usually just fear: fear that whatever project I'm attempting will go nowhere or fail miserably. Early on, I used to give in to that fear. Four books later, I know it's just a ghost, and I can blow right through it without looking back.

"You can be a juicy ripe peach and there'll still be someone who doesn't like peaches."

DITA VON TEESE
TW/IG/FB: @DitaVonTeese
dita.net

DITA VON TEESE is the biggest name in burlesque in the world since Gypsy Rose Lee (born 1911). Dita is credited with bringing the art form back into the spotlight. She is renowned for her iconic martini glass act and dazzling haute-couture striptease costumes adorned with hundreds of thousands of Swarovski crystals. This "Burlesque Superheroine" (*Vanity Fair*) is the performer of choice at high-profile events for designers such as Marc Jacobs, Christian Louboutin, Louis Vuitton, Chopard, and Cartier. She is the author of the *New York Times* bestseller *Your Beauty Mark: The Ultimate Guide to Eccentric Glamour* and has a namesake lingerie collection available internationally at prominent retailers.

If you could have a gigantic billboard anywhere with anything on it, what would it say and why?

"You can be a juicy ripe peach and there'll still be someone who doesn't like peaches." This is a quote that my friend's great-grandmother told to her, and she told it to me, and I've always loved it. In the public eye as a burlesque star, I've been called both brilliant and stupid, ugly and beautiful in equal measures. I've strived to let insults fall off me like water off a swan's back. Personally, I find that most things that are universally accepted are mediocre and boring.

What is the book (or books) you've given most as a gift, and why? Or what are one to three books that have greatly influenced your life?

Mae West's *On Sex, Health, and ESP* is a very rare book, but whenever I find a copy, I buy it to give as a gift. Mae was an incredibly witty woman. She wrote every line she ever said in any film and was responsible for countless memorable quips. She made her first film at age 40 and was the biggest sex symbol of her time. When I was living in Paris, my friends and I would sit around, drink champagne, and read aloud from this hilarious book.

I often give *It's Called a Breakup Because It's Broken* by Greg Behrendt and Amiira Ruotola-Behrendt to friends going through a tough breakup. It's a humorous, clever book with great advice on how to maintain one's dignity during a split.

I obviously give a lot of people my own book, *Your Beauty Mark*. Yes, it's my book, but one reason I love to gift it is for the insightful profiles on eccentric people who go against mainstream standards of beauty. They share their inspiring stories about how they made their beauty marks on the world.

How has a failure, or apparent failure, set you up for later success? Do you have a "favorite failure" of yours?

For as long as I can remember, I wanted to be a ballet dancer. When I was a little girl, I had this 1950s-era vinyl record, and on it, there was a photograph of a ballerina with dramatic winged eyeliner, red lipstick, and she was wearing a pale blue tutu, flesh-toned fishnet tights, and blue satin pointe shoes. I wanted to be her! I took ballet classes all my life, even cleaning the studio bathrooms in exchange for lessons. By the time I was a teenager, I realized I was never going to be a good enough dancer to be a professional ballerina, no matter how badly I wanted it, or how much I practiced. My ballet teachers thought that I had great presence, elegance of carriage, nice feet, and I was strong en pointe . . . but I just couldn't remember choreography, and I couldn't jump or perform turns in certain directions.

When I was 19, I started wearing that 1950s-style winged eyeliner and red lipstick and dressing in vintage style. It wasn't long after that I began creating vintage-style burlesque shows. A few years ago, someone asked me if there was a dream that I knew I would never realize, and I mentioned my childhood dreams of being a ballerina. I suddenly realized that, in a way, I had been given everything that I *really* wanted . . . I wanted to be that woman on the album cover.

Truthfully, I never really *loved* dancing per se; I loved what ballet stood for. I loved the glamor, the femininity, the elegance, the drama, not to mention the sparkling costumes and pink spotlights. Showbiz. That's what I wanted. If I hadn't been a lousy ballet dancer, I doubt I would have pursued the obscure idea of being a 1940s-style burlesque dancer.

I believe that sometimes, our shortcomings can lead to greatness, because those of us who have intense desire but lack natural God-given talent sometimes find roundabout ways of realizing dreams. I never expected to become famous for doing my little feather fan dances and for bathing in a giant champagne glass. But I strongly feel that with integrity and a real love for showbiz and burlesque, I've made my mark in a more significant way than I might have had I just been a good ballet dancer.

What purchase of $100 or less has most positively impacted your life in the last six months (or in recent memory)?

Mylola.com has changed my life . . . conscientious 100 percent-organic cotton feminine products that you can curate according to your needs, delivered to your door every month in elegant packaging. They also donate products to low-income and homeless women (and girls) across the U.S. This company and their approach has been life-changing for me and for every woman I know who has started using their products.

What is one of the best or most worthwhile investments you've ever made?

Collecting vintage has been a good investment. I originally started wearing vintage clothes in the '90s because I couldn't afford designer things, and now, as dressing in vintage style has become all the rage, my collection has become quite valuable. I like to spend money on things that bring me pleasure but that are also easily resold, whether it be artwork, vintage clothing, or antique furniture. I've always been able to trade up, break even, or turn a profit on the antiques I collect. My vintage cars have greatly appreciated in value, and although I do need a modern daily driver, I control my car lust and only buy a modern car when I really need to, every 10 or 15 years or so.

I also bought several famous 1940s- and '50s-era original pinup paintings a while back that have become more valuable, along with vintage Hollywood and pinup memorabilia from silver screen, burlesque, and pinup icons of the past. I love being the caretaker for these relics, and I know that as time goes by, they will keep their mystique and their value.

Also, I was on a plane with Richard Branson once and he had this very weathered Louis Vuitton duffel bag that he said he'd used for more than 30 years. I travel a lot, and after years of funneling money into cheap luggage, I saved up for a Louis Vuitton carry on, and it's going strong 17 years later. Generally speaking, I don't shop for status bags, but some things are worth the splurge if you can swing it.

What is an unusual habit or an absurd thing that you love?

I'm a natural blonde, but I've been dyeing my hair black and wearing my signature red lipstick and cat-eyeliner for over two decades. Every Halloween I go "natural," with beige, light makeup and a light-colored wig, all worn with a jeans look of some kind. I'm so unrecognizable that it's hilarious to everyone who knows me, and it's a real psychological experiment! I begin to notice how overlooked I become, how vulnerable I feel, and how I'm approached by the kind of men who would *never* dare try to pick me up. It's my favorite Halloween costume . . . people think I'm the annoying girl who didn't bother dressing up for the party.

In the last five years, what new belief, behavior, or habit has most improved your life?

I've become more involved in my business, looking over all my financials. I remember the 1950s sex symbol Mamie Van Doren telling me, "I know it's not fun, but you have to look at all of your financials, because people *will* try to fleece you." I'd love to just do the artistic part of my work, and she's right, it isn't fun to look at the numbers, but now that I know everything about the financials of producing my show tours and my deals, I can engage in the business conversations in an educated way.

"What would you do if you weren't afraid?"

JESSE WILLIAMS
TW/IG: @iJesseWilliams
jessehimself.tumblr.com

JESSE WILLIAMS is an activist, actor, entrepreneur, and former high school teacher. He plays Dr. Jackson Avery on ABC's hit series *Grey's Anatomy* and has appeared in films such as *The Butler*, *The Cabin in the Woods*, and *Band Aid*. He is the co-founder of the Ebroji company and Ebroji mobile app, a popular cultural language and GIF keyboard. He's also a partner and board member of Scholly, a mobile app that has directly connected students to more than $70 million in unclaimed scholarships. He executive-produced the documentary *Stay Woke: The Black Lives Matter Movement*. Jesse co-hosts the sports and culture-themed podcast *Open Run* on Lebron James' and Maverick Carter's Uninterrupted network. He is founder of the production company farWord Inc. and the executive producer of "Question Bridge: Black Males," a series of transmedia art installations. Jesse gained international attention for his 2016 BET Humanitarian Award acceptance speech.

What is the book (or books) you've given most as a gift, and why? Or what are three books that have greatly influenced your life?

Guns, Germs, and Steel by Jared Diamond: This text helped rid me of the nagging incompleteness in my understood connection between the successes and failings of ancient and modern civilizations. Power needs tools and circumstance. Neither need be earned.

A Confederacy of Dunces by John Kennedy Toole: At the time in my life that I cracked this book open, it brought me tremendous, dare I say, glee! It was f*cking funny, vivid, and adventurous. Sometimes that's what we need.

Song of Solomon by Toni Morrison: The characters' dilemmas just rocked my world in high school. I bought a second copy, "just in case," and I was so grateful for the classroom discussions throughout the rich layered poetic journey.

The Souls of Black Folk by W. E. B. Du Bois: A seminal work in American and African-American literature. Du Bois, a brilliant writer and sociologist, introduced notions like "double-consciousness" and the "veil of race" while examining what it means to spend lifetimes primarily viewing ourselves through the eyes of other people, power, and cultures.

The Fountainhead by Ayn Rand: The protagonist's audacious self-confidence and refusal to compromise his artistic vision—which was to say, himself—was a fascinating thing to survey.

In the last five years, what new belief, behavior, or habit has most improved your life?
Transcendental Meditation is something I'd long heard about but only stepped into this year, and it's transformed my ability to center my mind and recharge in short periods of time. The David Lynch Foundation has made it so digestible without any of the rigidity or easier-said-than-done elements that I expect many of us find intimidating about beginning a meditation practice.

Going to therapy has opened a portal into the how and why of my own thoughts and behaviors. I can see and act with a new level of honesty, which helps cut a path to clearer communication with myself and others. For me, these are among the more critical tools to personal freedom.

My therapist operates from a psychodynamic/psychoanalytic orientation. He utilizes a psychoanalytic approach in his clinical conceptualizations and considers his approach to be a little eccentric. Less "homework" and more getting to the root of the issue and, over time, reprocessing for a more "authentic-self" approach to one's life.

When you feel overwhelmed or unfocused, what do you do? What questions do you ask yourself?

I tend to lose focus for one of two reasons: exhaustion or distraction. Or both. Sometimes I look to the cold for remedy: a walk in the crisp air, a cold drink, a shower. The shower doesn't have to be cold; the ceremony itself is kind of a reset button. If it's exhaustion, I'll just take a nap or, more recently, meditate. If the problem isn't exhaustion, I might just pick up whatever novel I'm reading and go off on that journey. Reading creative writing stimulates my creative thoughts. I get big ideas, I'm reminded of something I meant to act on—an incomplete task or story idea of my own.

My friend Adepero likes to ask, "What would you do if you weren't afraid?" That's a good one.

"We can't control the fact that bad things are going to happen, but it's how we react to them that really matters."

DUSTIN MOSKOVITZ
TW: @moskov
asana.com

DUSTIN MOSKOVITZ is the co-founder of Asana, which helps you track your team's work and manage projects. Prior to Asana, Dustin co-founded Facebook and was a key leader within the technical staff, first in the position of CTO and then later as VP of engineering. He is also the co-founder of Good Ventures, a philanthropic foundation whose mission is to help humanity thrive.

What is the book (or books) you've given most as a gift, and why? Or what are one to three books that have greatly influenced your life?

The 15 Commitments of Conscious Leadership by Jim Dethmer and Diana Chapman. Though most people will typically blame other people or circumstances in their life when they are unhappy, Buddhists believe that we are the cause of our own suffering. We can't control the fact that bad things are going to happen, but it's how we react to them that really matters, and *that* we can learn to control. Even if you don't accept that this is true in all cases, giving it consideration in moments of unhappiness or anxiety will often give you a new perspective and allow you to relax your grip on a negative story. This book is an approachable manual for how to do that tactically, and the lessons it teaches have transformed the way I engage with difficult situations and thus reduced the suffering I experience in big and small ways. Though it is written with leaders in mind, I find myself recommending it to everyone, and we give it to every new employee at Asana.

What purchase of $100 or less has most positively impacted your life in the last six months (or in recent memory)?

The Back Buddy by the Body Back Company is my favorite purchase from the past five years, bar none. Most basically, it allows you to administer self-massage anywhere on your back with the full leverage of two hands, but I've also really gotten to know and appreciate all the little knobs and other features over the years. I've even learned how to manipulate parts of my skeletal structure (i.e., self-chiropracty) and incorporate it into my yoga practice. It only costs $30, so I have purchased several: one for the living room, one for my desk at the office, and a collapsible version for traveling (though I do bring the full-size one if I'm checking a roller bag). With 4,500 reviews and a 4.5-star average review on Amazon, I'm far from alone in my appreciation of this product.

In the last five years, what have you become better at saying no to?

The first no is by far the easiest and cleanest. Declining a request is uncomfortable, so it's tempting to equivocate, say you'll hear someone out before deciding, or agree to a smaller version of the request, even when you're confident that you would rather not engage at all. As soon as you open that door, however, you've almost always ensured at least one more request that you'll have to accept or decline in the future and thus haven't saved yourself the discomfort at all. Worse still, you've crossed a psychological boundary by establishing yourself to the asker as someone who is interested in the type of request being made. Research shows we're remarkably committed to maintaining a consistent sense of external identity, even if we only established it to begin with out of politeness. The asker will see this as an opportunity to press harder, or ask you about similar requests that come up in the future, and you'll have even more discomfort declining those requests versus if you had simply declined the first one. They may even start handing out your contact information to other people in their network, multiplying the problem.

"You have to lift off the back foot while taking a step forward, or you will not be able to move ahead."

RICHA CHADHA
TW: @RichaChadha
IG: @therichachadha

RICHA CHADHA is an award-winning Indian actress who works in Hindi films. She made her debut in the comedy *Oye Lucky! Lucky Oye!*, and her major breakthrough was a supporting role in the film noir gangster saga *Gangs of Wasseypur*. Richa's role as the bellicose and extremely foul-tongued wife of a gangster earned her a Filmfare award (India's equivalent of an Oscar). In 2015, Richa made her debut in a leading role with the drama *Masaan*, which received a standing ovation when screened at the Cannes Film Festival.

What is the book (or books) you've given most as a gift, and why? Or what are books that have greatly influenced your life?

The book I give out the most is *Autobiography of a Yogi* (by Paramahansa Yogananda). It reminds me that human beings are the only species that have become conditioned to doubt survival. Plants grow, trusting nature to provide nutrition; animals thrive in the wild despite dangerous conditions. This book reminded me to have faith at a low point in my life, hence I share it as widely as possible to pull others out of their misery.

I was greatly influenced by *Alice's Adventures in Wonderland* in my formative years. I still live my life wide-eyed in childlike wonder. Even though it was heavy for me at 15, I was greatly impacted by Salman Rushdie's *Shame*. It made me kinder. Naomi Klein's *No Logo* made me reassess consumerism and greed.

What purchase of $100 or less has most positively impacted your life in the last six months (or in recent memory)?

In my case, it would be buying a pro subscription to my IMDb account, enabling people from all over the world to find me easily.

How has a failure, or apparent failure, set you up for later success? Do you have a "favorite failure" of yours?

I was conned into doing a film where my role was later severely edited, leaving me with only one speaking scene. Even though the film was a colossal box-office disaster, it didn't fare well for me. My colleagues began to assume that I was up for smaller, inconsequential parts out of desperation, which was far from the truth. It set me back a couple of years. Even though this kind of blatant corruption is not new to the Hindi film industry, I was shocked and depressed.

When the reviews came out, they lauded my work, and I saw it as a blessing in disguise. If a single scene could have this impact, what could an entire film do? A year later, I am on a roll. I was top-billed cast for India's first original series, *Inside Edge*, and I have regained credibility with a slate of releases from India and around the world.

I think I needed this shock. Trusting blindly in my business, or any business for that matter, is never a good idea. Most people are driven by self-interest or profit, and we can't judge them for it. What we can be is provokable, so people know we won't be sitting ducks if they mess with us.

If you could have a gigantic billboard anywhere with anything on it, what would it say and why?

"Be so good that they can't ignore you" is the motto I live by. I start afresh with each project. I forget who I am and my past laurels. It keeps me grounded and makes me work harder.

There is a lot of nepotism in my industry. If you were to Google who the top stars are, undoubtedly most stars, particularly the male actors, would have been born into the movie business. It takes time, but if you are consistently good at what you do, at least you get to call your success your own.

What is one of the best or most worthwhile investments you've ever made?

My father encouraged me to take a course called "Money and You," devised around the ideas of Buckminster Fuller. I attended the four-day course in Kuala Lumpur. The first two days focused on money and the next two on "you." It was very balanced, taught me to look at money differently, and imbued me with a sense of enterprise at a young age. It cost me $500.

What is an unusual habit or an absurd thing that you love?

I use a different perfume for every film. Of the five senses, I figured the only sense I could play with was the sense of smell. I select the perfume based on the world and milieu of the film and the attributes of the character.

I played the character of a village woman in a film called *Gangs of Wasseypur*. For that I used Elizabeth Arden's Green Tea Lotus parfum. I played a gangster in a film called *Fukrey*, in which I wore Provocative Woman from Elizabeth Arden. For my Amazon series, *Inside Edge*, I used Chanel No. 5 because I play a movie star in it.

This is a quirk I enjoy, because I love to smell good. I am not a method actor, but this allows me to slip into my character with ease. When I walk out of my trailer, the assistants know that it's me, walking in character toward the set.

Cheap thrills, I guess!

In the last five years, what new belief, behavior, or habit has most improved your life?

I find that I tend to look at the larger picture.

Cinema as a business model in Hindi-speaking India is suffering. There aren't enough screens to accommodate the output, taxation is at a debilitating 51 percent for entertainment, and the turnover of piracy is three times that of [other] films.

All this while digital penetration is growing at an unprecedented rate. When I chose to work on a digital series, many people thought it to be a demotion. They were wrong.

Looking at the larger picture gives you perspective. Like when a plane takes off, you realize how small your little cocoon of problems, in fact, is.

What advice would you give to a smart, driven college student about to enter the "real world"? What advice should they ignore?

The education system, by and large, gears everyone up to adhere to set industry standards. While this is a foolproof way to get a job and live a normal life, very few people can break out of the cycle of the mundane to be adventurous, inventive, and selfless. The safety net of a regular job is too comfortable.

When I declared to my middle-class Indian academic parents that I intended to not make use of my degree in journalism and instead move to Mumbai to become an actor, they were apprehensive but supportive.

My mother told me, "You have to lift off the back foot while taking a step forward, or you will not be able to move ahead."

What are bad recommendations you hear in your profession or area of expertise?

I have been blessed with "well-wishers" and "advisors" throughout my career. They teach me what not to do. People make recommendations based on what they think is safest for you, or based on their understanding of who you are and what you ought to be. They set invisible limits on how much you can achieve in your life and pass those limitations on to you inadvertently.

I was told to not do independent films (the films I owe my career to), to dress like others (making me a fashion-friendly homogenized clone with no identity), date or marry rich (again, safety net), and not be vocal about political issues (no matter where you are, you have to pay a price for voicing your concerns, and that's a price I was willing to pay).

This stuff is simple; it may not always be easy.

In the last five years, what have you become better at saying no to?

I have become better at saying no to things and people (including friends and family) that drain my energy. This isn't easy, especially if you are a people-pleaser.

When I am straightforward and sincere about my needs, I find that no one is offended when I say no. Those who are offended perhaps don't value my needs.

When you feel overwhelmed or unfocused, what do you do?

I have a few approaches. First, I journal. It gives me clarity. I have had a diary ever since I was about ten. Today, when I look back at my scribbles from when I was in high school, it gives me great joy to notice how far I have come intellectually and career-wise. I am living my dream. I used to journal frequently as a student, growing up. My diary looked like a scrapbook, with illustrations and quotes that inspired me. I journal at least thrice a week now, and the time dedicated to it is proportional to my state of mind. If I am contemplative or confused, it tends to be a long session. I maintain one diary that has everything: my to-do list (which I divide into personal and professional), contemplations, how I felt about an incident that perhaps triggered me to journal, and sometimes just plain gratitude. I always buy interesting journals and colorful pens. Right now I am using a Wonder Woman journal and neon pens. People may think it's childish, but the different colors help me retain more and keep it fun.

I meditate. This is a challenge when I feel like my head is in turmoil. I generally start by focusing on my breath. I could count back from ten to one while exhaling and I drift into meditation. It takes about 20-odd minutes to become somewhat thoughtless. Sometimes I feel like I am asleep, but I realize that lucidity is meditation. It always helps. There has not been a single time in my life when I have meditated on something and it hasn't been useful. I meditate either first thing in the morning or post-lunch if I am at a stressful film shoot.

I talk to my father. He is my friend and mentor, and being a life coach and behavioral psychologist, he keeps me grounded and on track.

I take a break. I de-tick my cat, take long baths, go on a trek, spend time in nature, read, eat yummy food, and do a life/career detox. This time off usually gifts me with several epiphanies, always works. A life detox is me delegating my responsibilities to an assistant or manager for a while and seeking help before I turn my phone off and wander and think and relax. A career detox means I turn my phone off, don't read about how films/shows/plays are faring, and be a regular person.

I also do a "so what" exercise. I make a statement and ask myself "so what?" at the end of it. For instance,

X was rude.
So what?
I felt disrespected.
So what?
I don't like being disrespected.
So what?
What if everyone stops respecting me?
So what?
I will be alone and loathed.
So what?
I don't want to be alone.
So what?
I have an irrational fear of loneliness.
So what?
It's irrational.
So what?
So nothing. I'm good.
So what?
So nothing.

QUOTES I'M PONDERING

(Tim Ferriss: Dec. 11, 2015–Jan. 1, 2016)

"Grudges are for those who insist that they are owed something; forgiveness, however, is for those who are substantial enough to move on."

–CRISS JAMI
American poet and author of *Salomé: In Every Inch in Every Mile*

"One does not accumulate but eliminate. It is not daily increase but daily decrease. The height of cultivation always runs to simplicity."

–BRUCE LEE
Martial artist, actor, and author of *Tao of Jeet Kune Do*

"It is vain to do with more what can be done with less."

–WILLIAM OF OCKHAM
English philosopher and originator of Occam's Razor

"Learning to ignore things is one of the great paths to inner peace."

–ROBERT J. SAWYER
Hugo and Nebula Award-winning science fiction writer

"Whenever there is any doubt, there is no doubt."
—David Mamet, *Ronin*

MAX LEVCHIN
TW: @mlevchin
affirm.com

MAX LEVCHIN is the co-founder and CEO of Affirm, which uses modern technology to reimagine and rebuild core components of financial infrastructure from the ground up. Previously, Max co-founded and was first chief technology officer of PayPal (acquired by eBay for $1.5 billion). He then helped start Yelp as its first investor and served as chairman for 11 years. Max also founded and was CEO of Slide, which Google acquired for $182 million. *MIT Technology Review* named him "Innovator of the Year" in 2002, when he was 26 years old.

What is the book (or books) you've given most as a gift, and why? Or what are one to three books that have greatly influenced your life?

The Master and Margarita, by Mikhail Bulgakov (translated by Pevear, et al.), which is I think is one of the finest works of fiction of the last century. It's a fairly short novel, remarkable in its exceptional depth, exploring everything from fundamentals of Christian philosophy to the fantastical (and hilarious) satire of soul-corrupting 20th-century Soviet socialism. I usually buy *M&M* in batches of five or ten and give as gifts to new friends. There are always a few copies on my desk at work, just in case someone wants to borrow one.

Next, not a book, but a movie. I've watched the Kurosawa classic *Seven Samurai* more than 100 times (really), and used to give DVD copies of the Criterion Collection remaster to young CEOs I mentored. I love the movie (and am generally a bit of a Japanophile), but I recommend it to new managers and CEOs especially because it is fundamentally about leadership: A small band of courageous leaders risks everything to organize a ragtag group in a fight for its life. Sound familiar? To me, this timeless story is a near-perfect metaphor for startups. What would Kambei Shimada do?

If you could have a gigantic billboard anywhere with anything on it, what would it say and why? Are there any quotes you think of often or live your life by?

I have several candidates for this one:

"Whenever there is any doubt, there is no doubt." The line is from the inimitable David Mamet, a quote from *Ronin*, one of my all-time favorite movies. A laconic reminder to always be decisive in battle and in business, and at a most basic level, to trust your gut. In my line of work, this often enough translates to "fire early," too. When you aren't sure about a key employee or a co-founder, odds are exceedingly low your mind will be changed for the better.

"The difference between winning and losing is most often not quitting." This famous line from Walt Disney on willpower cannot be more true when it comes to entrepreneurship. The only predictable thing about startups is their unpredictability, and powering through the lows of the startup roller coaster ultimately just takes grit—yours and your team's.

But if my billboard were in Marin County (or another big cycling destination) it would just say, "When my legs hurt, I say, 'Shut up, legs! Do what I tell you to do!'" This gem is from Jens Voigt, a legendary cyclist who is famous for his willingness to work extra hard for his team, no matter how fatigued or injured.

Building a startup is very much an endurance sport, and cycling never fails to provide an inspirational anecdote, quote, or metaphor. Another Voigt favorite is, "If it hurts me, it must hurt the other ones twice as much."

"Look for a partner you'll try to impress daily, and one who will try to impress you." Over the last couple decades, I've noticed that the best, most enduring partnerships in business (and in life) are among people who are constantly growing together. If the person you choose to depend on is constantly striving to learn and improve, you too will push yourself to new levels of achievement, and neither of you will feel like you have settled for someone you eventually outgrow.

What is an unusual habit or an absurd thing that you love?

Genetic algorithm cooking. I like to obsess over how certain foods are made, and will recreate and rework them until they are perfectly adapted to my palate. When it comes to cooking, I am not exactly creative, but I can follow a well-stated recipe pretty precisely. But tweaking a recipe to better suit my personal taste is fun, and feeds my innate obsessiveness. I approach a recipe as if it were a genome, where every ingredient and step in the process is a gene that I modify based on the results of previous attempts and also randomly. I taste-test the results and "crossbreed" the "genes" from the tastiest outcomes. I've thrown together a few bits of code to make and track the modifications for me, so it's a pretty precise process (more or less).

There's something very therapeutic about it, though it also means occasionally taste-testing copious amounts of (very slightly) different kimchi, kombucha, or kefir in the course of a week. Fermented foods (especially if they start with a "K") are a big favorite of mine in general, and they also lend themselves particularly well to such experimentation.

In the last five years, what new belief, behavior, or habit has most improved your life?

Focusing on my strengths. After PayPal, my most important "career" goal was to diversify, to do something not in fin-tech, not in payments, not in anti-fraud, not in anything I really enjoyed doing in my first successful project. I really wanted to diversify my skills and experiences.

And while the next few startups were all fun (and some turned out fairly well), I never achieved the same startup "high" I had while building PayPal. For years, I blamed that on the fact that the companies I helped start after PayPal didn't exceed it in market value or broad appeal, but it was more fundamental than that.

When the time came to start another company, my wife (who continues to impress me every day!) pointed out that I was happiest when working on building PayPal, not when it went public or was acquired. She suggested I consider going back to my entrepreneurial roots in financial services. Having stayed far away from financial services for over a decade, I co-founded Affirm. Very different from PayPal, but with many overlapping concepts and related challenges.

Daily work at Affirm can be just as challenging and difficult as it was during PayPal, but I am once again working in my sweet spot and loving every minute of it.

What advice would you give to a smart, driven college student about to enter the "real world"? What advice should they ignore?

[My advice is to] take risks, now. The advantages that college students and new grads have are their youth, drive, lack of significant responsibilities, and, importantly, lack of the creature comforts one acquires with time. Nothing to lose, everything to gain. Barnacles of the good life tend to slow you down, if you don't get used to risk-taking early in your career.

I started numerous companies in my early 20s only to see them all fail, but I never thought twice about starting the next one. I knew after the first one that I loved the feeling of starting something, and I had almost no other responsibilities. Eventually, one of the startups did work out, but I was prepared to try as many times as it would take to win.

If you are your sole responsibility, this is the time to step outside of your comfort zone, to start or join an exciting, risky project; to drop everything else at the chance to be part of something really great. So what if it fails? You can always go back to school, take that job at an investment bank or a consulting company, move into a nicer apartment.

The advice to ignore (in certain situations) is to strive to become "well-rounded"—to move from company to company, looking to pick up different types of experience every year or two, when starting out. That's useful in the abstract, but if you find that strength of yours (as an individual contributor or a team leader) at a company whose mission you are truly passionate about, take a risk—commit and double down, and rise through the ranks. Maybe you'll be running the place before you know it!

"Learn more, know less."

NEIL STRAUSS
TW: @neilstrauss
IG: @neil_strauss
neilstrauss.com

NEIL STRAUSS is an eight-time *New York Times* best-selling author. His books, *The Game* and *Rules of the Game*, for which he went undercover in a secret society of pickup artists, made him an international celebrity and an accidental hero to men around the world. In his follow-up book, *The Truth: An Uncomfortable Book About Relationships*, Strauss dives deep into the worlds of sex addiction, nonmonogamy, infidelity, and intimacy, and explores the hidden forces that cause people to choose each other, stay together, and break up. He most recently co-authored with Kevin Hart the instant #1 *New York Times* bestseller *I Can't Make This Up: Life Lessons*.

What is the book (or books) you've given most as a gift, and why? Or what are one to three books that have greatly influenced your life?

The book that's most influenced me is James Joyce's *Ulysses*. I read it in senior year of high school, and it awakened me to the power and possibilities of language. It's hypertext before hypertext existed. I reread it every three years, and each time it's a different book.

The book I've given most as a gift is *Under Saturn's Shadow* by James Hollis, a Jungian analyst. I've underlined ideas on every single page. The thrust of the book, in his words: "Men's lives are as much governed by role expectations as are the lives of women. And the corollary is that those roles do not support, confirm, or resonate to the needs of men's souls."

The *audiobook* I've given away most is *Nonviolent Communication* by Marshall Rosenberg. Though "nonviolent communication" is poorly named (it's the equivalent of calling cuddling "nonmurderous touching"), the central idea is that, unbeknownst to us, there's a lot of violence in the way we communicate with others—and with ourselves. That violence comes in the form of blaming, judging, criticizing, insulting, demanding, comparing, labeling, diagnosing, and punishing.

So when we speak in certain ways, not only do we not get heard, but we end up alienating others and ourselves. *NVC* has a magical way of instantly defusing potential conflicts with anyone, from a partner to a server to a friend to someone at work. One of its many great premises is that no two people's needs are ever in conflict. It's only the strategies for getting those needs met that are in conflict.

Disambiguation: The version you want is a 5-hour, 9-minute lecture. You can recognize it by the cover, which is a close-up of a hand flashing a peace sign. It starts slow, but then gets revolutionary. Do *not* get any versions of the printed book, which has the same title.

What purchase of $100 or less has most positively impacted your life in the last six months (or in recent memory)?

Tile Mate key finder on Amazon. It's given me hours of my life back that were previously spent dashing around the house, looking for my keys. Works great with pets, too!

How has a failure, or apparent failure, set you up for later success? Do you have a "favorite failure" of yours?

The best thing that ever happened to me was not getting accepted into journalism school. Because of that, I eventually ended up as a reporter and columnist at *The New York Times*. It allowed me to learn through experience rather than academics, and to take a route following my passion instead of how it's "supposed to be done."

Because of that, I realized that the outcome is not the outcome. In other words, what we think of as endpoints to a goal are really just forks in a road that is endlessly forking. In the big picture of our lives, we really don't know whether a particular success or failure is actually helping or hurting us. So the metric I now use to judge my efforts and goals is: Did I do my best, given who I was and what I knew at that particular time? And what can I learn from the outcome to make my best better next time?

Note that criticism is not failure. If you're not being criticized, you're probably not doing anything exceptional.

If you could have a gigantic billboard anywhere with anything on it, what would it say?

"Learn more, know less."

What is one of the best or most worthwhile investments you've ever made?

The best investment was the time I put in as an unpaid intern at *The Village Voice* in NYC. I must have spent a year just opening mail and doing people's expense reports, but I was so excited to be there. I probably interned there for years. They couldn't get rid of me. I loved writing, but I wasn't very good at it when I started. But by being around the writers and editors I admired, and spending all my free time reading back issues in the archives, I learned to be a writer, a critic, and a reporter.

In another question, I mentioned that the best failure was not getting into journalism school. This was my journalism school.

In the last five years, what new belief, behavior, or habit has most improved your life?

Without a doubt, finding a healthy community here in Malibu to work out with. Before, I'd go to the gym to achieve a certain weight or muscle goal, and I never stuck with it. Now I show up to see my friends, and we always exercise outdoors: at the beach, in a pool, on a lawn. We almost always end with a sauna/ice session. It's the highlight of the day. I have no outcome I want from it, and I've never been in better shape in my life. It helped me realize that the secret to change and growth is not willpower, but positive community.

In the last five years, what have you become better at saying no to?

We are in an arms race against distractions. Our devices and technology have gotten to know us so well that we now need devices and technology to protect us from them. Especially our time. So what's helped me say no to distractions is the app Freedom on my computer, which I've set to block the Internet 22 hours a day, and a Kitchen Safe [now called kSafe], which is a timed safe I can drop my cell phone into.

What's helped with saying no to others is asking myself first if I'm saying yes out of guilt or fear. If so, then it's a polite no.

When you feel overwhelmed or unfocused, what do you do?

Overwhelmed and unfocused seem like two different problems. I'm thinking that overwhelm is about mentally managing what's coming from outside yourself, while unfocused is about mentally managing what's going on inside.

Overall, what would work for both is to think of my mind as a computer, and the RAM is full. So best to shut it off for a little. For me, this means stepping away from work for anything from a cold shower to a surf to meditation to a breathing exercise outside to talking with someone I immensely enjoy.

Anything healthy that gets you out of your mind and into your body is ultimately good for your mind.

What is an unusual habit or an absurd thing that you love?

Kracie Fuwarinka (Beauty Rose) Candy, Calbee Honey Butter Chips, *Rick and Morty*, doing Richie's Plank Experience on the HTC VIVE with an actual elevated plank on the floor, Crack Butter from healthybutter.org, escape rooms, Tim Tam slams, picklebacks, skittykitts, saying age-inappropriate words like "lit," pretending like I know what someone's talking about when I really don't, ending sentences with prepositions, and playing a game my wife and I made up where we play our music on shuffle and then take turns making up movie scenes that each song could be the soundtrack to. Kinda hard to explain. Best if you're in the car with us.

"I've only ever had one house motto: 'Fuck you, pay me.' … Things like 'exposure,' or 'reaching new audiences,' or having a 'great experience' are all well and good, but they don't pay the rent or put food on the table. Know your worth."

VERONICA BELMONT
TW/IG/FB: @veronica
veronicabelmont.com

VERONICA BELMONT is a bot-obsessed product manager in San Francisco. She works for Growbot, helping to make sure employees get the recognition they deserve on their teams. She also helps to admin Botwiki.org and Botmakers.org, a huge community of bot creators and enthusiasts. As a writer, producer, and speaker, her primary goal has been to educate audiences of all types about how technology can enhance their lives. Through the years, her love of innovation has led to advising many startups on product, communications, and marketing, including Goodreads (acquired by Amazon), about.me (acquired by AOL), DailyDrip, SoundTracking (acquired by Rhapsody), Milk (acquired by Google), WeGame (acquired by Tagged), Forge, Chic CEO, and more. She is also a podcaster and hosts *IRL* for Mozilla and *Sword & Laser*.

What is the book (or books) you've given most as a gift, and why? Or what are one to three books that have greatly influenced your life?

10% Happier by Dan Harris made me totally rethink mindfulness and meditation. For me, it was always something that "other people do," but Dan's experience of suffering from anxiety and panic attacks (especially on-camera, which used to be my career) struck home in a major way. Plus, since he comes to it from the perspective of a skeptic, I wasn't worried that I was being sold to or recruited in some way! Just a great way to take stock of your thoughts and mood.

What purchase of $100 or less has most positively impacted your life in the last six months (or in recent memory)?

I switched to drugstore shampoo and conditioner. I discovered that a $4 bottle of Pantene works much better than a $25 bottle of the stuff from Sephora. Just because something is more expensive doesn't make it better!

What is an unusual habit or an absurd thing that you love?

I take photos of dogs and post them to the Dogspotting Facebook group. There are elaborate rules that you have to follow: must be a previously unknown dog, always try to crop out people, beware of "low-hanging fruit" dogs (a photo taken in a place where seeing a dog would be expected, like a dog park), etc. I find it weirdly cathartic, so much so that I started a mini-podcast on Anchor.fm called *Dogs I've Seen Today*. I'm finding my bliss, I guess.

In the last five years, what have you become better at saying no to?

I finally came to the understanding that my downtime is just as valuable as my uptime, and I have to schedule it in accordingly. Previously, if I saw a big chunk of free time on my calendar, it was a lot more difficult to turn down projects, speaking engagements, or even coffee meetings. Now, I see that block of time, and think, "Oh, that's my binge-watching Netflix time. Sorry."

How has a failure, or apparent failure, set you up for later success? Do you have a "favorite failure" of yours?

My favorite failure was hosting the Season 6 premiere of *Game of Thrones* for HBO. It was great, outwardly, but I made the mistake of going online afterward and reading the comments. Bad idea. I spent what should have been a magical evening sitting in my hotel room sobbing into the phone with my husband.

But with that feeling came certainty: I had been casually thinking about making a career switch for the previous six months or so, but I was scared of trying to do something I had never done before professionally. Sitting there in that hotel room, I thought, "Why am I spending my time doing something that consistently makes me miserable? Why not take a chance?"

So I did. I stopped taking any freelance gigs, wrapped up my video contracts, and spent all my time learning about product management and figuring out where I'd best fit in. It was a horrible night, but it was also the impetus for something completely new and wonderful.

If you could have a gigantic billboard anywhere with anything on it, what would it say and why?

I've only ever had one house motto: "Fuck you, pay me." After having been a freelancer for almost a decade, I'd seen every trick in the book when it came to people trying to get my work for free. Things like "exposure," or "reaching new audiences," or having a "great experience" are all well and good, but they don't pay the rent or put food on the table. Know your worth.

What are bad recommendations you hear in your profession or area of expertise?

I think people assume that you have to weigh all feedback on your product (whether it's a podcast, an app, etc.) equally. Not all feedback is created equal, and not all ideas from your users are good ones! Taking too much stock in feedback can change the vision for your own product, and suddenly it won't feel like yours anymore.

What advice would you give to a smart, driven college student about to enter the "real world"?

Don't wait until you get a job to do the thing you want to be doing. For most careers, showing that you have initiative by working on projects related to your future job is a great way to get a foot in the door. If you want to be a writer or journalist, start keeping a blog that you update regularly! If you want to be a programmer, create and maintain a project on GitHub. Anything that you can point to on your LinkedIn that screams, "Hey, I'm passionate about this!" works.

When you feel overwhelmed or unfocused, what do you do?

I always feel better after making a good list. It's a lot more satisfying for me to have something written down on paper that I can forcibly cross off when it's done. It gives me better focus on what I can get done in the short term, and actually feels like a completed task in and of itself.

If I'm feeling overwhelmed, nothing is better than taking my dog out to the park. Walking, fresh air, and seeing happy dogs always resets me in a really positive way. Also, it's nice knowing that your dog will always love you no matter how stressed out you are!

"My favorite failure is every time I ever ate it onstage as a comedian. Because I woke up the next day and the world hadn't ended."

PATTON OSWALT
TW/FB: @pattonoswalt
pattonoswalt.com

PATTON OSWALT is a standup comedian, actor, voice artist, and writer. For at least two years, I listened to his third comedy special, *My Weakness Is Strong*, on repeat in my car. I highly suggest tracks 8 and 9, "Rats" and "Orgy," respectively. He is also known for roles including Spence Olchin in the sitcom *The King of Queens;* Remy (voice) in the film *Ratatouille;* and playing multiple identical brothers, the Koenigs, on *Agents of S.H.I.E.L.D.* Patton has won a Primetime Emmy Award for Outstanding Writing for a Variety Special and a Grammy Award for Best Comedy Album for his Netflix standup special *Patton Oswalt: Talking for Clapping*. Patton is the author of the *New York Times* bestseller *Silver Screen Fiend: Learning About Life from an Addiction to Film* and *Zombie Spaceship Wasteland: A Book by Patton Oswalt.*

What is the book (or books) you've given most as a gift, and why?

The book I think I've given the most as a gift is Garret Keizer's *The Enigma of Anger*. It's an amazing meditation—but then again, so is everything Garret writes—on the dangers and benefits of blowing your stack. It's gotten me through some moments when I could have easily eaten myself alive with rage. And, I suspect, it was a safety net for some of my more, ahem, passionate friends.

What purchase of $100 or less has most positively impacted your life in the last six months (or in recent memory)?

ChicoBags, these reusable shopping bags for groceries. You throw a bunch in the back of your car. They're super-sturdy, they're cheap, and they're great for carrying everything. Nice heft and balance, too. If you fill one with cans of chili you have a nice, medieval-style mace.

How has a failure, or apparent failure, set you up for later success? Do you have a "favorite failure" of yours?

My favorite failure is every time I ever ate it onstage as a comedian. Because I woke up the next day and the world hadn't ended. I was free to keep fucking up and getting better. I wish at least one catastrophic failure on everyone pursing the arts. It's where you'll get your superpowers from.

If you could have a gigantic billboard anywhere with anything on it, what would it say?

"There is no Them."

What is one of the best or most worthwhile investments you've ever made?

The year of poverty-level living I did, burning off three years of savings (which wasn't much to begin with), from the summer of '92 to the summer of '93 in San Francisco. I got onstage at least once a night and grew ten years as a comedian in a year. I burned off any safety net I had becoming proficient. If you can swing it—and I know a lot of people can't—and you can scam a way to live off of nothing, it almost always pays off.

What is an unusual habit or an absurd thing that you love?

Meditative dishwasher loading. I love loading a dishwasher while I think through a problem. It's Tetris with dishes and silverware.

In the last five years, what new belief, behavior, or habit has most improved your life?

Daily meditation, twice a day. Just giving my brain a chance to power the fuck down and refresh. Makes all the difference.

What advice would you give to a smart, driven college student about to enter the "real world"? What advice should they ignore?

Embrace the suck for a while. Chances are your first job is going to stink and your living conditions won't be much better. Enjoy the scrappy years, 'cuz they'll make you self-sufficient way faster. Ignore anyone who tells you to go for security over experience.

What are bad recommendations you hear in your profession or area of expertise?

As far as comedians go, I see a lot of people telling comedians to try to have more of a social antenna rather than a moral or creative compass. Trying to second-guess what the masses will accept or reject always leads to stagnation.

In the last five years, what have you become better at saying no to?

I've definitely become better at saying no as a snap decision, rather than something I need to go think on and brood about. If something doesn't grab me, chances are it isn't worth pursuing. That certainly wasn't true in my younger years, but as I get older I know what's right for me and what I can't bring anything to. It doesn't even mean that something *I* say no to is necessarily not worth pursuing. It just means it isn't worth me pursuing it. There's a difference.

When you feel overwhelmed or unfocused, what do you do?

I meditate. I sit for 20 minutes and meditate. Best thing I ever learned how to do.

"We may be approaching a time when sugar is responsible for more early deaths in America than cigarette smoking."

LEWIS CANTLEY
cantleylab.weill.cornell.edu

LEWIS CANTLEY has made significant advances in cancer research, stemming from his discovery of the signaling pathway phosphoinositide 3-kinase (PI3K). His pioneering research has resulted in revolutionary treatments for cancer, diabetes, and autoimmune diseases. He is the author of more than 400 original papers and more than 50 book chapters and review articles. He conducted his postdoctoral research at Harvard University, where he became assistant professor of biochemistry and molecular biology. He later became a professor of physiology at Tufts University, but returned to Harvard Medical School as a professor of cell biology. He became chief of Harvard's new Division of Signal Transduction, and a founding member of its Department of Systems Biology, in 2002.

What is the book (or books) you've given most as a gift, and why? Or what are one to three books that have greatly influenced your life?

I read fairly widely, but particularly enjoy and give or recommend to my friends and family books written by three contemporary writers: Richard Rhodes, Neal Stephenson, and Philip Kerr.

The Making of the Atomic Bomb by Richard Rhodes is a masterpiece of explaining the sequence of discoveries that led to the development of the atomic bomb in an historical context. During my graduate studies at Cornell, I minored in theoretical physics and took courses from Hans Bethe and other luminaries, so I had met several of the physicists in the book. Yet I learned more physics from the book than I did in my courses.

Neal Stephenson (page 470) is an incredible writer who manages to create fictional characters who reveal the eccentricities and absurdities of real-life scientists and mathematicians as they go about their work of creativity. Were I to teach a course on the history of science, *The Baroque Cycle* would be required reading. It is way over the top in capturing the character of Newton and his contemporaries, and the science sometimes (intentionally) becomes magical, but with the interwoven sex and violence, it is way too much fun to put down.

Finally, I have read everything Philip Kerr has written about the fictional Berlin policeman Bernie Gunther, struggling to survive as the Nazis take over Germany. These books are a contemporary warning for our own future in America.

How has a failure, or apparent failure, set you up for later success? Do you have a "favorite failure" of yours?

An important failure for me was my failure to obtain tenure at Harvard in 1985. As an assistant and associate professor in the Biochemistry and Molecular Biology Department, I worked on the proteins and lipids that make up the barrier between the inside and outside of cells, and how they are involved in cell regulation. This was not very fashionable, as everyone was jumping onto the revolution of genetics and molecular biology. My move to Tufts Medical School and, later, Harvard Medical School led to collaborations with scientists at those institutions, notably Tom Roberts and Brian Schaffhausen, who appreciated the importance of understanding the biochemical pathways involved in cancer. Ultimately, it was work done at those institutions that led to the discovery of PI 3-kinase, a central mediator of cell growth, involved in both diabetes and cancer.

What is one of the best or most worthwhile investments you've ever made?

My best investment was the eight years I spent getting undergraduate and graduate degrees in chemistry and biophysical chemistry. While my current research focuses on developing cures for cancers, the insights I have into how cancers evolve and how to develop drugs to treat cancer come from my understanding of the rules of chemistry and biochemistry. This insight has not only facilitated breakthroughs in my own laboratory, but also allowed me to start companies such as Agios and Petra, which are developing drugs against novel targets for cancer therapy.

What is an unusual habit or an absurd thing that you love?

I relax by playing solitaire on my iPad. Trying to develop strategies to beat the odds focuses my mind and eliminates all other thoughts.

The even more nerdish thing that I do [in my work] is try to read the function of proteins from their linear sequence of amino acids. A protein is a string of amino acids with approximately the same amount of information as is found in the 500 or so letters that make up a typical paragraph in a book. There is no reason why we shouldn't be able to teach ourselves how to "read" the information in a protein the way we read paragraphs in English or French or Chinese. The problem is to establish the rules. My lab focuses on breaking down the protein into short strings of five or ten amino acids called "motifs" that are conserved through evolution and often found in multiple proteins. Often these motifs are ways for proteins to communicate with other proteins. So once we know the function of the motif, we can predict how the protein communicates with other proteins in our bodies. When someone tells me about the protein they are excited about in regard to a disease, I immediately look up the sequence and search for motifs that might help explain the link of the protein to the disease. This approach is responsible for many of the discoveries from my laboratory.

In the last five years, what new belief, behavior, or habit has most improved your life?

Moving from Cambridge to New York City has allowed me to live without having an automobile. My walk to work is ten minutes regardless of the weather or traffic. I don't need to shovel snow, scrape ice from a car window, or look for a parking spot. It's wonderful. It probably saves me at least an hour every day, and walking is healthy.

What advice would you give to a smart, driven college student about to enter the "real world"? What advice should they ignore?

My advice is to choose a profession that is really easy for you to do and that also allows you to be creative. If it is easy for you to do and somewhat difficult for your peers to do, you will not have to work too hard to be successful and you will have enough spare time to enjoy life. You will also be able to put in extra hours to blow out the competition every now and then, should that be necessary. If, on the other hand, you have to work long hours all the time just to be competitive, you will burn out and not enjoy life.

One should not pursue a profession just because it is viewed, at the time you begin college, as the one that will have the most jobs or where you will make the most money. Technologies and infrastructures in the world are changing at an unprecedented rate. No one can predict what will be the best profession four years from now. If you are uncertain of your talent, get a broad education that does not narrow your options. The best skill is to be able to communicate efficiently both in writing and speaking. The two college courses that were probably most important for my career were a course in literature and composition and a course in logic (an advanced math course). These courses taught me how to reach the correct conclusion from a set of facts and how to communicate that conclusion to a diverse audience.

If you could have a gigantic billboard anywhere with anything on it, what would it say and why?

My message would be: "Sugar is toxic." Sugar and other natural or artificial sweeteners are among the most addictive agents in our environment. When consumed in quantities that exceed the rate of metabolism in muscle or the brain, sugar is converted to fat, resulting in insulin resistance, obesity, and an increased risk of many other diseases, including cancers. While consuming fats and proteins evokes a feeling of satiety, consuming sugars induces a desire for more sugar within an hour or so. We evolved this addiction because, in the not-so-distant past, adding fat to our bodies at the end of a growing season when fruits were ripe was essential for surviving until the next growing season. But today, sugar is available all year round and is one of the cheapest foods available. So we continually add fat to our bodies. We may be approaching a time when sugar is responsible for more early deaths in America than cigarette smoking. I have written and lectured extensively on this subject over the past ten years as our understanding of the biochemical basis for the toxicity of sugar, especially the link to cancer, has become more clear.

What are bad recommendations you hear in your profession or area of expertise?

The worst recommendation is to keep your ideas and data secret until you have a paper describing these results accepted in a journal. Anytime I have a crazy idea or see an unexpected result, I talk about it with my colleagues to see if they have seen anything similar and whether they think my idea is crazy. This is the fun of science. Multiple scientists with different experiences and expertise can collaborate and get to the right answer much faster than a single scientist.

When you feel overwhelmed or unfocused, what do you do?

I play solitaire, which clears my mind, allowing me to fall asleep. After six hours of sleep I spontaneously wake up and everything seems simple and possible.

QUOTES I'M PONDERING

(Tim Ferriss: Jan. 8–Jan. 29, 2016)

"People say that what we're all seeking is a meaning for life. I don't think that's what we're really seeking. I think that what we're seeking is an experience of being alive."

–JOSEPH CAMPBELL
American mythologist and writer, known for *The Hero with a Thousand Faces*

"If you must play, decide on three things at the start: the rules of the game, the stakes, and the quitting time."

–CHINESE PROVERB

"There is nothing that the busy man is less busy with than living; there is nothing harder to learn."

–SENECA
Roman Stoic philosopher, famed playwright

"Creation is a better means of self-expression and possession; it is through creating, not possessing, that life is revealed."

–VIDA DUTTON SCUDDER
American educator, writer, and welfare activist

"Hard choices, easy life.
Easy choices, hard life."

JERZY GREGOREK
FB: tim.blog/happybody
(redirect)
thehappybody.com

JERZY GREGOREK emigrated from Poland to the United States as a political refugee with his wife, Aniela (page 121), in 1986. He subsequently won four World Weightlifting Championships and established one world record. In 2000, Jerzy and Aniela founded UCLA's weightlifting team. As co-creator of the Happy Body program, Jerzy has mentored people for more than 30 years. In 1998, Jerzy earned an MFA in writing from the Vermont College of Fine Arts. His poems and translations have appeared in numerous publications, including *The American Poetry Review*. His poem "Family Tree" was the winner of *Amelia* magazine's Charles William Duke Long Poem Award in 1998.

What is the book (or books) you've given most as a gift, and why? Or what are one to three books that have greatly influenced your life?

After I read this question, I raised my head and looked at the hundreds of books in my study, then I walked to my living room and looked at more books there, and then I looked at the piles in my bedroom, the kitchen, my gym, and my meditation room. I had a strong feeling that almost all of them contributed to the person I have become.

One book I've returned to throughout my life, so much so that it's now filled with underlining and notes, is *The Doctor and the Soul* by Viktor E. Frankl. A psychiatrist who emerged alive after six years in a concentration camp, Frankl's work is based on our search for meaning in life as a very personal task. This book helped me embrace hard choices and keep imagining a better future.

The Tao of Power by Lao Tzu [a translation of the Tao Te Ching by R. L. Wing] helped me see the relationship between "enough," health, and wealth. It sent me on a 30-year journey to find enough food, exercise, and rest; to learn how to live between too much and too little to create a youthful and happier existence.

And from *Letters from a Stoic* by Seneca, I learned self-mastery: to constantly improve myself so I would be ready for any possible disaster. I also learned that when disaster happens, it means that something is being asked of me. I need to improve. The whole scenario is so clear while aging. After 35 years old, no matter what we do, we'll get worse. Deterioration is automatic in the process of aging, and the result is that we get depressed. But if we live like a stoic, it does not affect us in a negative way. A stoic is always ready for any disaster and ready to embrace it, to turn it into opportunity. My wife used to ask me, "Why are you happy when something bad happens?" I am not happy, I am just not unhappy. I focus on removing what is wrong. One day my friend did something unethical, so I stopped being friends with him, but Aniela was curious why I was not more upset. I replied that I was happy because I did not have to be associated with him anymore. Can you imagine if it had happened five years later when I felt even closer to him?

What purchase of $100 or less has most positively impacted your life in the last six months (or in recent memory)?

When I was 19 years old, I had just become a fireman and was racing for the first time to a fire that had broken out in an apartment. As our fire engine raced through the city with the lights spinning and the siren blaring, I felt an overwhelming feeling of goodness. For the first time, I felt somebody needed me, and I really liked it. Since that time, I've kept educating myself and have tried to keep becoming an even better man so I can again help people in need and feel that goodness.

Five years ago, I decided to eliminate my reactive behavior to irritations, but at first none of my tricks worked. I placed philosophical and inspirational quotes on my iPhone wallpaper or wrote in my journal, but the proverbs always lost their effectiveness over time. Then, one day, I told one of my clients who blamed her husband for everything to take 100 percent responsibility for her part in their interactions. "This way," I said, "you will be free of trying to control him, and you will be able to find constructive solutions in your relationship." When she left, I realized that the same advice could help me as well. Taking 100 percent personal responsibility would help me to stop blaming or complaining and achieve a sense of flow. It would also give me the clarity in any conversation to locate the right words to help a person to accept a hard choice.

On March 8, 2017, I bought a bracelet on Amazon for $19.95 with the first letters of each word of a sentence: IARFCDP. Only I know what the letters mean, but I'll share them with you now. They are the key to my personal proverb, a line that brings awareness and helps me see through my own emotional storms. It means: I Am Responsible For Calming Down People. Sometimes it helps me to teach what I need to learn myself.

I never take it off. It reminds me many times a day what the letters stand for and lets me feel its goodness. Sometimes while reacting to an irritation, I notice the bracelet and stop myself before I get to the point where I'll be sorry. Then, I experience glimpses of flow.

How has a failure, or apparent failure, set you up for later success? Do you have a "favorite failure" of yours?

I became an alcoholic at the age of 15, and a bad one. After six months of drinking with friends, I was expelled from school. Over the next three years, I would have severe blackouts where I wouldn't remember what had happened for the previous two or three days. One day a friend, Mirek, mentioned that his dad had thrown all of his weightlifting equipment out of his house. "You can store it at my place," I offered casually, not expecting him to follow through. The next day, he showed up with his weights and convinced me to do a short workout with him before going out for a beer.

He was kind and persistent, and I noticed that he had a sense of contentment that I envied. After six months, I was spending most of my time with Mirek and his crowd of weightlifters and little time with my old friends, the town drunks. A year later, I was sober and felt reborn.

This dramatic early failure helped me in a few ways. It showed me how, with consistent effort, someone can turn their life completely around in the space of a year. I realized firsthand how important mentoring is in this process of deep change; it's why mentoring is so important in our work today. It also gave me insight into the mind of an alcoholic, or any addict. Today I can drink moderately without tipping into the reckless fatalism of addiction. Without having been there, though, I doubt I could find the right words at the right time for the alcoholics who need me to understand them.

If you could have a gigantic billboard anywhere with anything on it, what would it say and why?

"Hard choices, easy life. Easy choices, hard life."

Nothing truly meaningful or lasting has ever been created in a short period of time. If you learn the story behind any great success, you realize how many years went by and how many hard choices were made to achieve it. Reaching for more is not only an act of ambition, it also comes from passion and love. Nothing is achieved because of easy choices. I believe that people can endure any hardship if it is sensible and constructive. Hard choices means never retiring, because the brain has to be engaged in finding new solutions in the moment, not just remembering old formulas. Hard choices make us wiser, smarter, stronger, and wealthier, and easy choices reverse our progress, focusing our energies on comfort or entertainment. In every difficult moment ask yourself, "What is a hard choice and what is an easy choice?" and you will know instantly what is right.

What is one of the best or most worthwhile investments you've ever made?

After I recovered from my alcoholism, I realized that I'd missed out on my education, and I was determined to make up for lost time. I started studying 16 hours a day, seven days a week, hoping to pursue a medical career. University tuition was beyond the budget of my family, however, so I eventually entered the fire protection engineering academy. Even before this, I was studying English. Despite its unpopularity in Poland at the time, I was determined to become fluent. Little did I know that in a few years' time, I would be forced to flee Poland to save my life, eventually arriving in the U.S. as a political refugee.

Ever since those teenage years, when I discovered the power of learning and decided to educate myself, knowing more has been my path to personal power and happiness. When Aniela and I were refugees in Europe, books were like clothes. We couldn't be without them. We've never regretted investing in our education. When we were dissatisfied with a hired writer's work on the first draft of *The Happy Body*, we decided to pursue master's degrees in creative writing so we could better communicate our own stories and ideas. Our work is a synthesis of the thousands of books we have read over the years, and we will never stop learning. To us, books are what make us human.

What is an unusual habit or an absurd thing that you love?

Aniela and I have been married for 38 years, and we still have lots to talk about. We also have a tradition. At noon, we stop working and prepare ourselves for our date. After taking showers and dressing in our favorite clothes, we head to our favorite local restaurant. As soon as we walk in, the entire staff welcomes us with a smile and we head to our favorite table, guided by the chatting host. He offers a menu and a bottle of sparking water while Aniela reads the menu. She chooses a different lunch each time, but I stay with the same appetizer (French fries) and a double vodka for my entrée with a plate of veggies on the side. I love our dates. Nothing is better than sitting with your wife after 42 years of being together and still enjoying the moment.

In the last five years, what new belief, behavior, or habit has most improved your life?

When I was 55, I went to Poland and learned that my mother's five brothers died because of prostate cancer, each when they were close to 55 years old. As I stood looking at the grave of one of them, I realized I was 55 myself. When I returned to the States, I immediately visited my doctor, who informed me that my prostate was large and had nodules. She tested my PSA, and after seeing the result of 9.5, she sent me to the urologist. He was very fast and forceful with his recommendation: biopsy and possible removal. "Wait, wait," I said. "Let me think about it." The doctor urged me to make a quick decision, but I wanted to do some research first. The whole next week, I studied the literature about my condition and decided to change my diet, incorporating many more vegetables, before taking drastic medical action. The result? After six months my PSA was down to 5, and after another six months it reached 1. Another half a year later it hit 0.1, and it has been like this every year since.

It's a cliché that everyone hates to eat their vegetables, but during the last five years, I developed many creative ways to prepare them that are tasty. Now it's easy to eat a lot of them. Every day, I eat a bowl of veggie soup, drink veggie juice, and eat pâté made out of the post-juicing pulp mixed with garlic, lemon juice, kale, spinach, and avocado. I serve it on bananas and other fruits so it looks like sushi. But my favorite concoction, which I created three years ago, is a medley of cabbage, onion, avocado, and pear. It's incredibly delicious, extremely healthy, and fast to prepare. This dish also gave me a deep insight about eating: there was no way to make food better than this. I felt pride and a surge of energy, realizing that I actually ate the best in the world. Nobody could eat better than I, but only as good as I. Then, one day, I was sitting with a friend, discussing longevity and health. For the first time, I could not feel that deep fear of death inside me—I had lost it. I turned to him and I said, "I feel I will be living a long time," and then I told him my story of fear. He smiled and said, "I hope it's contagious."

What advice would you give to a smart, driven college student about to enter the "real world"?

When I started studying fire protection engineering, a professor gave a welcome speech and said something like this: "Up to today, you studied hard and repeated what the world told you. Our purpose in the next four years is to teach you how to think for yourself. If we succeed, you will create something this world has never seen before, but if we do not, you will just be stuck copying others and repeating. Take my words seriously, study hard, but also open your imagination. One day you will be designing a new world, and I hope it will be better than the one we live in."

What are bad recommendations you hear in your profession or area of expertise?

"You have to do endurance cardio." In the '90s, I coached an Olympic weightlifting team at Gold's Gym in Venice. There was a trainer there who asked to join the team. When I asked why he would take on such a big challenge, he said that he was impressed by what we could do and the tremendous skill of the team members. He wanted to learn our techniques so he could later use them in his coaching. I agreed, and he joined the team, following the program and attending all our practices. One day he cornered me and said, "I understand what you do and I think it is very valuable, but I train marathon runners and triathletes and I think that cardio is important. I also trained firemen in New York, and sometimes they have to run up 40 flights of stairs, so they needed cardio training." I told him that I would ask him one question. After that, if he still thought that cardio was important, then I would include it in the training. But if not, we would never discuss it again. He agreed, so I asked him, "If I put firefighting gear on the winner of a marathon and the winner of an Olympic sprint and sent them to the 40th floor, who would be faster?" He stared at me for more than a minute without saying anything. Then I said, "Now you know how you slowed down firemen in New York by training them for endurance and not power." He smiled, and we returned to the training.

In the last five years, what have you become better at saying no to?

I have finally learned to say no to the fatalist within me. If the fatalist wins, we get worse and our quality of life declines. It was my clients who made me aware of a dialogue that we all have running inside our minds between the fatalist and its opposite, the master. No matter what I said or did to inspire them to rise above the situations that hobbled them, they still failed. My clients kept watching themselves doing what they knew was wrong, yet they did not have the power to stop. After much meditation on this problem I realized that I had a fatalist too, and that the dialogue between the fatalist and the master is automatic and running constantly in my head. The only difference is that my fatalist is no longer strong enough to win. And the margin that leads to victory is small—it can be just 49 percent fatalist versus 51 percent master. By spending more than a year writing three books of dialogues between the master and fatalist, I observed that a 1 percent tipping point often comes through a bit of trickery on the part of the master. By exploring the dynamic over time I've been able to empower the master within, and I can trap the fatalist in new ways, creating a larger margin of victory — 5 or even 10 percent — which means failing about once a week as opposed to a few times a day.

When you feel overwhelmed or unfocused, what do you do?

Over the last half of my life, I've read hundreds of poetry books. Whenever I read a poem that I loved or felt a deep connection to, I added it to a collection I titled "200 Antidepressant Poems." Now, whenever I feel overwhelmed or feel I did something wrong, I go to the meditation room, randomly open my manuscript, then read a poem loudly. Usually two poems are enough to make me feel better and restore love in my heart. Here are my 11 favorite poems to read when I am feeling depressed (11 is the master power number):

1. "The Fish" by Elizabeth Bishop
2. "Leaving One" by Ralph Angel
3. "A Cat in an Empty Apartment" by Wisława Szymborska
4. "Apples" by Deborah Digges
5. "Michiko Nogami (1946–1982)" by Jack Gilbert
6. "Eating Alone" by Li-Young Lee
7. "The Potter" by Peter Levitt
8. "Black Dog, Red Dog" by Stephen Dobyns
9. "The Word" by Mark Cox
10. "Death" by Maurycy Szymel
11. "This" by Czeslaw Milosz

"Friendship is born at the moment when one person says to another: 'What? You too? I thought I was the only one.'"
—C. S. Lewis

ANIELA GREGOREK
FB: tim.blog/happybody
(redirect)
thehappybody.com

ANIELA GREGOREK came to the United States with her husband, Jerzy Gregorek (page 113), in 1986 as a political refugee during the persecution of the Polish Solidarity Movement. As a professional athlete, Aniela has won five World Weightlifting Championships and established six world records. In 2000, she and Jerzy founded the UCLA weightlifting team and became its head coaches. Aniela has an MFA degree in creative writing from Norwich University. She writes and translates poetry both from Polish to English and from English to Polish. Her poetry and translations have appeared in major poetry magazines. As co-creator of the Happy Body Program, Aniela has mentored people for more than 30 years. She is the co-author of *The Happy Body: The Simple Science of Nutrition, Exercise, and Relaxation*.

What is the book (or books) you've given most as a gift, and why? Or what are one to three books that have greatly influenced your life?

The one book that I've read and keep rereading is *Man's Search for Meaning* by Viktor Frankl. It's marked up with my thoughts, feelings, and comments. It is a book I have gifted to many people because it changed the way I think about human suffering and grace in life.

Most of us wonder and attempt to understand the miracle of being alive and having this human experience. We strive to find meaning and purpose in our brief existence. Viktor Frankl found his. His observations about reacting or acting in challenging situations are a constant wonder to me—how one chooses the hardship of goodness and grace, or the opposite, to be selfish and self-centered. After reading his book I was deeply affected by people's struggles and suffering in concentration and labor camps during World War II. One of the survivors said that "the best of us didn't come back." Reading *Man's Search for Meaning* inspired me to share the creative works of talented World War I and World War II Polish Jewish poets in a lecture at Vermont College. They were a lost generation of fellow poets, and I wanted to honor their lives and work. Afterward, I co-translated and published two books by these poets.

My other favorite book, *Musicophilia: Tales of Music and the Brain* by Oliver Sacks, reminds me of the connection of music with healing and its importance in memory. I gained a deeper understanding of how music affects our moods and our brains. I personally experienced the power of music and memory after my mother passed away. In a lecture for my creative writing program, I heard Bachianas Brasileiras No. 5 and started sobbing uncontrollably. The soft murmuring of the opera singer transported me to when I was maybe two or three years old, and my mother would sing in exactly the same way while cooking or doing the laundry.

How has a failure, or apparent failure, set you up for later success? Do you have a "favorite failure" of yours?

When I walked away from our first house, I felt like a failure. We had purchased a fixer-upper with money we had saved after working 10- to 12-hour days in the gym for several years.

Our monthly budget for food and other necessities had been a meager $67; we felt we had achieved the American dream. And we had fixed up the house, from the floors to the roof, ourselves. Our clients always knew what we were doing by the smell of paint lingering in our hair, or by the paint stuck under our fingernails.

Eight years later, the Northridge earthquake damaged our house and many others along our street. The value of real estate spiraled down as people moved out and the neighborhood deteriorated. About the same time, my mother passed away unexpectedly. This led me to reconsider my priorities in life—I no longer wanted to work for "things." I thought about my impossible childhood dream of becoming a writer and living close to water.

Together, my husband and I decided to take a loss and walk away from our dream house to begin again from scratch. We moved to the marina to pursue a more creative and purposeful life. Years later, I understood that my goal of owning a physical house was not going to satisfy me. What I really wanted was a spiritual house, a place inside me where I could feel fulfilled at any time.

If you could have a gigantic billboard anywhere with anything on it, what would it say and why? Are there any quotes you think of often or live your life by?
I have a few of them:

> "To laugh often and much, to win the respect of intelligent people
> and the affection of children . . . to leave the world a bit better . . .
> to know even one life has breathed easier because you lived. This is
> to have succeeded."—Ralph Waldo Emerson

> "Some men see things as they are and say 'why?' I dream of things
> that never were and say 'why not?'"—Robert Kennedy

> "Friendship is born at the moment when one person says to another:
> 'What? You too? I thought I was the only one.'"—C. S. Lewis

> "It is impossible to live without failing at something, unless you live
> so cautiously that you might as well not have lived at all—in which
> case you fail by default."—J. K. Rowling

What is one of the best or most worthwhile investments you've ever made?

"If I accept you as you are, I make you worse; however, if I treat you as though you are what you are capable of becoming I help you become that."
—Johann Wolfgang von Goethe

In my practice, when I see clients for the first time, I see them as the end product—the way they will be in the future. They are all beautiful. What stands between who they are and who they want to be is their willingness to change strong habits, belief systems, and the gracefulness to embrace a new way of living. I aid them in their pursuit of change and liberation from unwanted habits.

My best investment was spending money on mentors and personal education. I've spent time and energy to learn how to effectively help every person who walks through my door.

What purchase of $100 or less has most positively impacted your life in the last six months (or in recent memory)?

A sweet and curious yellow-green parakeet, which our daughter named Margarita. The new bird came to replace our 12-year-old "soul of the house" (as I call our birds), who had passed away.

In the last five years, what have you become better at saying no to?

I have become better at saying no to negativity. The first sign of negativity, for me, is irritation. When I recognize it, right away I save myself and my loved ones a lot of emotional pain by taking time alone. Breathing deeply helps. In between breaths, I have time to slow down and see the thoughts running through my mind as well as see the other person in front of me.

I say no to blame, no to complaints, and no to gossip. I also teach my daughter these three rules. If I have nothing positive to say, I don't say anything. It makes my life easier and happier. The moment I start one of these three behaviors—blaming, complaining, or gossiping—I become negative. It is a sign of avoiding what I am responsible for: my life. Negativity is like pollution. It pollutes the mind and relationships. It is passivity. When there is constructive criticism with an intention of helping someone to be better or do better, then the act becomes active. It is important how I convey the message, since the intention is not to offend or hurt someone's feelings. If I see negativity seeping through someone I interact with, a client or a friend, I guide that person toward positive solutions.

What is an unusual habit or an absurd thing that you love?

At first I thought I didn't have any unusual habits. So I asked my daughter, Natalie, about it because children know these things about their parents. She said, "Mom, you are the most normal person I know. But you do these weird things, like the jars you made."

She's referring to our Eating Out Jar, Happiness Jar, and others. The three of us are strong-willed individuals with distinct preferences, and the Eating Out Jar came out of a struggle. Each time we talked about going out to eat, we would spend so much energy bickering that we would be exhausted or discouraged by the time we finally chose. It was not fun. The same situation occurred with choosing an activity for the weekend.

I sat my family at the table and gave them pens and Post-it notes where we wrote all the ideas we had. It was fun to see my family's ideas. My husband and daughter realized that they both liked the same places and the same activities. Usually I was the one to introduce new ideas, which were met with resistance. Here was my chance to introduce things and activities I would like to experiment with and experience.

Creating jars eliminated the necessity of using force, manipulation, or persuasion. Now we don't waste time on making simple decisions, we just pull the jar out and randomly pick one, and we all love (or accept) the choice.

The Happiness Jar we created for those times when we were going through down times as family. We came up with ideas that we all like and enjoy—simple things such as bathing our dog Bella or making potato-zucchini pancakes.

When you feel overwhelmed or unfocused, what do you do?

The most helpful practice for me when I feel unfocused is to go for a walk in nature. Being near the water has a calming effect on my nervous system, and the rhythm of the waves coming and going pacifies me. Also, going for a walk among the trees has a similar effect. In Japanese, there is a term, "forest bathing," where you take a walk under the trees and the coolness, the smell, and the silence wash over you. I feel relaxed, cleansed, and clear-minded afterward. In nature I experience the opposite of sitting meditation. Sometimes trying to tame the mind and get focused in my Transcendental Meditation, which I have practiced for many years, just magnifies whatever is happening inside me. That makes me feel more tired and stressed out— this is when I turn to nature. I feel nature meditates me.

In the last five years, what new belief, behavior, or habit has most improved your life?
I have recently changed my beliefs about aging and parenting. When I was 25, I already thought that I was old and headed downhill, but then my life took some unexpected turns. I immigrated to the USA, learned a new language, competed in Olympic Weightlifting, finished an MFA in creative writing, and became a writer and a translator. I co-created the Happy Body Program, a practice that became my life's purpose and work. Then, at age 45, I was blessed to get pregnant and have a child. Deprived of sleep and struggling to raise a small child with no family close by, I felt I'd suddenly aged decades. But as my daughter grew, I began to find my own equilibrium as a parent and learned how to take care of myself along with her. Now I am 58, my daughter is 13, and I feel full of energy and enthusiasm about the future. I am on both ends of aging, as I watch my daughter grow into a young adult while I am growing older with a lifestyle that supports youthfulness. Now I know that parenting is also one way to stay young.

"No one owes you anything."

AMELIA BOONE
TW: @ameliaboone
IG: @arboone11
ameliabooneracing.com

AMELIA BOONE is a four-time world champion in the sport of obstacle course racing (OCR) and is widely considered the world's most decorated obstacle racer. She has been called "the Michael Jordan of obstacle racing" and "the Queen of Pain." Her victories include winning the 2013 Spartan Race World Championships and being the only three-time winner of the World's Toughest Mudder. In the 2012 World's Toughest Mudder competition, which lasts 24 hours (she covered 90 miles and ~300 obstacles), she finished second *overall* out of more than 1,000 competitors, 80 percent of whom were male. The one person who beat her finished just eight minutes ahead of her. Amelia is also a three-time finisher of the Death Race, a competitive ultra-marathoner, and has risen to the top of her sport while simultaneously working as a full-time corporate attorney. She has been selected as one of the "50 Fittest Women" by *Sports Illustrated*.

What purchase of $100 or less has most positively impacted your life in the last six months (or in recent memory)?

During a tough period in my life, I purchased a handmade wrap bracelet on Etsy inscribed with the quote "The struggle ends when the gratitude begins."

[Quote attributed to Neale Donald Walsch] I wear it on my wrist every day as a constant reminder to myself to live in a place of gratitude.

If you could have a gigantic billboard anywhere with anything on it, what would it say and why?

"No one owes you anything."

We live in a world that's rampant with entitlement, with many people believing that they deserve to be given more. My parents raised me to be self-sufficient, and impressed upon me that the only person you can really depend on in life is you. If you want something, you work for it. You don't expect it to be given. If others help you out along the way, that's fantastic, but it's not a given. I believe that the key to self-sufficiency is breaking free of the mindset that someone, somewhere, owes you something or will come to your rescue.

What is one of the best or most worthwhile investments you've ever made?

In 2011, I shelled out $450 to participate in the first World's Toughest Mudder, a brand-new 24-hour obstacle race. Saddled with law school debt, it was a big expenditure for me, and I had no business thinking I could even complete the race, let alone compete in it. But I ended up being one of 11 finishers (out of 1,000 participants) of that race, and it altered the course of my life, leading to my career in obstacle racing and multiple world championships. Had I not plunked down the cash for that entry fee, none of that would have happened.

What is an unusual habit or an absurd thing that you love?

For every major event in my life—everything from races to job changes to breakups—I assign a song. Most of these come organically: what I was listening to at the time, lyrics that spoke to me at a moment in my life, or a song I sang on repeat during a race (a common habit of mine). I keep these songs in a playlist, ordered chronologically. I can go back through and listen to that playlist and relive major experiences, both highs and lows, in my life. It has a profound impact on me and my ability to recall and relive memories and major milestones. Examples:

- World's Toughest Mudder 2012: Macklemore, "Thrift Shop" (rapped to myself to make sure I was lucid and coherent in the middle of the night)

- Studying for and taking the bar exam: Augustana, "Sunday Best"

Oh, and I eat a Pop-Tart before every race. Most folks consider that one strange.

What is the book (or books) you've given most as a gift, and why? Or what are one to three books that have greatly influenced your life?

Atlas Shrugged by Ayn Rand. Beliefs and feelings on objectivism aside, when I read the book in my teens, Dagny Taggart's character spoke to me on a level I'd never experienced with any other novel. It was life-changing for me during my formative years in figuring out who I was and what I wanted in life (granted, I'm still figuring that out).

A Tale of Two Cities by Charles Dickens. This one isn't necessarily because of the book itself (though it remains one my favorites to this day), but because of when and where I read it. My fifth grade teacher saw that I wasn't being challenged by our class reading, so she gave it to me as a side assignment. My ten-year-old self struggled mightily through it, but I'll never forget the feeling of accomplishment when I turned the last page. When I reread it later, I realized I didn't comprehend at least half of what was happening the first time around, but that wasn't the point—the point was that I had a teacher who believed enough in my intelligence to entrust me with it, and that gave my nerdy ten-year-old self all the confidence in the world. And since then, I've read every Dickens novel.

Brave Enough by Cheryl Strayed. I've kept collections of quotes since I was a young child. The beauty of quotes is that they can speak to you outside of the original context at different times in your life. I picked this up during a tough period in my life, and many of the quotes are still pinned to my bathroom mirror.

What are bad recommendations you hear in your profession or area of expertise?

"Resting is weakness." So many athletes have gotten into the mindset that more is better, which sets you up for burnout, injury, overtraining, and adrenal fatigue issues. While this mindset is common with athletes, it's applicable to high achievers in all areas of life. Growth and gains come from periods of rest, yet "rest" has become a four-letter word for high performers, and that needs to change.

When you feel overwhelmed or unfocused, what do you do?

This may sound odd, but I'll tackle a chore like scrubbing the bathtub or cleaning out the fridge. When I feel stuck, sometimes accomplishing a task, however mundane, gives me the momentum I need to refocus. Either that, or I'll work up a sweat, preferably in the form of a trail run. Nature and endorphins are always the answer.

What advice would you give to a smart, driven college student about to enter the "real world"? What advice should they ignore?

If you are struggling to figure out where you are headed in life or what you are passionate about, pay attention to activities, ideas, and areas where you love the process, not just the results or the outcome. We are drawn to tasks where we can receive validation through results, but I've learned that true fulfillment comes from love of the process. Look for something where you love the process, and the results will follow.

In the last five years, what new belief, behavior, or habit has most improved your life?

I'm risk-averse by nature, and in the last five years, I've learned how to run toward fear, instead of running away from it. My nature has always been to take the straight and narrow path, to take the path with fewer unknowns. But by forcing myself to face the unknown (e.g., Joe De Sena's infamous "Death Race") and embrace the uncomfortable, I've found that I actually thrive in it. So I now take fear and discomfort as a sign that I should be doing something. That's where the magic happens.

"Be a good wife/husband/ mom/dad/friend. Look at Paul Newman's life. Do that."

SIR JOEL EDWARD McHALE, LORD OF WINTERFELL
TW/IG: @joelmchale
joelmchale.com

JOEL McHALE is best known as host of E!'s *The Soup* and for his starring role on the hit comedy series *Community*. His film credits include *A Merry Friggin' Christmas, Deliver Us from Evil, Blended, Ted, What's Your Number?, The Big Year, Spy Kids 4: All the Time in the World,* and *The Informant!* Joel also performs standup comedy around the country to sold-out audiences. In 2014, he hosted the annual White House Correspondents' Association Dinner in Washington, D.C., and hosted the 2015 ESPYs on ABC. Born in Rome and raised in Seattle, Joel was a history major at the University of Washington, where he also was a member of their championship football team. He received his master of fine arts from UW's Professional Actor Training Program. He is the author of *Thanks for the Money: How to Use My Life Story to Become the Best Joel McHale You Can Be.*

What is the book (or books) you've given most as a gift, and why? Or what are one to three books that have greatly influenced your life?

Because this question is so big, Tim (I can't believe I'm not getting paid for this), I'm going to list five, you jerk. I'm not going to even recommend my book: *Thanks for the Money: How to Use My Life Story to Become the Best Joel McHale You Can Be* . . . because that would seem arrogant. In stores now!

Anyway, here are the books.

The Road by Cormac McCarthy. This book is poetry (it's not really). No novel has ever captured the love a parent has for his child better than this book. It also paints the closest picture to what a post-apocalyptic world would look like. It's fun!

The Blade Itself by Joe Abercrombie. Mark my words, Abercrombie will go down in history as one of the greatest fantasy novelists of all time. He's with Tolkien. These books are magical in how he creates a world out of nothing and characters so well drawn that you'll think Joe takes trips to this magical place and interviews these people. On top of all that, Joe has a hilarious sense of humor.

The Book of Strange New Things by Michel Faber. It's hard to describe the brilliance of this book. If you read it, keep in mind that it was written by an atheist.

How to Fly a Horse: The Secret History of Creation, Invention, and Discovery by Kevin Ashton. This book is so great. Among many, many other things that it illuminates, one of the most revelatory things is that being creative is not just a unique trait in a few select people—it's written in our DNA. Everyone's DNA.

Deep Survival: Who Lives, Who Dies, and Why, by Laurence Gonzales. I read this book 13 years ago, and I still think about it almost every week. The title explains exactly what it is and it is fascinating. This book taught me not to take things for granted. It taught me what to do in stressful and simple situations I would find myself in, and how to evaluate them in a levelheaded way. It teaches you how things really are, as opposed to what you want them to be. And that is the difference between life and death (ominous!).

What purchase of $100 or less has most positively impacted your life in the last six months (or in recent memory)?

Okay, it's more than the last six months (what are you gonna do to me, Tim Ferriss? Sue me? Please. I will bury you) but I'm going to go with Audible. com. (They are not paying me to write this. That said, please buy the Swiffer WetJet today! It's magic!) I'm dyslexic (yuo to2? This Time Frerris booak is me føreveer Takeing!), so when Audible came along—it changed my life. I've ultimately spent way more than the $100 Tim is holding us to for some godforsaken reason. Each book can be anywhere from $3 to $30. The world of the classics has been opened to me, and I thank God and the nerds that designed this app for it. I was assigned Dostoyevsky's *Crime and Punishment* in high school. The chances of me reading that whole thing back then were as good as me growing a tail. I blew through the unabridged Audible version in a couple weeks (36 hours for the whole book). It was so good I got shivers (might have been the flu). When I drive, work out, do the dishes, etc., I listen to that app and I get lost in the world's stories (either that or the Molly is really kicking in).

What advice would you give to a smart, driven college student about to enter the "real world"?

Hey smart, driven college student—

First of all, why am I hanging out with you? I never used to hang out with people like you. Do you want to go see that *Baby Driver* movie? I get it, you're busy, you're driven. Do you mind if I have a couple of beers while I answer Tim's question? It's cool, I'm going to anyways.

My advice for a college student who is about to enter the real world is not revelatory. You probably hear this all the time but I'm going to tell you anyway—again. Here it is: Pursue that dream or dreams that are planted in you already. Yes, some of you are saying you don't know what that dream is, but—it's there. Believe me.

That's the thing for you. Capital YOU. I believe you're supposed to follow your dreams. Like it's an order.

Don't just do the thing that people expect you to do or go for the money. That might work out for a while, but you will harbor some serious resentment as you get into your 40s if you do that. I see it all the time. It sucks. On top of that—and just as important—help people who are less fortunate than you and help the planet. Yep [takes long pull off a bottle of IPA]. At the end of your life, you will be much happier and good (good is more important) if you did something that wasn't just selfish, even if that selfish thing (your dream) was righteous.

Oh—and be a good wife/husband/mom/dad/friend. Look at Paul Newman's life. Do that. Do that. Do that.

"Don't believe anyone who tells you they know what they are doing. William Goldman, the screenwriter, once wrote 'nobody knows anything' in the movie business, and it is true. I know I don't."

BEN STILLER
TW: @RedHourBen
FB: /BenStiller
thestillerfoundation.org

BEN STILLER has written, starred in, directed, or produced more than 50 films, including *The Secret Life of Walter Mitty, Zoolander, The Cable Guy, There's Something About Mary,* the *Meet the Parents* trilogy, *DodgeBall, Tropic Thunder,* the *Madagascar* series, and the *Night at the Museum* trilogy. He is a member of a group of comedic actors colloquially known as the Frat Pack. His films have grossed more than $2.6 billion in Canada and the United States, with an average of $79 million per film. Throughout his career, he has received multiple awards and honors, including an Emmy Award, multiple MTV Movie Awards, and a Teen Choice Award.

What is an unusual habit or an absurd thing that you love?

I have a lot of unusual habits that I don't think I should go into here. I love stopping on the side of the road whenever I see a historical marker and reading the whole thing, and then sometimes exploring the site. While not absurd, I can sometimes go down the rabbit hole of this kind of thing and take big detours from my schedule.

I like to dunk my head in a bucket of ice in the morning to wake me up. I don't think it actually is therapeutic but it is definitely invigorating and probably absurd looking.

What is the book (or books) you've given most as a gift, and why? Or what are one to three books that have greatly influenced your life?

I was given *The Second Tree from the Corner,* a book of short stories by E. B. White, when I was a teenager by my older sister's friend. It has always been so inspiring . . . it's a simple inner monologue about a guy in his psychiatrist's office trying to answer the question of what he wants in life. It is simple and uniquely moving in that it distills how ephemeral and fleeting moments of happiness can be, yet that's what life's mystery is all about. The humor and emotion of the story moved me at a young age and connected with something inside I previously could not articulate.

When I was a teenager, my mother gave me *Nine Stories* by Salinger. The story "For Esmé—with Love and Squalor" affected me deeply. A simple story about a soldier dealing with posttraumatic stress disorder (though not called that at the time) and how a short encounter with two children while he was in the war comes back to help him after he is back. The gut punch of the ending, which is little more action than reading a letter, made me realize the power of storytelling. It encapsulates what art can do—move you, and in such a simple way. The story is about human kindness and how a small act can mean so much. This idea, coming to me at a formative age, really affected my attitude toward art.

The Jaws Log is a book written by Carl Gottlieb, the screenwriter of the movie Jaws. It is a day-by-day account of the making of the movie. It is filled with the details of making a movie on location. It was incredibly inspiring to me—I wanted to be a director and Jaws came out when I was ten years old. I loved the movie and was fascinated by everything having to do with it. I ingested the information and it sort of became my bible for filmmaking as I set out to make my Super 8 movies with my friends. A book like that at the right time, that feeds your desire for knowledge about a specific craft when you are just learning about it, can be formative. I still remember the texture of the tattered paperback cover and how excited I was to read and reread it. Also now, in this new age of digital filmmaking, it is a great chronicle of how movies were made back when the process was much more analog.

What purchase of $100 or less has most positively impacted your life in the last six months (or in recent memory)?

I found the right backpack [Incase City Collection]. It makes a big difference, since it is sort of my portable office/pocketbook. For a guy, unless you carry a "purse" (man purse), I think a backpack is essential. It always seems to end up getting overstuffed, and when it does, I remind myself I don't need to carry everything with me all the time. Getting one with a good top compartment for wallet, keys, etc., really makes life easier.

How has a failure, or apparent failure, set you up for later success? Do you have a "favorite failure" of yours?

I think the commercial and critical failure of The Cable Guy would be what I look back on as the most educational and spirit building. The making of it was a pure creative experience. We basically did what we wanted, and the power of Jim Carrey to take a chance with that movie afforded us that. So in making it, we felt fulfilled and excited. But when it came out, everyone hated it and no one went. It was pretty shocking, mainly because I never experienced such a high-profile project not doing well. It hurt, as failures always do, but I think the first time you go through something like that you don't know how to emerge. And when you finally do, it gives you a perspective you could never have [otherwise]. In terms of how people react to art or entertainment, you learn that it sometimes goes well and it sometimes doesn't. It doesn't mean that the cause and effect are connected. In other words, you always do the best you can in the moment, and then it either connects or it doesn't. Going forward, I was less innocent or maybe naive about that. Then, when I did something well received after that, it was always tempered by the knowledge that it didn't mean that the project itself was better or worse. I think that was very helpful. Also, with movies, you learn that the true mark of "success" is whether people still connect years later. If the movie has a "life." With *Cable Guy*, I have found it does, more so than other movies I made that were more "successful," when people mention it to me, I find it even more fulfilling.

If you could have a gigantic billboard anywhere, what would it say and why? Are there any quotes you think of often or live your life by?

"BE HERE NOW" (something I am constantly trying to do, though not always successfully).

Because life is short, and we only have the current moment. Our memories are precious but they are the past, and the future is not here now. As I get older, I am trying to live fully in moments with the people I love and care about. I have spent a lot of years focusing on the next thing, and, in so doing, stressed about things that ultimately don't matter or bring happiness. I keep trying to sort of "relax" into where I am now, whether it is where I want to be or not.

In the last five years, what new belief, behavior, or habit has most improved your life?

Taking time to breathe when I feel stressed. I will try to just breathe and concentrate on my breath. I find it really relaxing, and it helps me refocus and reset.

What are bad recommendations you hear in your profession or area of expertise?

I think people are too aware of trying to figure out what's "hot" and trying to emulate that. Ultimately, you need to develop your own voice as a film-maker or even as an actor. It takes time. In terms of bad recommendations, don't believe anyone who tells you they know what they are doing. William Goldman, the screenwriter, once wrote, "nobody knows anything" in the movie business, and it is true. I know I don't, and I have been doing it a long time. It's always starting from scratch each time.

So don't listen to anyone who tells you what kind of movie to write, or how you should look, or what kind of work to do.

QUOTES I'M PONDERING

(Tim Ferriss: March 11–March 25, 2016)

"A man is rich in proportion to the number of things he can afford to let alone."

–HENRY DAVID THOREAU
American essayist and philosopher, author of *Walden*

"What gets measured gets managed."

–PETER DRUCKER
Considered "the founder of modern management,"
author of *The Effective Executive*

"Morality is simply the attitude we adopt towards people we personally dislike."

–OSCAR WILDE
Irish writer, author of *The Picture of Dorian Gray*

"Yoga, and the community I came to know through my practice, saved my life."

ANNA HOLMES
TW/IG: @annaholmes
annaholmes.com

ANNA HOLMES is an award-winning writer and editor who has worked with numerous publications, including *The Washington Post*, *The New Yorker* online, and *The New York Times*, where she is a regular contributor to the Sunday Book Review. In 2007, in response to her work for magazines like *Glamour* and *Cosmopolitan*, she created the popular website Jezebel. com, which helped to revolutionize popular discussions around the intersections of gender, race, and culture. In 2016, she became SVP of Editorial at First Look Media, where she is spearheading the launch of Topic.com, the consumer-facing arm of Topic, the company's film, TV, and digital studio.

What advice would you give to a smart, driven college student about to enter the "real world"? What advice should they ignore?
They should ignore any advice from anyone who purports to tell them what the future will look like. No one knows. People have ideas, and those are

good to take on board and consider, but that's about the extent of it. I can't tell you how many media or political "experts" have made proclamations as to the next big thing in journalism or entertainment—or politics—and been proven horribly, embarrassingly wrong. In the whole scheme of things, no one knows anything, or rather, all of us have a lot to learn, and it takes a lifetime. Interrogate the information shared with you by others, and use it as a way to make up your own mind, not a path to follow.

If you could have a gigantic billboard anywhere with anything on it, what would it say and why?

"Follow your curiosity, wherever you can find it." Embracing a curious mind and always trying to learn more—about others, about yourself, about the world and our place within it—is an important way to express yourself, and it's pretty cheap, too, often free!

How has a failure, or apparent failure, set you up for later success? Do you have a "favorite failure" of yours?

I am a complete failure at the politics of the workplace. Probably because I just don't have the stomach for it. I like collaborative environments where people who work hard and do good work get rewarded for it, no matter who they are. I hate machinations and behind-the-scenes strategizing and bullshit. The first place I worked after college was a profoundly political place and I did not do well there, which, in the end, was a blessing, because it set me up to try my talents in more emerging, less conventional, and less conservative [not conservative politically, but conservative as in "cautious, by-the-book, doing things the way they are always done"] spaces.

What is the book (or books) you've given most as a gift, and why? Or what are one to three books that have greatly influenced your life?

My favorite children's book, *Miss Rumphius*, by Barbara Cooney. I have about ten copies in my apartment that I give out to friends (old and new) with daughters. It's a beautifully illustrated and written tale of a young girl in coastal Maine who grows up to travel the world and indulge her curiosity about other places and people. In her old age, she returns to Maine to make the world a more beautiful place. There's no mention of marriage or motherhood in the story; it's simply a portrait of the life of a woman who finds value and meaning in following her interests and an important lesson for all of us about what women are capable of.

What is an unusual habit or an absurd thing that you love?

Over the past few years, I've found myself more and more fascinated by flight—by birds and by airplanes. A few months ago, I did some plane spotting while staying at a hotel near Heathrow airport; I just ambled out to the parking lot and introduced myself to some young Englishmen who were on a small hill watching the planes come in. We'll see if it's a fascination that "takes." I don't think it's a particularly common fascination of women, from what I can tell.

In the last five years, what new belief, behavior, or habit has most improved your life?

Yoga. Specifically, vigorous vinyasa yoga. I began a yoga practice in 2011 as a way to get stronger and healthier and to deal with a very difficult period in my life—the estrangement from my then husband and later separation and divorce. I'd been a dancer as a child and had forgotten how much an understanding of my own body and belief in its capabilities could translate into better self-esteem, focus, and mental and emotional centeredness. Yoga, and the community I came to know through my practice, saved my life.

In the last five years, what have you become better at saying no to?

I've become much better at saying no to requests for assistance and advice, which sounds horrible! But there was a certain point a few years ago, where I was spending more time responding to queries from complete strangers than making sure I was allowing myself to be accessible and present to the actual people in my life—my friends and family. A few years ago, I gave a commencement speech to graduates of a private girls' boarding school in upstate New York. The thrust of the speech was why these accomplished young women should learn to say no more often. Females are socialized to be accommodating, to be caretakers, to not rock the boat, and to put others before themselves. What I told these graduates was not so much "fuck that," but that they should work to overcome the uncomfortable feelings they may encounter when telling someone else no, whether that is a friend, a romantic partner, a work colleague, etc.

When you feel overwhelmed or unfocused, what do you do?

Two things: I try to breathe deeply and I walk, preferably in some sort of natural setting: a park, along the NYC waterfront . . . if I'm lucky, someplace outside of the city, like paths and trails in Maine, the UK, or my beloved home state of California. I also like road trips. I find that long drives help me to put things in perspective and solve problems and blow off steam. (I sing in the car. Loudly.) Moving throughout the world, whether by foot or four-wheeled vehicle, gives me a different way of looking at things and inspires me to feel gratitude at even the smallest of pleasures: a fluffy cloud, a chipmunk scurrying across the road, a hawk sitting on a fencepost, a gaggle of teenagers making a ruckus and having the time of their lives.

"Things are never as good or as bad as they seem."

ANDREW ROSS SORKIN
TW: @andrewrsorkin
andrewrosssorkin.com

ANDREW ROSS SORKIN is a financial columnist for *The New York Times* and the founder and editor-at-large of DealBook, an online daily financial report published by the same. Andrew is also an assistant editor of business and finance news at the *NYT,* helping guide and shape the paper's coverage. He is a co-anchor of *Squawk Box,* CNBC's signature morning program, and he is the author of the *New York Times* best-selling book *Too Big to Fail: How Wall Street and Washington Fought to Save the Financial System—and Themselves,* which chronicled the events of the 2008 financial crisis. The book won the 2010 Gerald Loeb Award for Best Business Book and was shortlisted for the 2010 Samuel Johnson Prize and the 2010 Financial Times Business Book of the Year Award. Andrew co-produced the film adaptation of the book, which was nominated for 11 Emmy Awards. He began writing for *The New York Times* in 1995 under unusual circumstances: He hadn't yet graduated from high school.

If you could have a gigantic billboard anywhere with anything on it, what would it say?
"Things are never as good or as bad as they seem."

What purchase of $100 or less has most positively impacted your life in the last six months (or in recent memory)?

Earplugs for sleeping. I've tried them all. Hearos Xtreme Protection NRR 33 work best and are the most comfortable. If you really want to go to extremes to also control light, Lonfrote Deep Molded Sleep Mask is the best for airplanes or anywhere else.

What advice would you give to a smart, driven college student about to enter the "real world"?

Persistence matters more than talent. The student with straight As is irrelevant if the student sitting next to him with Bs has more passion.

When you feel overwhelmed or unfocused, what do you do?

Whenever I'm feeling like I need to prioritize what I'm doing or overthinking a particular situation that is making me anxious, I try to remember this great exchange in the film *Bridge of Spies*. Tom Hanks, who plays a lawyer, asks his client, who is being accused of being a spy, "Aren't you worried?" His answer: "Would it help?" I always think, "Would it help?" That is the pivotal question that I ask myself every day. If you put everything through that prism, it is a remarkably effective way to cut through the clutter.

"A good friend of mine once said: 'It's really easy to say what you're not. It's hard to say what you are.' … Anybody can talk about why something's bad. Try doing something good."

JOSEPH GORDON-LEVITT
TW/IG: @hitrecordjoe
hitrecord.org

JOSEPH GORDON-LEVITT is an actor whose career spans three decades, and ranges from television (*3rd Rock from the Sun*) to arthouse (*Mysterious Skin, Brick*) to multiplex (*Inception, 500 Days of Summer, Snowden*). He made his feature screenwriting and directorial debut with *Don Jon* (Independent Spirit Award nomination, Best First Screenplay). He also founded and directs HITRECORD, an online community of artists emphasizing collaboration over self-promotion. HITRECORD has evolved into a "community-sourced" production company that publishes books, puts out records, produces videos for brands from LG to the ACLU, and has won an Emmy for its variety show *HitRecord on TV*.

What is the book (or books) you've given most as a gift, and why? Or what are one to three books that have greatly influenced your life?

Remix: Making Art and Commerce Thrive in the Hybrid Economy by Lawrence Lessig. This book is about what it means to take something someone else has created and make it your own. He's a legal scholar, and he's talking about intellectual property laws, copyright, fair use, etc., but he's also quite insightful about the creative process in general. Our culture puts such a premium on the notion of originality, but when you really examine just about any "original" thought or work, you find it's a composite of previous influences. Everything's a remix. Of course, there's such a thing as being overly derivative, but I tend to mostly value sincerity over originality. I think I perform better when I focus less on being original and more on being honest.

How has a failure, or apparent failure, set you up for later success? Do you have a "favorite failure" of yours?

I started working as an actor when I was six. I quit at 19 to go to college, but when I tried to get back into it, I couldn't get a job. I spent a year auditioning and failing. It was painful. I had visions of never getting to do it again, which genuinely terrified me.

I did a lot of thinking. What exactly was I scared of? What would I be missing if I never got another acting job? I never really liked the glitz and glamor of Hollywood, so it wasn't that. At that time, I'd never even cared all that much what other people thought of the movies and shows I got to be in. Mostly, I just loved doing it. I loved the creative process itself, and I realized I couldn't let my ability to be creative depend on somebody else deciding to hire me. I had to take matters into my own hands.

I came up with my own little metaphorical mantra for this, something I'd think to myself when I needed encouragement, and that was "hit record." I'd always played around with my family's video cameras, and the red REC button became a symbol for my conviction that I could do it on my own. I taught myself to edit video and started making little short films and songs and stories.

My brother helped me set up a tiny website where I'd put up the things I'd made, and we called it HITRECORD.ORG. That was 12 years ago.

Since then, HITRECORD has grown into a community of more than half a million artists around the world. We've made all kinds of incredible things together, paid people millions of dollars, and won prestigious awards, but for me, the heart of it is still the same: the love of creativity for its own sake. It's that thing I had to find 12 years ago, dead in the thick of self-loathing, sloth-inducing, throat-sore-from-screaming failure.

If you could have a gigantic billboard anywhere with anything on it, what would it say and why? Are there any quotes you think of often or live your life by?

A good friend of mine once said: "It's really easy to say what you're not. It's hard to say what you are." In other words, you can spend all day undermining other people, and even if you're right, who cares? Anybody can talk about why something's bad. Try doing something good.

What is one of the best or most worthwhile investments you've ever made?

I think moving away from my hometown was one of the most fruitful things I ever did. We can't help but define ourselves in terms of how others see us. So being around nothing but new people allowed me to define myself anew. I've since moved back, but the growth I got out of living away was huge.

What is an unusual habit or an absurd thing that you love?

I like talking to myself. Often loudly.

In the last five years, what new belief, behavior, or habit has most improved your life?

My wife turned me on to Google Scholar. It's like Google, except it only searches academic and scientific studies. So when I want to know something, rather than reading some sensationalistic clickbait, I can find out what the actual evidence says. It takes way longer. Scientific studies are not easy to read. In fact, I usually need help, but it's worth it.

What advice would you give to a smart, driven college student about to enter the "real world"?

I kind of touched on this idea already, but for anybody out there reading this who wants to get into acting or entertainment, my advice is to first ask yourself: why? Try to be really honest with yourself about what exactly you're after. Fame is seductive. We've all seen and loved the movies about the young underdog becoming a star. I won't claim to be 100 percent immune to it. In fact, I think there's something natural about wanting to be famous, in terms of biological evolution. When our ancestors lived in the wild, having everyone know who you were probably helped you get the support you needed to brave the harsh environment and pass on your genes. So I'm not saying you're a bad person if you want to be famous. I'm just saying you might be heading down a path that won't lead to happiness. Of the famous people I know, the ones who are happy aren't happy because of the fame. They're happy for the same reasons everybody else is: because they're healthy, because they have good people around them, and because they take satisfaction in what they do, regardless of how many millions of strangers are watching. I think this applies outside of acting and entertainment. In any field, there's usually some kind of mythological reward you're supposed to receive if everybody considers you a success. But in my experience, there's a lot more honest joy to be had from taking pleasure in the work itself.

When you feel overwhelmed or unfocused, what do you do?

I like to write. I've gone through different phases in my life of writing in a journal more or less frequently, but it's something I turn to, especially when I'm trying to work through something that's vexing me. I sit down and describe my situation in writing. I type. I use complete sentences. I guess I write it as if it's for an audience, even though I never show it to anyone. By having to explain it to a "reader" with no prior knowledge, I'm forced to identify and parse all the elements and nuances of what's really going on. Sometimes I arrive at new answers or conclusions, but even when I don't, I'm usually thinking more clearly and breathing a bit more easily.

HOW TO SAY
NO

WENDY MacNAUGHTON
TW/IG: @wendymac
wendymacnaughton.com

WENDY MacNAUGHTON is a *New York Times* best-selling illustrator and graphic journalist based in San Francisco. Her books include *Meanwhile in San Francisco, The City in Its Own Words; Lost Cat: A True Story of Love, Desperation, and GPS Technology; Pen and Ink: Tattoos and the Stories Behind Them; Knives & Ink: Chefs and the Stories Behind Their Tattoos; The Essential Scratch & Sniff Guide to Becoming a Wine Expert; The Essential Scratch & Sniff Guide to Becoming a Whiskey Know-It-All;* and the newly released *Leave Me Alone with the Recipes: The Life, Art, and Cookbook of Cipe Pineles.* Wendy is the back page columnist for *California Sunday Magazine* and co-founder of Women Who Draw. Her partner is Caroline Paul (page 395).

Note from Tim: My beautiful reader, as you've no doubt noticed (being brilliant, as well as beautiful), one of the questions I like to ask is some variant of the following: "In the last five years, what have you become better at saying no to (distractions, invitations, etc.)? What new realizations and/or approaches helped?"

What's fantastic about this question is that it's hard to avoid answering. This is true even if—actually, *especially* if—someone refuses to answer! When I asked Wendy if she'd participate in this book, she sent a very thoughtful and perfect "I have to pass" response after much consideration. I loved it so much that I replied with, "Here is perhaps a very odd question—might you be OK with me printing this very polite decline email in the book?"

She agreed, so here's the email she sent me . . . to decline being in this book:

Hi Tim,

Gah. OK. I've been battling with this, and here's the deal: after five intense years of creative output and promotion, interviews about personal journeys and where ideas come from, after years of wrapping up one project one day and jumping right into promoting another the next . . . I'm taking a step back. I recently maxed out pretty hard, and for the benefit of my work, I gotta take a break. Over the past month, I've cancelled contracts and said no to new projects and interviews. I've started creating space to explore and doodle again. To sit and do nothing. To wander and waste a day. And for the first time in five years, I'm finally in a place where there is no due date tied to every drawing. No deadline for ideas. And it feels really right.

So, while I really want to do this with you—I respect you and your work and am honored that you'd ask me to participate—and as capital S stupid as it is for me professionally not to do it, I'm going to have to say thank you but . . . I gotta pass. I'm simply not in a place to talk about myself or my work right now. (Crazy for a highly verbal only child to say.) Hopefully we will get a chance to talk somewhere down the line—I promise any thoughts I'll have for you then will be far more insightful than anything I can share with you right now.

I hope the space created by my absence is filled by one of the brilliant people I suggested in my previous email.

And really, thank you so much for your interest.

I'll be kicking myself when the book comes out.

–W

"I'd rather give an understated good recommendation: be interdisciplinary . . . the interactions between [fields] tend to very often inform strategic and protocol decisions."

VITALIK BUTERIN
TW: @VitalikButerin
Reddit: /u/vbuterin

VITALIK BUTERIN is the creator of Ethereum. He first discovered blockchain and cryptocurrency technologies through Bitcoin in 2011, and was immediately excited by the technology and its potential. He co-founded *Bitcoin magazine* in September 2011, and after two and a half years looking at what the existing blockchain technology and applications had to offer, wrote the Ethereum white paper in November 2013. He now leads Ethereum's research team, working on future versions of the Ethereum protocol. In 2014, Vitalik was a recipient of the two-year Thiel Fellowship, tech billionaire Peter Thiel's project that awards $100,000 to 20 promising innovators under 20 so they can pursue their inventions in lieu of a post-secondary institution.

In the last five years, what new belief, behavior, or habit has most improved your life?

The largest one is probably understanding how to interpret things that other people are saying in situations where their goals do not fully align with yours. A common rookie error that inexperienced leaders make is always agreeing with the last person they talked to; this takes a while to get past, though it becomes easy once you get exposed to enough people who contradict each other. A good general strategy is reasoning counterfactually: if someone tells you that X is true, ask yourself—(i) what would they say if X really is true, and (ii) what would they say if X is false? If the answer to (i) and (ii) is "they will say roughly what they just said now," then their words provided you with exactly zero information. In general, know when it's really important not to take people's words at 100 percent face value.

What purchase of $100 or less has most positively impacted your life in the last six months (or in recent memory)?

A proper comfortable traveling backpack. I use it to carry all of my stuff (~10 kg) everywhere with me wherever I fly, and it has helped greatly in making the experience more convenient.

What is an unusual habit or an absurd thing that you love?

- I watch movies frequently on airplanes, but I make sure to only watch them in languages that I am not yet fully fluent in. Currently I cycle through French, German, and Chinese.

- 90 percent dark chocolate. Below 80 is too sweet, 95 is still a bit too dark for me . . . for now. Usually I go with Lindt because that's the one that's most often available, but I do mix it around from time to time. It's guided much more by what's available than my personal preferences.

- Cats.

What are bad recommendations you hear in your profession or area of expertise?

I'd rather give an understated good recommendation: be interdisciplinary. In my case, I follow quite a bit of research in computer science, cryptography, mechanism design, economics, politics, and other social sciences, and the interactions between these fields tend to very often inform strategic and protocol decisions.

When you feel overwhelmed or unfocused, what do you do?

It depends what kind of overwhelming situation it is. In general, it's always helpful to switch one's focus to something else at least for some time, perhaps by going on a walk. If it is because of a technical problem (i.e., how do we get task X done?) then the best way to get around an impasse is to put yourself in many different situations and environments to try to get some new inspiration. The more difficult kind to deal with is social situations. In this case, it's important to avoid falling into the trap of seeing things from the perspective of the last person you talked to, or even in general the people you spend more time with; you need to try to find ways to neutrally evaluate the situation, and perhaps talk to others who are outside of the circle that's currently in conflict.

QUOTES I'M PONDERING

(Tim Ferriss: Feb. 12–March 4, 2016)

"Do your own thinking independently. Be the chess player, not the chess piece."

–RALPH CHARELL
Author of *How to Make Things Go Your Way*

"Named must your fear be before banish it you can."

–YODA
Powerful Jedi master

"The best defense is a good offense."

–DAN GABLE
Olympic gold medalist in wrestling,
considered the greatest wrestling coach of all time

"Many a false step was made by standing still."

–FORTUNE COOKIE

"The single most important distinction in life ... is to distinguish between an opportunity to be seized and a temptation to be resisted."

RABBI LORD JONATHAN SACKS
TW/FB: @rabbisacks
rabbisacks.org

RABBI LORD JONATHAN SACKS is an international religious leader, philosopher, award-winning author, and respected moral voice. He was awarded the 2016 Templeton Prize in recognition of his "exceptional contributions to affirming life's spiritual dimension." Rabbi Sacks has been described by HRH The Prince of Wales as "a light unto this nation" and by former British prime minister Tony Blair as "an intellectual giant." Since stepping down as the chief rabbi of the United Hebrew Congregations of the Commonwealth—a position he held for 22 years—Rabbi Sacks has held a number of professorships at several academic institutions including Yeshiva University and King's College London. He currently serves as the Ingeborg and Ira Rennert Global Distinguished Professor of Judaic Thought at New York University. Rabbi Sacks is the author of more than 30 books.

His most recent work, *Not in God's Name: Confronting Religious Violence* was awarded a 2015 National Jewish Book Award in America and was a top ten *Sunday Times* bestseller in the UK. Rabbi Sacks was knighted by Her Majesty The Queen in 2005 and made a Life Peer, taking his seat in the House of Lords in October 2009.

What is the book (or books) you've given most as a gift, and why? Or what are one to three books that have greatly influenced your life?

Leadership on the Line by Ronald A. Heifetz and Marty Linsky, because it is the most honest book I have ever read on leadership, and you can tell that by the book's subtitle, *Staying Alive Through the Dangers of Leading*. It's deeply honest, and a book that I give to everyone, so they know exactly what they're letting themselves in for if they choose to be a leader.

What purchase of $100 or less has most positively impacted your life in the last six months (or in recent memory)?

Without a shadow of doubt, buying [Bose] noise-canceling earphones. These are the most religious objects I have ever come across, because I define faith as the ability to hear the music beneath the noise.

How has a failure, or apparent failure, set you up for later success? What event or thinking triggered the depths of the despair?

The lowest point in my life actually came about when I published in 2002 —on September 11, 2002, the first anniversary of 9/11—a book called *The Dignity of Difference*.

I stood at Ground Zero in January 2002. The World Economic Forum had been moved to New York from Davos for that year and the archbishop of Canterbury, the chief rabbi of Israel, imams, gurus from all over the world stood at Ground Zero and we said prayers together.

And I suddenly realized that this was the great defining choice that humanity would face for the next generation: religion as a force for coexistence, reconciliation, and mutual respect or religion as a force for hatred, terror, and violence.

I decided that I would write a personal response to 9/11 to be published on the first anniversary. It was called *The Dignity of Difference*. It was a very strong book and a very controversial book. Members of my own community believed that I had simply gone too far, and that I had actually been guilty of heresy.

This was in the beginning of 2002 and something rather funny happened. Rowan Williams had just been appointed as archbishop of Canterbury, and the week before his appointment he had attended a Druid service in Wales, which was regarded by some Church of England people as a pagan act.

So there was one newspaper headline, which said, and I doubt that this has ever been said before or will ever said be again, "Archbishop of Canterbury and Chief Rabbi Accused of Heresy."

Now, when you're the defender of the faith, it is a little challenging, to say the least, to be accused of being a heretic to the faith. There were calls for my resignation. I felt that many of my rabbinical colleagues did not understand the book and were critical of it.

It was simply unclear to me how I could move from here to there.

I could not see a scenario that would allow me to recover my standing and my reputation, my credibility as a Jewish leader, and that plunged me into total despair. When there is no light at the end of the tunnel, all you can see is the tunnel. I felt at that point there was no way forward. Probably the most important thing I had to do was resign.

It was then that I heard a voice. I'm not going to say this was God talking to me, but it was certainly a voice that said to me, "If you resign, you have given your opponents the victory. You have allowed yourself to be defeated in this first battle of what you see as the major challenge of the coming generation."

I couldn't do that.

Despite the fact that I was in almost unbearable personal pain, I could not resign. I could not hand my enemies, my opponents, the opponents of religious tolerance and reconciliation, that victory.

That was when I suddenly realized that it wasn't about me. It was about not letting down the people who had put their faith in me and not betraying the ideals that had led me to take the job in the first place and write the book in the second place.

So that was the turning point and, in the end, the fact that I survived and emerged stronger after than I had been before, was not only important for me. It was important for all the other rabbis, because they too could see that you can take a controversial stand, be widely criticized, and yet still come through and still be able to sing with Sir Elton John, "I'm Still Standing."

There was a 180-degree shift, a Copernican shift in my understanding of the nature of what I was doing. It wasn't personal at all; there was no self involvement here. It's about what you stand for, and the people that you care about. From that moment on, I became, in a sense, invulnerable, because I was no longer putting myself on the line.

If you could have a gigantic billboard anywhere, what would it say, and why?

It would say three words: "Live. Give. Forgive." They are by far the most important things in life.

What is one of the best or most worthwhile investments you've ever made?

It happened in 1979. Long time ago, 38 years ago, when my wife Elaine and I bought a house with a playroom at the bottom of the garden, which I could turn into a study. I had been laboring until then to write my PhD, to write my first book, completely without success. I used to dream of going off to a mountain retreat or a little cottage in the countryside, and it suddenly occurred to me: "Here's a house with a room at the bottom of the garden, and maybe there I will find peace and isolation." It worked like a dream, and it was in that room that I completed my doctorate and wrote my first five books. It completely changed my life. Expensive, but worth every penny.

What is an unusual habit or an absurd thing that you love?

The really ridiculous thing, which I find totally life-changing is, at little pauses in our life, or when we need rejuvenation, I call [my wife] Elaine, and we sit or stand, and revisit a moment in our past by watching a music video on YouTube. It's an extraordinary thing. If Proust had had YouTube, he wouldn't have had to write *À la recherche du temps perdu*, because thanks to it, none of our past is ever lost. We can revisit it any time we like. There is our *Back to the Future*, there is our little piece of personal time travel, back to a time and a place earlier in our life that is rich in emotion, and it's magically easy to do, and it takes almost no time at all.

Can you please share an example pairing of a past moment and a particular YouTube music video?

As just one example, in the summer of 1968, two very, very important things happened to me. Number one, I made a trip to America, where I had some life-changing encounters with some of the greatest rabbis of our time. And second, when I came back, I met Elaine, who was studying at the hospital at Cambridge. I was studying at the university in Cambridge, and pretty soon we got engaged and eventually married.

There was a film at the time that Elaine and I went to see, *The Graduate* with Dustin Hoffman. The girl he fell in love was called Elaine, and the music to the film was from Simon and Garfunkel. In '68 they released a very evocative song called "America," with young men and girlfriends and counting cars on the New Jersey turnpike.

So, whenever I want to recapture that moment when Elaine and I first met, when new horizons opened up in my life and the greatest romance of our lives became real, I just tune into YouTube and listen and watch Simon and Garfunkel singing "America."

In the last five years, what new belief, behavior, or habit has most improved your life?

Three and a half years ago, I gave up being chief rabbi and attempted to do something that, for all sorts of reasons, none of my predecessors were able to do, which is develop a new career, a new kind of challenge. I realized that leaving a job as public and as privileged as that was almost certain to bring withdrawal symptoms and risk of depression.

I took a decision to overschedule my diary in order to simply not have time to be depressed. It was magically effective. I recommend it to anyone.

In the last five years, what have you become better at saying no to? What new realizations and approaches have helped you to deal with that?

Quite simply, my team. My wife and my two people who run my office, because I realize that my biggest weakness is an inability to say no, so I simply delegate it away. Those people I've delegated it away to are a whole lot better at saying no than I am. I recommend this also to anyone.

What are bad recommendations you hear in your profession in your area of expertise?

In my area of business, that is in religion and public discourse, probably the thing I hear most often is fear and hence defensiveness. This is precisely the wrong way to face the future. Face it full of hope, knowing that whatever challenge lies ahead, you are equal to it, and just deliver a message that is precisely the opposite of fear and defensiveness.

When you feel overwhelmed or unfocused, what do you do?

What did I key into the sat-nav system of my life [where do I want to be 10, 20 years from now]? What is my ultimate destination? You have to look at that every time you feel overwhelmed. Remembering that destination will help you make the single most important distinction in life, which is to distinguish between an opportunity to be seized and a temptation to be resisted.

"One distraction I've learned to avoid is consuming media that's just telling me things I already know and agree with."

JULIA GALEF
TW: @juliagalef
FB: /julia.galef
juliagalef.com

JULIA GALEF is a writer and speaker who focuses on the question, "How can we improve human judgment, especially on complex, high-stakes decisions?" Julia is the co-founder of the Center for Applied Rationality, a nonprofit that runs workshops on improving reasoning and decision-making. Since 2010, she has hosted the *Rationally Speaking* podcast, a biweekly show featuring conversations with scientists, social scientists, and philosophers. Julia is currently writing a book about how to improve your judgment by reshaping your unconscious motivations. Her TED Talk, "Why You Think You're Right—Even If You're Wrong," has more than three million views.

In the last five years, what new belief, behavior, or habit has most improved your life?
When something goes badly, I don't automatically assume I did something wrong. Instead I ask myself, "What policy was I following that produced

this bad outcome, and do I still expect that policy to give the best results overall, occasional bad outcomes notwithstanding?" If yes, then carry on!

The reason this habit is so important is that even the best policies will fail some percent of the time, and you don't want to abandon them (or beat yourself up) as soon as one of those inevitable failures pops up.

Let's say you always aim to arrive at the airport 1 hour and 20 minutes before your flight. One day there's an accident on the highway that ends up delaying you, and you just barely miss your flight. Does that mean you should have left more time? Not necessarily. A policy of aiming to be two hours early to the airport would have saved you this time, but it comes with a different cost—lots more time spent waiting in airports. Aiming for 1 hour 20 minutes may still be the best policy going forward even though it occasionally, like today, causes a missed flight.

Similarly, I have a tendency to beat myself up over mistakes I make in a blog post, or in a meeting, or giving a talk, etc., and my impulse is always to think "Well, I should have spent more time preparing for that." Sometimes that's true. But other times, the right conclusion is, "No, actually, the amount of prep time I would have to spend before each talk, to avoid mistakes like that, is not worth it overall."

To give a somewhat different example, I was recently on a New Jersey Transit train during winter and, looking out the window, I thought I saw a fire on the train tracks. No one else was reacting, so I thought, "It's probably nothing to worry about," but I wasn't sure, so I went and hunted for a train conductor and told him about it. Turns out it was indeed nothing to worry about—apparently train companies use flames to de-ice their tracks during winter. My impulse was to feel silly for worrying about nothing, but upon reflection, I realized, "No, actually, I think it's good to continue checking on risks that would be really bad if I was right. Even if, most of the time, it turns out I was wrong."

What are bad recommendations you hear in your profession or area of expertise?

I think most recommendations are bad because they're one-size-fits-all. "Take more risks." "Don't be so hard on yourself." "Work harder." The problem is that some people need to take more risks, while others need to take fewer risks. Some people need to ease up on themselves, while others are already too self-forgiving. Some people need to work harder, while others are already skating on the edge of burnout. And so on.

So, I think the most useful kind of recommendations are about improving your general judgment—your ability to accurately perceive your situation (even if the truth isn't flattering or convenient), your possible options, and the tradeoffs involved. Good judgment is what allows you to evaluate whether a recommendation is appropriate to your situation or not; without it, you can't tell the difference between good and bad advice.

The books *Superforecasting* (by Philip E. Tetlock and Dan Gardner) and *How to Measure Anything* (by Douglas W. Hubbard) have some good advice on how to improve your ability to make accurate predictions. And *Decisive* (by Chip Heath and Dan Heath) explains four of the biggest judgment errors (like framing your decision too narrowly, or letting temporary emotions cloud your judgment) and gives tips for combating them.

In the last five years, what have you become better at saying no to?

One distraction I've learned to avoid is consuming media that's just telling me things I already know and agree with (for example, about politics). That stuff can be addictive because it feels so validating—it's like venting with a friend—but you're not learning from it, and over time, I think indulging that impulse makes you less able to tolerate other perspectives. So I broke my addiction by, essentially, reminding myself how much time I was wasting not learning anything.

When you feel overwhelmed or unfocused, what do you do?

I sometimes find myself torn between two options, and it's clear to me that the stakes are high, but it's not at all clear which option is better. So I keep agonizing over the choice, Ping-Ponging back and forth between my options, even though I'm not getting any new information.

Fortunately, at some point in this process, I remember this principle: Uncertainty over expected value (EV) just gets folded into EV. So, if I know that one of option A or B is going to be great, and the other's going to be a disaster, but I'm totally unsure which is which, then they have the same expected value.

That's a powerful reframe. Thinking to yourself, "One of these options is great and the other's terrible, but I don't know which is which" is paralyzing — but thinking to yourself, "These options have the same expected value as each other" is liberating.

(Of course this assumes you can't cheaply purchase more information about A and B to reduce your uncertainty about which is better. If you can, you should! This advice is about getting yourself to act in situations where there's no more cheap info left to purchase, and you feel paralyzed.)

Let's say you're agonizing over two possible jobs you could take, and you feel overwhelmed because you can't easily tell which one is a better option. Job A is more prestigious and higher-paying, but Job B has a more supportive culture and you'll have more freedom to choose your projects.

What you should ask yourself is, "Is there some way for me to get additional information that would settle this question?" Maybe you could talk to people at the respective companies about their job satisfaction, or you could look at what former employees of A and B go on to do.

But maybe you've done stuff like that already, and the answers didn't help settle it for you. If that's the case—if there's no additional information you could easily get that would make the "right choice" clear—then you should relax and just pick one without worrying anymore. And I know that "relax and stop worrying" is often easier said than done, but if I can't tell which one is the better choice, then for all intents and purposes, they're equally good choices.

> **"When I was younger, it's not like I was 'ungrateful,' but I never stopped to take the time to reflect on everything I had going for me. Now I do a gratitude practice every morning."**

ANNIE DUKE
TW/FB: @AnnieDuke
annieduke.com

TURIA PITT is one of Australia's most admired and widely recognized figures. In 2011 at age 24, Turia was an ex-model fitness junkie and successful mining engineer when she was caught in a freak firestorm while competing in a 100 km ultramarathon in Western Australia. She was choppered out of the remote desert, barely alive and suffering from full thickness burns to 64 percent of her body. Surviving against overwhelming odds, Turia came back stronger than ever. Turia completed the Ironman World Championship in Kona, Hawaii, in late 2016 and later wrote her memoir *Everything to Live For: The Inspirational Story of Turia Pitt*. Her popular TEDx Talk, "Unmask Your Potential," details her incredible story of triumph over adversity.

What is the book (or books) you've given most as a gift, and why? Or what are books that have greatly influenced your life?

My personal favorite book is *The Map That Changed the World* by Simon Winchester. A canal digger (William Smith) ended up creating the first geological map of England and Wales. You would think that this would earn him accolades and honors, but instead, he was accused of heresy and ended up in prison. Having said this, I know that most people aren't as fascinated by geology as I am (I used to be a mining engineer), so I try and give them a book based on their interests.

If they're interested in running, I give them *Born to Run* by Christopher McDougall. If they want to turn their finances around, I give them *The Barefoot Investor* by Scott Pape. If they want to find out more about me, I give them one of my books, and if they're doing a bit of soul searching, hands down it's Viktor Frankl's *Man's Search for Meaning*.

What purchase of $100 or less has most positively impacted your life in the last six months (or in recent memory)?

It cost me a bit more than $100, but it's completely changed my life. I got a pair of Beats Solo3 headphones while I was in the airport a couple of months ago. They're the goods! I love listening to the app Brain.fm using the headphones—it helps me to get into the zone and focus on the task at hand. I guess if I'm sticking to the "$100 or less" rule, the Brain.fm app has been life-changing, too. Really helps me to focus on my work. I use it every day.

How has a failure, or apparent failure, set you up for later success? Do you have a "favorite failure" of yours?

I've had plenty of f***-ups throughout my life, almost too many to count! I've owed the tax office a gigantic sum of money (yes, it's been paid now). I blew $10,000 on speech coaching and later realized I didn't need it. I've flown to conferences where I was presenting . . . only to realize that I flew to the wrong city. I've gotten extremely drunk at an awards night and made an idiot of myself.

None of these failures have "set me up" for success, but they have taught me that it's okay to make a mistake. Because you know what? The Earth doesn't stop spinning just because you made a mistake. In fact, mistakes are more useful than success in life. I've never learned anything from making a success happen. It's almost . . . too easy. Mistakes, on the other hand, point out your fallibility and, more important, you can learn and improve from them.

In the last five years, what new belief, behavior, or habit has most improved your life?

Gratitude. When I was younger, it's not like I was "ungrateful," but I never stopped to take the time to reflect on everything I had going for me. Now I do a gratitude practice every morning, every day, and I might even do it again throughout the day. I don't weigh in too much on the science behind it, I just know if I do it, I feel better. I'm not a believer in "quick fixes" but I know it's a very effective method to instantly change how you're feeling.

[Here's what it looks like:] First, I listen to my gratitude playlist on Spotify, any song on the list. For example, here are nine tracks as of today:

1. "Breathturn" by Hammock
2. "Your Hand in Mine" by Explosions in the Sky
3. "Devi Prayer" by Craig Pruess and Ananda
4. "Horizon" by Tycho
5. "Recurring" by Bonobo
6. "Hanging On" by Active Child
7. "Long Time Sun" by Snatam Kaur
8. "Angels Prayer" by Ty Burhoe, James Hoskins, Cat McCarthy, Manorama, and Janaki Kagel
9. "Twentytwofourteen" by The Album Leaf

Then, I think of three things that I'm genuinely grateful for. I've found the more specific the better. So for example, rather than just thinking, "my mum," it could be "my mum for making me spinach pie last night." Instead of "my partner," it could be "the run I went for with my partner yesterday." This morning, it was:

1. My son kicking me in my belly
2. My coffee
3. Seeing the sun rise

If I do this properly and genuinely (i.e., not just rattling them off in my head—that's why music helps me to get into the right frame of mind), I'll usually start crying from gratitude. If I feel frustrated or pissed off during the day, sometimes I'll do this again to center me.

"When two extreme opinions meet, the truth lies generally somewhere in the middle. Without exposure to the other side, you will naturally drift toward the extremes and away from the truth of the matter."

ANNIE DUKE
TW/FB: @AnnieDuke
annieduke.com

For two decades, **ANNIE DUKE** was one of the top poker players in the world. In 2004, she bested a field of 234 players to win her first World Series of Poker (WSOP) bracelet. The same year, she triumphed in the $2 million winner-take-all, invitation-only WSOP Tournament of Champions. Prior to becoming a professional poker player, Annie was awarded a National Science Foundation Fellowship to study cognitive psychology at the University of Pennsylvania. Annie regularly shares her observations on the science of smart decision-making (applied to much more than poker) on her blog, *Annie's Analysis,* and has shared her poker knowledge through a series of best-selling books, including *Decide to Play Great Poker* and *The Middle Zone: Mastering the Most Difficult Hands in Hold'em Poker* (both co-authored with John Vorhaus). Annie's latest book, *Thinking in Bets: Making Smarter Decisions When You Don't Have All the Facts,* focuses on strategies for great decision-making.

What advice would you give to a smart, driven college student about to enter the "real world"?

First, seek out dissenting opinions. Always try to find people who disagree with you, who can honestly and productively play devil's advocate. Challenge yourself to truly listen to people who have differing ideas and opinions than you do. Stay out of political bubbles and echo chambers as much as possible. Feel good about really hearing those who disagree with you. Try to change your mind about one thing every day.

The fact is that when two extreme opinions meet, the truth lies generally somewhere in the middle. Without exposure to the other side, you will naturally drift toward the extremes and away from the truth of the matter. Don't be afraid of being wrong. Because being wrong is just an opportunity to find more of the truth.

Second, stay flexible and be open to opportunities as they come your way. Most of the successful people I know did not know exactly what they wanted to do coming right out of college, and they changed their focus over the course of their careers. Be open to what the world brings your way. Don't be afraid to change jobs or careers, no matter how much time you have already put into something. There is no urgency to have it all figured out. And feeling like you have it all figured out can make you stuck and close-minded to change.

In the last five years, what have you become better at saying no to?

I have generally become better at saying no to just about everything, but particularly to obligations that make me travel away from home. The strategy I have implemented is to imagine it is the day I have to leave and think about how happy or sad I am on that day. Then to follow that by imagining it is the day after and I am back home and to ask myself: Was the travel worth it? Am I happy to have said yes and done what I did? By doing this kind of "time traveling," I am better able to imagine the downside of the things I don't like (being away from home, the hassle of traveling) and weigh that against the upside of what I am considering (giving a keynote that gets a great response from an audience, doing a charity event and feeling really good about the money raised).

I can achieve the same thing by imagining similar offers that I have accepted or rejected. Am I happy I accepted or happy I rejected the offer? This is a great technique for thinking about any decision, whether it is a small one like whether to accept a dinner invitation or a big one like whether to move to a new city. Doing some mindful time travel helps you get perspective.

How has a failure, or apparent failure, set you up for later success? Do you have a "favorite failure" of yours?

In poker, you do a lot of failing because you lose a lot of hands. There are two ways to fail in poker. First, you could define failing simply as having a losing outcome, like losing a hand. But one of the lessons poker teaches you is that this is an unproductive way to define failure because you can win a hand by making very poor decisions and lose a hand while making very good decisions. So you can put all your money in the pot with a mathematically dominant hand and still lose because the rest of the cards that are dealt don't go your way.

If you define failure as merely losing, then you will think failure is just an outcome. And you might try to adjust your play to avoid losing even though your decisions were great (or repeat poor strategies just because you won executing them once). This would be the equivalent of deciding it is wise to run red lights because you made it through one safely a few times. Or to decide not to go through green lights because you got in an accident once doing that.

Poker has taught me to disconnect failure from outcomes. Just because I lose doesn't mean I failed, and just because I won doesn't mean I succeeded —not when you define success and failure around making good decisions that will win in the long run. What matters is the decisions I made along the way, and every decision failure is an opportunity to learn and adjust my strategy going forward. By doing this, losing becomes a less emotional experience and more an opportunity to explore and learn.

"Every smart person and stable person I know both walks and meditates. The app Headspace is a fun way to start. Try and do it every day. But I suggest not doing it while you are walking . . . for now."

JIMMY FALLON
TW/IG: @jimmyfallon
tonightshow.com

JIMMY FALLON is an Emmy Award- and Grammy Award-winning comedian. He is known for his work as a cast member of *Saturday Night Live* and as the host of the late-night talk show *The Tonight Show Starring Jimmy Fallon*. He is the author of several books, including *Your Baby's First Word Will Be DADA*, and his latest, *Everything Is Mama*. Jimmy lives in New York City with his wife, Nancy, and their two daughters, Winnie and Franny. If you'd like to see him flying on top of my feet (seriously), check out tim.blog/jimmy

---

What is the book (or books) you've given most as a gift, and why? Or what are one to three books that have greatly influenced your life?

If I gave one to an adult, it would be *Man's Search for Meaning* by Viktor Frankl. I read it while spending ten days in the ICU of Bellevue hospital trying to reattach my finger from a ring avulsion accident in my kitchen. It talks about the meaning of life, and I believe you come out a better person from reading it. The lines I took from it are: "There is no exact answer to the question 'what is the meaning of life.' It's like asking a chess master 'what is the best move in the world?' It all depends on what situation you are in." It also reinforced the belief, that which does not kill me makes me stronger. If you read it, you'll get more from it.

The books I give most now are children's books, since I'm going to more and more parties for kids (I have a two-and-a-half- and a four-year-old). I think of the ones I loved as a kid—ones that stuck in my head. One is *The Monster at the End of This Book* by Jon Stone.

I remember laughing at Grover, who is the narrator, freaking out about turning the pages because there is a monster at the end—but I kept turning the pages—and he freaked out more: "YOU TURNED THE PAGE!!?!???? STOP TURNING PAGES!!!!??" And I'm not sure if I was trying to be brave for him or I just knew everything was going to be okay, but I kept turning the pages and reading this book until the last page where it's revealed—HE is the monster at the end of the book! Lovable furry old Grover! I think that book taught me that there is nothing to be afraid of.

In the last five years, what new belief, behavior, or habit has most improved your life?

The best new behaviors I've adopted in the last five years have to be walking and meditating (separately). My friend Lorne Michaels loves to walk, and anytime we hang out, we walk and talk, and we don't even really have a purpose for walking—it's just fun. One time in London, we walked almost eight miles without even thinking about it. My wife and kids love to walk, and I feel like it's something I can do forever. I'm kind of bummed that it took me so long to realize how great it makes me feel. Meditation? That is a tougher nut to crack, but if you can train your brain to do it (like learning anything—playing the guitar, doing impressions, driving stick shift) it's a great skill to have. It just takes practice. Every smart person and stable person I know both walks and meditates. The app Headspace is a fun way to start. Try and do it every day. But I suggest not doing it while you are walking . . . for now.

QUOTES I'M PONDERING

(Tim Ferriss: April 1–April 15, 2016)

"Genius is only a superior power of seeing."

—JOHN RUSKIN
Victorian polymath, art critic,
philanthropist, and social thinker

"As to methods there may be a million and then some, but principles are few. The man who grasps principles can successfully select his own methods. The man who tries methods, ignoring principles, is sure to have trouble."

—RALPH WALDO EMERSON
American essayist, leader of the
19th-century transcendentalist movement

"The first rule of any technology used in a business is that automation applied to an efficient operation will magnify the efficiency. The second is that automation applied to an inefficient operation will magnify the inefficiency."

—BILL GATES
Co-founder of Microsoft

"Multiplicity of perspectives is essential to making us who we are. Identity is always a two-way street— created from the inside out and the outside in."

ESTHER PEREL
IG: @estherperelofficial
FB: /esther.perel
estherperel.com

ESTHER PEREL has been called the most important game-changer in sexuality and relational health since Dr. Ruth. Her TED Talks on maintaining desire and rethinking infidelity have more than 17 million views, and she's both seen and tested everything imaginable in 34 years of running her private therapy practice in New York City. Esther is the author of the international bestseller *Mating in Captivity,* which has been translated into 26 languages. Fluent in nine of them (I've heard her in person), this Belgian native now brings her multicultural pulse to her new book *The State of Affairs: Rethinking Infidelity.* Her creative energy is currently focused on co-creating and hosting an Audible original audio series, *Where Should We Begin?*

What advice would you give to a smart, driven college student about to enter the "real world"? What advice should they ignore?

Life will present you with unexpected opportunities, and you won't always know in advance which are the important moments. Above all, it's the quality of your relationships that will determine the quality of your life. Invest in your connections, even those that seem inconsequential.

A friend of mine recently told me a story that spoke to this point. He had taken his daughter to visit a college, and they requested a tour of one particular center she was set on. The facilities manager showed them around with great pride—from the principal's office to the media center to the utility room. Surprised by the exhaustive tour, the daughter rolled her eyes but her father told her, "Just ask questions. You never know what will happen." When they were finally done, the facilities manager gave them his card, and my friend instructed his daughter to write a thank-you note, and to specifically mention two things that were memorable about the experience.

The next day, the daughter got a call from the president of the center. Evidently, the facilities manager had forwarded her email with a note telling him, "This is the kind of student we need here." You can guess what followed.

Always take the time to acknowledge people—and not just when you know you have something to gain. If you show interest in them, they will be interested in you. People react to kindness with kindness, to respect with respect. Relationships—even brief ones—are doorways to opportunity.

The advice to ignore is "What is your five-year plan?"

What is one of the best or most worthwhile investments you've ever made?

I got a head start with languages because I grew up in Belgium, which is a trilingual country (Flemish, French, and German). My parents were postwar Jewish refugees from Poland, and that added Polish, Hebrew, and Yiddish to the mix. From a very early age, I understood that a language is a doorway to another world—its culture, sensibility, aesthetic, and humor. The opposite of a refugee is an insider, and language was going to be my way in. Different parts of me come alive when I switch languages.

I learned my additional languages at school (English), on the road (Spanish), in a bossa nova band (Portuguese), and on the pillow (Italian). I would often watch the news in several different languages in one night.

Magazines were very helpful. And conversations on planes improved my vocabulary. I speak nine languages and work in at least seven of them.

The time I invested in learning languages was essential to my career. When I arrived in the U.S., with no papers and no fancy degrees, the only thing that differentiated me was my languages, and the multiple perspectives they afforded me.

I made sure to transmit the linguistic imperative to my sons. I often found it strange that in the U.S., to be bilingual is a sign of lower social status, and even in nursery school, children would refuse to speak the language of their parents. So I infected my kids with the travel bug. If they wanted to play with the other kids in Europe, Israel, or South America, they needed to learn the language.

In my work, I speak with people from all around the world about the most personal of matters. Language is intimate, and there is no way I could do the work I do if I had to communicate in translation.

When you feel overwhelmed or unfocused, what do you do?

I seek out people to help me regain my focus, my confidence, and my clarity. I live my life in a network of friends, family, colleagues, strangers, mentors, and students. When I get overwhelmed, I lose a sense of direction, and I need a human GPS to help me "recalculate" and find my path.

In moments when you don't believe in yourself, you need other people who believe in you. They can hold you up when you falter and keep you from hitting the ground. Other people see you differently from the way you see yourself. And that multiplicity of perspectives is essential to making us who we are. Identity is always a two-way street—created from the inside out and the outside in.

Many people feel that when they are overwhelmed or lose focus, they need to retreat into themselves and shut out the world. They think that there is greater merit and virtue in figuring things out alone. That doesn't work for me. I find myself, and activate my greatest creative capacities, in relationship with the beautiful diversity of other human beings.

"What makes a river so restful to people is that it doesn't have any doubt—it is sure to get where it is going, and it doesn't want to go anywhere else."

— Hal Boyle

MARIA SHARAPOVA
TW/IG: @MariaSharapova
MariaSharapova.com

MARIA SHARAPOVA is the winner of five Grand Slam titles and is an Olympic silver medalist in tennis. Maria was born in Nyagan, Russia, and turned professional at the age of 14. She is one of only a handful of players to hold all four Grand Slam titles—Wimbledon (2004), US Open (2006), Australian Open (2008), and the French Open (2012, 2014). She has held the world #1 ranking for 21 weeks and has won 35 singles titles in her career. *Forbes* named her the highest paid female athlete of all time in 2005, and she held that title for a record 11 years. She is the author of *Unstoppable: My Life So Far*.

What is the book (or books) you've given most as a gift, and why? Or what are one to three books that have greatly influenced your life?

I like to gift *The Beggar King and the Secret of Happiness: A True Story* by Joel ben Izzy. Some of today's books come as manuals, step-by-step guides, and although that's practical, it is not how life always turns out. You might have to take the tenth step before you take the second. I enjoyed this book because it doesn't give you answers; it makes you wonder what answers you might give yourself.

How has a failure, or apparent failure, set you up for later success? Do you have a "favorite failure" of yours?

In my profession, losses are often seen as failures. Not being the person who wins the last point, walking off the court first. All those visible things. But internally, losing sets you up for winning. Losing makes you think in ways victories can't. You begin asking questions instead of feeling like you have the answers. Questions open up the doors to so many possibilities. If a loss sets me up for those tough questions I might have to ask, then I will get the answers that will ultimately turn those losses into victories.

If you could have a gigantic billboard anywhere with anything on it, what would it say and why?

"Be original."

It's straightforward. It says what it is. Be you. Embrace you. Celebrate you. We are always influenced by external events, people we might have never met, and it steers us away from what we have and should always be, which is ourselves.

What is an unusual habit or an absurd thing that you love?

I have a few random things. I always put my left shoe on before my right. Not just a tennis shoe, but any shoe. If I am in a store and I am trying on shoes, if they hand me a right shoe, I might say, "I am sorry—I am fine with opening the box again myself, I'd rather get the left shoe." They give you a strange look.

For my match court outfits, I don't like to wear [the same outfit]. Usually people like to wear the same outfit that they did well in. They wash it, but then wear it again—or maybe they don't wash it. I do the opposite. I don't wear it again. I alternate. I do not want to wear the same exact outfit. I will wear the same-looking gear but I have a few different variations.

When you win a big tournament, do you have a favorite cheat food or anything that you celebrate with?

I love sweets. I love dulce de leche. We have this cake in Russia, it's called *medovik*. It's a soft, layered honey cake. I could eat that every day for breakfast, lunch, and dinner. When my grandma makes cherry jam, I could eat that by the spoonful. That's a childhood memory. I love sweets.

What advice would you give to a smart, driven college student about to enter the "real world"? What advice should they ignore?

You can't ever say the words "please" and "thank you" enough. And turn those words into actions, make people around you feel that those words are genuine, that it is exactly how you feel. The same goes for when you break through and make it. Don't eliminate those words from your pocket.

When you feel overwhelmed or unfocused, what do you do?

My best friend put a little quote in my birthday card a few years ago: "What makes a river so restful to people is that it doesn't have any doubt—it is sure to get where it is going, and it doesn't want to go anywhere else."—Hal Boyle.

There is so much going on in a day, actions and distractions, it's easy to get caught up and lose your vision. This quote brings me right back to where I want to be. It keeps me grounded.

"The 'problem' with meditation — I thought — was that it wasn't 'practical.' . . . But I eventually reframed meditation as a way to relinquish control of my conscious mind so that my more powerful unconscious mind could take over."

ADAM ROBINSON
TW: @IAmAdamRobinson
robinsonglobalstrategies.com

ADAM ROBINSON has made a lifelong study of outflanking and out-smarting the competition. He is a rated chess master and has been awarded a Life Master title by the United States Chess Federation. As a teenager, he was personally mentored by Bobby Fischer in the 18 months leading up to his winning the world championship. Then, in his first career, Adam developed a revolutionary approach to taking standardized tests as one of the two original co-founders of The Princeton Review. His paradigm-breaking—or "category killing," as they say in publishing—test-prep book, *Cracking the System: The SAT*, is the only test-prep book to have ever become a *New York Times* bestseller. After selling his interest in The Princeton Review, Adam turned his attention in the early '90s to the then-emerging field of artificial intelligence, developing a program that could analyze text and provide human-like commentary. He was later invited to join a well-known quant fund to develop statistical trading models, and since, he has established himself as an independent global macro advisor to the chief investment officers of a select group of the world's most successful hedge funds and ultra-high-net-worth family offices.

What is the book (or books) you've given most as a gift, and why? Or what are one to three books that have greatly influenced your life?

Our unconscious mind is working all the time, processing orders of magnitude more information, and with astoundingly greater facility, than is our conscious mind. Of course our entire education system, and indeed much of Western philosophy—is devoted to improving our conscious thinking and capacities rather than our unconscious ones.

I've read far and wide, consuming thousands of books. Five disparate books stand out from all the rest as the most influential, either in confirming my own intuitions or in suggesting promising avenues of inquiry in my quest to understand—or at least gain some control over—my unconscious thinking, to be able to tap into it on demand, and to direct it as far as possible.

And those books are *Zen in the Art of Archery* by Eugen Herrigel, *Drawing on the Right Side of the Brain* by Betty Edwards, *The Crack in the Cosmic Egg* by Joseph Chilton Pearce, *The Act of Creation* by Arthur Koestler, and, perhaps most of all, *The Origins of Consciousness in the*

Breakdown of the Bicameral Mind by Julian Jaynes. These books have been so seminal to my thinking that I have read each at least three times straight through, and continually dip into them as the years pass as triggers for further insights and inspiration.

And what they have confirmed, as well as my own explorations of the unconscious have revealed, is, to paraphrase Hamlet, that there is far, far more in our unconscious mind than is dreamt of in our philosophy.

In the last five years, what new belief, behavior, or habit has most improved your life?

The understanding—which has become a habit—that has most improved my life in the last five years, dramatically so, is recognizing the importance of others in not only changing the world, but in enjoying it!

By nature I am an introvert. So much so that some friends revealed years after school that we had mutual high-school classmates who had never seen me speak.

By the time I graduated from graduate school—Oxford University after doing my undergraduate work at The Wharton School of the University of Pennsylvania—I had emerged from my interior world to a great extent, but I was still 95/5 on the introvert/extrovert scale. I very much enjoyed the company of other people, but only for brief periods, beyond which I'd reach overload and need to seclude myself to recharge.

After college, in my career, my success in the world was the product of my insights and imagination and thinking, so I inhabited the world of ideas far more than I did the world of people. The more and better ideas I came up with, the more success I achieved.

So it came as a surprise relatively late in life, in fact only in the past year, that if you want to change the world, you have to enroll others in your plans and vision. Not only that, but the immense pleasures and satisfactions that can be derived from focusing on others, and the surprising discovery that the more I gave to others—which I'd always done—the more the universe gave me back in return.

Whereas in the past when I went outside and encountered others, I would invariably be lost in thought—now I am solely focused not inwardly, on my ideas, but outwardly, on connecting with others. I mentioned this discovery publicly for the first time in a live group podcast with Tim [Ferriss] in

December 2016, and was inspired shortly thereafter to write a book, *An Invitation to the Great Game: A Parable of Love, Magic, and Everyday Miracles,* in which I articulate my three guiding rules of life. First, whenever possible, connect with others. Second, with enthusiasm, strive always to create fun and delight for others. And third, lean into each moment and encounter expecting magic—or miracles.

This discovery so profoundly altered my life path—revealing for the first time my true mission on this planet—that I now divide my life into two periods: pre-discovery of "others" and post-discovery. Now, I so eagerly look forward to leaving my home each day, wondering what magic I'll create encountering others, that I can scarcely contain myself. My days now have a natural rhythm between introversion and extroversion that is akin to breathing: when I am alone, inhaling my ideas, and then exhaling with others.

The number of remarkable people and serendipities and successes that have come into my life since I adopted this awareness of others—which quickly developed into a reflexive habit of directing my attention solely on them when I am not alone—has been nothing short of astonishing.

What is one of the best or most worthwhile investments you've ever made?

I've made many investments in my life—of money, of time, of energy, of passion and emotion—and one of the best payoffs for the amount invested was learning to meditate.

I've always been driven, excited by the world, so my mind is continually racing at 1,000 miles per hour pursuing this question or that, creating this system or that. Nonstop. Twenty-four hours a day, 365 days a year, 366 on leap years.

Now all that nonstop mental and psychic stimulation gets exhausting, of course. And if you want to perform optimally, at anything, you need to find a way to recover from the stresses of that activity. So I knew I should find a way to "turn off" my mind and just relax, just enjoy—just be—for years, but I failed to find a way.

I tried everything. Yoga. Exercise. I even tried hypnosis. I researched the "best" hypnotist in New York City as a way to turn off my hyperactive mind, but after four attempted—and hugely expensive—sessions, the hypnotist gave up, saying, "Your mind is too active to submit to the hypnosis."

"Thanks a lot, Doc," I told him, not concealing my annoyance, "that's why I came to you!"

Then, about two years ago, my bestie Josh Waitzkin (page 195), recognizing that I couldn't unwind, or disengage from my unrelenting analyzing of the world—especially the financial world—recommended that I take up meditation.

"Doesn't work for me," I said. "Can't sit still long enough for any benefits of meditating to kick in."

"Have you ever tried heart rate variability training? HRV training?" he asked.

"No," I said.

"Well, I strongly recommend that you do," he said.

I told him I'd never even heard of HRV training. He said that you just focus on your breathing, using biofeedback to measure the "smoothness" and the amplitude—variability—of your heart rate. The heart registers all of our real-time emotions and stresses, so a normal heartbeat is highly erratic, staying within a tight band around an average. The goal with the biofeedback training is to gain control over your own heart rate by focusing on your breathing, making your "jagged" heart rate smooth out like a sine curve and to widen its amplitude.

That sounded interesting, but it wasn't until I reframed meditation that I submitted to trying it. The "problem" with meditation—I thought—was that it wasn't "practical." And worse, the time I spent meditating was time that I could have spent analyzing the world.

But I eventually reframed meditation as a way to relinquish control of my conscious mind so that my more powerful unconscious mind could take over, and my analysis of the world would improve.

Motivated by that reframing, I enthusiastically adopted biofeedback HRV training, and in a few weeks learned to quiet my mind after just a single deep, diaphragm belly breath—gaining the ability to achieve a Zen-like calm on demand.

Now, whenever I need to detach from the world or from the stresses of daily life and to allow my mind a rest, I simply get centered and inhale from my diaphragm. And I do so numerous times a day. A minute here. A few minutes there. At least once a day, I "waste" a larger 15- to 20-minute block of time meditating in this way. But it's not wasted time, of course, since the enhanced creativity and productivity from these mini restorative sessions is worth far more than the time I spend being "unproductive" while meditating.

Meditation is one of the most practical, powerful, productivity-enhancing tools ever created, and learning to meditate is one of the best investments I ever made.

What purchase of $100 or less has most positively impacted your life in the last six months (or in recent memory)?

This purchase is not less than $100, but at $159, it is too close to pass up: the HeartMath Inner Balance biofeedback monitor. It detects your heart's minutest rhythms and sends a graph to your smartphone, facilitating HRV training.

What are bad recommendations you hear in your profession or area of expertise?

Virtually all investors have been told when they were younger—or implicitly believe, or have been tacitly encouraged to do so by the cookie-cutter curriculums of the business schools they all attend—that the more they understand the world, the better their investment results. It makes sense, doesn't it? The more information we acquire and evaluate, the "better informed" we become, the better our decisions. Accumulating information, becoming "better informed," is certainly an advantage in numerous, if not most, fields.

But not in the field of counterintuitive world of investing, where accumulating information can hurt your investment results.

In 1974, Paul Slovic—a world-class psychologist, and a peer of Nobel laureate Daniel Kahneman—decided to evaluate the effect of information on decision-making. This study should be taught at every business school in the country. Slovic gathered eight professional horse handicappers and announced, "I want to see how well you predict the winners of horse races." Now, these handicappers were all seasoned professionals who made their livings solely on their gambling skills.

Slovic told them the test would consist of predicting 40 horse races in four consecutive rounds. In the first round, each gambler would be given the five pieces of information he wanted on each horse, which would vary from handicapper to handicapper. One handicapper might want the years of experience the jockey had as one of his top five variables, while another might not care about that at all but want the fastest speed any given horse had achieved in the past year, or whatever.

Finally, in addition to asking the handicappers to predict the winner of each race, he asked each one also to state how confident he was in his prediction. Now, as it turns out, there were an average of ten horses in each race, so we would expect by blind chance—random guessing—each handicapper would be right 10 percent of the time, and that their confidence with a blind guess to be 10 percent.

So in round one, with just five pieces of information, the handicappers were 17 percent accurate, which is pretty good, 70 percent better than the 10 percent chance they started with when given zero pieces of information. And interestingly, their confidence was 19 percent—almost exactly as confident as they should have been. They were 17 percent accurate and 19 percent confident in their predictions.

In round two, they were given ten pieces of information. In round three, 20 pieces of information. And in the fourth and final round, 40 pieces of information. That's a whole lot more than the five pieces of information they started with. Surprisingly, their accuracy had flatlined at 17 percent; they were no more accurate with the additional 35 pieces of information. Unfortunately, their confidence nearly doubled—to 34 percent! So the additional information made them no more accurate but a whole lot more confident. Which would have led them to increase the size of their bets and lose money as a result.

Beyond a certain minimum amount, additional information only feeds —leaving aside the considerable cost of and delay occasioned in acquiring it—what psychologists call "confirmation bias." The information we gain that conflicts with our original assessment or conclusion, we conveniently ignore or dismiss, while the information that confirms our original decision makes us increasingly certain that our conclusion was correct.

So, to return to investing, the second problem with trying to understand the world is that it is simply far too complex to grasp, and the more dogged our attempts to understand the world, the more we earnestly want to "explain" events and trends in it, the more we become attached to our resulting beliefs—which are always more or less mistaken—blinding us to the financial trends that are actually unfolding. Worse, we *think* we understand the world, giving investors a false sense of confidence, when in fact we always more or less *mis*understand it.

You hear it all the time from even the most seasoned investors and financial "experts" that this trend or that "doesn't make sense." "It doesn't make sense that the dollar keeps going lower" or "it makes no sense that stocks keep going higher." But what's really going on when investors say that something makes no sense is that they have a dozen or whatever reasons why the trend should be moving in the opposite direction . . . yet it keeps moving in the current direction. So they believe the trend makes no sense. But what makes no sense is their model of the world. That's what doesn't make sense. The world always makes sense.

In fact, because financial trends involve human behavior and human beliefs on a global scale, the most powerful trends won't make sense until it becomes too late to profit from them. By the time investors formulate an understanding that gives them the confidence to invest, the investment opportunity has already passed.

So when I hear sophisticated investors or financial commentators say, for example, that it makes no sense how energy stocks keep going lower, I know that energy stocks have a lot lower to go. Because all those investors are on the wrong side of the trade, in denial, probably doubling down on their original decision to buy energy stocks. Eventually they will throw in the towel and have to sell those energy stocks, driving prices lower still.

When you feel overwhelmed or unfocused, what do you do? What questions do you ask yourself?

When I am feeling unfocused, the first question I ask myself is, "Am I rehearsing my best self?" And if the answer is no, I ask myself how can I reset. Each day presents us with 86,400 seconds, which means each day presents us with virtually countless opportunities to reset, recover our balance, and continue rehearsing our best selves.

If I realize my focus is off, and certainly when I'm experiencing any negative emotions, I ask myself, "Where should my attention be right now?"

Almost always, the answer is "my mission," which is like a beacon that always beckons.

But sometimes I take on too many commitments. Because I sometimes have trouble saying no to others eager to work with me, I can become over-committed and overwhelmed.

When that happens, rather than attempting to do everything badly, I ask myself, "What activity or commitment can I cut out right now that will free up the most time?" It reminds me of this news story I read ages ago about a small European town (I won't say what country, lest I offend it unnecessarily) in which the postal workers had trouble keeping up with their deliveries.

On Monday they'd do their best to deliver the mail, but they'd have some pieces left over, which they'd add to Tuesday's delivery pile. Tuesday they'd fall further behind, of course, and Wednesday and Thursday further still. By Friday, they'd have an enormous pile of undelivered mail, which they'd burn so they could start "fresh" on Monday. The process would repeat the next week, a small bonfire every Friday purging their delivery vans of that week's undelivered mail.

Now that was a highly dubious way of "resetting" each week, which I don't recommend! But the idea of having a fresh restart whenever over-whelmed is excellent. So, let's say by noon on any given day I'm running behind, and it's clear I'm in danger of becoming overwhelmed in short order. Rather than attempting to keep all of my afternoon appointments, which I'd reach later and later as the day progressed, I scan my calendar, asking myself which is the earliest appointment I can "burn" by postponing it to another day. I'd rather reschedule one appointment and make the other three on time than be late and frazzled for all four appointments that afternoon.

Speaking of which, each week I leave one day completely open and schedule a pretend trip out of the city so that I'm not tempted to fill it in any way, not even with meeting friends or other fun diversions. Then, if an emergency arises or I fall behind and become overwhelmed, I know I have a "free day" to use any way I'd like.

So, when I get overwhelmed trying to juggle too many balls simultan-eously, I ask myself which one or two I can set down—for the moment—so I get caught up on all the others.

What is an unusual habit or an absurd thing that you love?

In the old television show *Candid Camera*—reprised by Ashton Kutcher's (page 250) *Punk'd* in more recent times—unsuspecting people were video-taped coping in real time with an insane prearranged situation, usually to great ensuing hilarity.

I get endless delight covertly "ambushing" unsuspecting strangers with random acts of kindness. So, for example, after ordering my iced latte, I'll give a Starbucks barista a $20 bill and tell him to comp the person after the person behind me for whatever he or she wants, and to give that person the change as well. I don't do the person behind me, who might suspect that I was the mystery benefactor.

Then I sip my latte from afar and watch the confusion give way to smiles when the random beneficiary realizes the unexpected bounty. Sometimes the person leaves all the change as a tip. Sometimes he or she will pay it forward and "gift" the next person a free coffee. But the beneficiary always leaves smiling broadly, and I know that I've unleashed a positive ripple effect into that person's community and to anyone he or she encounters that day.

Spreading magic!

"Life is fucking beautiful."

JOSH WAITZKIN
joshwaitzkin.com

JOSH WAITZKIN was the basis for the book and movie *Searching for Bobby Fischer*. Considered a chess prodigy, he has perfected learning strategies that can be applied to anything, including his other loves of Brazilian jujitsu (he's a black belt under phenom Marcelo Garcia) and tai chi push hands (he's a world champion). These days, he spends his time coaching the world's top athletes and investors, working to revolutionize education, and tackling his new passion of paddle surfing, often nearly killing me (Tim) in the process. I first met Josh many years ago after reading his book, *The Art of Learning*.

What is the book (or books) you've given most as a gift, and why? Or what are books that have greatly influenced your life?

On the Road by Jack Kerouac: Opened up the ecstatic beauty of life's little moments to me as a teenager.

Tao Te Ching, Gia-Fu Feng and Jane English translation: Inspired my study of softness and receptivity as a counterpoint to my mad passions.

Zen and the Art of Motorcycle Maintenance by Robert Pirsig:
Inspired my cultivation of dynamic quality as a way of life.

Ernest Hemingway on Writing: The most potent little book of
wisdom on the creative process that I have run into.

What purchase of $100 or less has most positively impacted your life in the last six months (or in recent memory)?

Stay Covered Big Wave SUP leash ($36). It doesn't break, which I have been
immensely grateful for in some hairy paddle surfing moments way offshore.

How has a failure, or apparent failure, set you up for later success? Do you have a "favorite failure" of yours?

The most painful loss of my life was the last round of the Under-18 World
Chess Championship in Szeged, Hungary. I was tied for first place with the
Russian representative, who offered me a draw early. I declined, pushed for
a win, and lost. In the critical moment of the game, I had to make a decision
that was completely outside of my conceptual scheme. I only discovered the
right decision after more than a hundred hours of study three months after
the game. Essentially, I had to remove my final defensive piece in front of
my king, because his attack actually needed my defense like fire needs fuel to
burn. Without my defensive pieces in the way, my pawn structure was actually enough to defend my king and his attack had nothing to bite into. The
principle: the power of empty space—or responding to aggression with a
void. The lesson felt like a complete paradigm shift, and I ended up devoting
a huge part of my life to its practice.

Twelve years later, I harnessed it to win the finals of the Tai Chi Chuan
Push Hands World Championship. So, the worst loss of my chess life
taught me one of the most important thematic lessons of my life and ended
up winning me a world championship in martial arts over a decade later.
It's so beautiful how life unfolds, if we lay it all on the line and keep our
pores open.

If you could have a gigantic billboard anywhere with anything on it, what would it say?

"Life is fucking beautiful."

What is an unusual habit or an absurd thing that you love?

I love rain, storms, inclement conditions, chaos with hidden harmonies. Is that absurd?

In the last five years, what new belief, behavior, or habit has most improved your life?

I have had countless "failures." Tim has seen a lot of them on our surf trips. Early in my life as a competitor, there was often a long interval between a painful loss and my recognition of how valuable the lesson was. I was always pretty good at making the technical correction, but I've improved two things quite a bit in recent years: finding the thematic or psychological lesson hidden in the technical error (which hugely amplifies the ensuing growth), and having a sense of the beauty and potency of how the loss is actively improving me while I'm still in the thick of the pain of the blow.

What advice would you give to a smart, driven college student about to enter the "real world"?

Do what you love, do it in a way that you love, and pour your heart and soul into every moment of it. Do not be subject to inertia. Challenge your assumptions and the assumptions of those around you as a way of life. Notice how you are unconsciously fighting to maintain your conceptual scheme even as it mires you in quicksand and immense pain. Harness the body to train the mind.

Advice they should ignore: Follow the beaten path. Avoid risk. Play it safe. Wear a suit.

What are bad recommendations you hear in your profession or area of expertise?

Just about anything that comes from someone who has not lived and been tested in the trenches. Beware the philosophologist.

In the last five years, what have you become better at saying no to?

I say no to just about everything public. I say no to more than 99 percent of professional opportunities that people approach me with. A core operating principle is that there is no better investment than in my own learning process, and so I only engage in partnerships that will challenge and improve me. I am exponentially better when I am all in than when I am 99 percent in, so I only engage with what inspires me to be all in. And I only team with people I have love for, or who I believe I could have love for.

When you feel overwhelmed or unfocused, what do you do?

I change my physiology. If I am near waves, I go surf them. If not, a short, intense kettlebell workout, a bike ride, a swim, a cold shower or ice plunge, Wim Hof or heart rate variability breathing [see Adam Robinson, page 185, for a description]. It's remarkable how the mind follows the body. Honestly, I think a lack of understanding or desire to understand that simple evolutionary reality is what inhibits so many people from rapidly improving their lives.

"This may come as strange advice from someone who majored in electrical engineering and got a PhD in math modeling of computer security, but I tell students I encounter to spend the remainder of their time in college filling their minds with the best of the humanities their school has to offer."

ANN MIURA-KO
TW: @annimaniac
IG: @amiura
floodgate.com

ANN MIURA-KO is a partner at Floodgate, a venture capital firm specializing in micro-cap investments in startups. She has been called "the most powerful woman in startups" by *Forbes* and is a lecturer in entrepreneurship at Stanford. The child of a rocket scientist at NASA, Ann is a Palo Alto native and has been steeped in technology startups since she was a teenager. Prior to co-founding Floodgate, she worked at Charles River Ventures and McKinsey and Company. Some of Ann's investments include Lyft, Ayasdi, Xamarin, Refinery29, Chloe and Isabel, Maker Media, Wanelo, TaskRabbit, and Modcloth.

How has a failure, or apparent failure, set you up for later success? Do you have a "favorite failure" of yours?

As a 12-year-old, I stood on a stage next to my brother, who confidently pointed to me and announced, "This is Ann Miura. She will be playing a Chopin Nocturne in C sharp minor." I stood next to him, mute, and then strode over to the piano and started to play. Even though I could play a piano recital in front of many people, [my brother spoke for me because] I was absolutely terrified of speaking in public. Compounding that fear was the fact that I spoke Japanese at home and, while I was very confident of my abilities in other subjects, English was never particularly a strong suit. In high school, I decided to confront these insecurities headfirst by signing up for the speech and debate team and devoting almost all of my extracurricular hours to this endeavor. Two years in, finishing up my sophomore year in high school, my parents pointed out that this experiment had been a miserable failure. While other teammates had racked up trophies and accolades, I had a losing record and not much else to show for the time I had put in. My parents, rightfully concerned that I had put all of my eggs into a very sad and empty basket, suggested gently that I change course starting junior year. "Perhaps fencing?" my mother suggested, clearly unaware of my complete lack of athletic skills. "I hear that if you're good at fencing, you can get into a great college!"

While their intentions were sound, my parents didn't take into account that I absolutely loved debate. I loved the competition. I loved constructing arguments. I loved the preparation. I loved everything about it, and my losing record had yet to dampen my ardor for it. I begged for a summer to figure out a new approach. While my mother labeled me stubborn, I spent the entire summer between my sophomore and junior year of high school holed up at the local library researching next year's potential debate topics. I doubled or even tripled the effort I had previously put in by reading philosophy books, sociology texts, journal articles—literally anything I could get my hands on. I promised my parents that I would quit debate if I didn't place in the first two tournaments of the year.

That summer was an absolute gift to me. I learned more about myself and how I might find success than in any moment where I have actually experienced a more traditional measure of success. First, if you love something enough, it is far easier to really commit to something. Through true commitment and hard work, you can out-prepare the competition. When I walked into my first debate round in the fall of my junior year, I had already won the round before my opponent spoke a single word. I had out-prepared and out-planned my opponent. For every argument he gave, I had thought through a multitude of responses. There were literally no surprises. Second, I learned that I alone know my personal capabilities better than anyone else. It is so difficult for people to measure grit, determination, hard work, and human potential. When given the chance, we can potentially see them more clearly than anyone else. We just need to make sure we listen and hear that inner voice. I went on to take second that junior year in the state of California and won the national Tournament of Champions my senior year. I myself couldn't have predicted that in the summer of my sophomore year.

What is an unusual habit or an absurd thing that you love?

I am absolutely nuts about office supplies. My mother's side of the family has a small office supply store in Kanazawa, Japan, and I spent summers as a kid manning their store. I loved comparing the latest and greatest pencils and pens. I knew the model of the pencil case with the greatest set of features including a built-in pencil sharpener, matching rulers and scissors, and hidden compartments for candy or money. I loved the smell of a new notebook whose binding had yet to be cracked for the first time. I loved that people in Japan used stamps in place of signatures and came to this store to replace a stamp they may have lost. Today my obsession for the very best pens (Muji 0.38mm gel pens and Pilot Juice Up 0.4 mm gel pens) and notebooks (Leuchtturm1917 Medium Hardcover) is an echo of those hot summer days I spent in my uncle's office supply store. I'm only mildly embarrassed by how much I love to take notes on paper with an endless supply of colored pens and pencils at my fingertips.

What advice would you give to a smart, driven college student about to enter the "real world"?

There are two pieces of advice I typically give to students who are in their final year of college. This may come as strange advice from someone who majored in electrical engineering and got a PhD in math modeling of computer security, but I first tell students I encounter to spend the remainder of their time in college filling their minds with the best of the humanities their school has to offer. While classes I took in digital circuits in 1995 have long become outdated, the timeless lessons on fundamental human nature (e.g., John Locke, Thomas Hobbes), the rise and demise of great societies and the inspirational examples set by real-life heroes (e.g., Alexander Hamilton) found in the literature and history classes I took are ones I draw upon even to this day. In a world where we emphasize the creation of new products through rapid iteration and experimentation, we often forget to step back and make sure that the future we are racing to is one we truly want to create. The practice of judgment and reasoning found in philosophy (e.g., Kantian ethics), history, and literature are skills we should continue to hone even when we are out of college, but if we do not start the practice there, it is a process that is difficult to pick up after the fact.

Second, in the first month of starting to work in New York City, my manager at work dispensed free advice that he told me was deeply personal but profoundly important: Develop a philosophy of giving as soon as you enter the working world. He said that I should develop this philosophy when I had few obligations outside of the student debt I had taken on. He suggested that I commit to a percentage of my income and that I consistently donate that amount to charities of my choosing every year. What I didn't realize then but have come to know in my life is that charitable giving is as much a habit as it is a conscious act. While in any moment, it may feel like there are countless other places where you could use those precious dollars saved up for charitable giving, simply making and keeping such a personal commitment can carry tremendous meaning. I kept that promise to myself from the time I was first working out of college, even into leaner years in graduate school, and my husband and I have reaffirmed that commitment together for our future.

> "The fairest rules are those to which everyone would agree if they did not know how much power they would have." —John Rawls

JASON FRIED
TW: @jasonfried
basecamp.com

JASON FRIED is the co-founder and CEO of Basecamp (previously 37signals), a Chicago-based software firm. The company's flagship product, Basecamp, is a project management and team communication application trusted by millions. He is the co-author of *Getting Real: The Smarter, Faster, Easier Way to Build a Successful Web Application,* which is available for free at gettingreal.37signals.com. He is also the co-author of the *New York Times* bestseller *Rework* and *Remote: Office Not Required.* Jason writes a regular column for *Inc.* magazine and is a frequent contributor to Basecamp's popular blog, *Signal v. Noise,* which offers "strong opinions and shared thoughts on design, business, and tech."

What is the book (or books) you've given most as a gift, and why? Or what are one to three books that have greatly influenced your life?

I think this one's out of print, but I always tell people to find it and read it: *Seeking Wisdom: From Darwin to Munger* by Peter Bevelin. I think any book that reviews Charlie Munger's ideas is worth reading, and this one in particular weaves in wisdom from some of history's greatest minds. It's a bit meandering and loose, but that's fine with me.

How has a failure, or apparent failure, set you up for later success? Do you have a "favorite failure" of yours?

Way back in the '90s, when I was getting started as a web designer, I sent my work into an awards site called HighFive.com. At the time, it was the shit. If you were awarded a High Five award, you were recognized.

Now . . . I sent my stuff in, and David Siegel, the guy who ran it, emailed me back. I don't have the original email anymore, but basically he told me I sucked, I had no business being in the web design business, and that I should never email him again.

That rejection filled me with so much fire. Not anger. Not resentment. Not disappointment. But fire. Fire to kick ass and prove his impression wrong.

I loved the rejection. It made me.

If you could have a gigantic billboard anywhere with anything on it, what would it say and why? Are there any quotes you think of often or live your life by?

One of these quotes:

"If you think you are too small to be effective, you have never been in the dark with a mosquito."—Betty Reese

"Every great cause begins as a movement, becomes a business, and eventually degenerates into a racket."—Eric Hoffer

"The fairest rules are those to which everyone would agree if they did not know how much power they would have."—John Rawls

"In theory there is no difference between theory and practice. But, in practice, there is."—Jan L. A. van de Snepscheut

"Price is what you pay. Value is what you get."—Warren Buffett

"Everybody is somebody, but nobody wants to be themselves."
—Gnarls Barkley

"Life does not ask what we want. It presents us with options."
—Thomas Sowell

"Watch what people are cynical about, and one can often discover what they lack."—George S. Patton

"Do what you can, with what you have, where you are."
—Theodore Roosevelt

"It's not what you look at that matters, it's what you see."
—Henry David Thoreau

"Beware the investment activity that produces applause; the great moves are usually greeted by yawns."—Warren Buffett

"The hole and the patch should be commensurate."—Thomas Jefferson

"In all affairs, it's a healthy thing now and then to hang a question mark on the things you have long taken for granted."—Bertrand Russell

"Bureaucracy is the art of making the possible impossible."
—Javier Pascual Salcedo

"It is very important what not to do."—Iggy Pop

"Don't pay any attention to what they write about you, just measure it in inches."—Andy Warhol

"Knowledge is the beginning of practice; doing is the completion of knowing."—Wang Yangming

"There is nothing so useless as doing efficiently that which should not be done at all."—Peter Drucker

"In the hopes of reaching the moon men fail to see the flowers that blossom at their feet."—Albert Schweitzer

"Our fears are always more numerous than our dangers."
—Seneca the Younger

"It is amazing what you can accomplish if you do not care who gets the credit."—Harry Truman

"Don't worry about people stealing an idea. If it's original, you will have to ram it down their throats."—Howard H. Aiken

"Don't hire a dog, then bark yourself."—David Ogilvy

"All good work is done in defiance of management."—Bob Woodward

"Put one dumb foot in front of the other and course correct as you go."—Barry Diller

"A cynic is a man who knows the price of everything and the value of nothing."—Oscar Wilde

"A complex system that works is invariably found to have evolved from a simple system that worked. A complex system designed from scratch never works and cannot be patched up to make it work. You have to start over, beginning with a working simple system."—John Gall

"Whenever there is a hard job to be done, I assign it to a lazy man; he is sure to find an easy way of doing it."—Walter Chrysler

"Not everything that can be counted counts, and not everything that counts can be counted."—William Bruce Cameron

"You must be the change you wish to see in the world."
—Mahatma Gandhi

"Most of the wonderful places in the world were not made by architects but by the people." — Christopher Alexander

"I notice increasing reluctance on the part of marketing executives to use judgment. They are coming to rely too much on research, and they use it as a drunkard uses a lamp post: for support, rather than for illumination." — David Ogilvy

"Lose an hour in the morning, chase it all day." — a Yiddish saying, author unknown

"Communication usually fails, except by accident." — Osmo Wiio

What is one of the best or most worthwhile investments you've ever made?

Every time I've given without any expectation of return. Money, time, energy, whatever. Whenever I've expected something in return, the investment was stunted. Whenever I've given purely for giving, for helping, for supporting, for aiding, for encouraging — with zero expectation or interest in any return whatsoever — it's been thoroughly fulfilling.

Most recently, my friend Krys was opening his own personal training gym. He'd just left his father's business, money was tight, and he was taking a big risk. I had full faith in him, I knew he would be great at it, and I wanted to remove some worry for him. So I paid his first year's rent for him. No equity, no payback, no financial interest at all. It was just a gift. His business is thriving and it's such a pleasure to see him and his young family (wife and two kids) so happy. I couldn't be more thrilled for them.

In the last five years, what new belief, behavior, or habit has most improved your life?

I started working out twice a week versus three times. Small change, but something great happens when you work out less: you realize that you have to eat better, sleep better, and live better on your off days. Working out more frequently can cover up bad habits, but when you work out less frequently, everything else matters more. That really helps me make better decisions about how I take care of my health.

What advice would you give to a smart, driven college student about to enter the "real world"?

Focus on your writing skills. It's the one thing I've found that really helps people stand out. More and more communication is written today. Get great at presenting yourself with words, and words alone, and you'll be far ahead of most.

Also, most of the stuff you'll worry about doesn't matter anyway. You'll sweat so many details that no one will care about. It's not that details don't matter—they do—but only the right details matter. Pay close attention to what you're spending your time on.

Time and attention are very different things. They're your most precious resources moving forward. Just like you walk through the air and you swim through the water, you work through your attention. It's the medium of work. While people often say there's not enough time, remember that you'll always have less attention than time. Full attention is where you do your best work, and everyone's going to be looking to rip it from you. Protect and preserve it.

What are bad recommendations you hear in your profession or area of expertise?

There are so many. "Scale." No, don't scale. Start small, stay as small as possible for as long as possible. Grow in control, not out of control.

"Raise capital to launch a software/services business." No, bootstrap. As in life, we form business habits early on. If you raise money, you'll get good at spending money. If you bootstrap, you'll be forced to get good at making money. If there's one habit/skill an entrepreneur should practice, it's making money. So force yourself into it.

"Fail early, and fail often." No. What's with the failure fetish in our industry? I don't get it. Of course, most businesses don't make it, but the idea that failure is a prerequisite for success has never made sense to me. I don't think it's a notch in the belt. It's just a failure. Further, many people will tell you there's a lot to learn from failure. Maybe . . . But there's more to learn from success. Failure may tell you what not to do again, but it doesn't help you figure out what to do the next time around. I'd rather focus on the things that work, and try those again, than try to take lessons from the things that didn't.

There are really so many. I could go on and on and on . . .

In the last five years, what have you become better at saying no to?

I've always been pretty good at saying no, but over the last couple of years I've come up with a new rule. If the ask is more than a week away, I almost always say no, regardless of what is it. Exceptions include family things I need to attend, and a conference or two I really want to speak at, but other than that, if the "yes" would tie me to something further than a week or so out, it's almost always a no.

I keep it simple and direct. Unless there are special circumstances, I always explain why and say something like, "Thanks for the invitation, but I just can't commit to anything more than a day or so in advance. I need to keep my schedule open for me and the people I work with on a regular basis. Best bet is to hit me up a day or two before you wanted to get together. If I'm available we can set up a time."

This is loosely modeled on Warren Buffet's purported "can I get a meeting with Warren" policy, as I wrote about on *Signal v. Noise*.

I've simply realized that the further out the yes, the more I regret the moment when it comes due. Because there's no cost now, it's simply too easy to say yes about something deep in the future. Further, a future "yes" ultimately means that the past controls your schedule. By the time you get around to later, your calendar is already filled with prior engagements. That limits what's possible in the moment. Few things bother me more than wanting to actually say yes to something today but being blocked by a previous yes I said weeks or months ago.

When you feel overwhelmed or unfocused, what do you do?

I go for a walk. Preferably on a route I've never taken before. If it's a routine route, I tend to ignore the surroundings and slip back into thinking about the stuff I'm unfocused on. But if it's a new route, I focus outward and my mind clears up quickly. Seems like it has to be about 30 minutes or more to really do the job, but nothing refreshes me like walking in a new direction, toward something or somewhere I haven't headed before.

QUOTES I'M PONDERING

(Tim Ferriss: April 22–May 13, 2016)

"Action may not always bring happiness, but there is no happiness without action."

—BENJAMIN DISRAELI
Former prime minister of the United Kingdom

"It is fatal to know too much at the outset. Boredom comes as quickly to the traveler who knows his route as the novelist who is over certain of his plot."

—PAUL THEROUX
American novelist, travel writer, and author of *The Great Railway Bazaar*

"I prefer to be true to myself, even at the hazard of incurring the ridicule of others, rather than to be false, and to incur my own abhorrence."

—FREDERICK DOUGLASS
African-American social reformer, leader of the abolitionist movement

"All courses of action are risky, so prudence is not in avoiding danger (it's impossible), but calculating risk and acting decisively. Make mistakes of ambition and not mistakes of sloth. Develop the strength to do bold things, not the strength to suffer."

—NICCOLÒ MACHIAVELLI
16th-century Italian philosopher, dubbed
"the father of modern political science," author of The Prince

"Burnout is not the price you have to pay for success."

ARIANNA HUFFINGTON
TW: @ariannahuff
thriveglobal.com

ARIANNA HUFFINGTON has been named to *Time* magazine's list of the world's 100 most influential people and *Forbes'* "Most Powerful Women" list. Originally from Greece, she moved to England when she was 16 and graduated from Cambridge University with an MA in economics. In May 2005, she launched *The Huffington Post*, a news and blog site that quickly became one of the most widely read, linked-to, and frequently cited media brands on the Internet, and in 2012 won a Pulitzer Prize for national reporting. In August 2016, she launched Thrive Global with the mission of ending the stress and burnout epidemic by offering companies and individuals sustainable, science-based solutions to well-being. Arianna serves on numerous boards, including Uber and The Center for Public Integrity, and she is the author of 15 books, including her most recent, *Thrive: The Third Metric to Redefining Success and Creating a Life of Well-Being, Wisdom, and Wonder,* and *The Sleep Revolution: Transforming Your Life, One Night at a Time.*

What is the book (or books) you've given most as a gift, and why? Or what are one to three books that have greatly influenced your life?

One of my favorite books that I often give is *Meditations* by Marcus Aurelius. He spent 19 years as the emperor of Rome facing nearly constant war, a horrific plague, an attempt at the throne by one of his closest allies, and an incompetent and greedy stepbrother as co-emperor, and he still had the presence of mind to write one of my favorite quotes, "People look for retreats for themselves, in the country, by the coast, or in the hills. There is nowhere that a person can find a more peaceful and trouble-free retreat than in his own mind. . . . So constantly give yourself this retreat, and renew yourself." And stoicism, as we can see from the almost daily articles about its revival, has never been more relevant. I find the book so inspirational and instructive, it lives on my nightstand.

I also love *Memories, Dreams, Reflections* by Carl Jung. It's a great guide to how important dreams are as a gateway to our own intuition and wisdom.

How has a failure, or apparent failure, set you up for later success? Do you have a "favorite failure" of yours?

One of my "favorite failures," which was actually a collection of many smaller failures, was when my second book was rejected by 37 publishers. I remember running out of money and walking, depressed, down St. James Street in London, where I was living at the time. I looked up and saw a Barclays Bank and, without giving it much thought, I decided to walk in and asked to speak to the manager. I asked him for a loan, and even though I didn't have any assets, the banker—whose name was Ian Bell —gave it to me. It wasn't much, but it changed my life because it meant I could keep things together for a few more rejections, and after number 37, I finally got my book published. And I still send Ian Bell a holiday card every year.

My mother taught me that failure is not the opposite of success but a steppingstone to success.

What is one of the best or most worthwhile investments you've ever made?

One of the best investments I've made is, as they tell us on airplanes, putting my own oxygen mask first—sleeping, meditating, walking, working out, etc. In 2007 I collapsed from exhaustion. After that, I made changes to my life, and became more and more passionate about the connection between well-being and productivity. A lot of people think they don't have time to take care of themselves, but it's an investment that will pay off in so many ways.

In the last five years, what new belief, behavior, or habit has most improved your life?

I would say it's a reformulation of how I think about my time. Before, I separated time into work time and non-work time, and I always wanted to maximize work time. Now I realize that you can't separate the two—time spent taking breaks, taking a walk, unplugging, meditating—that's all work time, too, in the sense that time spent unplugging and recharging makes me better, more effective, and happier in my work and in my life.

What advice would you give to a smart, driven college student about to enter the "real world"?

I would advise them to be much more mindful and deliberate about their relationship with technology. Technology allows us to do amazing things, but we have become addicted to it. And that's by design—product designers know how to addict us in the race to dominate the attention economy. But there are ways to—as Tristan Harris, a former Google design ethicist, puts it— "unhijack your mind."

[For example] one tip is to scramble apps regularly, which interrupts the conditioning we all have to the pattern of apps on our phones. Creating this pattern interrupt will make it easier to be more mindful about phone use, creating just a little bit of space and time in which people can decide for themselves whether they really need to use their phone or whether they're grabbing it out of boredom or habit.

What purchase of $100 or less has most positively impacted your life in the last six months (or in recent memory)?

The $100 product that has most positively impacted my life in the last six months is the Thrive Global phone bed. I know, I know, it's a product from my own company, so I may be breaking some unwritten Tim Ferriss Q&A rule, but as so many people reading this book know, when you can't find something in the market, you have to create it. The phone bed lives on the bureau outside my bedroom, and makes disconnecting a regular part of my nightly ritual. It has up to 12 ports, so it can charge phones and tablets for the whole family. Our phones are useful for many things, but as the repositories of our to-do lists, our anxieties and our worries, they're definitely not sleep aids. So to make it easy to put our phones away—by giving them their own bed where they can charge outside our bedroom—we can say good night to our day and get the sleep we need to wake up fully recharged.

When you feel overwhelmed or unfocused, what do you do?

I love taking even five minutes for a short meditation. It helps me move beyond the surface and go deeper, and after just a few moments of focusing on my breath, I feel recentered.

If you could have a gigantic billboard anywhere with anything on it, what would it say and why?

I'd have it say, "Burnout is not the price you have to pay for success." And I hope billions truly would see it, since so much of the world is still living under the collective delusion that they have to choose between their own well-being and success. Science tells us the complete opposite—when we prioritize our well-being, our performance goes up across the board. Three-quarters of all startups fail, and entrepreneurship is about making decisions. Nothing impairs the quality of your decisions faster than running on empty.

"Macro patience, micro speed."

GARY VAYNERCHUK
TW/IG: @garyvee
garyvaynerchuk.com

GARY VAYNERCHUK is a serial entrepreneur and the CEO and co-founder of VaynerMedia, a full-service digital agency servicing Fortune 500 clients. Gary rose to prominence in the late '90s after establishing one of the first e-commerce wine sites, Wine Library, which helped his father grow the family business from $4 million to $60 million in annual sales. He is a venture capitalist, four-time *New York Times* best-selling author, and an early investor in companies such as Twitter, Tumblr, Venmo, and Uber. Gary has been named to both *Crain*'s and *Fortune*'s "40 Under 40" lists. Gary is currently the subject of *DailyVee,* an online documentary series highlighting what it's like to be a CEO and public figure in today's digital world.

What purchase of $100 or less has most positively impacted your life in the last six months (or in recent memory)?
My random assortment of 1980s wrestling T-shirts.

How has a failure, or apparent failure, set you up for later success? Do you have a "favorite failure" of yours?
I believe that being a small guy, being an immigrant, peeing my bed until I was 12, all of these things really set me up for macro success. I was a terrible student and I sucked shit at school.

I think the extremities of my educational life set me up for the extreme winnings that I'm having in real life, because the market—a.k.a. my friends, parents, and the teachers who always razzed on me, and put me down, and anticipated losses from me—forced me to become better.

[People write] something about me [on the Internet] and compare me to awful human beings, tell me that I'm a con artist and a horrible person, which is one of the most difficult things who a noble person can deal with. But they don't penetrate me at all, because I'm so used to it.

I feel like so much of why I'm able to leverage my personality as a gateway to business achievements is predicated on all the losses. There's no specific story. I think I grew up as a loser by standards, because schooling was the only way you judged kids. It was either class or athletics, and I was doing neither. I was on no teams, achieving nothing, and I was getting Ds and Fs. I was as cliché of a 1982–1994 school system loser as it gets.

Yet here I am.

What advice would you give to a smart, driven college student about to enter the "real world"?

Macro patience, micro speed. They should not care about the next eight years, but they should stress the next eight days.

At a macro, I think everybody's super impatient. I think I'm unbelievably patient in years and decades, and unbelievably sporadic and hyper every minute on a day-to-day basis. I genuinely think everybody's the reverse. Everybody's making decisions about, like, "What am I going to do at 25? I better do that. . . ." In years, they're impatient and making dumb decisions, and then in days, they're watching fucking Netflix. They're super worried about 25 when they're 22, yet they're drinking every Thursday night at 7 P.M. They're playing Madden. They're fucking watching *House of Cards*. They're spending four and a half hours on their Instagram feed every single day.

This is super important.

Everybody's impatient at a macro, and just so patient at a micro, wasting your days worrying about years. I'm not worried about my years, because I'm squeezing the fuck out of my seconds, let alone my days. It's going to work out.

In the last five years, what new belief, behavior, or habit has most improved your life?

My health regimen. Three years ago, I got much more serious about my health regimen. However, this is a great place to state the following: I have picked up zero energy from it. Zero. It's just that it's the right thing to do. I sit here today at 41 with less energy. I can pick up my luggage and kids more easily. I'm stronger, but I have zero extra energy, or all the other things that people like to throw around when you work out. But there is just absolutely no debating that I should, in theory, have a lot of things work out positively for me in my 60s, 70s, 80s, and 90s that are benefitted by me putting in the work now.

My initial ambition was to improve my aesthetics, which quickly turned into "How can I feel good and build for the long term?" I now work with a trainer seven days a week. I usually train three or four days doing a split of upper-body and lower-body compound exercises. The remainder of my workouts focus on flexibility and soft tissue. I do a lot of mobility work for my hips, back, and neck. It has tremendously improved the way I feel. Now I am focused on building muscle and establishing a strong foundation. I dead-lift, I bench press, I squat, and everything in between. It is not my goal to get ripped; it is my goal to feel good and remain strong, flexible, and healthy.

Whenever I can squeeze in 30 minutes to an hour I do. My personal trainer, Jordan, travels with me a lot. I primarily work out in the morning before I get to the office. I am usually in the gym by 6:15 and out within an hour.

In the last five years, what have you become better at saying no to?

Everything. One of the great issues for anybody who starts gaining success is they become crippled by opportunity, and the no's becoming imperatively important versus the yeses.

On the flip side, as Tyler or any of my other assistants will tell you, I still need a healthy balance of 20 percent yeses to things that seem dumb, because I believe in serendipity, and that's an important balance that people struggle with.

I do believe that most people reading this either go too far into one or the other extreme. They become super disciplined and say no to everything, and they think that's the right use of time, or they're just saying yes to everything and giving it no thought, no strategy.

I want to be closer to the no's and be good at that, and really value my time. However, I do think that there's a nice healthy balance of doing things on spec that aren't obvious ROI on intuition, because one of those things in that 20 percent usually makes the entire investment worth it.

When you feel overwhelmed or unfocused, what do you do?

I pretend that my family has died in a horrific accident. Honestly, that's what I do. It's probably weirder than a lot of people's answers in this book, but it's absolutely what drives me. I go to a very dark place, really feel it, feel that pain in my heart, and then realize no matter what I'm dealing with right now, that it's not even in the same universe of something like that. Then I become grateful for losing that client, missing that opportunity, getting made fun of, etc.

"Money in a business is like gas in your car. You need to pay attention so you don't end up on the side of the road. But your trip is not a tour of gas stations."

TIM O'REILLY
TW/FB: @timoreilly
LI: linkedin.com/in/timo3/
tim.oreilly.com

TIM O'REILLY is the founder and CEO of O'Reilly Media. His original business plan was simply "interesting work for interesting people," and it seems to have worked out well. O'Reilly Media delivers online learning, publishes books, runs conferences, urges companies to create more value than they capture, and tries to change the world by spreading and amplifying the knowledge of innovators. He has been dubbed the "Trend Spotter" by *Wired* magazine. Tim has now turned his attention to implications of AI, the on-demand economy, and other technologies that are transforming the nature of work and the future shape of the business world. This is the subject of his new book, *WTF?: What's the Future and Why It's Up to Us*.

What is the book (or books) you've given most as a gift, and why? Or what are one to three books that have greatly influenced your life?

It is very hard to limit this list to three books, because books and the ideas I've taken from them are such a large part of my mental toolbox.

I have to start with *The Meaning of Culture* by John Cowper Powys, because it explains something about my relationship to literature (and the other arts). Powys makes the point that the difference between education and culture is that culture is the incorporation of music, art, literature, and philosophy not just into your library or your CV but into who you are. He talks about the interplay of culture and life, the way that what we read can enrich what we experience, and what we experience can enrich what we read.

The Way of Life According to Lao Tzu, the Tao Te Ching as translated by Witter Bynner. This book is close to the heart of my personal religious and moral philosophy, stressing the rightness of what is, if only we can accept it. Most people who know me have heard me quote from this book. "Seeing as how nothing is outside the vast, wide-meshed net of heaven, who is there to say just how it is cast?" "I find good people good, and I find bad people good, if I am good enough."

Rissa Kerguelen by F. M. Busby. I read this now largely forgotten science fiction book at about the time I was starting my company, and it influenced me deeply. One key idea is the role of entrepreneurship as a "subversive force." In a world dominated by large companies, it is the smaller companies that keep freedom alive, with economics at least one of the battlegrounds. This book gave me the courage to submerge myself in the details of a fundamentally trivial business (technical writing and publishing) and to let go of my earlier hopes of writing deep books that would change the world. Those hopes came back around later.

The other wonderful idea in this book is "the long view." Well before the Long Now Foundation popularized the idea, Busby hinged his plot on the science fiction trope that in a world of near-light-speed travel, time passes more slowly for those at near-relativistic speed than for those left behind. The characters must set events in motion and travel to meet up with them decades hence. That was also a useful framing as I set out to build a business that would allow me to affect the world of the future in ways that I couldn't yet as a young entrepreneur.

If you could have a gigantic billboard anywhere with anything on it, what would it say and why?

I do actually have gigantic billboards of this sort. They are just online rather than by the side of the road. A number of things I've said have been turned into Internet memes, complete with a stunning variety of imagery (and sometimes a butchery of the text). Three of the most popular are:

"Work on stuff that matters."

"Create more value than you capture."

"Money in a business is like gas in your car. You need to pay attention so you don't end up on the side of the road. But your trip is not a tour of gas stations."

If I had to pick just one, it would probably be "Create more value than you capture," because so much of what's wrong with our economy comes from a failure to do that. In a rich society, or a rich, complex ecosystem . . . Brian Erwin, at the time my VP of marketing, came up with this line at a company executive retreat in about 2000, when I remarked wryly that more than one Internet billionaire had told me that he'd started his business with what he'd learned from an O'Reilly book. Brian suggested we embrace that principle, and I've never looked back.

I once tried to explain to Eric Schmidt why I thought this would be a better guiding light for Google than "Don't be evil!" It's measurable—you can actually compare what you get out of an activity to what others do. Google actually does do some of that measurement in its annual economic impact report, but I don't think they'd be heading into antitrust trouble right now if they had spent more time thinking about the health of their ecosystem as they develop new services. It isn't enough just to think about yourself and your users or customers. You have to think of your company as part of a web of life, just like an organism in an ecosystem. If you become too dominant, you suck all the life out of the ecosystem. It gets out of balance, and everyone suffers, eventually even the creatures that think themselves safe at the top of the pile.

What is an unusual habit or an absurd thing that you love?

Every morning, on my run, I try to take a picture of a flower and share it on Instagram. I was inspired to do this by a passage I read many years ago in a book by C. S. Lewis (I think it was *The Great Divorce*), in which a character, after death, only sees the flowers as blobs of color, and his spirit guide tells him, "That's because you never really looked at them when you were alive." As the line from *Hamilton* says, "Look around. Look around. How lucky we are to be alive right now!"

In the last five years, what new belief, behavior, or habit has most improved your life?

When I roll out of bed, I do the plank for two minutes right off, followed by downward dog for the same, then a series of stretches. It gets my metabolism going, and makes me much more likely to start with a more vigorous bout of exercise. I used to start the day by getting on my computer, getting sucked in, then looking up and realizing it was too late to get out before the day started in earnest.

In the last five years, what have you become better at saying no to?

I have profited greatly from Esther Dyson's (page 243) advice about accepting speaking engagements: "Would I say yes if it were on Tuesday?" Because the day will come when it *is* on Tuesday, and you'll be saying, "Damn, why did I say yes to that?" Forethought is a virtue; remember that one day, that distant future will be now, and the choices you make today will have shaped the choices you are able to make then. This obviously has wide applications to social and environmental issues (ahem, climate change or income inequality) as well.

What are bad recommendations you hear in your profession or area of expertise?

"Disrupt!" When Clayton Christensen introduced the term "disruptive technology" in his 1997 business classic, *The Innovator's Dilemma: When New Technologies Cause Great Firms to Fail*, he was asking a very different question than "How can I get funded by convincing VCs that there's a huge market I can blow up?" He wanted to know why existing companies fail to take advantage of new opportunities. He discovered that breakthrough technologies that are not yet mature first succeed by finding radically new markets, and only later disrupt existing markets.

The point of a disruptive technology is not the market or the competitors that it destroys. It is the new markets and the new possibilities that it creates. Just like transistor radios or the early World Wide Web, these new markets are often too small for established companies to consider them worth pursuing. By the time they wake up, an upstart has taken a leadership position in the emerging segment.

But more important, the idea that we should focus on disruption rather than the new value that we can create is at the heart of the current economic malaise, income inequality, and political upheaval. The secret to building a better future is to use technology to do things that were previously impossible. That was true in the first industrial revolution, and it is true now. It isn't technology that eliminates jobs, it is the shortsighted business decisions that use technology simply to cut costs and fatten corporate profits. The point of technology isn't to make money. It's to solve problems!

This is the master design pattern for applying technology: Do more. Do things that were previously unimaginable.

For all its talk of disruption, Silicon Valley too is often in thrall to the financial system. The ultimate fitness function for too many entrepreneurs is not the change they want to make in the world, but "the exit," the sale or IPO that will make them and the venture capitalists who funded them a giant pile of money. It's easy to point fingers at "Wall Street" without realizing our own complicity in the problem or in finding a way to bring it under control.

What advice would you give to a smart, driven college student about to enter the "real world"? What advice should they ignore?

"Let life ripen and then fall. Will is not the way at all." — Lao Tzu, from *The Way of Life According to Lao Tzu*

We equate being smart and being driven as the ways to get ahead. But sometimes, an attitude of alert watchfulness is far wiser and more effective. Learning to follow your nose, pulling on threads of curiosity or interest, may take you places that being driven will never lead you to.

My own life has been shaped by happy coincidences. When I was barely out of college, a friend asked if I'd write a book about science fiction writer Frank Herbert. I'd never written a book, but Dick Riley, the editor of a new series about science fiction authors, knew I loved science fiction and was a good writer. I remember talking to my thesis adviser at Harvard, Zeph Stewart, who was still a friend, about whether it would take me "off course." He laughed, and said, "You're only 21. If you don't know what you're doing by the time you're 30, that might be something to worry about."

Because I said yes, I came to think of myself as a writer. And because I thought of myself as a writer, a few years later, I agreed to help a programmer friend write a computer manual (even though I knew nothing about computers). That lucky break led me to start what was to become O'Reilly Media.

And even later in my career, there were moments when waiting for the right moment led to the perfect outcome. Take "the freeware summit" that I organized in April 1998. I'd been thinking about bringing together people from the Linux community, the Perl community, and the Internet all through the fall of 1997, but something kept me from pulling the trigger. Then Netscape announced that they were going to release their browser as free software, and when I organized the meeting in April of 1998, the timing was perfect. The term "open source" software had been coined by Christine Peterson only a few weeks earlier. If I'd held my meeting in the fall of the previous year, I wouldn't have had the chance to persuade the assembled leaders to agree to the new name and to showcase it to the assembled press.

Listen to your inner voice, which tells you what to choose. Socrates called it his "*daimon.*" Lao Tzu said of the wise man that "He has his no, and he has his yes." It is this ability to wait quietly for the right moment, rather than rushing about aimlessly, that can lead even an ambitious success-hunter to capture the biggest game.

"Excellence is the next five minutes. . . . Forget the long term. Make the next five minutes rock!"

TOM PETERS
TW: @tom_peters
tompeters.com

TOM PETERS is a co-author of *In Search of Excellence: Lessons from America's Best-Run Companies,* which is often referred to as "the best business book ever." Sixteen books and more than 30 years later, he's still at the forefront of the "management guru" industry he helped invent. As CNN has said, "While most business gurus milk the same mantra for all it's worth, the one-man brand called Tom Peters is still reinventing himself." His most recent book is *The Little BIG Things: 163 Ways to Pursue Excellence.* Tom's bedrock belief is: "Execution is strategy—it's all about the people and the doing, not the talking and the theory." Tom has given more than 2,500 speeches, and his speech and writing materials are available for free at tompeters.com.

What is the book (or books) you've given most as a gift, and why? Or what are one to three books that have greatly influenced your life?

Susan Cain's (page 10) book *Quiet: The Power of Introverts in a World That Can't Stop Talking,* Frank Partnoy's *Wait: The Art and Science of Delay,*

Linda Kaplan-Thaler's *The Power of Nice: How to Conquer the Business World with Kindness* and *The Power of Small: Why Little Things Make All the Difference*, and Cathy O'Neil's *Weapons of Math Destruction: How Big Data Increases Inequality and Threatens Democracy*.

Cain's book embarrassed me. It suggests that most of us undervalue introverts and, thus, effectively take a pass on about 40 percent of the population. In particular, introverts tend to be more thoughtful and deliberate. And it's not that they don't like people—in fact, they tend to have deeper relationships with fewer people relative to extroverts.

Speed is everything! Right? Frank Partnoy says . . . NO! The ability to pause and reflect separates us from the rest of the animal kingdom. Given the acceleration frenzy, "slow down" is no less than profound advice.

As to Ms. Kaplan-Thaler's books . . . Wow! She built a large ad agency from scratch and is in the Advertising Hall of Fame. I happen to believe that "nice" and "small" rule! These ideas animate and have animated my life. (She also mocks the idea of a "vision"—the point is instead the quality of today's work.)

Then there's Kathy O'Neil's book: It gives "big data" a much-needed punch in the nose. Bravo! Big data can be invaluable but can do incalculable harm as well. We need to be much more wary of the latter than we currently are.

Okay, a couple more: I happen to believe that economic success lies in the hands of SMEs, small and medium-sized enterprises. Four books I give away on SMEs are: George Whalin's *Retail Superstars: Inside the Twenty-five Best Independent Stores in America* (Favorite line: "Be the best, it's the only market that's not crowded."), Bo Burlingham's *Small Giants: Companies That Choose to Be Great Instead of Big*, Bill Taylor's *Simply Brilliant: How Great Organizations Do Ordinary Things in Extraordinary Ways*, and Hermann Simon's *Hidden Champions of the Twenty-first Century: The Success Strategies of Unknown World Market Leaders*.

I love giving books away! I bet, crazy as it may sound, I've given away a minimum of 25 to 50 of each of these books. FYI: One of the world's great investors once said to me, "Tom, what do you consider the number-one failing of CEOs?" After I hemmed and hawed, he said, *"They don't read enough."*

What purchase of $100 or less has most positively impacted your life in the last six months (or in recent memory)?

I love to row, and I've been doing it since about age five. I don't mean competitive rowing—I mean jumping into a rowboat and spending an hour or two on a river. I grew up on the Severn River, near Annapolis. After 60 years of row-row-row your boat, I discovered paradise: my sleek, light (Kevlar) 14-foot Vermont Dory. The maker is Adirondack Guide Boat of North Ferrisburgh, Vermont.

(FYI: It was a lot more than $100 . . . but it sure as heck was my favorite purchase in a long, long time.)

What is one of the best or most worthwhile investments you've ever made?

I'd like to think I spent a couple of decades a half step ahead of the pack. But about four years ago, I felt as if I couldn't even see the tail end of the pack because I was so far behind. So I took a de facto one-year sabbatical, and . . . READ and READ and READ some more. When it comes to tech change, where I felt so out of it, I think I can now effectively deal with its implications with some degree of confidence.

What is an unusual habit or an absurd thing that you love?

It's an annoying habit that really drives my wife nuts. I am trained as a civil engineer, and engineers love redundancy. We expect the worst and design to deal with it.

Translation into real life: For even short trips, my bags weigh a ton. I have duplicates or triplicates of everything. If you stole my bag, you could, for example, open a small electronics store on the spot.

What advice would you give to a smart, driven college student about to enter the "real world"? What advice should they ignore?

All sorts of people will give you this or that approach to your job. My advice is of a different sort: Good manners pay off big time. I assume you're smart and I assume you work hard. But being civil and decent and kind is the bedrock of career success, as well as personal fulfillment. (And if anybody tells you that's a "soft" idea, send 'em to me and I'll give 'em a "hard" punch in the nose.)

Oh, and two other things: First, become a superstar, all-pro listener. How? Work on it. It does not come naturally. Read up on it. Practice it. Have a mentor grade you on it. Second: Read. Read. Read. Read. In short, the best student wins, whether at age 21 or 51 or 101.

What are bad recommendations you hear in your profession or area of expertise?

They say: "Think big! Have a compelling vision!" I say: Think small. Do something super cool by the end of the day! I write about "excellence." Most see excellence as some grand aspiration. Wrong. Dead wrong. My two cents: Excellence is the next five minutes or nothing at all. It's the quality of your next five-minute conversation. It's the quality of, yes, your next email. Forget the long term. Make the next five minutes rock!

When you feel overwhelmed or unfocused, what do you do?

Walk. Walk. Walk. A 30-minute (or even 15-minute) out-of-the-office walk with no devices almost invariably clears my head.

My book *In Search of Excellence* got its de facto theme during a single 1977 meeting with Hewlett-Packard president John Young. He said the HP mantra was "MBWA." Translation: Managing By Wandering Around. It stands for being in touch, being human—and learning from everyone. Years ago, I worked with a wildly successful Nordstrom store manager. She said (approximately), "When I'm stuck or down, I stand up from my desk and take a 30-minute ramble on the floor. Just talking with our gang for a few minutes clears my head and unfailingly inspires me."

"The good, the painful — it is all a privilege."

BEAR GRYLLS
TW/IG: @BearGrylls
FB: /RealBearGrylls
beargrylls.com

BEAR GRYLLS is one of the most recognized faces of outdoor survival and adventure. Bear spent three years as a soldier in the British Special Forces, serving with 21 SAS. It was there that he perfected many of the skills he now showcases on television. His Emmy-nominated show *Man vs. Wild/ Born Survivor* became one of the most-watched programs on the planet with an estimated audience of 1.2 billion. On his hit NBC adventure show *Running Wild*, he takes some of the world's best-known stars on incredible adventures, including former president Barack Obama, Ben Stiller (page 135), Kate Winslet, Zac Efron, and Channing Tatum. He has authored 20 books, including the #1 best-selling autobiography, *Mud, Sweat & Tears*.

What is the book (or books) you've given most as a gift, and why? Or what are one to three books that have greatly influenced your life?

Rhinoceros Success by Scott Alexander. I read this at age 13, and it basically told me that life is tough and like a jungle, and that life rewards the rhinos who charge hard at their goals and never give up. And above all, not to follow the cows of life who drift aimlessly and suck purpose and joy out of the journey. I give it often to people I think would love or need it.

How has a failure, or apparent failure, set you up for later success? Do you have a "favorite failure" of yours?

I failed selection for the British SAS on my first attempt, and it ripped my heart out at the time. I had never given so much for anything and to fall short was soul-destroying. But I went back and tried a second time and eventually passed. Four out of 120 will generally make it, and they often say the best soldiers pass the second time. I like that. It tells me that tenacity matters more than talent, and in life, that is certainly true.

To prepare the second time around for SF selection I basically hit the hills even harder and trained with ever more intensity. A typical day was either a fast-paced mountain trek carrying 50 pounds for three hours max speed, or 60 minutes of bodyweight circuits mixed with hill sprints. Basically, I got mad with focus.

Failure means struggle, and it is struggle that has always developed my strength.

If you could have a gigantic billboard anywhere with anything on it, what would it say and why?

Simple one for me to answer: "Storms make us stronger." If I had one message for young people embarking on life, it would be this. Don't shy away from the hard times. Tackle them head-on, move toward the path less trodden, riddled with obstacles, because most other people run at the first sign of battle. The storms give us a chance to define ourselves, to distinguish ourselves, and we always emerge from them stronger.

The other key is to be kind along the way. Kindness matters so much on that journey of endeavor. It is what separates the good from great.

In the last five years, what new belief, behavior, or habit has most improved your life?

Learning to enjoy the process, rather than always striving for the future. Sometimes in these jungles or deserts, I am desperately trying to get through it, do my best, work hard, work fast, and get back to my family. But I realized I was spending so much time dreading what was ahead, or striving to be out of where I was. Learning to embrace the moment changed a lot for me. The good, the painful—it is all a privilege. I figure that so many people never get to live beyond 30, so we are already the blessed.

When you feel overwhelmed or unfocused, what do you do?

Hold tight, focus the effort, dig deeper, and never give up. It isn't rocket science but it is hard, as most people, when it gets tough, start to look around for an excuse or a different tactic. Often, though, when it starts to get tough, all it requires is for you to get tougher and hold on. The magic bit is that when it gets like this, it often means you are near the end goal! One big heave of focus, dedication, and grit, and you often pop out the other end. Look around you, though, and you see that most people are gone— they gave up in that final bit of hurting.

"Courage over comfort."

BRENÉ BROWN
IG/FB: @brenebrown
brenebrown.com

DR. BRENÉ BROWN is a research professor at the University of Houston Graduate College of Social Work. Brené's 2010 TEDxHouston Talk, "The Power of Vulnerability," has been viewed more than 36 million times and is one of the top five most viewed TED Talks in the world. She has spent the past 14 years studying vulnerability, courage, worthiness, and shame. Brené is also the *New York Times* best-selling author of *Daring Greatly, The Gifts of Imperfection, Rising Strong,* and *Braving the Wilderness: The Quest for True Belonging and the Courage to Stand Alone.*

What is the book (or books) you've given most as a gift, and why? Or what are one to three books that have greatly influenced your life?

I give out a lot of books. My go-to list includes *The Dance of Anger* by Harriet Lerner (so helpful for couples in that "I'm screaming and he's/she's shutting down" cycle) and her new book, *Why Won't You Apologize?* (Turns out that most of us are pretty terrible apologizers—this really changed me.) For new parents, I love the Positive Discipline series by Jane Nelsen (empowering for kids and parents) and the Touchpoints series by T. Berry Brazelton (you really can't guide your children if you don't understand what's happening developmentally). I buy everyone on my team books a few times a year. Our next reads are *Stretch* by Scott Sonenshein and *Lead Yourself First* by Kethledge and Erwin.

If you could have a gigantic billboard anywhere with anything on it, what would it say and why?

"Courage over comfort." Just a simple reminder that there's nothing comfortable about being courageous. Everyone wants to be brave, but no one wants to be vulnerable.

What purchase of $100 or less has most positively impacted your life in the last six months (or in recent memory)?

Easy. My ten-foot iPhone charger from Native Union and my Fierce lip balm from Tata Harper.

What is one of the best or most worthwhile investments you've ever made?

Problem identification is always a sound investment of time, money, and energy. Einstein said, "If I had an hour to solve a problem, I'd spend 55 minutes thinking about the problem and five minutes thinking about solutions." It feels uncomfortable to spend time and resources trying to figure out exactly what the problem is—we want to jump to fixing way too fast. Most of us are plagued with action bias and really struggle to stay in problem identification. I've found that getting clear about what's wrong and why it's a problem is the best investment you can make at home or work.

In the last five years, what new belief, behavior, or habit has most improved your life?

Sleep. Diet, exercise, and work ethic don't hold a candle to how sleep can revolutionize the way you live, love, parent, and lead.

When you feel overwhelmed or unfocused, what do you do? What questions do you ask yourself?

Always these questions:

1. Sleep?
2. Exercise?

3. Healthy food?
4. Am I resentful because I'm not setting or holding a boundary?

How has a failure, or apparent failure, set you up for later success? Do you have a "favorite failure" of yours?

One of my biggest mistakes was not understanding or owning how involved I wanted and needed to be in my businesses. I convinced myself early on that I could "download ideas" and our kick-ass teams would execute against those ideas while I was off doing other things. I wanted to believe it because my time is so scarce. I research, write, speak, facilitate leadership programs, lead three businesses, and maintain nonnegotiable boundaries around my family time. It didn't work. I've got the best people in the world—they're committed, creative, and smart. But downloading ideas is not leading. The real work is the constant iteration, incorporating consumer feedback, troubleshooting, figuring out when to push and when to bail, and helping everyone reset after a setback and learn. I want and need to be involved in all of that. I want to rumble on how we pack a box and the note that comes with it. I want to see the photos we're going to use on the website—do they have emotional resonance and convey connection? Not being there created unnecessary frustration for all of us and, ironically, led to the worst kind of micromanaging on my part. Now I spend a lot of time with teams at the start of a project defining what "done" looks like, and I'm involved in their standups once a week. Team leads have access to me on Slack. Our roundup team has also worked to make sure that there's solid alignment between responsibility and authority for everyone. You can feel the shift. We're becoming more productive and effective than we've ever been and we're having fun. Key learning: Magical thinking is incredibly dangerous and will cost you more time, money, and energy than digging in ever will.

QUOTES I'M PONDERING

(Tim Ferriss: May 27–June 16, 2016)

"The simple willingness to improvise is more vital, in the long run, than research."

–ROLF POTTS
American travel writer and author of *Vagabonding*

"There is no way to happiness — happiness is the way."

–THICH NHAT HANH
Vietnamese Buddhist monk and Nobel Peace Prize nominee

"The reasonable man adapts himself to the world; the unreasonable one persists in trying to adapt the world to himself. Therefore all progress depends on the unreasonable man."

–GEORGE BERNARD SHAW
Irish playwright, Nobel Prize recipient

"Perfection is not when there is no more to add, but no more to take away."

–ANTOINE DE SAINT-EXUPÉRY
French writer, author of *The Little Prince*

> **"I ask myself, 'What's the most loving thing I can do for myself and others right now?' Then I get to it."**

LEO BABAUTA
TW: @zen_habits
zenhabits.net

LEO BABAUTA is the founder of *Zen Habits*, a website dedicated to finding simplicity and mindfulness in the daily chaos of our lives. *Zen Habits* has more than two million readers, and *Time* magazine named it one of the "Top 25 Blogs" for 2009 and one of the "Top 50 Websites" for 2011. Leo is the author of *The Power of Less: The Fine Art of Limiting Yourself to the Essential . . . in Business and in Life, Essential Zen Habits: Mastering the Art of Change, Briefly,* and several other books.

What purchase of $100 or less has most positively impacted your life in the last six months (or in recent memory)?
I got a Manduka PRO black yoga mat for about $100 (on sale). It is such a heavy, luxurious mat that it encourages me to practice at home, which is frankly a miracle.

How has a failure, or apparent failure, set you up for later success? Do you have a "favorite failure" of yours?

In 2005, I was stuck—deeply in debt, overweight, addicted to junk food, no time for my family, couldn't stick to an exercise plan. I felt like an absolute failure. But this led to me researching habits and how to change them, and I put my entire being into making one single change. And then another. It led to my entire life changing, and to me helping others to change habits. It felt horrible, but it was one of the most incredible lessons of my life.

The first change I made was quitting smoking, which turned out to be one of the hardest changes I've made and I don't recommend starting with it. But I put everything I had into it, and I learned a lot about changing habits. The next change was adding running—as a way to cope with stress after I quit smoking—and to start getting healthier. After that, I became vegetarian and started meditating.

If you could have a gigantic billboard anywhere with anything on it, what would it say and why?

"You are good enough, just as you are. Breathe, and relax into the moment."

What is an unusual habit or an absurd thing that you love?

I am absurdly fond of minimalist aesthetics. I get a ridiculous amount of pleasure from an empty room with just one piece of furniture and a plant. Sometimes I fantasize about owning nothing but an empty room!

In the last five years, what new belief, behavior, or habit has most improved your life?

Zen Buddhism has profoundly influenced me—not only in meditation and mindfulness, but in believing in the pureness of experience, in my inter-connectedness with all other beings, in my wanting to devote my life to helping others be happy. I'm now devoted to helping others turn suffering into mindfulness, openness, and joy.

The book I started with is *Zen Mind, Beginner's Mind* by Shunryu Suzuki, which is a classic. But I think the best book for beginners is *What Is Zen?: Plain Talk for a Beginner's Mind* by Norman Fischer. It's a wonderful intro and answers most of the questions I had when I started.

What advice would you give to a smart, driven college student about to enter the "real world"?

Embrace uncertainty, groundlessness, and fear as the place where you'll really learn and grow. Go into that place, rather than shrinking from it. It'll help you overcome procrastination, social anxiety, fear of launching your own business or pursuing your dreams, fear of failure and ridicule, and more. Those fears will still be there, but you'll find the deliciousness in them.

When you feel overwhelmed or unfocused, what do you do?

I drop into my breath and the sensations I'm feeling in my body. When I feel overwhelmed, I ask myself, "What does this feeling feel like as a bodily sensation, right now?" Not a narrative about my feeling, but actual sensations in my body. I try to stay with those sensations for as long as possible and be curious about and open to them. This works with fear, distraction, procrastination, frustration, and more. Once I've meditated on this, I ask myself, "What's the most loving thing I can do for myself and others right now?" Then I get to it.

"For me [meditation] is a great safe place where I can go deeply into my own trauma and drama, free from fear — decreasing being reactive and clearing space to be proactive."

MIKE D
IG: @miked
beastieboys.com

MICHAEL "MIKE D" DIAMOND is a rapper, musician, songwriter, drummer, and fashion designer, best known as a founding member of the pioneering hip-hop group The Beastie Boys. The Beastie Boys have been included in *Rolling Stone*'s "Top 100 Greatest Artists of All Time" and were inducted into the Rock and Roll Hall of Fame in April 2012. Eminem said, "It's obvious to anyone how big of an influence the Beastie Boys were on me and so many others." The Beastie Boys disbanded in 2012 after the death of one of the group's founding members, Adam "MCA" Yauch. Mike currently hosts a Beats 1 radio show, *The Echo Chamber.*

How has a failure, or apparent failure, set you up for later success? Do you have a "favorite failure" of yours?

Wow, there are so many instances of moments that either didn't go as we wanted at all as a band—ideas imagined and not realized, shows that seemed to last a lifetime because nothing would click—but perhaps the most "liberating" failure I can think of is an album of ours: *Paul's Boutique*. Over time it turned out not to be such a failure, as a lot of people cite it as their favorite of our albums. But it does make us wonder what all of these people were so busy with at the time of its release that they couldn't make it to a record store (really a CD store at the time) to part with $9.99.

So let's set this up correctly and give some context: *Paul's Boutique* was a huge commercial disappointment. We are talking major floperino here. *Licensed To Ill* had sold millions and millions of copies, and its songs and videos had been in microwave rotation for many months. A lot of people were waiting for us to just go away, to prove to them and the world that it was all a fluke. But on the other side, there were many people at a big record label penciling in *Paul's Boutique* to the good in their profit line. Waiting for lightning to strike twice. Oops, their bad! Sadly, with no repeat anthem, videos, or even remotely similar songs to *Licensed To Ill*, *Paul's* was too different for anyone except for a core contingent of freaks and weirdos: our true fans. At first, we were sort of in disbelief. We had worked so hard and believed in what we were making, and it was pretty much all over just some weeks after being released. No big hit songs or videos or arena tours. It was heartbreaking to let go of something that we had put all this effort and time into. So many words written, so many studio hours spent on so many vocal takes, endless different versions of songs, hours and hours of digital samples fussed over, not to mention the many Ping-Pong matches and air hockey games. We were gutted.

On the bright side of things, the album was critically well received. But this didn't seem to do much for its popularity. After a bunch of the Capitol Records top staff had been let go, largely due to this very flop, we went to the label to plead our case, asking them to still focus on marketing our record. No dice. They had other things to focus on.

So why was this liberating? Because it allowed us to fully retreat from the world. To withdraw and just spend time. All that was left was the three of us. Our relationship and trust in each other. Hanging out and having very little to do. Waking up, having breakfast, smoking pot, buying some records, listening to those records, and maybe playing some music. We now had total artistic freedom. Nobody, including us, was wed to any commercial expectation. This gave us the creative freedom to make whatever we wanted, completely free from fear and expectation. In hindsight this was a *huge* gift.

Of course, this story isn't totally fair. Like I said, *Paul's Boutique* was not only critically well received but, over time, people caught on in their own way on their own time, and it went on to sell millions of copies, which is still huge for three white kids from NYC who were a hardcore punk band that decided to rap.

In the last five years, what new belief, behavior, or habit has most improved your life?

For me, Transcendental Meditation is the biggest gift that keeps on giving. The older I get, the more I realize you never know when and where different lessons and practices are going to come from. I was on a surf trip on a boat in the middle of the Indian Ocean. The waves were firing, and things couldn't have been better in a lot of ways. I was super fortunate and grateful to be where I was, but I was going through a great deal of emotional turmoil and drama. Thankfully, the core of the people on this trip were TM practitioners. I immediately felt the benefit before being given a proper initiation. As soon as I got back home, I was in the studio working on a record. Not only did I learn and get initiated, all of us working on the record did as well. It made it a more powerful shared experience. And practically speaking, it made it more viable to get the practice time in when working long hours in the studio. It is amazing what a great "reset" TM can be. The structural demands of TM are very doable in the context of our current lives. Twenty minutes when we get up and 20 minutes toward the end of the day when we really need it anyway. For me, it is a great safe place where I can go deeply into my own trauma and drama, free from fear—decreasing being reactive and clearing space to be proactive. My relationships with everyone benefit. Sometimes my kids are like, "Dad, why are you spending this time meditating?" But I am much better in my relationship as a dad with it. I'm much better in all my relationships with it.

When you feel overwhelmed or unfocused, what do you do?

Interesting question. My first tendency, especially when working on a song or music, is to keep going. Keep banging my head against the wall, hoping for a breakthrough, even if my poor head really f-ing hurts! *But*, I think with maturity (I am scared to admit to any maturity at all) I have learned that a reset is needed at times. This can take a few different forms. Here are some that have helped me:

TM: See above. Especially when I am overwhelmed, overtired, or just can't figure something out and am becoming increasingly frustrated, spending 20 minutes doing TM can help me completely refocus and recharge. It often allows me to see things differently and be productive for hours, which equals a good return on investment.

Surfing: I am a lucky duck. I live in Malibu, California, with waves within walking distance. I spend a good amount of my time surfing with my kids all around the world, and it is worth every damn minute. I am well aware that most people are landlocked and are not afforded this luxury, but surf offers me a great reset. I instantly become so much more grateful and appreciative, and by being in nature's playground, it offers perspective. The ocean and the wave are in control, not me. I am just a little speck trying to breathe and do the best I can.

Hanging with my kids: They won't be kids forever, that is for damn sure! And sometimes I need a distraction from them! But I am always so grateful when we have amazing experiences and conversations together. It really does put things into perspective. One thing I am so grateful to be able to model: I was always included in my parents' and their adult friends' conversations, and I try to practice the same with my kids, valuing their ideas and thoughts.

Walking my dogs: By just taking a break and walking my dogs, I can usually figure a couple of things out.

"Ask yourself, 'Would you say yes if this were next Tuesday?' It's so easy to commit to things that are weeks or months out, when your schedule still looks uncluttered."

ESTHER DYSON
TW: @edyson
wellville.net

ESTHER DYSON is the founder of HICCup and chairman of EDventure Holdings. Esther is an active angel investor, best-selling author, board member, and advisor concentrating on emerging markets and technologies, new space, and health. She sits on the boards of 23andMe and Voxiva (txt-4baby), and is an investor in Crohnology, Eligible API, Keas, Omada Health, Sleepio, StartUp Health, and Valkee, among others. From October 2008 to March 2009, Esther lived in Star City outside Moscow, Russia, training as a backup cosmonaut.

What is the book (or books) you've given most as a gift, and why? Or what are one to three books that have greatly influenced your life?

The Biology of Desire: Why Addiction Is Not a Disease by Marc Lewis. Addiction is short-term desire. Purpose is long-term desire.

Scarcity: Why Having Too Little Means So Much by Sendhil Mullainathan and Eldar Shafir. An explanation of scarcity for rich intellectuals, showing how poor people do stupid things for lack of money, while rich people do stupid things for lack of time.

From Bacteria to Bach and Back: The Evolution of Minds by Daniel C. Dennett. How consciousness arises, and how much it depends on a sense of past, present, and future (plus a lot of other interesting insights).

How has a failure, or apparent failure, set you up for later success? Do you have a "favorite failure" of yours?

Many over the years! Most recently, one of the five communities my ten-year nonprofit project Way to Wellville was working with just wasn't engaged—like someone who hires a personal trainer but just never makes it to the gym. We politely cut ties and selected a different community. Not only has that worked out, but it has made it clear to everyone—the communities, potential funders, and partners, et al.—that we hold ourselves and others accountable. With this move, we honored those communities who are willing to take risks and work hard to make a difference.

If you could have a gigantic billboard anywhere with anything on it, what would it say and why?

"Always make new mistakes!" I actually get royalties of about $50 per year from Quotable Quotes for this one.

What is an unusual habit or an absurd thing that you love?

Well, I don't think it's absurd—space travel. I hope to retire on Mars, but not too soon! I have trained as a backup space tourist, for six months in Star City, Russia.

In the last five years, what new belief, behavior, or habit has most improved your life?

I started using Audible and now I'm reading books regularly again. (Or perhaps the 30-year period when I was *not* reading books should go into the "failure" question.) It's great. Even as I work in the weeds with Wellville, I'm reading intellectual books about poverty, neuroscience, nutrition, complex systems, addiction, and the like. The two strands — highly abstract and intimately, personally concrete with real humans — complement one another.

What advice would you give to a smart, driven college student about to enter the "real world"?

Always take jobs for which you are not qualified; that way you will inevitably learn something. And do not drop out of college unless you truly have a better alternative. Some notable individuals have succeeded in spite of doing so, but it's a serious obstacle to overcome for most people.

In the last five years, what have you become better at saying no to?

I have become slightly better at avoiding conferences that are fun but not terribly useful.

My tip: Ask yourself, "Would you say yes if this were next Tuesday?" It's so easy to commit to things that are weeks or months out, when your schedule still looks uncluttered.

When you feel overwhelmed or unfocused, what do you do?

[When I'm] overwhelmed: Ask, "What is the worst thing that could happen?" Fear of the unknown is generally far worse than fear of something specific. If it's not the death of yourself or those you are responsible for, there's probably some reasonable set of options you should consider calmly and thoughtfully.

"I started my first business with $200.... I learned far more about business from that $200 than from a debt-inducing MBA."

KEVIN KELLY
TW: @kevin2kelly
kk.org

KEVIN KELLY is "senior maverick" at *Wired* magazine, which he co-founded in 1993. He also co-founded the All Species Foundation, a non-profit aimed at cataloging and identifying every living species on Earth, and the Rosetta Project, which is building an archive of all documented human languages. In his spare time, he writes best-selling books and serves on the board of the Long Now Foundation. As part of the last, he's investigating how to revive and restore endangered or extinct species, including the woolly mammoth. He might be the real-world "most interesting man in the world." His latest book is *The Inevitable: Understanding the 12 Technological Forces That Will Shape Our Future*.

What is the book (or books) you've given most as a gift, and why? Or what are books that have greatly influenced your life?

Here are the books that altered my behavior, changed my mind, redirected the course of my life. These books have been levers for me (and others). I list them in the order they entered my life.

Childhood's End by Arthur C. Clarke: For a kid growing up without TV in the boring enclaves of suburbia in the '50s and early '60s, science fiction opened up my universe. I devoured any and all science fiction our public library contained. Arthur C. Clarke's stories in particular birthed a lifelong interest in science and a deep respect for the power of imagination. This story of a singularity always stuck with me as something to prepare for.

The Whole Earth Catalog by Stewart Brand (page 332): When I was 17, this big catalog of choices gave me permission to have my own ideas, make my own tools, and unabashedly follow my two loves of art and science. I used it to invent my own life. Decades later, I worked at the *Catalog* in my first real job.

The Fountainhead by Ayn Rand: I got sucked into reading this over-the-top manifesto of self-reliance during finals of my first year of college. By the end of the book, I decided to drop out of school. I never returned. It was the best decision of my life.

Leaves of Grass by Walt Whitman: While reading this classic poetic ode to America and possibilities ("I am multitude!") my gasket blew, and I became seized with an unstoppable urge to travel. I set the book down and bought a ticket to Asia. I roamed there, off and on, for eight years. It was my university.

The Story of My Experiments with Truth by Mahatma Gandhi: This autobiography of Gandhi curiously led me to Jesus. Gandhi's stance of radical honesty prompted me to attempt the same. It started my spiritual awakening.

The Bible: Reading this all the way through, beginning to end, shattered all expectations I had of such a foundational text. It was weirder, stranger, more disturbing, and more powerful than I was led to believe. I've read it through several times more and it never fails to disturb me, in good ways and bad.

Gödel, Escher, Bach by Douglas R. Hofstadter: I was amazed and impressed by the brilliance of *GEB* when I first read it, but it didn't alter my life at first. However, over the years, I kept finding myself returning to its insights, and each time I would arrive at them at a deeper level. Now I find these insights as my own thoughts, and I realize I now see the world through a similar lens.

The Ultimate Resource by Julian Simon: Another book whose influence took time to establish itself in my view. Simon's clarifying insight — that mind and intelligence can overcome any physical limitations, and are therefore the only scarce resource — has become a big idea that colors much of what I look at today.

Finite and Infinite Games by James P. Carse: This small, short book provided me a vocabulary to think about the meaning of life — not just my life, but all life! It gave me a mathematical framework for my own spirituality. As it says, the game is to keep the game going forever, to rope all beings into playing infinite games versus finite (win-lose) games, and to realize that there is only one infinite game.

What purchase of $100 or less has most positively impacted your life in the last six months (or in recent memory)?

I recently upgraded to a team/family plan for 1Password, the password management tool. Now all the security, ease, and relief of a good password system can be shared with all my family and people I work closely with. We can safely share appropriate passwords.

What is one of the best or most worthwhile investments you've ever made?

I started my first business with $200. I bought an ad in the back of *Rolling Stone* magazine advertising a catalog of budget travel guides by mail for $1. Neither the catalog nor the book inventory existed. If I hadn't gotten enough orders I would have returned the money [from any orders], but it all worked out by bootstrapping. I learned far more about business from that $200 than from a debt-inducing MBA.

In the last five years, what have you become better at saying no to?

Whenever I am trying to decide whether to accept an invitation, I just pretend it is going to happen tomorrow morning. It is easy to say yes to something happening six months from now, but it has to be super fantastic to get me to go tomorrow morning.

In the last five years, what new belief, behavior, or habit has most improved your life?

I avoid working on things that someone else could do, even if I enjoy doing it and would get paid well to do it. I try to give my best ideas away in the hope that someone will do them, because if they do them, that means I was not the only one who could have. I encourage competitors for the same reason. In the end, I'm left with projects that only I can do, which makes them distinctive and valuable.

What advice would you give to a smart, driven college student about to enter the "real world"? What advice should they ignore?

Don't try to find your passion. Instead master some skill, interest, or knowledge that others find valuable. It almost doesn't matter what it is at the start. You don't have to love it, you just have to be the best at it. Once you master it, you'll be rewarded with new opportunities that will allow you to move away from tasks you dislike and toward those that you enjoy. If you continue to optimize your mastery, you'll eventually arrive at your passion.

"Be polite, on time, and work really fucking hard until you are talented enough to be blunt, a little late, and take vacations and even then ... be polite."

ASHTON KUTCHER
FB: /Ashton
aplus.com

ASHTON KUTCHER is a prominent actor, investor, and entrepreneur. He began his acting career in the popular sitcom *That '70s Show*, which aired for eight seasons, and he starred in the comedy and box office hit *Dude, Where's My Car?* He is a renowned technology investor, with investments in Airbnb, Square, Skype, Uber, Foursquare, Duolingo, and others. He is currently a co-founder and chairman of the board of A Plus, a digital media company devoted to spreading the message of positive journalism, where he leads strategic partnerships with brands and influencers. In 2009, he became the first Twitter user to reach one million followers, and he now has close to 20 million.

What is the book (or books) you've given most as a gift, and why? Or what are one to three books that have greatly influenced your life?

The Happiest Baby on the Block by Harvey Karp. If you want to be a hands-on parent and also have some version of a career, this book is gold. I usually send it with another book called *The Sleepeasy Solution*, written by Jennifer Waldburger and Jill Spivack.

The brainy book I seem to be sharing or talking about the most lately is *Sapiens* by Yuval Noah Harari (page 554). The more that I study people and the way systems work, the more I realize that it's all made up. It's easy to spout philosophies, or quote books, well-known people, or doctrines as if they are somehow of more credence than others, but the deeper you dig, the more you realize we are all just standing on piles of collective fiction. This book does a great job of illustrating that point.

How has a failure, or apparent failure, set you up for later success? Do you have a "favorite failure" of yours?

When I was 18, I went to jail and was charged for a third-degree burglary felony offense (thankfully, I got a deferred judgment, which expunged it from my record, so I can still vote and own a firearm). The shame of that event pushed me to prove, to everyone who judged me, that I wasn't *that* guy. Because of this event, I took risks that I never would have taken otherwise, because I knew that the low of failure would never match the low of shame.

If you could have a gigantic billboard anywhere with anything on it, what would it say and why?

"Shit or get off the pot." Too many people are waiting to get shit set up just right so they can do the thing they are gonna do. It's time.

Or: "Posting about it isn't doing anything. It's just like talk . . . it's cheap!" Too many people think they are supporting a cause, and the only thing they are doing is posting about it on social media. Doing something is doing something, everything else is just talk.

In the last five years, what new belief, behavior, or habit has most improved your life?

I finally started to value sleep. I've realized that if I don't sleep responsibly, I'm performing below optimal state in [nearly] every aspect of life.

When you feel overwhelmed or unfocused or have lost your focus temporarily, what do you do?

Take a walk or run. Have sex. Or eat. Then I make lists.

Generally the cure for feeling overwhelmed is getting to a state of appreciation. Walking helps you appreciate the world around you. Running helps you appreciate oxygen, health, life. Sex . . . I mean, come on, it's sex. Food is really just to make sure that you aren't hangry. And making lists brings organization to the chaos and generally turns big things into little actionable things.

What advice would you give to a smart, driven college student about to enter the "real world"?

Be polite, on time, and work really fucking hard until you are talented enough to be blunt, a little late, and take vacations and even then . . . be polite.

QUOTES I'M PONDERING

(Tim Ferriss: June 24–July 15, 2016)

"Love of bustle is not industry."

–SENECA
Roman Stoic philosopher, famed playwright

"Service to others is the rent you pay for your room here on earth."

–MUHAMMAD ALI
Legendary American professional boxer and activist

"There are many things of which a wise man might wish to be ignorant."

–RALPH WALDO EMERSON
American essayist, leader of the
19th-century transcendentalist movement

"If you don't make mistakes, you're not working on hard enough problems. And that's a big mistake."

–FRANK WILCZEK
American theoretical physicist, Nobel Prize winner

"Sometimes you need to allow life to save you from getting what you want."

BRANDON STANTON
IG: @humansofny
FB: /humansofnewyork
humansofnewyork.com

BRANDON STANTON is the creator of the #1 *New York Times* best-selling books *Humans of New York, Humans of New York: Stories,* as well as the children's book, *Little Humans of New York*. In 2013, he was named one of the "30 Under 30 People Changing the World" by *Time* magazine. Brandon has told stories from around the world in collaboration with the United Nations, and was invited to photograph President Obama in the Oval Office. His photography and storytelling blog, *Humans of New York,* is followed by more than 25 million people on several social media platforms. He is a graduate of the University of Georgia and lives in New York City.

How has a failure, or apparent failure, set you up for later success? Do you have a "favorite failure" of yours?

At the time I was fired from my trading job, I was convinced that I wanted to be a successful bond trader. Sometimes you need to allow life to save you from getting what you want.

In the last five years, what new belief, behavior, or habit has most improved your life?

Be very careful with the moral high ground. It helps to resolve conflict when you realize that everyone has different moral codes, and very few people intentionally make immoral decisions. Chase Jarvis once told me: "Everyone wants to see themselves as a good person." No matter how egregious the crime, the criminal usually has a reason for viewing it as morally acceptable.

What are bad recommendations you hear in your profession or area of expertise?

The most baffling tendency I've found in media is the pressure to "follow what works." My main motivation as an artist has always been to create something different. I think the most that any of us can achieve is to find a way to say something new. But this type of thinking is rarely rewarded when it's time to publish. Newness is seen as a liability. Publishers want something that has been proven to work. This means that the best art will always be the riskiest.

"When 99 percent of your life is your work, either you are really bad at what you do or you are completely off balance with the rest of your life; neither is something to be proud of."

JÉRÔME JARRE
TW/FB/SC/YT: @jeromejarre

JÉRÔME JARRE dropped out of business school at age 19 and moved to China. After failing in six startups, he focused all of his energy on cracking social media, and within 12 months, his videos about happiness and challenging fears reached 1.5 billion views, making him a pioneer of the mobile video industry. In 2013, Jérôme co-created the first mobile-only advertising agency with Gary Vaynerchuk (page 215) and helped advise some of the largest companies in the world, pairing influencers with brands. In 2017, after supporting local NGOs across the globe, Jérôme united 50 of the largest mobile influencers through LOVE ARMY, which raised $2.7 million for the drought in Somalia and spent every penny directly on the ground.

What is the book (or books) you've given most as a gift, and why? Or what are one to three books that have greatly influenced your life?

Propaganda by Edward Bernays, along with the documentary *The Century of the Self*. This book opened my eyes to the marketing industry in a time when I was blindly playing my role in it. Essentially, Edward Bernays is the ancestor of the entire marketing space, he is the father of all the marketing gurus and agencies. He became fascinated at the beginning of the last century by what Hitler's army had created—a complete illusion, "propaganda" that millions of people in Europe believed. So he moved to New York and decided to apply this technique to business. And because of the bad reputation of the word "propaganda," he renamed it "public relations" and created the first PR firm in America.

Unfortunately for humanity, he was choosing his clients based on how much money they were willing to give him, like 99.9 percent of the agencies today. So he ended up helping the pork industry by convincing people that bacon for breakfast made a man stronger, and he helped the tobacco industry by making cigarettes the symbol of the women's rights movement.

I am passionate about the life of Bernays because he did everything wrong. He chased money over purpose. Fame over impact. And he had massive regrets on his deathbed. I read that, on his deathbed, he was preaching against the use of tobacco. I know the marketing and PR industry is not going anywhere, and it's probably too late to reverse the effect this guy and all the marketing gurus have had on the world, but my hope is one day Bernays' books and the documentary on his life will be the first things students have to read and watch in business/marketing school. Right now, his life is being ignored by everyone for a very specific reason: It is hard to look at yourself in the mirror. I recall speaking about Bernays' life and legacy at a marketing conference in Germany. The organizers were furious —they were hoping I would give them tools to sell products on Snapchat to "millennials."

What purchase of $100 or less has most positively impacted your life in the last six months (or in recent memory)?

I spent four dollars to park near a beautiful lake in Oregon. I took a swim and had a trillion-dollar moment with the water.

How has a failure, or apparent failure, set you up for later success? Do you have a "favorite failure" of yours?

Most of what I do looks like a failure at first. When I dropped out of business school to create my first startup, 75 percent of the people I knew thought I was going to regret it all my life, and some even said that I would end up homeless. When I quit my struggling tech startup to start making videos online, everyone around me saw it as a shameful escape and a waste of my time. When I quit the influencer marketing agency Gary Vaynerchuk and I co-created to pursue using social media for good instead, everyone thought I was completely crazy and losing not only my mind but a huge source of income and a guaranteed future. Turns out they were the best decisions of my life. Because each one of those difficult decisions that looked like failures (at first) took me a bit closer to my real self. Each one of them empowered the real me. Each one of them woke me up from the illusion. At this point, I can see a clear pattern of rejection every time I try to get closer to my real self, so the feeling of "looking like a failure" has become more of a fuel than a burden.

If you could have a gigantic billboard anywhere with anything on it, what would it say and why?

Somehow having an audience on social media feels like having a giant bill-board for millions of people every day. I wish we could all start seeing it that way. I know so many people, for example, who were against Trump but were talking about him, criticizing, on their social every day. Would you put up a giant billboard of someone you don't want to see elected? Probably not. We truly don't understand social media. A good book that would help us is *Understanding Media* by Marshall McLuhan. It should be the online behavior bible of the 21st century. We all use media 24/7 but most of us have never truly studied it.

Back to your question: I would like two billboards. One for something I tell myself when I have a difficult decision to make that goes against the odds. And it is "Make yourself proud." I think we spend too much of our time trying to please everyone. And we forget that it's all already within. Your instinct, your inner child, your soul, all of those know what's good for you and the world. The public opinion of your friends and strangers online, not so much.

The second is a quote from a very special man, Christopher Carmichael, "You are 99 years old, you are on your deathbed, and you have a chance to come back to right now: what would you do?" I have used this one many times when faced with difficult questions. When I met him in China seven years ago, I didn't speak any English. So he gave me a couple of books to read to practice and get used to the English language. One of the books was *The 4-Hour Workweek*. I read it so many times to practice that I think I was speaking a bit like you [Tim] for a while.

What is one of the best or most worthwhile investments you've ever made?

Four years ago, just before Vine was about to take off, I decided to pursue it full-time. If I wanted to make it happen, I needed to leave Toronto where I was living and move to New York. New York is one of the prime cities for marketing/advertising, and I had this desire to create the first mobile influencer marketing firm. So I took a leap of faith and asked my business partners at the time how much money was available for me to move to New York. We had nothing. But one of our associates said I could borrow $400 from him. Imagine that—moving to New York City with $400. I knew nobody in the entire United States. All I knew was that I felt a call to go, and I had to trust my gut. I booked a bus ticket from Toronto to New York for $60. I slept on the floor of a friend of a friend of a friend. And here I was, "living" in New York.

Within seven days, Gary Vaynerchuk and I started GrapeStory, the first mobile-only influencer agency. I was so broke and didn't want Gary to know, so I started sleeping at the office of his company VaynerMedia, showering at the nearby gym, eating the leftovers that his team was forgetting in the company fridge. This lasted for months, and during that period my posts on Vine started to intensify. I was inspired by New York, so inspired that I didn't mind the struggle of being broke in such an expensive city. I think it took just about one year before I moved into an apartment. My goal had never been to grow a huge following, only to study the app by using it, but in New York I somehow found my style and the audience liked the content. In June 2013, just a couple weeks after moving to New York, I grew from 20,000 followers to 1 million in a month. That same month, our agency started being profitable. Even though we were making money, I kept sleeping at the office because I didn't really have the time to find a place, and I think I enjoyed for a while the hustle of sleeping on the floor in a Park Avenue South office in New York. It had its charm while it lasted. When I was able to take my first paycheck from the company, I bought the iPhone 5. That was the first time I had bought a new phone instead of secondhand. I did it as an investment to improve the image quality of my Vines. This was also a really good investment.

What is an unusual habit or an absurd thing that you love?

Not absurd, but it's something I didn't do for most of my life, and I don't see many friends doing it, so I assume it may not be very usual. Before eating, I pray. Not religiously, but more for setting intentions. I try to feel truly grateful for the food on my plate, especially if I happen to have an animal product on it. Maybe it's an egg or a chicken. Most of the time, my nutrition is plant-based, because it makes me feel the best and it costs the least to our planet and environment. But, for example, when I spent roughly four months in Somalia for our Love Army mission, we didn't have the luxury there to eat plants. We had to eat chickens. I am fine with eating animals when we have to, as long as it is done respectfully. Feeling gratitude for the animal's life is a good way to honor it. Everything we eat, be it a tomato or a chicken, is carrying light within. This light feeds us a lot more than the calories or protein. By acknowledging this light, by acknowledging the divinity of everything created by Mother Nature, we can feed ourselves twice. It's like when you are a kid and have a stuffed animal. They say stuffed animals only become real if you believe they are real. Same thing with the light in your food.

In the last five years, what new belief, behavior, or habit has most improved your life?

A belief: the belief that we are all mini gods. I mean this in the sense of creators, in a way that should not feed our ego but our consciousness. This means the entire universe is not just outside but also within us. We have unlimited power—the power to solve any problems facing us or facing others. We get to create our realities. It's a simple and small belief, but it can change the course of humanity. Being mini gods means we never lack. We know we already have everything. We don't need a million dollars. We don't need a trillion followers. We are complete. We are full. So full that we can give without counting. The day we will all start acting like mini gods is the day there will be peace in the world.

What advice would you give to a smart, driven college student about to enter the "real world"?

Don't trust the gurus, whether a marketing guru or a life guru. Anybody telling you he knows better is—more than anything—disempowering you, because he is placing you below and himself above. The guru separates himself from the rest of us. Anything that creates separation is an illusion. In reality, we are all united, all the same, all small parts of the same bigger thing, the universe. I am especially thinking of all the online personalities telling you to work harder, telling you they are working more than anybody. When 99 percent of your life is your work, either you are really bad at what you do or you are completely off balance with the rest of your life; neither is something to be proud of. Anytime you see someone preaching, remember that this is smoke and mirrors.

My other advice is to enter the real world as soon as you can. And by "real world," I don't mean for you to do an internship in a marketing company. I mean for you to get off of social media, to get out of the big cities, and to reconnect with what's real: nature, your soul, your inner child. Respect yourself. Most of the world is asleep today, playing a small role in a gigantic illusion. You don't have to be. You can choose a different life. It's all within. You will know the answers when you take the time to find yourself and trust yourself. If you are studying business/PR/marketing, then drop out today. The world is already full of marketers and businessmen. The world doesn't need more of that. The world needs healers and problem-solvers who use their hearts. Your heart is a million times more powerful than your brain.

What are bad recommendations you hear in your profession or area of expertise?

I have my feet in two industries right now, social media "influence" and the humanitarian industry. The worst recommendation that I hear in the influencer world is coming from marketing gurus who preach that if you build an audience and you start promoting brands to them, you can be extremely rich and successful. That's cute, but remember the story of Bernays. Promoting unethical or unhealthy companies for money is not success, it is actually called "corruption." Not corruption at the political level, like we are used to hearing, but corruption of your belief system. Corruption of your legacy. I know so many "influencers" who promote products they would never ever consume. But when the paycheck is half a million dollars for a couple Instagram photos, what would you do in their shoes?

I have been in those shoes, and I am proud to say I had to take some of my own medicine that day. Around the time I was starting to really question the advertising industry, two years ago, I was offered a million-dollar contract for a big Snapchat series for Sour Patch Kids. I told them I didn't eat those candies and would never eat them in front of the camera. They were fine with it. I even remember telling myself, "I would never ever eat one of those candies, even if their marketing director, who was signing the deal, asked me." That day was a difficult battle between the illusion of needing money and the incorruptible inner voice that told me to not do it. I turned down that million-dollar contract. I even recorded the scene of the meeting and put it on my YouTube. Gary Vee was in the room; he was negotiating that contract. I made myself proud that day. The worst advice anyone with an online audience can ever receive is from marketers. Gary says it himself, "marketers ruin everything."

When it comes to the humanitarian space, the worst advice you will ever receive is "Trust the big NGOs; they know what they are doing." As sad as it sounds, humanitarianism is, at this point, a giant industry. I have seen so many people raising money for a cause, hundreds of thousands of dollars, millions sometimes, and feeling like they aren't good enough to organize the relief mission themselves. They believe that if they trust a big, well-known NGO, things will be okay. Sure, it is a safe choice for you, because it totally drops the ball; suddenly your work is over. But is it really going to help the people who need it? Not so sure. When we raised money for Somalia, we decided to organize everything ourselves, to ask advice from local NGOs but to never drop the ball. And that's why our mission has been one of the most impactful relief missions ever organized in Somalia. Even though we had a relatively small amount of money compared to other big players in this space, we ended up having a massive impact. They will tell you good intentions are not enough, but I can promise you that if you keep your intentions pure through the entire process, then you will learn extremely fast and you will change lives, not only with the action but also with this intention. Humans who need food or water are still humans, and they can tell when the hand feeding them respects them and empowers them or disrespects them and treats them as a commodity. The NGOs that have been around for decades know that the humanitarian system is broken and that there are new, more efficient approaches.

For example, in many countries in Africa, like Somalia, mobile wire transfer is totally adopted by the population. This means there is no need to bring food to villages, but it is now simply possible to wire the money raised directly into people's phones. This has been ready for almost ten years but no NGO nor the UN will talk about it, as it scares them. Because if the humanitarian space suddenly gets disrupted like every other industry, it will bring massive change into those NGOs and for all the people that work in them. Think of what Uber did to taxi companies. When we discovered that all the infrastructure for this new model was ready, my team and I started raising and distributing money directly into people's phones. It was a game-changer for the people. They were empowered and could buy their own food like normal people. My point is this: give your money to people who need it, not to charities.

In the last five years, what have you become better at saying no to?

Somalia was a challenging time for me, as I had to separate my time between organizing our mission and updating/communicating with our 95,000 donors. I had to be very mindful of where I was putting my energy, and in this process, I started taking a different approach to my phone. Instead of considering every DM, every email as the most important thing in my life, I started looking at things as energy. Is this email empowering or is this email taking power out? I realized most of the time the answer was taking power out. Remember most people are asleep and forgetting their inner powers, so they think they need to take power out of others to feed themselves. I have now learned to say no to any of those solicitations.

When you feel overwhelmed or unfocused, what do you do?

I simply try to ground, and to ground you need to touch something real. This can be by swimming—water is real; by meditating—your heart is real; by being in contact with an animal—animals are real; or by enjoying a delicious meal by yourself under the sun. I love being alone with food. By eating slowly and putting so many intentions into my food, I have started to develop a stronger sense of taste than I used to have. So when I eat, I tend to get very emotional with the taste of the food. These types of little, real moments get you out of your head.

"Whether you think you can or you think you can't, you're right."
— Henry Ford

FEDOR HOLZ
TW: @CrownUpGuy
IG: @fedoire
primedgroup.com

FEDOR HOLZ is widely regarded as one of the best poker players in the modern era. In July 2016, he won his first World Series of Poker bracelet in the $111,111 High Roller for One Drop, securing $4,981,775. He was ranked by PocketFives as the best online multitable tournament player in 2014 and 2015. He has more than $23.3 million in earnings from live events. Fedor is the co-founder and CEO of Primed, a startup and investment company based in Vienna. Their first product is Primed Mind, a mindset coaching app, which helps you experience the same visualization and goal-setting techniques used to train the world's most notable poker phenoms.

What is the book (or books) you've given most as a gift, and why? Or what are one to three books that have greatly influenced your life?

Man's Search for Meaning by Viktor E. Frankl. His descriptions of his life in Nazi death camps, while everyone he loved around him perished, had a lasting impact on me and especially on how I decide what I want to spend my time on. [From it] I interpreted that we cannot avoid suffering, but we can choose how to cope with it, and that having meaning in our life is essential.

What purchase of $100 or less has most positively impacted your life in the last six months (or in recent memory)?

A Deuserband Original has been an amazing discovery for me. Especially when I spend long sessions in a chair, it feels great to stretch my arms and back, and it improves your posture.

How has a failure, or apparent failure, set you up for later success? Do you have a "favorite failure" of yours?

My "favorite failure" is that at the age of 18, I dropped out of university after nine months of studying to focus on poker. At that time, my family and most people around me were very concerned about me and my future. Another nine months of half-assing poker later, I moved out of my apartment, got rid of all of my belongings, and traveled the world to fully focus on poker. I met two great guys on my travels, moved in with them in Vienna, and in the next nine months made my first million dollars playing online poker.

If you could have a gigantic billboard anywhere with anything on it, what would it say and why?

"Whether you think you can or you think you can't, you're right." —Henry Ford

That's hands down my favorite quote of all time. My core values in life are a positive mindset, focusing on your priorities, and being passionate and determined to reach your goals.

What is one of the best or most worthwhile investments you've ever made?

I only invest in people I strongly believe in. I've invested tens of thousands of dollars in my close poker friends and they turned it into millions. They are some of the best in the game now.

There are lots of different deals and structures. Generally there are two main options: 1) long-term staking: which means you bankroll someone and you split the profit about 50/50, and keep playing until you're profiting. 2) Buying shares: you buy 50 percent of the action in one tournament for 50 percent + x percent bonus (called "markup") of the buy-in. That's what I've been doing a lot and where I've been very successful. It's comparable to sports betting. You assume the ROI of a player in a tournament and have to beat the "rake" of paying him something extra: the markup. Most players charge markup because they believe they are winning and want to split that potential profit with investors. If it's too high, even though he's a winning player, you'll lose money on your investment in the long run. The optimal case is that it's a fair split between player and buyer. Fifty percent was an example. It could be any amount. My biggest win was turning $2,500 into $750K in one tournament with one of my closest friends.

Besides that, I've always spent a lot of money on all kinds of experiences and rarely on materialistic things.

What is an unusual habit or an absurd thing that you love?
I can think better when my hands are busy—that's why I'm constantly playing with and throwing around little toys like a fidget cube, spinner, ball, or [small microbead neck] pillow.

In the last five years, what new belief, behavior, or habit has most improved your life?
Especially recently, I strongly realized the value of asking the *right* questions. So many times we are just scratching the surface by exchanging these scripted sentences. Diving deeper and discovering *why* someone behaves the way he or she does and what motivates him or her has a lot more meaning to me. Specifically in conversations, really asking someone how they feel and why they think they behaved in a certain way gives you (and them) a very different perspective.

What are bad recommendations you hear in your profession or area of expertise?
"You just have to keep playing." There is a lot more to poker than just continuously playing. Try to understand all the different facets of it and give your mind time to recover by taking time off and doing other things you enjoy. It's about a lot of money, so it's key to be fresh and sharp. Don't overdo it.

When you feel overwhelmed or unfocused, what do you do?
I work with my mindset coach, Elliot Roe, and/or use our app Primed Mind. After ten minutes, I'm in the zone, recharged, and ready to focus on my upcoming challenges.

"Do no harm to others. Be true to yourself. To me, being a good human being, and the way to true inner happiness, is through altruistic actions, being mindful of others."

ERIC RIPERT
TW/IG: @ericripert
TW/IG: @lebernardinny
le-bernardin.com

ERIC RIPERT is recognized as one of the best chefs in the world. In 1995, at just 29 years old, he earned a four-star rating from *The New York Times*. Twenty years later and for the fifth consecutive time, Le Bernardin, where Eric is the chef and a co-owner, again earned the *New York Times'* highest rating of four stars, becoming the only restaurant to maintain this superior status for such a marathon length of time. In 1998, the James Beard Foundation named him Top Chef in New York City and in 2003, Outstanding Chef of the Year. In 2009, *Avec Eric*, his first TV show, debuted and ran for two seasons, earning two Daytime Emmy Awards. It returned for a third season on the Cooking Channel in 2015. Eric has also hosted the show *On the Table* on YouTube, which debuted in July 2012, and he has appeared in media worldwide. He is the author of the *New York Times* best-selling memoir *32 Yolks: From My Mother's Table to Working the Line*, *Avec Eric*, and several other books.

What is the book (or books) you've given most as a gift, and why? Or what are one to three books that have greatly influenced your life?

My two standby books to gift are *The Alchemist* by Paulo Coelho and *A Plea for the Animals* by Buddhist monk Matthieu Ricard. Easy to read, *The Alchemist* speaks of everyone having an ultimate goal in life, but most of us are too afraid to pursue it. The encouragement to fulfill your dreams is very inspirational! Reading *A Plea for Animals* raised many personal struggles for me. As a Buddhist, I've always been deeply conflicted between an appreciation for meat and fish as ingredients and taking responsibility for the death of another creature. Matthieu Ricard's staggering facts and passionate argument challenged me emotionally and intellectually.

Most recently, I've been gifting my memoir *32 Yolks*. It's an honor for me to share my experience, and I hope that it serves as a source of lessons for young chefs.

What purchase of $100 or less has most positively impacted your life in the last six months (or in recent memory)?

An orb of shungite stone. Its incredible protective and healing qualities—mental, emotional, spiritual, and physical—can be felt by even the most skeptical people. One benefit relevant for many of us today: it diffuses negative waves from electronics.

How has a failure, or apparent failure, set you up for later success? Do you have a "favorite failure" of yours?

At about 15, I was kicked out of school for poor performance and told that I would need to find a vocation. I remember sitting next to my mother, across from the headmaster, trying to look sad, but internally I was delighted! From a very young age, I had a passion for eating that I learned in my mother's kitchen. This "failure" meant I could attend culinary school at last! Vocational school led to training under some of the greatest chefs, which led to me becoming the chef that I am today, living my passion.

If you could have a gigantic billboard anywhere with anything on it, what would it say and why?

My billboard would say: "Do no harm to others. Be true to yourself." To me, being a good human being, and the way to true inner happiness, is through altruistic actions, being mindful of others. I believe that to find contentment and to be at peace with yourself, you must have a positive impact on anyone you interact with each day. You also must not allow others' negative energy to lessen or alter you; you should stay true to your beliefs.

I came across a quote by the Dalai Lama recently that deeply spoke to me and the way I wish to live my life: "Happiness is not something readymade. It comes from your own actions."

What is one of the best or most worthwhile investments you've ever made?

In the early 1990s, I read the Dalai Lama's *Cent éléphants sur un brin d'herbe*, which translates to "One Hundred Elephants on a Blade of Grass" and opens with the Dalai Lama's Nobel Prize speech. I was a young man searching for guidance and spirituality. . . . It was a revelation for me and started me on my journey to Buddhism.

What is an unusual habit or an absurd thing that you love?

In my pocket at almost all times, I carry with me a mini crystal Buddha statue or a stone with protective qualities.

In the last five years, what new belief, behavior, or habit has most improved your life?

Giving up diet sodas. I've switched to more teas—saffron, lotus—which give me the same energy but don't have the negative health side effects.

When you feel overwhelmed or unfocused, what do you do?

To avoid feeling overwhelmed or unfocused, I spend about one hour meditating each morning. It's taught me to make space for happiness and calm in my day. In stressful moments, I try to take distance from the situation, take time to reflect. Whatever the problem, I typically ask myself, "Am I able to make a difference right now?" If I don't see a clear way to make a positive impact, I reflect further. I think that patience in problem-solving can often be underrated.

[Elaboration from Cathy Sheary on Eric's team: "Eric practices different types of meditation [usually every morning], including Samatha when he needs to focus, and Vipassana, which is a guided meditation and can be more religious, which he might use to contend with any anger. He can practice in most environments, but it's usually in his meditation room. Sometimes it's in his office, and sometimes when he's walking."]

In the last five years, what have you become better at saying no to?

Five or six years ago, I decided that I was going to live my life in three parts —one-third for my business, one-third for my family, one-third for myself. The distinction and prioritization helps me to find balance and contentment in each area. It has become very easy to say no now. . . . If something does not add meaning or fun to one segment, then I don't participate.

What are bad recommendations you hear in your profession or area of expertise?

There's often a drive to open many restaurants very quickly, which some people correlate with success. The weak spot in any restaurant is consistency —you cannot be great one day, then be only okay the next. Attempting to manage multiple spaces and maintain the same caliber of service and food is nearly impossible. We could not run two Le Bernardins and have both be equally good. The more you divide your focus, the more each endeavor can suffer from your lack of attention.

"You do not have to earn love. You simply have to exist."

SHARON SALZBERG
TW: @SharonSalzberg
sharonsalzberg.com

SHARON SALZBERG has played a crucial role in bringing meditation and mindfulness practices to the West and mainstream culture since 1974, when she first began teaching. She is the co-founder of the Insight Meditation Society and the author of ten books, including the *New York Times* bestseller *Real Happiness,* her seminal work, *Lovingkindness,* and her new book, *Real Love: The Art of Mindful Connection.* Renowned for her down-to-earth teaching style, Sharon offers a secular, modern approach to Buddhist teachings, making them instantly accessible. She is a regular columnist for *On Being*, a contributor to *The Huffington*, and the host of her own podcast: *Metta Hour.*

How has a failure, or apparent failure, set you up for later success? Do you have a "favorite failure" of yours?

In my early teaching career I was too petrified to give lectures. The structure of our intensive meditation retreats is one where people meditate throughout the day, with question-and-answer sessions, small group and individual teacher contact, and a formal lecture each night. The first retreats I taught in this country, I couldn't give a single talk—my colleagues had to do them all.

This lasted for well over a year. I was afraid that in the middle of speaking, my mind would just go blank, and I would sit there, looking stunned, disappointing everyone. After a long time, I realized that people weren't sitting out there waiting to cruelly judge me. They also weren't sitting out there waiting to hear me expound on my incredible expertise. What they wanted more than anything else was a sense of connection, and I could provide that by being genuine and present. I realized that what I also wanted was connection, and I didn't need to be a perfect speaker for that to happen. If it hadn't been for my initial fear, I wouldn't have looked deeper, and I might not have learned as much about authenticity.

What is the book (or books) you've given most as a gift, and why? Or what are one to three books that have greatly influenced your life?

Zen Mind, Beginners Mind by Shunryu Suzuki greatly influenced my life. There is a line in there something like, "We practice (meditation) not to attain Buddhahood but to express it." Even though I first read it over 40 years ago, I still feel a thrill move through my body as I think about that line. I've often thought the best kind of teaching is an articulation of what we already know, but don't know how to put into words or, most crucially, how to live. From the first time I read it, I sensed the vital difference between practicing to get something you think you lack, and practicing to express the fullness of who you are.

If you could have a gigantic billboard anywhere with anything on it, what would it say and why?

"You are a person worthy of love. You don't have to do anything to prove that. You do not have to earn love. You simply have to exist." It's easy for us to confuse real love for ourselves with narcissism or conceit, but I think they are very different. Instead of the inner bleakness or hollowness narcissism is designed to conceal, I've seen that real love for myself comes from a sense of inner abundance or inner sufficiency. It comes from feeling whole, which is innate to us, hidden underneath our fears and cultural conditioning and self-judgments. So it's not going to take learning tennis or creating a video that goes viral or becoming a world-class chef to be worthy of love. Those are all great things, but we are worthy whether or not we accomplish them.

In the last five years, what have you become better at saying no to? What new realizations and/or approaches helped? Any other tips?

I've gotten better at saying no to invitations, though I still have a ways to go! I picked up this tip from a friend, who felt she could hardly ever say no when she really needed to. In her meditation, she consciously brought up situations where she might have better said no, and she looked at what was happening in her body as she replayed the questioning. She tuned into the sensations spiraling through her stomach up into her chest, restricting her breathing. It was almost a kind of panic, a visceral expression of "maybe they won't like me anymore." She learned the feeling of those sensations, and the next time she was at work, or with her family, and that very kind of question was asked and she felt those sensations beginning, she used that as her feedback to say, "I'll have to get back to you on that." With a little space, she could then say no. Awareness of the emotional expression in her body was key. I'm trying to follow in her footsteps.

When you feel overwhelmed or unfocused, what do you do?

I stop and ask myself, "What do you need right now in order to be happy? Do you need anything other than what is happening right now in order to be happy?" That orients me right away toward what I care about. I also try to remember to breathe. I've seen that if I feel overwhelmed, I freeze, and my breath gets quite shallow. "Just breathe" is also something I say to myself if I feel chaotic. Or I shift my attention to feel my feet against the ground. Mostly we tend to think of our consciousness residing up in our heads, behind our eyes. What I've learned I have to do is start by gently bringing my energy down, so I'm feeling my feet from my feet. Try it! It's a little weird at first, but consciousness doesn't have to be seen as limited to our heads, peering out at the world, disconnected. The more my awareness can pervade my body, the more I remember to breathe, the more focused I naturally become.

QUOTES I'M PONDERING

(Tim Ferriss: July 22–Aug. 12, 2016)

"Anything you build on a large scale or with intense passion invites chaos."

—FRANCIS FORD COPPOLA
Award-winning director, best known for *The Godfather*

"Do not seek to follow in the footsteps of the wise, instead, seek what they sought."

—MATSUO BASHŌ
Japanese poet of the Edo period

"The things you own end up owning you."

—CHUCK PALAHNIUK
American author, best known for *Fight Club*

"If you set your goals ridiculously high and it's a failure, you will fail above everyone else's success."

—JAMES CAMERON
Renowned Canadian director, best known for *Titanic* and *Avatar*

"I lived the first 33 years of my life actively trying to avoid failure. More recently, I've worried less about failing and more about not risking failure enough, because I'm reasonably sure that there's not a failure I can't survive."

FRANKLIN LEONARD
TW: @franklinleonard
IG: @franklinjleonard
blcklst.com

FRANKLIN LEONARD has been described by *NBC News* as "the man behind Hollywood's secret screenplay database, 'The Black List.'" In 2005, Franklin surveyed almost 100 film industry development executives about their favorite scripts from that year that had not been made into feature films. Since then the voter pool has grown to 500 film executives. Now, more than 300 Black List screenplays have been made as feature films. Those films have earned more than $26 billion in worldwide box office sales, have been nominated for 264 Academy Awards, and have won 48, including Best Pictures *Slumdog Millionaire, The King's Speech, Argo*, and *Spotlight*, and ten of the last 20 screenwriting Oscars.

How has a failure, or apparent failure, set you up for later success? Do you have a "favorite failure" of yours?

Arguably, the first three years of my career were a catalog of failed attempts at careers I thought that I might like: The congressional campaign I helped run was unsuccessful. My writing in the *Trinidad Guardian* newspaper was good but unremarkable. I was a mediocre analyst at McKinsey and Company. Those nonsuccesses led me to give Hollywood a shot, and ironically, my work at the Black List is, in many ways, a synthesis of helming a movement, driven by writing, that requires a real understanding of corporate systems and operations.

What is an unusual habit or an absurd thing that you love?

I'm not sure how unusual or absurd it is, but I'm a degenerate soccer fan. I play every Friday night in Los Angeles. I'm up at 4 A.M. on Saturday and Sunday mornings during the English Premier League season to watch every match. I play Fantasy Premier League religiously, and I often plan international travel around the opportunity to see big games live. Fundamentally, I love the game, but it's also about an unapologetic disconnect from everything that goes into my day job. Ironically, though, my sincere love of the game has bonded a number of professional relationships with folks who share my interest.

When you feel overwhelmed or unfocused, what do you do?

I give myself a day off (or, if a full day isn't possible, a few hours, or even a few minutes) with permission to not think about wherever I'm failing. That day usually includes some sort of strenuous activity and re-watching at least one of my favorite films (usually *Amadeus* and *Being There*, both, possibly unsurprisingly, films about how genius is found in unusual places).

I'll take a pickup soccer game wherever I can get it. I instinctively hate the gym, but it's both necessary and valuable as a way for me to keep fit and lose myself in physical pain as a distraction from the emotional pain that comes with being overwhelmed or unfocused. I'm also lucky enough to live blocks from Griffith Park in Los Angeles, so a long walk into the hills is easy.

In the last five years, what new belief, behavior, or habit has most improved your life?

There are probably two:

The absolute necessity of travel. I was an army brat. I didn't live in the same place for more than 12 months before I was nine years old, and I suspect that I have wanderlust as a consequence. I resisted it for at least a decade, trying very hard to focus on work as defined by being in my office and shuffling papers. Over the last three years, I've tried to say yes to every travel opportunity presented to me for work and commit to spending at least a month outside of the U.S. during the year. It's done extraordinary things for my mental health and ability to maintain perspective on what's important and not important when I'm back in the office grinding away.

Trusting that I can weather most failures that might befall me. I lived the first 33 years of my life actively trying to avoid failure. More recently, I've worried less about failing and more about not risking failure enough, because I'm reasonably sure that there's not a failure I can't survive. Even if the Black List blows up in my face tomorrow, I'm sure someone will offer me a job.

What are bad recommendations you hear in your profession or area of expertise?

The biggest one is that international audiences won't see films about people of color. It's particularly insidious, but it's reflective of a broader issue wherein Hollywood accepts conventional wisdom that is more convention than wisdom without interrogating whether there's any evidence to support those assumptions.

What advice would you give to a smart, driven college student about to enter the "real world"?

Try everything you think you might want to do professionally before accepting whatever backup plan you have in the back of your head but are very much hoping to avoid.

"The great majority of that which gives you angst never happens, so you must evict it. Don't let it live rent-free in your brain."

PETER GUBER
TW: @PeterGuber
LinkedIn Influencer: peterguber
peterguber.com

PETER GUBER currently serves as chairman and CEO of Mandalay Entertainment Group. Prior to Mandalay, he was chairman and CEO of Sony Pictures Entertainment. He has produced or executive produced (personally or through his companies) films that have garnered five Best Picture Academy Award nominations (winning for *Rain Man*) and box office hits that include *The Color Purple*, *Midnight Express*, *Batman*, *Flashdance*, and *The Kids Are All Right*. Peter is also co-owner and co-executive chairman of the 2015 and 2017 NBA Champions, the Golden State Warriors, an owner of the Los Angeles Dodgers, and an owner and executive chairman of Major League Soccer's Los Angeles Football Club (LAFC). Peter is a noted author whose works include *Shootout: Surviving Fame and (Mis)Fortune in Hollywood* and his most recent book, *Tell to Win: Connect, Persuade, and Triumph with the Hidden Power of Story*, which was an instant #1 *New York Times* bestseller.

How has a failure, or apparent failure, set you up for later success? Do you have a "favorite failure" of yours?

When I was a young executive at Columbia Pictures in the '70s, the company was ferociously trying to stop the onslaught of the video cassette industry, believing that the motion picture incumbency as producers and distributors of filmed content to movie theaters was threatened by this new challenge. I argued that this was a new way to reach audiences who could now time-shift content to their schedule and would only be a value-add to our business and to our audience. The executives had a narrow view of their offering. When they finally succumbed to seeing its value, they began to see it not as a time bomb but a treasure.

Later, all of the studios jumped at the proposition of a windfall when the folks who challenged their dominance offered to acquire their entire old libraries at the end of their theatrical and TV run for their exclusive distribution in packaged media. I argued vociferously not to take the money or to let them build a distribution system of great value off of our back, but rather to leverage our content to be in this new business. They went for the gold and gave up an enterprise that turned out to be the golden goose.

I never forgot that my failure was not convincing them that short-term thinking is not good in a marathon. Ironically, over two decades later as the CEO of Sony (who had acquired Columbia Pictures) I bought back the library and all distribution rights at an expensive ransom. I felt that controlling the content and the right to distribute it was critical to the vitality of our brand and enterprise.

If you could have a gigantic billboard anywhere with anything on it, what would it say and why?

I would need three billboards:

"Don't let the weight of fear weigh down the joy of curiosity." Fear is really false evidence appearing real.

"The great majority of that which gives you angst never happens, so you must evict it." Don't let it live rent-free in your brain.

"Attitude puts aptitude on steroids." Attitude is the soft stuff, but when the chips are down, as they so often are, it's the soft stuff that often counts.

What advice would you give to a smart, driven college student about to enter the "real world"?

The seminal change in the business from then to now is that a young person should view the career pyramid differently rather than traditionally. Put the point at the bottom where you are now (at the start of your career) and conceive your future as an expanding opportunity horizon where you can move laterally across the spectrum in search of an ever-widening set of career opportunities. Reinvent yourself regularly. See your world as an ever-increasing set of realities and seize the day.

"Your dreams are the blueprint to reality."

GREG NORMAN
IG: @shark_gregnorman
FB: /thegreatwhiteshark
shark.com

GREG NORMAN is widely known as the "Great White Shark" and has won more than 90 golf tournaments worldwide, including two Open Championships. He holds the distinction of defending his #1 position in the world golf rankings for 331 weeks. In 2001, he was inducted into the World Golf Hall of Fame with a higher percentage of votes than any other inductee in history. He currently serves as chairman and CEO of the Greg Norman Company, which has a diverse portfolio of well-established companies, including lifestyle-driven consumer products, golf course design, and asset-based debt lending. His philanthropic efforts have quietly raised more than $12 million for charities including CureSearch for Children's Cancer and the Environmental Institute for Golf, which promotes sustainability and environmental responsibility.

What is the book (or books) you've given most as a gift, and why? Or what are books that have greatly influenced your life?
The Way of the Peaceful Warrior by Dan Millman, Tools of Titans by Tim Ferriss, On China by Henry Kissinger.

The Way of the Shark as it provides a very open and honest view on the transitions that have taken place in my life. Part two coming soon . . .

If you could have a gigantic billboard anywhere with anything on it, what would it say?

"Your dreams are the blueprint to reality."

What is one of the best or most worthwhile investments you've ever made?

Investing in Cobra back in the early '90s. My $1.8 million investment earned me $40 million after the company was bought by Acushnet. I rolled that money back into my business. The decision was a no-brainer for three reasons:

1. My investment got me 12 percent of Cobra and the allocation of my investment was put to R&D. During this era, Callaway was the first to go to market with an oversize driver but neglected to follow up on oversize irons. We/Cobra decided to attack this virgin market immediately by producing oversize irons for men and women, and we catered for the senior player, which had been left neglected. This decision was a solid rocket booster for Cobra's massive growth in the marketplace.

2. I was to remain an endorsed player representing Cobra for years to come, receiving an annual payment that would quickly recoup my initial investment. So, my ROI was always guaranteed, leaving me with 12 percent of a company that had hyper growth.

3. I was the #1 player in the world during these halcyon times — a global player. So, fortunately for us, I was a needle-mover in regards to exposure in a sport that was booming in the '80s, hence product promotion and awareness.

What is an unusual habit or an absurd thing that you love?

I brush my teeth standing on one leg, alternating each time. It is great for your legs, core, and stabilization!

In the last five years, what new belief, behavior, or habit has most improved your life?

Traveling to Bhutan in December 2016 and discovering Buddhism, which is more than a religion. It's rather a way of life that is so rewarding.

What are bad recommendations you hear in your profession or area of expertise?

"It cannot be done."

When you feel overwhelmed or unfocused, what do you do?

First, I yell "FUCK!" as loud as I can! Then, I compartmentalize and DIN and DIP ("do it now" and "do it proper").

I also go to the gym to disappear into my alone time, to allow myself to self-analyze and decompress by removing the stress of the moment and day.

When I am on my ranch, long trail rides on my horse, Duke, are also very cathartic, as nature is a great therapist.

"If you dare, then you have already gotten further ahead than 99 percent of all the others."

DANIEL EK
TW/FB: @eldsjal
spotify.com

DANIEL EK is the co-founder and CEO of Spotify, the widely popular streaming platform, which has more than 140 million monthly active users. Daniel has been called "the most important man in music" by *Forbes* magazine. As a teenager, he created websites for businesses and ran web-hosting services out of his bedroom. He dropped out of college and worked for several web-based companies before founding Advertigo, an online marketing firm that he sold in 2006 to the Swedish company Tradedoubler. He then established Spotify with Tradedoubler's co-founder, Martin Lorentzon, and became CEO.

What is the book (or books) you've given most as a gift, and why? Or what are books that have greatly influenced your life?

> *Black Box Thinking: The Surprising Truth About Success*, by Matthew Syed. Since reading this book, I've literally incorporated

this approach to problem-solving into every day. I've always encouraged those around me not to be scared of failure because I believe it's the most valuable learning tool.

The Alchemist, by Paulo Coelho. I spent an inspiring evening with Paulo in Switzerland, around the time we were launching Spotify in Brazil. It was fascinating to talk to him about how this book came to be such a hit—he never backed down, and he allowed people to read it for free in order to then boost sales—much like how Spotify's freemium model was perceived in the early days.

The Minefield Girl, by Sofia Ek. My wife, Sofia, recently published her first book. I'm incredibly proud of her for all her hard work and dedication in writing this. I don't know how she did this while being a great mom to both our daughters. The book is about her experiences being a young Western woman living and doing business in a dictatorship, and it's a story of love and hustle in a land where nothing is what it appears to be.

Poor Charlie's Almanack, by Charles T. Munger. I've been enjoying Charlie Munger's speeches online for years; this is the ultimate collection of the best of them. Watching *Becoming Warren Buffett* on a recent flight reminded me how much of a legend Charlie is.

In the last five years, what new belief, behavior, or habit has most improved your life?

I like to take at least two of my meetings every day as a "walk and talk." Even if my meeting isn't with someone physically in the same location, I meet them on a Google Hangout on my phone and hold the screen in front of me as I walk, with headphones in. It helps me to focus and be inspired, plus the obvious health benefits.

How has a failure, or apparent failure, set you up for later success? Do you have a "favorite failure" of yours?

I dropped out of university to start my own company, helping businesses build websites. At the time, my friends and family thought I was mad. But my mother has been the person who's given me the security to do what I do today. Of course she would have preferred that I had gone to university and had a solid educational foundation to stand on. But most of all she says to me: "Do what you really feel like doing, and I'll be here for you no matter what." It's probably this support that's made me feel like there's nothing in the world that's impossible. You just have to dare to do it. If you dare, then you have already gotten further ahead than 99 percent of all the others.

What are bad recommendations you hear in your profession or area of expertise?

"Good things come to those who wait." If I'd listened to that, Spotify would never have become anything more than an idea. We had so many knock-backs in the early days. Bono once said to me, "Good things come to those who work their asses off and never give up." That speaks to me much more.

"Always ask: What am I missing? And listen to the answer."

STRAUSS ZELNICK
IG: @strausszelnick
zmclp.com
take2games.com

STRAUSS ZELNICK founded Zelnick Media Group (ZMC) in 2001, which specializes in private equity investments in the media and communications industries. He serves as CEO and chairman of the board of Take-Two Interactive Software, Inc., ZMC's largest asset and the video game developer of blockbuster hits including *Max Payne*, the *Grand Theft Auto* series, and *WWE 2K*. Strauss is also a director of Education Networks of America, Inc., and sits on the board of Alloy, LLC. Prior to forming ZMC, he was president and CEO of BMG Entertainment, at that time one of the world's largest music and entertainment companies with more than 200 record labels and operations in 54 countries. Strauss holds a BA from Wesleyan University, as well as an MBA from Harvard Business School and a JD from Harvard Law School.

What is the book (or books) you've given most as a gift, and why? Or what are one to three books that have greatly influenced your life?

How to Win Friends and Influence People, by Dale Carnegie, the founder of the business self-help movement. Archaic references and overweening title to the side, it's actually a great guide to leadership and salesmanship.

If you could have a gigantic billboard anywhere with anything on it, what would it say?

"Always ask: What am I missing? And listen to the answer."

In the last five years, what new belief, behavior, or habit has most improved your life?

Exercising seven to 12 times weekly, in a diverse and disciplined way, often with a group of like-minded people. Our team is called #TheProgram. It's changed my approach to fitness and vastly enhanced my life.

I'm a big believer in starting slowly. Magazines that promise washboard abs in three weeks are just selling magazines. If you're not in great shape, that didn't happen overnight; don't expect to reverse it overnight either. One good and gentle way to begin an exercise program is by doing about ten minutes of calisthenics three days a week: push-ups, sit-ups, jumping jacks, air squats, and the like. Then take a brisk walk for half an hour. After a few weeks of that, go to a gym and try an easy exercise class, or hire a trainer, or pick any number of online programs. Don't work out more than two or three times a week until your body feels ready for more. If you start slowly and develop the habit of doing exercise for about three months, it's very likely to stick.

And remember, you can't out-exercise your overeating. There are no magic exercises. I like Marc Perry's BuiltLean program a lot. It's very approachable for everyone and highly effective, especially when paired with his dietary recommendations.

How has a failure, or apparent failure, set you up for later success? Do you have a "favorite failure" of yours?

I make loads of mistakes daily. But mistakes can be identified and corrected (or at least addressed) in the moment. A failure is a collection of small mistakes that haven't been identified or corrected along the way. My "favorite" failure was when I unwittingly had an ethical lapse in business—and my personal approach and our corporate brand relies first and foremost on integrity. Specifically, my company owned a business with a partner, and our agreement precluded us from owning another business that was competitive. Despite that, we looked seriously at a different deal that, while not identical, operated in a similar space. I convinced myself—mostly because I wanted to build my business and not deal with a potentially difficult situation—that the new deal really didn't represent a conflict. Ultimately, as were getting close to buying the company in question, I went to my partner and told them what were about to do. Basically their heads exploded. So, what did I do? I took personal, public responsibility. I apologized profusely and repeatedly. I did the best I could to make things right. And most important, I relearned a lesson I thought I already knew: Never compromise your integrity. It's all you have. For what it's worth, the deal to buy the new company never happened in the end.

While it can feel embarrassing and uncomfortable to apologize, it's a sign of maturity and good character. Unfortunately there is no particular magic to saying "I'm sorry." Just do it.

What is one of the best or most worthwhile investments you've ever made?

Education. I spent four years in college and four more in graduate school. It seemed like an eternity at the time, but it was well worth it.

What advice would you give to a smart, driven college student about to enter the "real world"?

Figure out what success means to you. Don't accept others' views or conventional wisdom. Write down what your successful personal and professional life looks like in 20 years. Then roll the clock back to today. Make sure your choices are in service of those goals.

When I was in my early 20s, I created a sort of watercolor picture of what life would look like decades later. For me, professional success meant having a significant equity stake in a large diversified media and entertainment company that I control. Personal success meant having a wife and kids I love, and living comfortably in the New York area. And that's what my life looks like today. It's not perfect, and it's not for everyone, but I did get much of what I set out to get. Today I'm pretty content most of the time.

When you feel overwhelmed or unfocused, what do you do?

I try to take a break and not be too hard on myself. Get some (more) exercise. Having done that, I'll ask: Am I on the right track and just frustrated at today's lack of progress, or do I need to reconsider my approach? If that doesn't yield anything helpful, I'll pose those questions to close friends I trust and my wife. And if none of that helps, I'll try to put the thoughts aside for 24 hours. A day later, the smoke usually clears and things make more sense.

QUOTES I'M PONDERING

(Tim Ferriss: Aug. 12–Sept. 9, 2016)

"Often when you think you're at the end of something, you're at the beginning of something else."

–FRED ROGERS

Creator of the famous television series *Mister Rogers' Neighborhood*

"When I let go of what I am, I become what I might be."

–LAO TZU

Chinese philosopher, author of *Tao Te Ching,* founder of Taoism

"Anything worth doing is worth doing slowly."

–MAE WEST

One of the greatest female stars of classic American cinema

"If you find yourself in a fair fight, you didn't plan your mission properly."

–COLONEL DAVID HACKWORTH

Former United States Army colonel and prominent military journalist

"Celebrate the childlike mind."

STEVE JURVETSON
TW: @DFJsteve
FB: /jurvetson
dfj.com

STEVE JURVETSON is a partner at DFJ (Draper Fisher Jurvetson), one of the top venture capital firms in Silicon Valley. Steve has been honored as a "Young Global Leader" by the World Economic Forum, and as "Venture Capitalist of the Year" by Deloitte. *Forbes* has recognized Steve several times on the Midas List, and named him one of "Tech's Best Venture Investors." In 2016, President Barack Obama announced Steve's position as a Presidential Ambassador for Global Entrepreneurship. He sits on the boards of SpaceX, Tesla, and other prominent companies. Steve was the world's first owner of a Tesla Model S and the second owner of a Tesla Model X, following Elon Musk.

What is the book (or books) you've given most as a gift, and why? Or what are one to three books that have greatly influenced your life?

Gift #1: *The Scientist in the Crib* by Alison Gopnik. I give this to any fellow geek about to have their first child. Gift #2: *Ready Player One* by Ernest Cline. A gift to all of my Apple][programming buddies from high school and Dungeons & Dragons comrades. So many of the geek references from the early days of personal computing brought back a Rush 2112 of Proustian 16K memories, from the Trash-80 to cassette-loading games.

Most influential books on me:

Out of Control by Kevin Kelly (page 246). Introduction to the power of evolutionary algorithms and information networks inspired by biology.

Age of Spiritual Machines by Ray Kurzweil. What Moore observed in the belly of the early integrated-circuit (IC) industry was a derivative metric, a refracted signal, from a longer-term trend, a trend that begs various philosophical questions and predicts mind-bending futures. Ray Kurzweil's abstraction of Moore's law shows computational power on a logarithmic scale, and finds a double exponential curve that holds over 110 years! Through five paradigm shifts—such as electromechanical calculators and vacuum tube computers—the computational power that $1,000 buys has doubled every two years. For the past 30 years, it has been doubling every year. In the modern era of accelerating change in the tech industry, it is hard to find even five-year trends with any predictive value, let alone trends that span the centuries.

I have been maintaining this graph ever since I read Kurzweil, and I show it in every presentation I give. Here is the latest version:

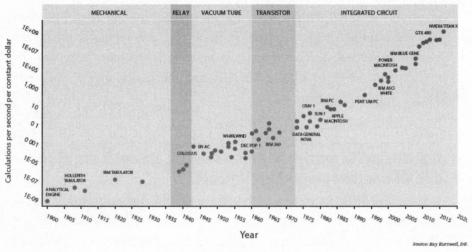

120 Years of Moore's Law

I would go further and assert that this is the most important graph ever conceived. Every industry on our planet is going to become an information business. Consider agriculture. If you ask a farmer in 20 years' time about how they compete, it will depend on how they use information, from satellite imagery driving robotic field optimization to the code in their seeds. It will have nothing to do with workmanship or labor. That will eventually percolate through every industry as IT innervates the economy.

Nonlinear shifts in the marketplace are also essential for entrepreneurship and meaningful change. Technology's exponential pace of progress has been the primary juggernaut of perpetual market disruption, spawning wave after wave of opportunities for new companies. Without disruption, entrepreneurs would not exist.

Moore's law is not just exogenous to the economy; it is why we have economic growth and an accelerating pace of progress. At DFJ, we see that in the growing diversity and global impact of the entrepreneurial ideas that we see each year. The industries impacted by the current wave of tech entrepreneurs are more diverse, and an order of magnitude larger than those of the '90s—from automobiles and aerospace to energy and chemicals.

In the last five years, what new belief, behavior, or habit has most improved your life?

The Whole30 diet. After the 30-day cleanse, I have removed bread and [non-naturally occurring] sugar from my diet and have more energy than ever before, I sleep through the night, and I dropped back to my high school weight.

And now, having tasted synthetic meat, I believe it will accelerate the development of human morality, much like an economic alternative to slavery helped society acknowledge the horrors of slavery. When we look back 2,000 years, we can see how much we have changed as culture matures. It's much more difficult to identify something that we do in our current lives and the mainstream considers moral, but our future selves will consider immoral. As a meat eater, I can now see that in myself for the first time. I believe that in a few years we will look back and marvel at the barbarism and stunning environmental waste (water consumption and methane production) of meat harvesting today.

Our circle of empathy generally expands over time . . . but sometimes as a retrospective rationalization. We don't typically discuss the meat industry in polite conversation because we don't want to face the inevitable cognitive dissonance (because bacon tastes so good). We don't really want to know why almost all USDA meat inspectors become vegetarian. I think all of that will change when viable meat products are grown from cell cultures, not in the field. We will switch, and condemn our former selves.

What is an unusual habit or an absurd thing that you love?

Launching big homemade rockets with my kids and collecting Apollo space artifacts. (I have converted DFJ into a space museum.)

If you could have a gigantic billboard with anything on it, what would it say and why?

"Celebrate the childlike mind." From what I can see, the best scientists and engineers nurture a childlike mind. They are playful, open-minded, and unrestrained by the inner voice of reason, collective cynicism, or fear of failure.

What is so great about the "childlike" mind? Once again, I highly recommend Alison Gopnik's *Scientist in the Crib* to any geek about to have a child. Here is one of her key conclusions: "Babies are just plain smarter than we are, at least if being smart means being able to learn something new. . . . They think, draw conclusions, make predictions, look for explanations and even do experiments. . . . In fact, scientists are successful precisely because they emulate what children do naturally."

Much of the human brain's power derives from its massive synaptic interconnectivity. Geoffrey West from the Santa Fe Institute observed that across species, synapses/neuron fanout grows as a power law with brain mass.

At the age of two to three years old, children hit their peak with ten times the synapses and two times the energy burn of an adult brain. And it's all downhill from there.

The UCSF Memory and Aging Center has graphed the pace of cognitive decline, and finds the same slope of decline in our 40s as in our 80s. We just notice more accumulated decline as we get older, especially when we cross the threshold of forgetting most of what we try to remember.

But we can affect this progression. Professor Michael Merzenich at UCSF has found that neural plasticity does not disappear in adults. It just requires mental exercise. Use it or lose it. Bottom line: Embrace lifelong learning. Do something new. Physical exercise is repetitive; mental exercise is eclectic.

"Skateboarding can change the world. Enjoy the ride."

TONY HAWK
TW/IG/FB: @tonyhawk
birdhouseskateboards.com

TONY HAWK is arguably the best-known skateboarder of all time. He was the first skateboarder to land "The 900," a 900-degree aerial spin, which he did at the 1999 X Games. The *Tony Hawk's Pro Skater* video game franchise is one of the most popular in history and has surpassed $1.4 billion in sales. Tony's other enterprises include Birdhouse Skateboards, Hawk Clothing, and Tony Hawk Signature Series sporting goods and toys. The Tony Hawk Foundation has given away more than $5 million to more than 500 skate park projects throughout the United States, which serve more than 4.8 million kids annually.

How has a failure, or apparent failure, set you up for later success? Do you have a "favorite failure" of yours?

When I first set out to help create a video game that features skateboarding, I had very discouraging meetings with various publishers. Some bordered on contentious, and I found myself defending skateboarding in general, as opposed to pitching a game based on the sport I love. In hindsight, it wasn't the right timing anyway. A couple of years later, I was approached by Activision to be involved with what would eventually become *THPS* [*Tony Hawk's Pro Skater*]. If that first round of pitches had worked, I believe that we would have released a game to an audience that wasn't interested in skating . . . yet. As crushing as those first meetings seemed, they were exactly the motivation I needed to set myself up for the right opportunity.

If you could have a gigantic billboard anywhere with anything on it, what would it say?
"Skateboarding can change the world. Enjoy the ride."

What is an unusual habit or an absurd thing that you love?
Pinball! I will travel to great lengths to play good vintage machines. I have a couple of tables at home and at my office.

In the last five years, what new belief, behavior, or habit has most improved your life?
To not keep myself so busy that I miss out on the small, yet hugely important, moments with my family. To stay present and make myself available to my loved ones instead of chasing every business opportunity and keeping myself constantly distracted with work, skating, or travel. Having true intimacy with my wife and kids is a relatively new concept for me, but it has provided a more meaningful life than ever before.

What advice would you give to a smart, driven college student about to enter the "real world"?
Success should not be measured by financial gain; true success is doing something you love for a living. Learn every aspect of your chosen field or craft, as it will give you an advantage over any competitors, and set you up for more—often better—job opportunities.

Can you offer any advice or warnings to entrepreneurs?
We have partnered with some big companies (McDonald's, Frito-Lay, Mattel, etc.) to do collaborations and licensing deals. Each time, I had to fight for final approvals over creative direction, advertising, and products. Sometimes it stalled the release of the product or campaign, but it was ultimately worth the trouble in order to maintain the integrity of my brands. My advice is to remain steadfast in your values and product direction, especially when working with other companies.

And if things blow up faster than you expected, keep control of your brand (or idea) no matter what.

"The actual consequences of your actions matter far more than your actions themselves."

LIV BOEREE
TW/IG: @liv_boeree
https://reg-charity.org

LIV BOEREE is a poker player, TV presenter, and writer. As a European Poker Tour and World Series of Poker Champion with more than $3.5 million in tournament winnings, she is one of the best-known faces on the international poker circuit and has been nicknamed the "Iron Maiden." Liv is a member of Team PokerStars Pro and is a four-time winner of European Female Player of the Year. Her biggest passion is science, and she holds a first class honors degree in physics with astrophysics from the University of Manchester. Liv is a strong supporter of the Effective Altruism movement, the philosophy of using evidence and rational decision-making to achieve the most good. In 2014, she co-founded Raising for Effective Giving, a fundraising organization that raises money for the world's most cost-effective and globally impactful charities.

What is the book (or books) you've given most as a gift, and why? Or what are one to three books that have greatly influenced your life?

The Passion Trap: How to Right an Unbalanced Relationship by relationship therapist and psychologist Dean C. Delis. This was given to me by a friend when I was on the tail end of a very difficult relationship, and it was utterly illuminating. The author examines the psychological forces behind human attraction and explains the most common drivers of conflict in intimate relationships. A key takeaway is that it's rarely any given partner who's the cause for a poor relationship; more often unbalanced dynamics are to blame. The book offers numerous tactics to overcome these imbalances and I'd recommend it to anyone, whether you're single, about to break up, or in a perfectly happy relationship.

Map and Territory and *How to Actually Change Your Mind* by Eliezer Yudkowsky. These two books are hands-down the best insight into modern-day rational thinking I've ever read, written by (in my opinion) one of the greatest minds of our time. Yudkowsky manages to explain highly complex philosophical and scientific concepts to the reader in a remarkably entertaining and palatable way. I came away feeling like I'd finally found the tools with which to understand both myself and the world around me. These two books are actually parts one and two of a six-part collection called *Rationality: From AI to Zombies,* sourced from Yudkowsky's blog posts from the site LessWrong.com over the last decade.

What purchase of $100 or less has most positively impacted your life in the last six months (or in recent memory)?

Blinkist—an app that condenses nonfiction books into 15-minute reads.

What is one of the best or most worthwhile investments you've ever made?

Learning about modern-day rationality—I've found it's added value in all domains of my life.

Poker is all about making optimal decisions, so I learned the hard way how costly my irrational screw-ups could be. This gave me extra motivation to truly identify my inherent mental flaws. Rationality (and poker) teaches you how to think more quantitatively—how to make better predictions and evaluate your beliefs more effectively so you can better achieve your goals. It also teaches you how to better control and work with your emotions, and I've found it made a huge improvement on my general happiness.

If you could have a gigantic billboard anywhere with anything on it, what would it say and why?

If I had a billboard, it would read: "The actual consequences of your actions matter far more than your actions themselves."

One of my biggest "duh, of course!" moments was when a philosopher friend explained to me the difference between deontological and consequentialist thinking. A deontologist believes that for something to be ethically correct, it must abide by a predefined set of moral rules or ideologies, and if an action breaks those rules then it is immoral, regardless of the outcome. A consequentialist believes that the moral value of an action purely depends on its outcome—the act itself doesn't carry moral weight, all that matters is whether its consequences are good or bad overall.

For example, say there's an axe-murderer who's about to kill a number of victims unless you kill the murderer first. A strict deontologist would say, "Killing a person is always wrong, regardless of why it is done." A consequentialist would say, "Killing a person is wrong, because the outcome usually causes suffering. However, it is okay to do if it clearly prevents greater suffering." Most of us can easily identify with the second mindset in that situation—we're all familiar with the idea of the greater good—and thus it's easy to appreciate the value in thinking consequentially.

Moral heuristics (rules of thumb) had societal benefits, especially in pre-scientific times where superstitions and evidence-less beliefs ruled and education was very poor. However, in this age of readily available scientific data, we are now able to evaluate consequences of actions more accurately than ever before, and therefore should be more open to re-evaluating many of the ideological rules of thumb we still live by.

What is an unusual habit or an absurd thing that you love?

Erm . . . Instead of shaving my legs I like to pluck the hairs one by one, and it has been my favorite form of meditation for many years. Takes forever, but it's the most effective way for me to get into a quiet mind state!

In the last five years, what have you become better at saying no to?

I used to be an enormous social butterfly—my preferred gatherings involved as many new faces as possible. If there was a dinner being organized, I'd want to invite everyone who was around. I hated the idea of anyone I knew being left out or not getting to know one another, and I definitely enjoyed being the center of attention a little too much!

These days, I say no to most big group dinners. I prefer situations where one conversation happens at a time. Any more than five or six people and discussions tend to fragment and lose flow. I've found my focus has shifted to quality over quantity—I value more time with a few people as opposed to less time with more people.

In the last five years, what new belief, behavior, or habit has most improved your life?

Whenever I have to make a prediction about something uncertain, such as "Will I make this flight?" or "How likely is my partner to get mad about me not doing the dishes?" I now try to assign a numerical percentage to fuzzy words like "maybe," "sometimes," "occasionally," and "probably." Whenever I use one of those words, I try to picture exactly what I mean as a number on a sliding scale between 0 to 100 ("never" to "always"). Even though those numbers often feel very vague, I've found the outcomes of my decisions have improved significantly since I started the habit. After all, the physical reality we live in is governed by mathematics, so it makes sense to train our minds to think in line with that reality as much as possible.

What are bad recommendations you hear in your profession or area of expertise?

In poker, the most common error people make is overestimating their ability to read people—classic bad advice usually involves statements like "watch for their eye movements" (humans are generally very aware of their eyes when lying) or "he looked nervous, so he must be bluffing" (nervousness and excitement appear very similar). Physical tells are far less consistent and reliable than we're taught to believe, and to truly excel at the game it's far more important to have a solid understanding of the mathematical theory behind the game.

When you feel overwhelmed or unfocused, what do you do? What questions do you ask yourself?

It's essential to identify the root cause of that lost focus—am I just having a bad day, or is the task itself something I simply hate doing? If it's clearly the former, and time pressures allow, I'm a big fan of just packing it in and doing something more fun until my focus comes back, even if it's not until the next day. If it's the latter, it's probably relevant to investigate why I'm feeling so unmotivated. Given that I know the upsides of getting it done, feeling so icky about it might mean there's more going on than I'd fully considered. It then helps to list those reasons to see if I can find a new way of getting the task done, avoiding the crappy parts entirely. If that's not possible, I can now at least do a more effective cost-benefit analysis and decide whether to continue at all. If I decide the payoff is still worth it, then the motivation will be more likely to come back by itself.

"Somewhere behind the athlete you've become, and the hours of practice, and the coaches who have pushed you, is a little girl who fell in love with the game and never looked back . . . play for her."

ANNÍE MIST ÞÓRISDÓTTIR
IG/FB: @AnnieThorisdottir
anniethorisdottir.com

ANNÍE MIST ÞÓRISDÓTTIR first entered the CrossFit scene in 2009, when she finished eleventh at the CrossFit Games. At the 2010 Games, she took home an incredible second-place win before becoming the world's first back-to-back female champion, claiming the title of "Fittest Woman on Earth" in both 2011 and 2012. After recovering from a severe back injury in 2013, Anníe returned to the big stage and finished second at the 2014 CrossFit Games.

What is the book (or books) you've given most as a gift, and why? Or what are one to three books that have greatly influenced your life?

I mostly give books about Icelandic nature: *Iceland Small World* by Sigurgeir Sigurjónsson or *Iceland in All Its Splendour* by Unnur Jökulsdóttir, with photographs by Erlend and Orsolya Haarberg. I feel like that is such a big part of who I am and where I come from. I believe in the energy, strength, and freedom that nature gives.

What purchase of $100 or less has most positively impacted your life in the last six months (or in recent memory)?

The Five-Minute Journal gives focus to each day. I got it at Urban Outfitters. And maybe the Spiralizer, too. It makes salad so much more fun and interesting to eat.

How has a failure, or apparent failure, set you up for later success? Do you have a "favorite failure" of yours?

I injured my back, bulged out disc L5-S1 in 2013, and it made me realize how much I love training and competing. I didn't know just how important that was to me until then.

If you could have a gigantic billboard anywhere with anything on it, what would it say and why?

"Dreams come true. You just have to be willing to work for them."

What is an unusual habit or an absurd thing that you love?

I love watching cartoons. I even go see them at the movies. They make me happy. I never get tired of *Despicable Me*.

In the last five years, what new belief, behavior, or habit has most improved your life?

I've tried to stop worrying too much about the future. I focus on making the most out of every single day with the belief that it will bring me to where I want to be.

What is a favorite exercise (or a valuable one) that most CrossFitters or athletes neglect?

Lower intensity long endurance. Most CF workouts are high intensity, but we tend to forget hitting some of the other energy systems needed to build endurance and speed up recovery.

When you feel overwhelmed or unfocused, what do you do?

I try to stay centered, focus on myself, and remember why I do this in the first place. My favorite quote is "Somewhere behind the athlete you've become, and the hours of practice, and the coaches who have pushed you, is a little girl who fell in love with the game and never looked back . . . play for her."

QUOTES I'M PONDERING

(Tim Ferriss: Sept. 16–Oct. 14, 2016)

"I not only use all the dreams that I have, but all that I can borrow."

–WOODROW WILSON

28th president of the United States, recipient of the Nobel Peace Prize

"Life shrinks or expands in proportion to one's courage."

–ANAÏS NIN

Renowned essayist and memoirist, author of *Delta of Venus*

"The writer should never be ashamed of staring. There is nothing that does not require his attention."

–FLANNERY O'CONNOR

American writer, recipient of the National Book Award for Fiction

"Anger is often what pain looks like when it shows itself in public."

–KRISTA TIPPETT

Peabody Award-winning broadcaster and best-selling author

"The way to get the strongest is to lift what is optimal and not what is maximal."

MARK BELL
IG: @marksmellybell
YT: supertraining06
HowMuchYaBench.net

MARK BELL is the founder of Super Training Gym in Sacramento, which is often referred to as "the strongest gym in the West." Prior to opening his own gym, he studied and trained under the legendary Louie Simmons at Westside Barbell. Mark's best "geared lifts" in competition include a 1,025-pound (465 kg) squat, an 832-pound (377 kg) bench press, and a 738-pound (335 kg) deadlift. Mark is also a multimillion-dollar entrepreneur and the inventor of the patented Sling Shot, a device used to assist with proper bench press form while also increasing weight and reps.

What is the book (or books) you've given most as a gift, and why? Or what are one to three books that have greatly influenced your life?

Crush It! by Gary Vaynerchuk: Gary V. (page 215) had the forethought to recognize the importance of Twitter and technologies that hadn't come yet to maturity. He talked about how all the then-current forms of advertising would be left in the dust. He also predicted that there was going to be a marketing shift from professional athletes and celebrities to social media influencers. This book made me recognize that I have enough access to make a very large company, even from my house, since everyone has the same access to the Internet.

The 4-Hour Workweek by Tim Ferriss: It taught me better ways to manage my time and the value of not making myself too busy.

5/3/1 by Jim Wendler: Getting stronger can be as simple or as complex as you want to make it. Jim Wendler did a great job of presenting a condensed, simplified, but effective method for getting stronger.

If you could have a gigantic billboard anywhere with anything on it, what would it say and why?

"Either you're in, or you're in the way." Often, we chase after people who aren't "in," who, for whatever reason, don't fit into our lives or our business. We waste time with these people when our focus should be on the people who *are* in.

"Part of knowing who you are is knowing who you're not." This gem comes from my pops, Mike Bell. In the sport of powerlifting, like many competitive sports or fields, it is extremely difficult to be number one. I was so entrenched in powerlifting that I would do anything to be as strong as Ed Coan (page 313). My dad said this to me at just the right time in my life. He made me realize that maybe my impact on powerlifting would be quite different than that of the greatest lifter of all time.

How has a failure, or apparent failure, set you up for later success? Do you have a "favorite failure" of yours?

A few torn pecs. I'm an inventor who has earned the right to say that I have torn muscles for my patents. If it were not for my torn pecs, I would not have thought to invent the Sling Shot, which has sold more than 500,000 units to date. The Sling Shot is a supportive upper body device that allows you to train through and around injuries. It also allows you to safely over-load your body with more weight. By being able to handle more weight in the Sling Shot, you will be able to handle more weight without it. It also promotes lifting with better form, which, in the long run, will ingrain this movement pattern into your bench press and push-ups permanently.

What is one of the best or most worthwhile investments you've ever made?

I spent $1,200 on learning how to be a professional wrestler. The way that you entertain is through your wrestling promos that are done in front of a camera or live audience. This form of public speaking was one of the hardest things I've ever had to do. Since you're talking in front of a peer group, as well as a live audience, it forces you to think on your feet and improv. To make matters even worse, you are given direction on how many seconds you can talk, and you're fed things to say that you have to remember for the duration of your promo. Professional wrestling also taught me to cut down on nervous tension by going up to people, introducing myself, and shaking their hands.

What purchase of $100 or less has most positively impacted your life in the last six months (or in recent memory)?

A pair of Groucho Marx glasses I bought in Japan for 200 yen [about $2 U.S.]. It moved everyone's focus from my fellow wrestlers to me. It's all in the way you market yourself.

What is an unusual habit or an absurd thing that you love?

I like feeling sore. I like beating the sh*t out of myself with workouts. I don't necessarily love the pain, but I love the results I get out of it over a long period of time.

I write down my goals on my bathroom mirror. I've done it with my target body weight, to how much I want to bench, etc. By writing it down every single day, it turns those dreams into obtainable goals.

What are bad recommendations you hear in your profession or area of expertise?

The name of the game in what I do is lifting the most weight. However, the way to get the strongest is to lift what is optimal and not what is maximal.

In general, lifters and coaches tend to lift too heavy, too often. I think it's human nature in some ways to try to take on more than we can handle. But to make progress, you need to lift and do things that are more realistic. Any time you overreach, you are putting yourself in a compromised position.

What advice would you give to a smart, driven college student about to enter the "real world"? What advice should they ignore?

I would tell them to invest time in themselves, to make sure they have some sort of physical activity in their life, and adhere to some form of nutrition that keeps them healthy. When that stuff falls apart, it can make other things more difficult.

Things to ignore: what other people or businesses are doing. When you're not looking at what's in front of you, you could have a very tragic misstep. That's why racehorses have blinders on. If they look to the left or right, not only will they end up hurt, but everyone else will, too.

"I love my routine and when nothing upsets my routine. My dad used to tell me, 'I know never to die and have my wake or funeral on a lifting day, because I know you won't be there.'"

ED COAN
IG: @eddycoan
FB: /EdCoanStrengthInc

ED COAN is widely regarded as the greatest powerlifter of all time. He has set more than 71 world records in powerlifting. Ed's best single-ply lifts are a squat of 1,019 pounds (~462 kg), bench press of 584 pounds (~265 kg), and deadlift of 901 pounds (~409 kg), for a total of 2,504 pounds (1135.79 kg). His 901-pound deadlift was achieved at a bodyweight of 220 pounds. Ed became the lightest person in history to cross the 2,400-pound barrier in the powerlifting total, which is the sum of three competitive lifts: the deadlift, bench, and squat.

Note from Tim: This profile is a bit different from the rest. Ed is a childhood hero of mine and one of the best lifters the world has ever seen. I couldn't resist asking a bunch of training-specific questions. Find his answers to the tried-and-true set of questions toward the end.

Were you always good in sports?

When I was a little kid, I had no hand-eye coordination. I had to go to Illinois Institute of Technology at night and wear something like horse blinders because I couldn't even bounce a ball. I was really little. My freshman year in high school, I was 4-foot-11 and 98 pounds, so I never went out for baseball and never went out for football. I was scared. [Eventually], I wrestled, because there was a 98-pound weight class. That's when I found lifting.

I could dive into lifting by myself. It was only me and the weights. I'd sit in the basement at midnight on these ad hoc machines with little weights, going nuts for hours because no one was watching me. It was just me.

Were there any counterintuitive or particularly surprising findings that you found when looking at your notes from 28 years of training?

At the time I wrote the notes down, no. But when I look back at them, yes. The biggest surprise was that I took my time and made a little, tiny bit of progress four or five times a year. When you make a little progress four times a year over 28 years, you're going to be pretty good at what you do. I never thought, "Oh, I have to lift X amount of weight or accomplish Y." I just thought, "I'm going to get better, and this is what I have to do to get better. These are my weaknesses; let me correct my weaknesses."

What are some of the most common novice mistakes you see in lifting?

They don't take their time. They don't look at the long-term goals, the big picture. I'll ask kids an old question that every old guy asks: "Where do you want to be in five years? Where do you see yourself?" If I apply that question to lifting, a lot of people don't get it. They're only thinking, "What am I going to do within six months?" They don't realize that if you make the whole body strong in every aspect that you possibly can over a period of just three years, you've created an impenetrable machine that won't get hurt, that won't break down, that you can have for the rest of your life because you followed what you're supposed to at the beginning.

They don't take the time to dot their i's and cross their t's. By analogy, they can write the best paper in the world and turn it in to the teacher, but based on grammar, they're going to get a D. They don't take the time to do the little things: the assistance work, extra technique work, proper diet, prehab [injury prevention] exercises, etc.

I was fortunate because I was introverted—I realized what all of my weaknesses were. I only did two contests a year because I like to get better and have all that time to work on my weaknesses. So, for instance, my strength is my back and my hips. During my long off-season (roughly December to mid-June), I would do a high-bar Olympic close stance squat. Instead of regular deadlifts, I would do deadlifts with no belt and off of a deficit [an elevated platform] or use stiff legs off of a deficit.

For the bench press, I would ask myself, "How can I make this harder so it will help with my lockout?" I'd then bench with my feet up and do more close-grip and incline benches, things like that.

What do I know will help me not only get [generally] strong but also transfer over to the main lifts [of squat, deadlift, and bench press]? It doesn't matter if you have a pretty peak on your bicep if it doesn't do anything.

When is it okay to max out with a lift?

Twice a year at meets [competitions].

Usually, when people max out in a gym, they're pretty insecure and not confident about what their end results are going to be. Years ago, I went to Russia with Fred Hatfield [the first person to squat more than 1,000 pounds in competition] and a few other people. This is before perestroika, and the USSR was incredibly powerful. I was in one of their old gyms, something you might see in a Rocky movie. I talked with the guys about training and they said, "You only have so many max attempts in your body over your lifetime. Why waste them in the gym?" I tend to agree with that.

Are there any particular exercises that you think are neglected or that more people should incorporate?

Usually it's the hard ones like sets of pause [at the bottom] squats. Guys can't use as much weight, it's harder, and a lot of the time, they don't do them. The only way to get out of the bottom once you stop is for your whole body to push and sync at the right time. You can't have bad technique or you fall forward right away. I don't pause to a box . . . I taught myself how to stay tight with the barbell.

What are the most common mistakes you see in a barbell squat?

People don't focus on the body as a whole when they squat. Everyone thinks you just use your legs. They think, "You don't want to hurt your back, so don't use your back." But you need an equal amount of push going down through the floor, which is your legs, and push going up, which is your back driving against the bar. This dual action is what allows your hips to activate and move forward like a hinge on a door. If one of those is not working, you fall forward. So I concentrate on hitting the whole, driving with my legs and driving straight up with my back into the bar. That makes the hips react. It's the same principle in the deadlift.

Are there any particular prehab exercises that you like or dislike?

Layne Norton has suffered hip and back injuries over the last four years, and he came back. He has a tutorial of hip exercises on his Instagram account (@biolayne) that really helped him. I tried them, and they work phenomenally well.

I also do some Kelly Starrett stretching with bands to open things up, and I use a lacrosse ball to work on the pecs, rhomboids, etc.

For the pecs, for instance, you stand at the side of a door frame, place the lacrosse ball directly on the pec tendon, then lean against the wall. If you're working on your right pec, you'd stand in front of the left side of a door frame, and your right arm would be straight out in front of you, inside the door frame, the right pec (inside your shoulder) pressing the ball into the wall. The key is that you don't move the ball. Instead, you move your straight arm up and down while pushing against the ball, and you'll feel that sucker roll over the tendon. You're causing your own pain, which is more tolerable.

During your competitive career, did you find anything unusual to help with recovery?

Four times per week, I received chiropractic care from a friend of Dr. Bob Goldman. Every time I went to him, he worked on me from my feet up. Now you see a lot of people like Chris Duffin and Kelly Starrett rolling out the bottoms of their feet and doing ankle prep. At the time, we used something that looked like an abacus. Right after using it, I'd walk around and, all of a sudden, my knees didn't hurt and my back wasn't tight. These days, I use a lacrosse ball.

I've heard you never missed lifts in training, which is rare. Where did you learn that approach?

I'm pretty sure it was on my own. I used to read *Powerlifting USA* when I was younger, but my routine was a basic linear periodization with a lot of thought put into picking assistance exercises. So here's what I would do: If I had a 12-week training cycle, I would start from week 12—sets, reps, weights—and work my way back all the way to week one. I would have every set, every rep, and every weight for every single exercise predetermined. I didn't care if it was a leg curl or pause squat or shoulder press or bent row; whatever it was, my weight, sets, and reps were all figured out for the entire training cycle.

Then I would stop and I would look at that routine, all written in pencil, of course. I would ask myself, "Okay, is every single thing here doable?" If you have to think about it, change it. Make it so that you know 100 percent everything is doable. When you start that routine, imagine how positive your mental outlook is. It's huge.

I was never depressed. I was never stressed. I never worried about "Can I do this next week?" I always knew I could.

Looking back at your peak training, what did your weekly split look like during that period of time?

Mondays would be squats and all other leg assistance. Tuesdays would be off. Wednesdays would be bench with chest assistance and a lot of tricep work. I would come in Thursdays, after pre-fatiguing the triceps on Wednesday, and only hit shoulders [primary go-to exercises: seated behind-the-neck barbell press, working up to 400-plus pounds]. I would deadlift on Friday [with light squats as a warmup], do all of my back work. Saturday would be a light bench day for recovery using wide-grip bench, flies, etc., with occasional smaller exercises like light curls and grip work. [Sundays were off.]

If you could have a gigantic billboard anywhere with anything on it, what would it say and why?

"BE NICE!"

As angry and "focused" as I was as a younger man, I found that those two words made my life much easier.

I used to have a scowl on my face if anything differed from what I believed in any way, shape, or form. I don't know if was because it was hard for me—as such an introvert—to express things outwardly, or if I was just a jerk. I don't think I was a jerk because I never acted on much.

Then, one day, there was this idiot in the gym who really, really used to get under my skin.

I took a deep breath, let it go, walked up, and said, "Hey, how are you doing? You look great. Congratulations on finishing school." Suddenly, I thought, "Holy crap! This is amazing!" It was like I'd set myself free. It was gone. So even now, I just try to relax [with something like] "Hey, how are you doing? Nice to see you." If I really don't like something, or if something doesn't agree with me, I just walk away or talk to someone more positive.

I see this a lot with [powerlifters] Mark and Stan Efferding. They don't let anybody or anything get to them. It's like water off a duck's back.

When you feel overwhelmed or unfocused, what do you do?

When I travel and I'm on long plane rides, I'll go through my last two weeks: What I did, what I thought of it, how I can improve it, and what I'm going to do so I don't make mistakes. Stan Efferding actually taught me how to do that by writing lists [and it might only take 30 minutes]. . . . When I put it on paper, it takes the emotion out and makes it easier to follow.

For instance, it's usually my procrastination and fear that has stopped me from doing things. I tend to think of [things] as a big whole and get overwhelmed. If I break it down, put it down on paper, then look at it a half hour later, all of those smaller things don't seem like a big deal. When I write it down on paper, it looks so much easier, because the fear in my mind is externalized. I can look at it and realize that it's not so scary.

In the last five years, what new belief, behavior, or habit has most improved your life?

I have been doing JKD [Jeet Kune Do] counter-violence training for some years since I stopped competing, and I love it. That would be on the short list. I had to teach myself how to move again, because I wanted to be an athlete and not a one-dimensional gorilla.

What purchase of $100 or less has most positively impacted your life in the last six months (or in recent memory)?

It's a picture of my parents that I had framed. I've never heard my mom and dad badmouth anybody. The picture makes me think about how I should treat everyone I love.

The picture was only taken a few years ago, and it's my mom and dad together, next to each other—an upper torso shot. I'd never really seen them showing that much affection. My whole life, I never really saw it because of the five kids, and now the grandkids. They hadn't really had a chance to show it. They're both around 87 years old now, and they've had their health problems, but they're still kicking. They love life, they love their kids and grandkids, and it keeps them going.

I think what they instilled in me without me even knowing it was the ability to observe. Still today, I think that's one of the things I'm really good at: just sitting back and observing. I've never been one to try to be the life of the party or to be too loud. I usually just sit back and observe with a smirk on my face. I don't think you realize [how much your parents have given you] until you get older and can reflect on it.

What is an unusual habit or an absurd thing that you love?

I love my routine and when nothing upsets my routine. My dad used to tell me, "I know never to die and have my wake or funeral on a lifting day, because I know you won't be there."

I've also taken a nap every day since I was a kid. I still try not to miss it. Usually it's 45 minutes to an hour and ideally around 3:30 or 4 P.M.

What is the best purchase you've made in recent memory?

Not too long ago, [right after a surgery,] the pulmonary doctor and anesthesiologist came in my room, and it was like the TV show *Intervention*. I said, "What's up, guys? You're not smiling." They said, "We have to talk. Your surgery took a little longer than usual because of the density of your bone and the size of your muscles and tendons."

Now, that's fine with me. I'm happy. Then they said, "The hardest part of your whole surgery was keeping you breathing." Subsequently, I went in for a sleep study. They figured out that when I fall asleep on my side, I stop breathing eight times a minute. When I fall asleep on my back, I stop breathing 24 times a minute.

So I got a CPAP [machine], and it changed my life. It's helped me improve my focus, overcome negative thoughts akin to depression, and more. Your blood pressure comes down, your blood work starts changing, everything starts to happen because of it. I guarantee I'd been dealing with sleep problems my entire life. I just didn't realize it.

What are bad recommendations you hear in your profession or area of expertise?

"The newest training ideas are the best!" Wrong. Tried-and-true basics lay the foundation for everything we do in and out of the gym.

I hope this doesn't sound offensive, but why do you spell your name "Eddy"? It's an unusual spelling.

The reason I don't spell it E-D-D-I-E is because of the first guest lifting appearance I ever did. I did a deadlift exhibition when I was young in Pittsburgh, Pennsylvania. It was on St. Patrick's Day of all days, and I already look like a freaking leprechaun. I pulled a deadlift and, after, some lady came up to me with Bill Pearl's book *Keys to the Inner Universe*, which is a gigantic book, and she said, "Would you sign this for me? I think you're going to be famous someday in powerlifting." I said, "Sure," but my hand was still shaking from the adrenaline of having just lifted. I still had my belt on and chalk on my hands. So I went to sign it, and out came E-D-D-Y. I thought to myself, "You know what? I have to sign my name E-D-D-Y for the rest of my life so I don't negate the signature that I did for this lady."

"Think for yourself while being radically open-minded."

RAY DALIO
TW: @RayDalio
bridgewater.com

RAY DALIO is the founder, chair, and co-chief investment officer at Bridgewater Associates, a global leader in institutional portfolio management and the largest hedge fund in the world ($150+ billion). Bridgewater is known for its culture of "radical transparency," which includes encouraging dissent, openly airing disagreements, and recording all meetings. His estimated net worth is nearly $17 billion. Along with Bill Gates and Warren Buffett, Ray has signed "The Giving Pledge," committing half of his net wealth to charity over the course of his lifetime. He has created the Dalio Foundation to channel his philanthropic contributions. Ray has appeared on the *Time* 100 list of the "Most Influential People in the World," as well as the *Bloomberg Markets* list of the "50 Most Influential People." Ray is the author of *Principles: Life and Work*, in which he shares the unconventional principles that he's developed, refined, and used over the past 40 years to create unique results in both life and business.

What is the book (or books) you've given most as a gift, and why? Or what are one to three books that have greatly influenced your life?

The Hero with a Thousand Faces by Joseph Campbell, *The Lessons of History* by Will and Ariel Durant, and *River Out of Eden* by Richard Dawkins.

What purchase of $100 or less has most positively impacted your life in the last six months (or in recent memory)?

A pocket notepad to jot down good ideas when they come to me.

How has a failure, or apparent failure, set you up for later success? Do you have a "favorite failure" of yours?

My most painful failures have been my best teachers, because the pain prompted me to change. My "favorite failure" was in 1982, when I predicted a depression on *Wall Street Week* (a popular TV show) and to Congress just before a great bull market and economy.

If you could have a gigantic billboard anywhere with anything on it, what would it say?

"Think for yourself while being radically open-minded."

What is one of the best or most worthwhile investments you've ever made?

Learning to meditate. I faithfully practice Transcendental Meditation but also dabble and am interested in other types of meditation.

What is an unusual habit or an absurd thing that you love?

Enjoying reflecting on my painful mistakes. I do this by writing down my reflections. I've also developed an iPad app to help people reflect on the pain they experience that I call the Pain Button.

In the last five years, what new belief, behavior, or habit has most improved your life?

The belief that I'm at a stage in life when making others successful without me is the most important thing I can do.

What advice would you give to a smart, driven college student about to enter the "real world"?

Love looking at what you don't know, your mistakes, and your weaknesses, because understanding them is essential for making the most of your life.

What are bad recommendations you hear in your profession or area of expertise?

"The markets that have done great are great investments." In other words, when someone says, "Buy this because it's doing well," you should be thinking, "Be careful, because it's become more expensive."

When you feel overwhelmed or unfocused, what do you do?

I meditate.

"Have the moral courage to live in the gray. . . . Live the questions so that, one day, you will live yourself into the answers."

JACQUELINE NOVOGRATZ
TW: @jnovogratz
FB: Jacqueline Novogratz
acumen.org

JACQUELINE NOVOGRATZ is the founder and CEO of Acumen, which raises charitable donations to invest in companies, leaders, and ideas that are changing the way the world tackles poverty. Prior to Acumen, Jacqueline founded and directed the Philanthropy Workshop and the Next Generation Leadership programs at the Rockefeller Foundation. She also co-founded Duterimbere, a microfinance institution in Rwanda. She began her career in international banking with Chase Manhattan Bank. Jacqueline currently sits on the advisory boards of Sonen Capital and the Harvard Business School Social Enterprise Initiative. She also serves on the Aspen Institute Board of Trustees and the board of IDEO.org, and is a member of the Council on Foreign Relations, World Economic Forum, and the American Academy of Arts and Sciences. Jacqueline was recently awarded the Forbes 400 Lifetime Achievement Award for Social Entrepreneurship.

What is the book (or books) you've given most as a gift, and why? Or what are one to three books that have greatly influenced your life?

Invisible Man by Ralph Ellison. I read it as a 22-year-old, and it made me think deeply about how society doesn't "see" so many of its members. I'm still reminded to pay attention, to recognize people as I pass them, to say hello. It sounds so simple. It changes everything.

Things Fall Apart by Chinua Achebe. The first book I read by an African author. Achebe is unflinching in his portrayal of the challenges of change, the relationships of colonialism, and power/powerlessness. It is still so relevant today.

A Fine Balance by Rohinton Mistry. A Dickensian novel that captures the essence of being poor in urban India in ways extraordinary and deeply human. It brought new layers of understanding though I'd read many works of nonfiction and had spent years working in India.

How has a failure, or apparent failure, set you up for later success? Do you have a "favorite failure" of yours?

As a 25-year-old, I wanted to save the world, and thought I'd start with the African continent. I left a career on Wall Street, thinking I had so many skills to share and so much to give, but soon discovered that most people don't want saving. The skills I needed most were moral imagination or the ability to put myself in another's shoes, to listen, and to recognize there are few easy solutions but that building trust is a powerful door to possibility. Learning to balance (and hold) the audacity to dream a different world with the humility to start with the world as it is has been one of the most important lessons of my life. It is an essential attribute of leading for anyone who wants to bring about change. And right now, that needs to be all of us.

If you could have a gigantic billboard anywhere with anything on it, what would it say and why?

A single bottom line of profit motive no longer serves our interdependent world. We must move from a focus on shareholders to one on stakeholders, take a long-term view, and measure what matters, not just what we can count. That's a lot easier to say than to do. So we created a manifesto at Acumen, a moral compass to guide our decisions and actions. It is an aspirational document, one I think about daily, though I don't always live up to it. It is long for a billboard, but maybe if we put it in the right place and encouraged people to pause for just a moment, which in itself wouldn't be so bad. Here it is:

> It starts by standing with the poor, listening to voices unheard, and recognizing potential where others see despair. It demands investing as a means, not an end, daring to go where markets have failed and aid has fallen short. It makes capital work for us, not control us. It thrives on moral imagination: the humility to see the world as it is, and the audacity to imagine the world as it could be. It's having the ambition to learn at the edge, the wisdom to admit failure, and the courage to start again. It requires patience and kindness, resilience and grit: a hard-edged hope. It's leadership that rejects complacency, breaks through bureaucracy, and challenges corruption. Doing what's right, not what's easy. It's the radical idea of creating hope in a cynical world. Changing the way the world tackles poverty and building a world based on dignity.

Or else, I might borrow Rilke's gorgeous mantra to "Live the Questions," which is a simple reminder to have the moral courage to live in the gray, sit with uncertainty but not in a passive way. Live the questions so that, one day, you will live yourself into the answers. . . .

What advice would you give to a smart, driven college student about to enter the "real world"?

Don't worry all that much about your first job. Just start, and let the work teach you. With every step, you will discover more about who you want to be and what you want to do. If you wait for the perfect and keep all of your options open, you might end up with nothing but options. So start.

What are bad recommendations you hear in your profession or area of expertise?

"Do well by doing good." Who wants to do well by doing bad? We have to do better. This moment in history demands that we put purpose before profit, that we take more seriously the fact that we have the tools, the imagination, and the resources to solve our toughest problems. So it is time to get on with it.

When you feel overwhelmed or unfocused, what do you do?

I go for a very long run and remind myself of the beauty of the world, that the sun will rise again tomorrow, that what matters is to be in the arena.

"Almost all advice given to writers by supposed experts is wrong."

BRIAN KOPPELMAN
TW/IG: @briankoppelman
briankoppelman.com

BRIAN KOPPELMAN is a screenwriter, novelist, director, and producer. Prior to his hit show *Billions*, which he co-created and executive produced (and co-wrote on spec), he was best known as the co-writer of *Rounders* and *Ocean's Thirteen*, as well as a producer of *The Illusionist* and *The Lucky Ones*. He has directed films such as *Solitary Man*, starring Michael Douglas. Brian also hosts *The Moment* podcast. One of my favorite episodes is with John Hamburg, who wrote and directed *I Love You, Man* and wrote *Meet the Parents*, among many other films. It's like film school and an MFA in screenwriting wrapped into one conversation.

What is the book (or books) you've given most as a gift, and why? Or what are one to three books that have greatly influenced your life?

These are the books I have given away/recommended the most. They have all also been crucial in my life.

What I Talk About When I Talk About Running by Haruki Murakami
  The Artist's Way by Julia Cameron
  Awaken the Giant Within by Tony Robbins
City of Thieves by David Benioff

I know that's four books, but each one is worth talking about a bit. The Murakami book is the single best distillation of the kind of focus, commitment, and sense of mission it takes to become a great artist. He is ostensibly writing about his running life—and he is widely regarded as a great distance runner—but what he's really talking about is how to strip away everything you don't need in order to achieve your purpose. It's a rigorous, inspiring book that challenges the reader to step up. It's also gorgeously written nonfiction by, to me, the world's best writer of fiction.

The Artist's Way contains the single best tool for becoming unblocked that I have ever come across [which is morning pages]. If you have the sense, deep inside you, that you are running away from your true purpose, this book will help you break through.

Tony Robbins' work has always been useful to me. That's one of the reasons my creative partner, David Levien, and I executive produced *I Am Not Your Guru*, the documentary about Tony. This book was the first of his I read, and it asked me crucial questions about the stories I was telling myself that were limiting my growth. I don't know anyone who couldn't benefit from a little Tony.

And, lastly, *City of Thieves* by Benioff. This book is just a joy. Fiction has a real utility, and it's one I think high achievers sometimes forget, and that is: fictions stirs you up inside, unsettles you, forces you to engage with that which isn't easily solved. This book does all that and delights along the way. I've given it to 100 people. All of them thanked me and gave away a bunch themselves.

How has a failure, or apparent failure, set you up for later success? Do you have a "favorite failure" of yours?

For a period of time, we sold one pilot idea a year to a premium cable network. We would tell them the idea, they would pay us to write it, and then we'd deliver the script, only to have them tell us they no longer wanted to make that kind of show. Each time they flushed one of these scripts, it killed me. I fell in love with each show and saw how to make it, but I didn't own it anymore. The last time this happened, it hurt in a different way. The way that makes you sit up and say: no more. So the next time we had a great idea for a show, we decided to write it on spec instead of selling it in advance. The notion being, if someone wanted to buy the finished pilot script, we'd have some leverage in the dealmaking, might be able to insist on them actually making it. Turned out that the next idea was *Billions*.

[*Billions* ended up costarring Emmy and Golden Globe winners Paul Giamatti and Damian Lewis. It had the best-ever series debut as a Showtime original series, and it has recently been renewed for a third season.]

What is an unusual habit or an absurd thing that you love?

Ping-Pong. I love everything about the game. Jerome Charyn's great book about pong, *Sizzling Chops and Devilish Spins*, captures the way the game makes me feel. I know it seems like a silly sport, but when you are inside of it, it's the opposite of that. It moves fast, requires deep strategy, asks you to control your fear, to commit to your shots, to bounce back and get ready for the next shot the moment you hit the first. I have been playing four or five times a week for almost a year, and I only wish I'd committed this deeply years before.

What purchase of $100 or less has most positively impacted your life in the last six months (or in recent memory)?

My Butterfly Petr Korbel table tennis racket. Because when I bought it, I knew I was really committing to my training as a Ping-Pong player. I have always loved the game, always told myself I'd try to get good someday. Buying it said that day is now.

What are bad recommendations you hear in your profession or area of expertise?

Almost all advice given to writers by supposed experts is wrong. Because almost all of it tells the aspirant to engage in some kind of calculation about marketing before setting out to write. Now, in nonfiction, this may make sense. But that's not my thing. For artists, the most important thing is total engagement. So I always tell writers to follow their curiosity, obsessions, and fascinations.

"Back when I was 75 (I'm 78 now), I checked out the local CrossFit 'box' and was enchanted by the absence of mirrors and machines, and by the presence of free weights."

STEWART BRAND
TW: @stewartbrand
reviverestore.org

STEWART BRAND is the president of the Long Now Foundation, established to creatively foster long-term thinking and responsibility in the framework of the next 10,000 years. He leads a project there called Revive and Restore, which seeks to bring back extinct animal species such as the passenger pigeon and woolly mammoth. Stewart is well known for founding, editing, and publishing *The Whole Earth Catalog* (1968–85), which received a National Book Award for its 1972 issue. He is the co-founder of The WELL and Global Business Network, and the author of books including *Whole Earth Discipline*, *The Clock of the Long Now*, *How Buildings Learn*, and *The Media Lab*. He was trained in biology at Stanford and served as an infantry officer in the U.S. Army.

What is the book (or books) you've given most as a gift, and why? Or what are books that have greatly influenced your life?

Four books:

Finite and Infinite Games: A Vision of Life as Play and Possibility
    by James P. Carse
One True God: Historical Consequences of Monotheism
    by Rodney Stark
The Idea of Decline in Western History by Arthur Herman
The Better Angels of Our Nature: Why Violence Has Declined
    by Steven Pinker (page 475)

These are the fundamental guidebooks for understanding and helping civilization. The *Decline* book shows the consequences of believing romantic, tragic narratives of societies becoming degraded, while *The Better Angels* chronicles how humanity has in fact become less violent, less cruel, and more just with every passing millennium, century, and decade. *One True God* demonstrates how lethally competitive and regimented monotheistic religions inevitably become, while *Finite and Infinite Games* makes a thrilling case for getting beyond obsession with winning zero-sum outcomes and focusing on improving the games we play, infinitely.

In the last five years, what new belief, behavior, or habit has most improved your life?

CrossFit. Swagger in, stagger out. Repeat.

Back when I was 75 (I'm 78 now), I checked out the local CrossFit "box" and was enchanted by the absence of mirrors and machines, and by the presence of free weights. For an hour at a time, twice a week, I lose myself in the intense workout, different every time, pushing my strength, stamina, and agility in measured competition. Result? Over a year, I lost 30 pounds, back to my youthful fighting weight of 155 pounds, and I feel great, which makes me proud, which makes me happy.

What advice would you give to a smart, driven college student about to enter the "real world"?

All I know is what worked for me. After college, I learned a whole array of marketable skills through classes and jobs. By the time I was 24, I could have earned my living as a logger, writer, field biologist, commercial photographer, Army officer, museum exhibit researcher, or multimedia artist. I also learned to live happily on almost nothing. I stayed with none of those things, but the skills served me in everything I eventually did, such as publish *The Whole Earth Catalog*.

I was fortunate to base my college education on a science (biology), but I do wish I had taken some anthropology and trained in theater skills (introverts need them). For me, far better than graduate school was two years active duty as a military officer. Any kind of national service (Peace Corps, etc.) is a boon, both for you and for society.

QUOTES I'M PONDERING

(Tim Ferriss: Oct. 21–Nov. 18, 2016)

"The privilege of a lifetime is being who you are."

—JOSEPH CAMPBELL
American mythologist and writer, known for *The Hero with a Thousand Faces*

"When jarred, unavoidably, by circumstance, revert at once to yourself, and don't lose the rhythm more than you can help. You'll have a better group of harmony if you keep on going back to it."

—MARCUS AURELIUS
Emperor of Rome and Stoic philosopher, author of *Meditations*

"Everyone thinks of changing the world, but no one thinks of changing himself."

—LEO TOLSTOY
One of the greatest Russian writers, author of *Anna Karenina* and *War and Peace*

"Why do you go away? So that you can come back. So that you can see the place you came from with new eyes and extra colors. And the people there see you differently, too. Coming back to where you started is not the same as never leaving."

—TERRY PRATCHETT
English fantasy writer, best known for his Discworld series of 41 novels

"The main thing is to keep the main thing the main thing."

TW: @sarahelizalewis
IG: @sarahelizabethlewis1
sarahelizabethlewis.com

SARAH ELIZABETH LEWIS is an assistant professor of history of art and architecture and African and African American studies at Harvard University. She received her bachelor's degree from Harvard, an MPhil from Oxford University, and her PhD in the history of art from Yale University. Before joining the faculty at Harvard, she held curatorial positions at the Museum of Modern Art in New York and the Tate Modern in London and taught at Yale University School of Art. Sarah was the guest editor of the landmark "Vision & Justice" issue of *Aperture*, which received the 2017 Infinity Award for Critical Writing and Research. She is also the author of the *Los Angeles Times* bestseller *The Rise: Creativity, the Gift of Failure, and the Search for Mastery*. Sarah has served on President Obama's Arts Policy Committee and currently serves on the board of the Andy Warhol Foundation for the Visual Arts, Creative Time, and the CUNY Graduate Center.

What is the book (or books) you've given most as a gift, and why? Or what are one to three books that have greatly influenced your life?
There are two I tend to give: Rebecca Solnit's *A Field Guide to Getting Lost* and James Baldwin's collection of essays, *The Price of the Ticket*, with

one [essay] that should be a map for any innovator called "The Creative Process." I won't spoil it by describing it here, but it's Baldwin. It's brilliant. Any questions you didn't know you had about the purpose of the creative spirit for society will likely be answered. Solnit's book is perfect for someone trying to unlock their passion and is getting up the nerve to chart a new path.

What purchase of $100 or less has most positively impacted your life in the last six months (or in recent memory)?

Studies tell us that spending that yields the greatest happiness is the kind that buys you time or experiences, not things. I think that's true. But I will say that I'm a sucker for a good plain, no-lined notebook from Moleskine.

How has a failure, or apparent failure, set you up for later success? Do you have a "favorite failure" of yours?

Personally, the kind of failure I experience is more about assumptions. Being a woman of color who is paid to think, teach, and write, I'm underestimated a lot if people know nothing about my work. Meaning, people expect me to fail more often than I actually do. That perception of potential failure is a kind of fuel. I've learned to be grateful for it.

I wrote *The Rise* and gave my TED Talk about it because I believe so strongly in the power of so-called failure, or being assumed as a failure, for pathbreaking innovative achievements. Martin Luther King Jr. did well in school, but his worst grades were in public speaking. Yes. Two Cs, in back-to-back terms. The list goes on, and I loved writing about them all in the book. The most impactful kind of failures are "near wins" because of the propulsion we get from coming just shy of reaching a goal. I never really use the word "failure" though. Once you learn from an experience, it's tough to assign it that word because it has become useful to you, or so we hope.

If you could have a gigantic billboard anywhere with anything on it, what would it say and why?

The quote I would emblazon on a billboard is: "The main thing is to keep the main thing the main thing." Simple. So important. I think we often get distracted by, well, life, or social media, or whatever. At the end of the day, we can see that we haven't really moved the needle on what we truly care about. Women out there in particular know this is true. How do you keep the main thing the main thing? For me, it means guarding my mornings tightly for the time I need to create. Other people have other ways, but I find if I put my priorities on the agenda first thing during the day, I'm more likely to find time that day to focus on them.

What is one of the best or most worthwhile investments you've ever made?

I love keeping a meditation and workout regime. I added something new lately, a breathing technique that I learned from Brian Mackenzie, which I've found really helps me handle stress. Amazing. The work is based on some precise science. Brian does an intake that assesses emotional reactivity and CO_2 tolerance and that creates a specific nasal apnea sequence. The one he has designed for me feels like some stress-relieving magic. From what Brian tells me, the apnea allows for more parasympathetic tone in the body. This opens vasculature and brings more nitric oxide (NO) into the body. After the apnea sequence, I go into meditation for about 15 or 20 minutes. The whole regime takes about 35 minutes in the morning.

What is an unusual habit or an absurd thing that you love?

Privacy when I'm at a peak point of creative work. I tend to go off of social media during those times and not take many meetings at all. This is only unusual in today's climate, but it's crucial. Having a sense of privacy when we work is one of the ways that we foster risk-taking in ourselves. Part of why shutting out social media helps is because you stop worrying about what others might think of some unusual idea you're pondering, and you give it a chance to grow and mature.

In the last five years, what have you become better at saying no to?

Oh, this is a big one. Doing too much out of obligation can deplete you. Responsibilities that are borne of passion give you more energy. If a request would give me another responsibility that I'm passionate about, I'll do it. If not, I've found ways of saying no. My Harvard colleague Robin Bernstein has this great piece on artful ways of saying no, titled: "The Art of 'No.'"

When you feel overwhelmed or unfocused, what do you do? What do you tell or ask yourself?

"There is no earth-spinning committee." It helps me to relax and remember that I am, as we all are, a part of something larger. Larger forces so precise that we know how much of the moon will be visible in the sky on a given night, with certainty, even if someone's to-do list is not done! Yes, even then. That is to say, we can impact the laws of nature with how we treat the planet, and we can work with the laws of nature to manifest things in our world (sometimes without even knowing it), but we can't create these laws or destroy them. We live in a world governed by them. So when I'm overwhelmed, I try to get myself out into nature, a place that reminds me of the surrounding with a set of systems and laws that govern movements. If I'm city-bound, I'll stargaze and then return to the work with a sense of relaxation and support.

"'Just say no' (to drugs, gambling, eating, sex, etc.) is the least helpful advice one can say to a human being caught up in any addiction. If they could say no, they would."

GABOR MATÉ
FB: /drgabormate
drgabormate.com

DR. GABOR MATÉ is a physician who specializes in neurology, psychiatry, and psychology. He is well known for his study and treatment of addiction. Dr. Maté has written several best-selling books, including the award-winning *In the Realm of Hungry Ghosts: Close Encounters with Addiction*. His works have been published internationally in 20 languages. Dr. Maté has received the Hubert Evans Non-Fiction Prize, an honorary degree from the University of Northern British Columbia, and the 2012 Martin Luther King Humanitarian Award from Mothers Against Teen Violence. He is an adjunct professor in the Faculty of Criminology at Simon Fraser University.

What purchase of $100 or less has most positively impacted your life in the last six months (or in recent memory)?

A version of Béla Bartók's string quartets recorded in 1954 by the Végh Quartet. Perhaps I say so because I'm listening to this CD as I write these words, but I am moved and inspired by the modesty, the dedication to art, and the sheer purity of the performance.

What is the book (or books) you've given most as a gift, and why? Or what are one to three books that have greatly influenced your life?

The first book to deeply influence me was *Winnie-The-Pooh* by A. A. Milne. The Bear of Very Little Brain was a beloved companion of my Budapest childhood. (I happen to think the Hungarian translation is even funnier and livelier than the English original, if that's possible.) Milne's little universe of characters speaks to the playful child in all of us, who must, eventually, grow up and face life, hopefully with some of our Pooh-like humor and innocent wisdom intact.

The second was *The Scourge of the Swastika*, by E. F. L. Russell, a British baron, lawyer, and historian. The book was among the first to document the Nazi horrors, giving me, at age 12, a shocking glimpse into the history that had beset my family around the time of my birth. (I lived my first year in Nazi-occupied Budapest; my grandparents were murdered in Auschwitz.) More universally, it brought about my first awareness of the injustices and cruelty that are possible in our world, the ways completely innocent people can be made to suffer — an awareness that has never left me.

Third is The Dhammapada, containing the sayings of the Buddha. It teaches the importance of inner exploration if we are to see beyond the programmed prejudices and limitations of the egoic mind. In other words, if we are to see life clearly. It points to the impossibility of finding peace in the world outside of ourselves if we can't locate it within, an insight my own experience has corroborated over and over again. In a sense, this brief text is the template for the many later spiritual and psychological writings that have influenced me and nourished my own growth.

And to cheat, I'll add a fourth: *The Drama of the Gifted Child* by Alice Miller, the first book to teach me about the devastating lifelong impact of childhood trauma, the healing and integration of which has become my work's primary focus. If the editors are looking the other way, I'll also sneak in *Don Quixote*, the most beautiful and sanest madman in all of world literature.

How has a failure, or apparent failure, set you up for later success? Do you have a "favorite failure" of yours?

In 1997, I was fired from my job as medical coordinator of the Palliative Care Unit at Vancouver Hospital. I loved the work, loved working with dedicated medical colleagues and nurses in the care of the dying—and yet, what I first perceived as the humiliating failure of being fired was one of the best things that ever happened to me. After my initial shock, outrage, and sense of injustice, the experience became a source of invaluable learning. I was able to see how my narcissism had blinded me to the needs and concerns of the people I worked with. I realized what a poor listener and collaborator I'd been. And it opened the door unexpectedly to a new and profound professional calling. My next job, working with the traumatized addicted population in Vancouver's Downtown East Side, provided me with the experience, insight, and inspiration for the most recent and perhaps most significant chapter of my professional experience: writing and educating about addiction.

If you could have a gigantic billboard anywhere with anything on it, what would it say and why? Are there any quotes you think of often or live your life by?

On the billboard would be the words of my greatest contemporary teacher, A. H. Almaas: "Ultimately, your gift to the world is being who you are. It is both your gift and your fulfillment."

What is one of the best or most worthwhile investments you've ever made?

The greatest investment of time I ever made was attending an Enlightenment Intensive led by a close friend of mine, Murray Kennedy, many decades ago. Not that I got enlightened then, or since. In fact, I came away with self-imposed resentment and frustration at missing out on some spiritual experience I was convinced I needed. But it did open me to the world of spiritual inquiry, and it gave me my first experience of differentiating my sense of self from my busy, driven, and chronically dissatisfied mind. This is an endeavor still very much in progress, and one I'm grateful for. Over the years, my friend Murray has become a master teacher and an inspiration to me and many others in spiritual work.

What is an unusual habit or an absurd thing that you love?

Trying to seduce my wife with a Hungarian accent. The seduction is occasionally successful; the accent, not so much.

In the last five years, what new belief, behavior, or habit has most improved your life?

Having been a lifelong yoga agnostic/cynic—as in, "You'll never see me doing yoga"—I have now acquired, and continue to do, an almost daily yoga practice, developed by the Indian yogi Sadhguru Jaggi Vasudev. It has been transformative, granting me access to a sense of inner spaciousness and lightness I was hitherto little familiar with.

What advice would you give to a smart, driven college student about to enter the "real world"? What advice should they ignore?

If you're really smart, you'll drop the drivenness. It doesn't matter what's driving you; when you're driven, you are like a leaf, driven by the wind. You have no real autonomy. You are bound to be blown off course, even if you reach what you believe is your goal. And don't confuse being driven with being authentically animated by an inner calling. One state leaves you depleted and unfulfilled; the other fuels your soul and makes your heart sing.

What are bad recommendations you hear in your profession or area of expertise?

"Just say no" (to drugs, gambling, eating, sex, etc.) is the least helpful advice one can say to a human being caught up in any addiction. If they could say no, they would. The whole point of addiction is that people are compelled to it by suffering, trauma, unease, and emotional pain. If you want to help people, ask why they are in so much pain that they are driven (there's that word again) to escape from it through ultimately self-harming habits or substances. Then support them in healing the trauma at the core of their addiction, a process that always starts with nonjudgmental curiosity and compassion.

In the last five years, what have you become better at saying no to?

Not in the last five years, but in the last five *weeks*, I have been (at long last!) learning to say no to compulsively serving other people's needs, to healing everyone's pain, to accepting all invitations to teach my work. It was taking a toll on my inner peace and on my marriage. Ironic or not, I finally had to accept my own prescriptions, the ones I offered others in my own book on stress and disease, *When the Body Says No*. All very new, but I am feeling joy and vitality returning to me. I have gained a much-needed opportunity to explore who I am when I'm simply *being*, without constantly having to *do* something.

When you feel overwhelmed or unfocused, what do you do? What questions do you ask yourself?

Having a mind characterized by ADHD patterns, it's easy for me to lose focus, to succumb to distraction. The question that helps me return to the present is, simply, "Is what I am doing right now aligned with my life's calling?" My calling—what lights me up and inspires me the most—is freedom for everyone, including myself: politically, socially, emotionally, and spiritually. If I am being compelled to distract myself from emotional unease, I am not free. Then again, if I'm harshly judging my distractibility, I'm not free either. The freedom always comes from the renewed awareness of choice: my choice, in every moment.

"Remember, Babe Ruth was not only the home run king, he was also the strikeout king."

STEVE CASE
TW: @SteveCase
FB: /stevemcase
revolution.com

STEVE CASE is one of America's best-known entrepreneurs and chairman and CEO of Revolution LLC, an investment firm he co-founded. He is a pioneer in making the Internet part of everyday life. Steve's entrepreneurial career began in 1985 when he co-founded America Online (AOL). Under his leadership, AOL became the world's largest and most valuable Internet company. AOL was the first Internet company to go public and among the best-performing stocks of the 1990s, delivering a 11,616 percent return to shareholders. At its peak, nearly half of Internet users in the United States used AOL. Steve is the author of the *New York Times* best-selling book *The Third Wave: An Entrepreneur's Vision of the Future*. Steve is also chairman of the Case Foundation, which he established with his wife, Jean, in 1997. In 2010, Steve and Jean joined The Giving Pledge and publicly reaffirmed their commitment to give away the majority of their wealth to philanthropic causes.

What is the book (or books) you've given most as a gift, and why? Or what are one to three books that have greatly influenced your life?

The Third Wave by futurist Alvin Toffler had an enormous impact on my life. It was his vision of a global electronic village that helped put me on the path to co-founding AOL. I read Toffler's *Third Wave* as a senior in college and was mesmerized by the idea of connecting people through a digital medium. I knew it was inevitable and wanted to be a part of building that future. The book was so influential, when I decided to write a book, I borrowed the title: *The Third Wave: An Entrepreneur's Vision of the Future.* Toffler's three waves were the agricultural revolution, the industrial revolution, and the technology revolution. I focused on the three waves of the Internet: building the platforms to get the world connected, then building apps on top of the Internet, and then integrating the Internet throughout our lives in increasingly pervasive—and sometimes even invisible—ways.

What advice would you give to a smart, driven college student about to enter the "real world"?

First, I'd say it's important to lean into the future, and position yourself for what's happening next, versus what's happening now. Wayne Gretzky was a great hockey player because he didn't focus on where the puck was, he focused on where it was going, and he got there first. Do that!

Second, if, like many people, you got a liberal arts degree, be proud of it, and own it. While the conventional wisdom says that coding is the key to success, that's not as likely to be as true in the Third Wave, when major industries will be disrupted, as it was in the Second, when the focus was on building apps. Sure, coding will continue to be important, but creativity and collaboration will be as well. Don't try to be something you're not. Be confident in the skills you have, as they may be make-or-break for the journey you pursue.

And third, be fearless. I recognize this is easy to say and hard to do, particularly for a generation that has been raised by hovering helicopter parents who may have encouraged you to stay in the box, and in a world that has been unsettled by job loss and terrorism. But despite all of that, you have to get out of your comfort zone and swing for the fences, knowing that sometimes you will fail. Remember, Babe Ruth was not only the home run king, he was also the strikeout king. If you take risks, you will sometimes fail, but that doesn't mean you're a failure. It just means you have to dust yourself off, get up, and redouble your efforts to succeed.

What are bad recommendations you hear in your profession or area of expertise?

There are three things that have become conventional wisdom, especially in places like Silicon Valley, that worry me. First, the idea that naiveté is a competitive advantage. PayPal's founders famously said the fact they knew nothing about the credit card industry gave them an edge in disrupting it. That was true in their case, but it's now become a truism. This notion that ignorance is a strength is likely to lead to stumbles in a new era of innovation and disruption of major industries. For example, if you want to disrupt health care, it's not just about the software, it's about how you work with doctors, integrate with hospitals, get paid by health plans, and deal with regulations. Knowing something about health care is likely to be helpful—perhaps instrumental—in figuring out how to push forward, and having the credibility to get things done. Domain expertise is likely to also be important in AgTech [agricultural technology], as understanding the culture of farming is going to be important. Or in EdTech [educational technology], to be sure what you're building can really help students learn and teachers teach. The trick will be balancing that expertise with fresh out-of-the-box thinking. The people who do both well will be the victors in the Third Wave.

The second concern is the idea that it is better to do everything yourself —what some call a "full-stack" solution. There will be examples of this working, but going it alone will not work as well when it's not just about the app. Partners will likely be needed and, indeed, could be pivotal. There's a proverb that will become increasingly important: "If you want to go fast, go alone, but if you want to go far, you must go together." That could very well emerge as the mantra of the Third Wave.

And the third piece of bad advice is that it's best to ignore regulations and just plow ahead. Sure, Uber was successful in ignoring local laws. Rather than waiting for approvals that may have never come, they raced forward and built up a very successful and very valuable two-sided rider/driver marketplace. Hats off to them. But that worked for Uber because the laws were set locally, not nationally. That won't be the case for most innovations in sectors like health care; if you launch a drug or medical device without getting approval, you'll be stopped in your tracks. That will be the case with driverless cars on the roads and drones in the sky. It will be true with Smart Cities innovations. The list goes on. The bottom line is—like it or not —innovators in the Third Wave need to engage with policymakers to drive real innovation. In summary, the playbook that worked in the Second Wave, when the focus was on building software and services and driving viral adoption, generally won't work in the Third Wave, as the Internet starts impacting some of the most fundamental aspects of our lives.

"If you're *not* called crazy when you start something new, then you're not thinking big enough!"

LINDA ROTTENBERG
TW: @lindarottenberg
lindarottenberg.com

LINDA ROTTENBERG is the co-founder and CEO of Endeavor Global, a cutting-edge nonprofit supporting high-impact entrepreneurs worldwide. She has been named one of "America's Best Leaders" by *U.S. News & World Report* and one of *Time* magazine's "100 Innovators for the 21st Century." A frequent lecturer at Fortune 500 companies, Linda is the subject of four case studies by Harvard Business School and the Stanford Graduate School of Business. ABC and NPR have called her "the entrepreneur whisperer" and Tom Friedman dubbed her the world's "mentor capitalist." She is author of the *New York Times* bestseller *Crazy Is a Compliment: The Power of Zigging When Everyone Else Zags.*

How has a failure, or apparent failure, set you up for later success? Do you have a "favorite failure" of yours?

Around the time that Endeavor reached its ten-year anniversary and I thought we were finally out of the woods, a forest fire swept in that nearly felled me. My husband, a best-selling author known for adventure travel, was diagnosed with life-threatening bone cancer, which somehow robbed me of my motor function. Suddenly, I couldn't get on planes anymore and could barely even show up to the office. I wasn't sure if Bruce would survive and, honestly, I wasn't sure if Endeavor would either. Fortunately, our incredible team stepped up and we grew faster than ever. Perhaps the fact that I wasn't around to micromanage had something to do with it! But the lesson went deeper than learning not to micromanage. I gained a valuable leadership and life lesson when I returned to work after Bruce was thankfully cured. As a female CEO, I had made a point to lead with strength and confidence. . . . Never let them see you sweat, or—even worse—cry, right? After I returned to work, that stonefaced posture no longer worked. Team members wanted to know how Bruce was doing, how our young twin daughters were doing, and how I was doing. I had no choice but to let my guard down and be vulnerable for the first time. Shockingly, rather than drive my employees away, it drew them closer. Young team members actually pulled me aside and confessed that they used to think I was "superhuman," meaning I was unrelatable. Now that I was showing my vulnerability, they said, they would follow me anywhere. The lesson: Rather than striving to be superhuman, I would aspire to be *less* "super" and *more* "human."

If you could have a gigantic billboard anywhere with anything on it, what would it say and why?

My billboard would say, "Crazy is a compliment!"

I was called "la chica loca" (the crazy girl) so many times when I launched Endeavor that I finally decided to own it. I hope others will too, because if you plan to try something new, especially if that something new disrupts the status quo, then you should expect to be called nuts. You can't rock the boat without being told you're off your rocker. The greatest asset of entrepreneurs is their contrarian way of thinking, their tendency to zig when others zag, to go in a new direction. But many people don't give themselves permission to get going for fear that they will be called crazy. I say not only is crazy a compliment, but if you're *not* called crazy when you start something new, then you're not thinking big enough!

When you feel overwhelmed or unfocused, what do you do?

My twin daughters, Tybee and Eden, help me achieve perspective. They have greatly impacted both my personal and my professional growth. Just by virtue of being born, they changed my whole leadership style. I used to be a perfectionist, a micromanager, and a nonstop global traveler, but I had to learn to let go and occasionally say no in order to be with them. As Eden wisely pointed out at the ripe young age of five, "You can be an entrepreneur for a short time, but you're a mommy forever!"

What is an unusual habit or an absurd thing that you love?

Perhaps my most unusual habit is (nicely) stalking people. My ability to "stalk" (investors, board members, entrepreneurs, etc.) served me well when I was getting started with Endeavor. I even waited for a potential mentor outside the men's room once, just to get a few minutes of face time with him. [The opener was] "Hi, my name is Linda, and I've started an organization to support entrepreneurs in emerging markets. I'd love to come by your office for a few minutes to tell you more about it."

Get over the sense that you might be perceived as aggressive. Women especially have to learn this. Estée Lauder was one of the greatest stalkers, and many other successful entrepreneurs got their start not with huge existing networks, but with a little well-placed chutzpah. Find a little courage and reach out to a mentor you admire. People respond to passion and a clear articulation of why you are approaching them in particular. The victim of my stalking did: He ultimately agreed to co-chair Endeavor's global advisory board. In other words: Stalking is an underrated startup strategy!

What advice would you give to a smart, driven college student about to enter the "real world"? What advice should they ignore?

People always tell recent graduates and budding entrepreneurs that they should keep their options open; "don't close any doors." But keeping every option open winds up leading to paralysis or, worse than that, self-deception. How many of my former classmates who took a job at Goldman Sachs or McKinsey for "a few years" before they pursued their real passions like cooking or starting their dream company are actually now chefs or entrepreneurs? Most are still banking and consulting, believing that those doors are still open. My advice to college students: *Close doors.*

This advice also applies to entrepreneurs who have one foot in the business and one foot out. That's okay at the outset (heck, Phil Knight of Nike worked as an accountant for years, and Sara Blakely of Spanx sold fax machines until she was certain her idea would take off). But at some point after your idea has launched, the hedging has to stop. You can't build a significant business with one foot out the door. Entrepreneurs often cling to their conventional work like a security blanket—out of fear rather than necessity—even after they can afford to pursue their venture full-time.

My advice to entrepreneurs: Once your idea has gained traction, cut the umbilical cord. Your idea can't take flight if you don't leave the nest.

"It will never get easier than right now to recklessly pursue your passion. Do it."

TOMMY VIETOR
TW: @Tvietor08, @PodSaveAmerica
crooked.com

TOMMY VIETOR is a founding partner at Fenway Strategies, a creative strategic communications and public relations agency. He is also a co-founder of Crooked Media and a co-host of the political podcast *Pod Save America*. Tommy worked as a spokesman for President Barack Obama for nearly a decade. He served as spokesman for the National Security Council from 2011 to 2013, acting as the media's primary contact on all foreign policy and national security issues. He joined Obama's Senate campaign in 2004 and served as Obama's U.S. Senate spokesman. He was a visiting fellow at the University of Chicago Institute of Politics, and was named one of the top ten communicators of 2014 by *Campaigns and Elections* magazine.

What is the book (or books) you've given most as a gift, and why? Or what are one to three books that have greatly influenced your life?

A book that really impacted me was *The Nightingale's Song* by Robert Timberg. He follows five graduates of the United States Naval Academy

(John McCain, Bud McFarlane, Oliver North, John Poindexter, and Jim Webb) through the Vietnam War and into politics. It's an extraordinary story of courage and sacrifice and also a cautionary tale about how easy it is to lose your way and go down the wrong path, even if you think what you're doing is in service of a noble goal.

How has a failure, or apparent failure, set you up for later success? Do you have a "favorite failure" of yours?

I graduated from college in 2002 and moved down to D.C. to intern for Senator Ted Kennedy. I instantly fell in love with politics and knew it was what I wanted to do for a living. When my internship ended, I applied for every job opening I could find in D.C. Then Democrats got creamed at the midterm elections, and half of the jobs I'd applied for no longer existed, so I kept interning for free. Eventually a position opened up answering phones and greeting visitors in Senator Kennedy's front office, and I was convinced that I would get it. I applied, I interviewed, several people put in a good word for me, and it went to someone else. I was devastated, but if I had gotten that job and stayed in D.C., I would never have wound up on Barack Obama's Senate campaign, and my life would be very different. That failure was the most important step in my career.

What is one of the best or most worthwhile investments you've ever made?

The smartest investment I've ever made was forgoing jobs that paid well for positions that gave me invaluable experiences. [One such] experience was taking a campaign job. You make no money. You work insane hours. If you lose, you're unemployed. But making that sacrifice in the short term to learn was the smartest thing I've ever done.

My broke ass slept on an air mattress for two years. It came with me to three different states (North Carolina, Illinois, Iowa), and every morning it would end up half-deflated and my butt would be touching the ground. I overdrew my bank account countless times (thanks for all those overdraft fees, Bank of America!), but the experience was worth more than any paycheck then or since.

What advice would you give to a smart, driven college student about to enter the "real world"?

Don't worry about making money. Don't stress about having a plan. Don't think about networking or setting yourself up for the next thing. Try as hard as you possibly can to find something you love, because the depressing reality is that most people never find a career that they're truly passionate about. For many people, the real world is a slog and they live for the weekends. It will never get easier than right now to recklessly pursue your passion. Do it.

When you feel overwhelmed or unfocused, what do you do?

I get paid to read and comment on the news for a living, and I still wake up every morning completely overwhelmed by all that's going on. I can feel my blood pressure go up as I try to figure out what to focus on first. The way I manage it is to remember that the world will go on if I don't read everything. Newspapers will publish again the next day. I will always be better off consuming a smaller amount of high-quality information than trying to consume it all. I think that lesson can apply to a lot of things. For instance, you're better off spending quality time with one friend on a given night than trying to run around and see everyone.

If you could have a gigantic billboard anywhere with anything on it, what would it say and why?

My billboard would say "STOP LOOKING AT YOUR PHONE," both as a message to others and a reminder for me.

QUOTES I'M PONDERING

(Tim Ferriss: Nov. 25–Dec. 30, 2016)

"Don't believe everything you think."

—BJ MILLER, MD

A hospice care physician, quoting a well-known Buddhist saying

"It's so hard to forget pain, but it's even harder to remember sweetness. We have no scar to show for happiness. We learn so little from peace."

—CHUCK PALAHNIUK

Famed American author, best known for *Fight Club*

"Talk less, listen more."

—BRENÉ BROWN

Research professor, author of *Daring Greatly*

"Reality is merely an illusion, albeit a very persistent one."

—ALBERT EINSTEIN

German theoretical physicist, Nobel Prize winner

"You learn the secret of this business, which is there's no secret. Be yourself."

LARRY KING
TW: @kingsthings
ora.tv/larrykingnow

LARRY KING has been dubbed "the most remarkable talk-show host on TV ever" by *TV Guide* and "master of the mike" by *Time* magazine. He has done more than 50,000 interviews throughout his half century in broadcasting, including exclusive sit-downs with every U.S. president since Gerald Ford. *Larry King Live* debuted on CNN in 1985 and ran for 25 years. Described as the "Muhammad Ali of the broadcast interview," Larry has been inducted into five of the nation's leading broadcasting halls of fame and is the recipient of both a lifetime Emmy Award and the prestigious Al Neuharth Award for Excellence in the Media. Both his radio and television shows have won the George Foster Peabody Award for excellence in broadcasting. He is the author of several books, including his autobiography *My Remarkable Journey*. He is currently the host of *Larry King Now,* produced by Ora TV.

Note from Tim: My friend Cal Fussman (TW: @calfussman, calfussman. com) is a *New York Times* best-selling author and writer-at-large for *Esquire* magazine, where he is best known as a primary writer of the "What I Learned" feature. He's interviewed dozens of shapers of modern culture including Mikhail Gorbachev, Muhammad Ali, Jimmy Carter, Ted Kennedy, Jeff Bezos, and Richard Branson, among others. Cal also has breakfast with Larry King nearly every morning in L.A. Since Larry can be hard to nail down and I was dying to have him in this book, Cal was kind enough to interview him in my stead. We also wanted to focus on some of Larry's stories, so you'll notice that the format and questions are different. Thanks, Cal and Larry!

Larry King's first morning as a broadcaster:

Now it's Monday morning, May first, 1957. I get there like six o'clock, I go on at nine. My uncle hugs me and kisses me. It was a warm, muggy, sunny Miami Beach morning. Eight 41st Street, right opposite the police station. I would visit that last year, by the way. It's another station now.

But anyway, I walk in as a secretary comes in at about eight and say hello to the all-night guy and stack up my records. I'm ready to play and Marshall [Simmons, the general manager,] says, "Come into my office," like quarter to nine.

And he says, "This your first day on the air, the best of luck to you." And I said, "Thank you." He said, "What name are you going to use?" "What are you talking about?" "Well, Larry Zeiger"—that was my name—"ain't going to work." Now, it would work. Now, any name would go. Engelbert Humperdinck. Any name would go.

So he says it won't work, it's a little too ethnic. And people won't know how to spell it and we got to change your name.

I said, "I'm going on the air in 12 minutes." He said, "Well . . ." He had the *Miami Herald* open, I would later write a column for them. All these things are like miracles. And there was an ad for King's Wholesale Liquor on Washington Avenue. He looked and said, "How about Larry King?"

I said, "Okay, it sounds good." [. . .] Anyway, so now I got a new name. I'm about to go on the air.

Nine o'clock.

I start the record, [hums] I lower the record, put on the microphone, and nothing comes out.

CF: Nothing comes out of your mouth?

LK: Nothing. I bring the record back up, lower down, bring up, lower down and I am panicked. I am sweating. I'm looking at the clock, and I literally said to myself, "I can't do it. I can do a lot of things, but I'm nervous and maybe my whole career is done." And Marshall Simmons, God rest him, kicked open the door of the control room and said, "This is a communications business, dammit. Communicate!"

He closed the door. I turned down the record, put the mic on, and said, "Good morning. My name Is Larry King, and that's the first time I've ever said that because I just been given this name, and let me tell you, this is my first day ever on the air. And all my life I dreamed of this. When I was five years old, I would imitate announcers. [. . .]

"And I'm nervous. I'm very nervous here. So please bear with me." And I play the record and was *never* nervous again.

And later in life that's a story I told Arthur Godfrey, Jackie Gleason, others, and they said, "You learn the secret of this business, which is there's no secret. Be yourself." So what I did that day, I wasn't conceiving this, carried through me for 60 years, which is, be yourself. Don't be afraid to ask a question, don't be afraid to sound stupid.

Cal Fussman's favorite Larry King story:

I just started radio. I was on the air two months and working nine to 12 in the afternoon and I'm loving every second of it.

I mean, I can't wait to get there. I can't wait to be on. God, I loved it.

And general manager Marshall Simmons called me in and said, "Al Fox, the all-night guy, is sick tonight. Would you do the all-night show?" and I said, "Sure." He said, "You'll be here alone, you know. It's a very small station. We don't have an engineer at night. You just record the meter readings, play music, and talk. You are on from midnight to six. And then you'll hang around, will be on again at nine and then get some rest."

"Oh boy, sure, I'll be fine." Now I'm alone in the station, I'm playing records and I'm talking to people about the time and the weather and what's going on in the world. And the phone rings and I pick it up and I said, "W-A-H-R."

And this woman's voice—I could tell you the truth, Cal, I can almost hear it now.

This sexy woman voice says, "I want you."

Remember, I'm 22 years old. I think the pimples on my face are from Hershey bars. I am a Jew in heat. No one has ever said to me, "I want you."

And I suddenly said to myself: There are more than two benefits to being in this business.

So I said, "Whoah whoah whoah whoah whoah. What do you want?" She says, "Come over. Come over to my house." I said, "I'm on the air. I get off at six. I'll be over at six." "I live only ten blocks away. I have to go to work at six, so it's now or never. Here's my address. Try to come over."

I've got this moral dilemma now. My career, my radio, but no one has ever said, "I want you." So here's what the radio audience heard: "Ladies and gentlemen, I'm just filling in tonight. So I'm going to give you a particularly good time. I'm going to play the entire Harry Belafonte at Carnegie Hall album uninterrupted."

I had 23 minutes, which is all the time I needed, which is still true to this day.

Anyway, I put the record on—we didn't have tapes then—zoom out to the car, drive to her house, and there's the car she described in the driveway. I pull into the house, the light is on over the door. I go into a little dark room, and there's this woman in a white negligee sitting on the couch. She opens her arms, I grab her, I hold her, my cheek's against her, and she's got the radio on.

And I'm hearing Harry Belafonte and he's singing "Jamaica Farewell" and he sings, "Down the way where the nights, where the nights, where the nights . . ."

The record gets stuck. I place the girl back at the end of the couch, run out to my car. Jewish masochism, I keep the radio on all the way driving to the station, "where the nights, where the nights, where the nights . . ."

I get in, and all the lights are going, flashing from people calling in. I'm totally embarrassed. I'm picking up, I'm apologizing to people, and the last caller was an older Jewish man. And I just said, "W-A-H-R, good morning," and all I hear was "Where the nights, where the nights, where the nights . . . I am going crazy with "'where the nights.'" I say, "Gee, I'm sorry, why didn't you just change the station?" And he said, "I'm an invalid. I'm in bed and a nurse takes care of me. She leaves at night and she sets it to your station.

The radio is up on the bureau, I can't reach it. I'm stuck." I say, "Gee, can I do anything for you?" He says, "Yeah, play 'Hava Nagila.'"

Can you name one to three books that have massively impacted your life?

The Catcher in the Rye would be one. *Lou Gehrig: A Quiet Hero,* by Frank Graham.

What is an unusual habit or absurd thing that you love?

I try to total up words [or letters] in a phrase or a sentence and then divide it to see if I get an even number, like: "True love" divided by 2 is 4. Four letters in each thing. I don't want an odd number, I want an even number. I do that a lot in my head.

Everyone has little unusual [things]. For example, my pills—I take a lot of prescription pills and vitamins—have to be in order in the closet. And when I lay them out for the next day, I have to take them in the same order. That's a rule.

"Take it easy, ya azizi."

MUNA ABUSULAYMAN
TW: @abusulayman
FB: /Muna.Abusulayman.Page
haute-elan.com

MUNA ABUSULAYMAN is a leading media personality in the Middle East. She is the former founding secretary general of the Alwaleed bin Talal Foundation, the philanthropic arm of HRH Prince Alwaleed bin Talal's Kingdom Holding Company and co-host of one of MBC TV's most popular social programs, *Kalam Nawaem* ("Speech of the Soft"). In 2004, Muna was named a "Young Global Leader" by the World Economic Forum. In 2007, she became the first woman from Saudi Arabia to be appointed by the United Nations Development Program as a goodwill ambassador. In 2009 and 2010, she was selected as one of the 500 most influential Muslims in the world. In 2011, she was listed as the 21st Most Powerful Arab Woman, and 131st most Influential Arab in the World by *Arabian Business* magazine.

What is the book (or books) you've given most as a gift, and why? Or what are one to three books that have greatly influenced your life?

For every stage in life, you discover books that speak to you, that help you change, to become the version of yourself that you need to be. It's so very difficult to choose *one* book. But, if I must, it will be *The Power of a Positive No* by William Ury.

It allowed me to understand the reasons why I was saying yes to things I did not want to do. More important, it gave me the tools for how to say no consistently and without guilt.

Other books have allowed me to discover myself, guide myself to changing, but I would not have had the time to do that if I had not said no to time-sucking activities that I was accepting before.

If you could have a gigantic billboard anywhere with anything on it, what would it say and why? Are there any quotes you think of often or live your life by?

There are two sayings I live by that I got from my father, who knew that I always wanted to be the best in whatever I did: "You can only do your best" and "Take it easy, ya azizi." *Azizi* means "my dear" in Arabic.

Do your best, trust your abilities, and if it does not happen, then "Take it easy, ya azizi." This has helped me a lot on dark days when there were too many responsibilities, when I was trying to deliver perfect results in all aspects of my life.

It has also taught me to be accountable to myself. Do your best, take it easy, and live to battle another day, tomorrow.

What is an unusual habit or an absurd thing that you love?

I have to try weird ice cream flavors in countries that I travel to. I love ice cream. It should be its own food group. The weirdest flavor is probably durian ice cream in Malaysia, an exotic fruit that smells like sewage but which has a nice kick to it, once you get past the smell. [On the other hand,] my favorite flavor is almost any fruit flavor from Venchi Gelato in Rome.

When you feel overwhelmed or unfocused, what do you do?

I have learned that when I overcommit, I lose focus and desire to do the work at hand. So this is why learning to say no is very important to me.

Sometimes, however, loss of focus is a symptom of something else, that you really don't care for your work. This needs a lot of reflection and discussions with mentors to figure out whether you need a break, a vacation, or a change of career.

What is one of the best or most worthwhile investments you've ever made?

Investing in my children when they were young. Due to my busy schedule and long hours at work, it meant that almost every free minute was devoted to being with them, rather than adult social activities. It helped us get closer to each other, have bedtime stories, take vacations, and build memories.

Now that I am more established and have more time, they have flown the nest. I am glad that I truly made the time commitment to enjoy daily mundane activities with them, because now, when I do have the time, they don't.

I had also taken them with me when I traveled for work, if it was more than a three-day work trip. Sometimes, it cost an arm and a leg, but it allowed me to spend time with them and discuss issues that rose from those different cultures.

I always made the time to discuss with them any business call that I made in their presence: what it was about, what the issue was, how I was trying to solve it. First, so they understood what took Mommy away from them, but also to help them understand the world they will enter one day.

"No society in human history ever suffered because its people became too reasonable."

SAM HARRIS
TW: @SamHarrisOrg
samharris.org

SAM HARRIS received a degree in philosophy from Stanford University and a PhD in neuroscience from UCLA. He is the author of the best-selling books *The End of Faith*, *Letter to a Christian Nation*, *The Moral Landscape*, *Free Will*, *Lying*, *Waking Up*, and *Islam and the Future of Tolerance: A Dialogue* (with Maajid Nawaz). He also hosts the popular podcast *Waking Up with Sam Harris*.

What is the book (or books) you've given most as a gift, and why? Or what are one to three books that have greatly influenced your life?

The Beginning of Infinity by David Deutsch greatly expanded my sense of the potential power of human knowledge, while Nick Bostrom's *Superintelligence* made me worry that machine knowledge could ruin everything. I strongly recommend both books. But if you just want to forget about the future and lose yourself in the book that forever changed how narrative nonfiction is written, read *In Cold Blood* by Truman Capote.

What purchase of $100 or less has most positively impacted your life in the last six months (or in recent memory)?

I found a great sleeve for my computer made by WaterField Designs (MacBook SleeveCase, $69). It is so well made that I carry my computer with me much more than I used to, and this has led to some very satisfying sessions of work in public places.

If you could have a gigantic billboard anywhere with anything on it, what would it say and why?

"No society in human history ever suffered because its people became too reasonable."

As a species, we live in perpetual choice between conversation and violence. So it's very important that we keep making sense to one another. Only a commitment to honest reasoning can allow us to cooperate with billions of strangers in an open-ended way. And this is why dogmatism and dishonesty are not merely intellectual problems but social ones as well. When we fail to reason honestly, we have lost our connection to the world and to one another.

In the last five years, what new belief, behavior, or habit has most improved your life?

Five years ago, I don't think I knew what a "podcast" was. Now I release an episode of the *Waking Up* podcast more or less every week. Having a podcast has allowed me to connect with a wide range of fascinating people whom I wouldn't otherwise meet—and our conversations reach a much larger audience than my books ever will. I feel extremely lucky that my career as a writer and speaker has coincided with the birth of this technology. We appear to be living in a new golden age of audio.

What advice would you give to a smart, driven college student about to enter the "real world"?

Don't worry about what you're going to do with the rest of your life. Just find a profitable and interesting use for the next three to five years.

In the last five years, what have you become better at saying no to?

Out of necessity, I've become very good at saying no to more or less everything. In particular, I decline most work-related requests—invitations to collaborate on projects, blurb books, do interviews, attend conferences, etc. This became very easy the moment I realized that I was being given a choice between working on one of my own projects (or spending time with my family) and working for someone else (generally for free). Documentary interviews are especially easy to pass on these days. After doing a few dozen of them, I realized that most of these films never see the light of day.

It's not that I don't do people favors. In fact, I often go out of my way to do them. But, in such cases, I am doing something that I genuinely want to do. An inability to say no is almost never the reason why.

When you feel overwhelmed or unfocused, what do you do?

Whenever I feel overwhelmed, I complain to my wife about it. After listening patiently for about 30 seconds, she generally tells me to STFU. Then I meditate or work out.

"I wake up each day with the firm conviction that I am nowhere near my full potential. 'Greatness' is a verb."

MAURICE ASHLEY
TW: @MauriceAshley
mauriceashley.com

MAURICE ASHLEY is the first African-American International Grandmaster in the annals of the game of chess, and he has translated his love to others as a three-time national championship coach, two-time author, ESPN commentator, iPhone app designer, puzzle inventor, and motivational speaker. In recognition for his immense contribution to the game, Maurice was inducted into the U.S. Chess Hall of Fame in 2016. His book, *Chess for Success: Using an Old Game to Build New Strengths in Children and Teens*, shows the many benefits of chess, particularly for at-risk youth. His TEDx Talk, "Working Backward to Solve Problems," has been viewed nearly half a million times. He also appeared with me in the Brazilian jujitsu episode of *The Tim Ferriss Experiment*, joined by our mutual friend Josh Waitzkin (page 195).

What is the book (or books) you've given most as a gift, and why? Or what are one to three books that have greatly influenced your life?

Quite a few books have caused fundamental shifts within my being. However, the first that still resonates to this day is *Passages* by Gail Sheehy. I read it as an 18-year-old, and it opened my eyes to the realization that I would be a different person at every stage of my life, all the way to my old age and eventual death. It led me to realize that I should try to live my life backwards, starting with the wisdom of the elderly and applying it to the energy of youth. I have not always been able to do it, but it has helped me immensely with keeping perspective on things that matter and things that don't.

I would also add *Sugar Blues* by William Dufty to the list, as it made me radically change my diet for the better. *Mastery* by George Leonard detailed the challenges that we all face on the road to expertise in any field. And *The 4-Hour Workweek* by Tim Ferriss made me ditch the average life in search of one with complete flexibility and freedom to live life on my terms.

How has a failure, or apparent failure, set you up for later success? Do you have a "favorite failure" of yours?

As a competitive chess player, failure is part and parcel of growth. My most important failure came at a tournament in Bermuda where I needed to win a crucial game in order to finally get the title of International Grandmaster, the highest and most prestigious title a player can attain. I was playing Grandmaster Michael Bezold from Germany, and in a crucial position, I had a choice between taking one of his important pieces or taking a mere pawn. It turned out that taking his pawn would have kept all my advantages intact while greedily taking his rook caused my attack to dry up in an instant. After I lost the game, Alexander Shabalov, a Grandmaster who won the U.S. title four times, reassuringly pointed out my mistake and then said words I will never forget: "In order to become a Grandmaster, you must already be one." I understood right there that I had to get back to work on perfecting myself before I could actually go about winning games. That idea has kept my eyes focused on the process over the result ever since.

If you could have a gigantic billboard anywhere with anything on it, what would it say and why?

"I wake up each day with the firm conviction that I am nowhere near my full potential. 'Greatness' is a verb."

These words came to me one morning in a flash of awareness and insight. I have miles to go before I sleep, and so I will spend my remaining years desperately looking to improve who I am from year to year. Greatness is not a final destination, but a series of small acts done daily in order to constantly rejuvenate and refresh our skills in a daily effort to become a better version of ourselves.

In the last five years, what new belief, behavior, or habit has most improved your life?

I recently took a self-help course called Landmark, and I learned more than anything to strive to be completely open and transparent in my relationships. That has led to fewer but higher-quality relationships over time, and it has freed me from worrying as much about what other people think. Now one of the most important buzzwords in my vocabulary is "authenticity." That is my measuring stick for whether I am saying a load of crap or I am speaking the truths that resonate from my soul.

HOW TO SAY
NO

DANNY MEYER
TW: @dhmeyer
ushgnyc.com

DANNY MEYER is the founder and CEO of Union Square Hospitality Group (USHG), which comprises some of New York's most beloved and acclaimed restaurants, including Gramercy Tavern, The Modern, Maialino, and more. Danny and USHG founded Shake Shack, the modern-day "roadside" burger restaurant, which became a public company in 2015. Danny's book, *Setting the Table: The Transforming Power of Hospitality in Business*, a *New York Times* bestseller, articulates a set of signature business and life principles that translate to a wide range of industries. Danny was included in the 2015 *Time* magazine "100 Most Influential People" list.

Note from Tim: For your reading pleasure and schadenfreude itch, here's another beautiful "polite decline" email, this time from Danny Meyer.

Jeffrey [my friend who asked on my behalf],

Greetings and thanks for writing.

I'm grateful for the invitation to participate in Tim's next book project, but am struggling at this moment to make time ends meet for all we're doing at USHG, including my ongoing procrastination with my own writing projects.

I thought carefully about this as it's clearly a wonderful opportunity, but am going to decline—with gratitude.

Know the book will be a big success!

Thanks again.

Danny

Union Square Hospitality Group

"There are many organizations that fret over small, direct expenses, yet have no misgivings about keeping superfluous staff tied up in a conference room for hours."

JOHN ARNOLD
TW: @JohnArnoldFndtn
arnoldfoundation.org

JOHN ARNOLD is a co-chair of the Laura and John Arnold Foundation. LJAF's core objective is to improve the lives of individuals by strengthening our social, governmental, and economic systems. John founded and was CEO of Centaurus Energy, a multibillion-dollar energy commodity hedge fund, until he shocked Wall Street by announcing his retirement in 2012. Prior to founding Centaurus, he held various positions within Enron's wholesale division, including head of Natural Gas Derivatives, and was known as "the King of Natural Gas." John holds a BA from Vanderbilt University, and serves on the board of Breakthrough Energy Ventures, an investor-led venture capital firm dedicated to funding transformational technologies that will reduce global greenhouse gas emissions.

What is the book (or books) you've given most as a gift, and why? Or what are one to three books that have greatly influenced your life?

Much of one's attitude toward life depends on their level of optimism. An optimistic person will invest more in him- or herself, as the deferred reward is expected to be higher. A pessimistic person prefers the immediate returns at the expense of the long-term outcomes. However, the news cycle, driven by negative stories of the day, is the proverbial missing the forest for the trees. The reality, best captured in *The Rational Optimist* by Matt Ridley (page 35) and *The Better Angels of Our Nature* by Steven Pinker (page 475), is that the long-term trend in almost every measure is resolutely positive. Optimism is a reflexive trait, with a circular relationship between cause and effect. The more optimistic society is about the future, the better the future is. These books serve as a reminder of the great advances society has made.

What advice would you give to a smart, driven college student about to enter the "real world"? What advice should they ignore?

The unfortunate truth is that advice is almost always driven by anecdotal experience, and thus has limited value and relevance. Read a sampling of college commencement addresses, and you quickly realize each story is unique. For every entrepreneur who thrived by resolutely working on a singular idea for many years, there is another who pivoted wildly. For every successful individual who designed a master plan for life, there is another who was deliberately spontaneous. Ignore advice, especially early in one's career. There is no universal path to success.

In the last five years, what have you become better at saying no to?

I had not appreciated the maxim "Time is money" until recently. But for those whose time is a scarce resource, learning to say no to meetings is a necessary skill. Sitting through an unproductive meeting has huge opportunity costs. It seems obvious, but people struggle with equilibrating time and money. There are many organizations that fret over small, direct expenses, yet have no misgivings about keeping superfluous staff tied up in a conference room for hours. In recent years, I have become better at judging the opportunity cost of time.

QUOTES I'M PONDERING

(Tim Ferriss: Jan. 6–Jan. 27, 2017)

"A schedule defends from chaos and whim. It is a net for catching days."

—ANNIE DILLARD
American author, professor, and Pulitzer Prize winner for
Pilgrim at Tinker Creek

"Those who are determined to be 'offended' will discover a provocation somewhere. We cannot possibly adjust enough to please the fanatics, and it is degrading to make the attempt."

—CHRISTOPHER HITCHENS
Author, journalist, and social critic

"Those who are easily shocked should be shocked more often."

—MAE WEST
One of the greatest female stars of classic American cinema

"If at first the idea is not absurd, then there is no hope for it."

—ALBERT EINSTEIN
German theoretical physicist, Nobel Prize winner

"The key to a great life is simply having a bunch of great days. So you can think about it one day at a time."

MR. MONEY MUSTACHE
TW/FB: @mrmoneymustache
mrmoneymustache.com

MR. MONEY MUSTACHE (Pete Adeney in real life) grew up in Canada in a family of mostly eccentric musicians. He graduated with a degree in computer engineering in the 1990s and worked in various tech companies before retiring at age 30. Pete and his wife live near Boulder, Colorado, with their now 11-year-old son, and they have not had real jobs since 2005. This begs the question of "How?" In essence, they accomplished this early retirement by optimizing all aspects of their lifestyle for maximal fun at minimal expense, and by using basic index-fund investing. Their average annual expenses total a mere $25,000 to $27,000, and they do not feel in want of anything. Since 2005, all three of them have explored a freeform life of interesting projects, side businesses, and adventures. In 2011, Pete started writing about his philosophy on the *Mr. Money Mustache* blog, which has grown to reach about 23 million people (and 300 million page views) since its founding. It has become a worldwide cult phenomenon with a self-organizing community.

What is an unusual habit or an absurd thing that you love?

Hanging my laundry on a clothesline to dry in the sun, harvesting and chopping firewood, and shoveling enormous quantities of snow after a big storm. I find it joyful to spend good solid hours on these real, traditional human activities to avoid getting sucked into the vortex of the more artificial layers of business, money, and Internet chatter.

In the last five years, what new belief, behavior, or habit has most improved your life?

The most important one by far is realizing that the real measure of a good life is "How happy and satisfied am I with my life right now?"

This turns out to be a lot simpler than you might think. We all have our ups and downs, so your goal is simply to maximize your "up" time and minimize those downs to as close to zero as possible.

If you ask yourself this question at the end of a thoroughly great day, the answer is very often positive. After a horrible day (or a string of them), you're more likely to say that life sucks. I came to realize that the key to a great life is simply having a bunch of great days. So you can think about it one day at a time.

And it turns out there are some pretty simple buttons you can press to give yourself a great day. Start by waking up from a good sleep, eating good food, leaving your phone/newspaper/computer behind, and simply writing down your plan for what will make the day great. Several hours of physical activity, some hard work, a chance to laugh with and help out other people —and you're pretty much there.

So the longer-term challenge is simply designing your life so that you have more of this stuff and less of the fluff. Look at every activity as you go through your day and think, "Is *this* contributing to getting me a better day—today—and if not, is there anybody in the world who has managed to design this activity out of their lives and still succeed beyond my level?"

What advice would you give to a smart, driven college student about to enter the "real world"? What advice should they ignore?

The worst piece of standard advice is more of an assumption that spans the entire middle class: "Get yourself into a nice, prosperous 40-year career of being completely dependent on your employer."

It's an assumption because it happens automatically if you follow the standard path: Spend 85 percent or more of your income and borrow freely if you ever want something that you don't yet have the money for. You'll spend most of your life with your head just above the financial water, if everything goes well.

Instead, rewind that story and think of it in terms of freedom: You are free for life once you have 25 to 30 times your annual spending locked up and working for you in low-fee index funds or other relatively boring investments.

If you save the standard 15 percent of your income, this freedom arrives roughly at age 65. If you can crank that up to 65 percent, you're free just after your 30th birthday, and you often end up a lot happier in the process.

Of course, there are other ways to solve the money problem: Own a profitable business, or find work that is joyful enough to do it for life. But even these things happen more quickly if you don't get mired in the earn-to-borrow-to-spend trap that is part of that big middle-class assumption.

So the one-liner is: A high savings rate (or "profit margin on life") is by far the best strategy for a great and creative life, because it's your ticket to freedom. Freedom is the fuel for creativity.

"Learn Transcendental Meditation as taught by Maharishi Mahesh Yogi and meditate regularly. This will end your suffering and give you happiness and fulfillment in life. Rock on!"

DAVID LYNCH
TW: @david_lynch
davidlynchfoundation.org

DAVID LYNCH is an award-winning director, writer, and producer. He has been described by the *Guardian* as "the most important director of this era," and his work includes iconic films and groundbreaking television shows such as *Eraserhead*, *The Elephant Man*, *Blue Velvet*, *Wild at Heart*, *Twin Peaks*, *Lost Highway*, and *Mulholland Drive*. He is also the founder and chairman of the board of trustees of the David Lynch Foundation for Consciousness-Based Education and World Peace, which teaches Transcendental Meditation to adults and children worldwide. Lynch has received three Academy Award nominations for Best Director and a nomination for best screenplay. He has won France's César Award for Best Foreign Film twice, as well as the Palme d'Or at the Cannes Film Festival and a Golden Lion award for lifetime achievement at the Venice Film Festival.

What is the book (or books) you've given most as a gift, and why? Or what are one to three books that have greatly influenced your life?

That Motel Weekend by James Donner, *The Srimad Devi Bhagavatam*, and *The Metamorphosis* by Franz Kafka.

How has a failure, or apparent failure, set you up for later success? Do you have a "favorite failure" of yours?

A real good failure gives a person tremendous freedom. You can't fall further down, so there's nowhere to go but up. There's nothing left to lose. So this freedom is almost like a euphoria, and it can open doors in the mind that lead to what you truly want to do. And, in the doing of what you truly want to do, there's a joy mixed with this unbounded freedom, and there's no fear. Just a great happiness in the doing. My favorite failure was the motion picture *Dune*.

What purchase of $100 or less has most positively impacted your life in the last six months (or in recent memory)?

1/8", ¼", and 5/16" by 36" unfinished hardwood dowels. These were ordered from Amazon Prime and delivered to my door. I used them as part of a side table I'm building, and they worked out very well for parts of wooden hinges.

In the last five years, what new belief, behavior, or habit has most improved your life?

Festool technology for accuracy in woodworking.

If you could have a gigantic billboard anywhere with anything on it, what would it say?

"Learn Transcendental Meditation as taught by Maharishi Mahesh Yogi and meditate regularly. This will end your suffering and give you happiness and fulfillment in life. Rock on!"

What is one of the best or most worthwhile investments you've ever made?

$35—at the time the price for students—to start Transcendental Meditation on July 1, 1973.

What is an unusual habit or an absurd thing that you love?

Smoking cigarettes.

In the last five years, what have you become better at saying no to?
Interviews like this. As you can see, I still have some work to do.

What advice would you give to a smart, driven college student about to enter the "real world"? What advice should they ignore?
Learn Transcendental Meditation as taught by Maharishi Mahesh Yogi and meditate regularly. Ignore pessimistic thinking and pessimistic thinkers.

What are bad recommendations you hear in your profession or area of expertise?
Even if you don't like it, do it for the money.

When you feel overwhelmed or unfocused, what do you do?
I sit and desire ideas.

"Trusted third parties are security holes."

NICK SZABO
TW: @NickSzabo4
unenumerated.blogspot.com

NICK SZABO is a polymath. The breadth and depth of his interests and knowledge are truly astounding. He's a computer scientist, legal scholar, and cryptographer best known for his pioneering research in digital contracts and cryptocurrency. The phrase and concept of "smart contracts" were developed by Nick with the goal of bringing what he calls the "highly evolved" practices of contract law and practice to the design of electronic commerce protocols between strangers on the Internet. Nick also designed Bit Gold, which many consider the precursor to Bitcoin.

What is the book (or books) you've given most as a gift, and why? Or what are one to three books that have greatly influenced your life?
Richard Dawkins, *The Selfish Gene*, explains more about life (including human behavior and myself) than anything else I've read.

What advice would you give to a smart, driven college student about to enter the "real world"?

Everybody is striving after social proof—from a close friend's adulation to online likes and upvotes. The less you need positive feedback on your ideas, the more original design regions you can explore, and the more creative and, in the long term, useful to society you will be. But it could be a very long time before people will love you (or even pay you) for it. The more original your ideas, the less your bosses and peers will understand them, and people fear or at best ignore what they do not understand. But for me, making progress on the ideas was very rewarding in itself at the time, even though they would have made the worst party conversation topics ever. Eventually, decades after, they generated more social accolades than I now know what to do with.

What are bad recommendations you hear in your profession or area of expertise?

The Silicon Valley mantra "move fast and break things" is very bad advice when one is dealing with sizable sums of money!

If you could have a gigantic billboard anywhere with anything on it, what would it say?

"Trusted third parties are security holes."

What purchase of $100 or less has most positively impacted your life in the last six months (or in recent memory)?

Nothing terribly profound (or alternatively nothing that I don't take for granted) for $100. Those little single-cup foamer/mixer things [Tim: like the PowerLix Milk Frother] are pretty cool for concocting my own custom cocoa, coffee, etc. Not taking things for granted, it may be something as mundane now (but unavailable before not much longer than a century ago) as a tankful of gas to drive up to San Francisco and do your podcast!

How has a failure, or apparent failure, set you up for later success? Do you have a "favorite failure" of yours?

[My favorite "failure" has been] making unemployment creative, and not getting a job or hanging out with people just because one is "supposed to." My best ideas came from when I was not distracted or tired from a job or social needs but had the freedom to think big and think crazy, yet had the time to think it through. That said, a good education (computer science and law) and the discipline that came from highly motivated job experience (I definitely needed the money!) were also essential.

What is one of the best or most worthwhile investments you've ever made?

Working on my own ideas instead of the ideas I was supposed to be working on, even though in the short term that meant trouble. For example, from ignoring my bosses' ideas . . . Another way to put this is giving priority to advancing the ideas I admired over my social and consumer desires — by combining these ideas in novel and useful ways, or by working out the consequences of new technological capabilities for often very old ideas.

Another great long-term investment was my theoretically oriented computer science education, by which I discovered great technological capabilities to apply to the big problems I wanted to solve. It also had a practical benefit in that my computer science account was how I discovered the Internet early and thereby met the rare people who were pursuing similar directions, who I never would have had the opportunity to meet in "real life."

What is an unusual habit or an absurd thing that you love?

The manual use of printer paper! I know you are a fan of Evernote, but even as a computer scientist and programmer, I still get a great kick and utility out of having a handy piece of paper on which to doodle and jot my latest brain flashes.

When you feel overwhelmed or unfocused, what do you do?

Hey, I too wish I could solve this. I look forward to your other folks' answers!

"If you can't laugh at it, you lose."

JON CALL
IG/YT: jujimufu
acrobolix.com

JON CALL is best known as Jujimufu, the anabolic acrobat. In 2000, he started teaching himself "tricking," an aesthetic blend of flips, twists, and kicks. In 2002, Jon launched trickstutorials.com, which he ran for 12 years and became one of the largest communities of online tricksters. He became famous from viral videos involving weighted splits between chairs, with massive barbell weights held overhead, and has appeared on *America's Got Talent*. *Men's Health* wrote that he "looks like a strongman, moves like a ninja, and performs the most insane fitness stunts you'll ever see."

What is the book (or books) you've given most as a gift, and why? Or what are one to three books that have greatly influenced your life?

Thinking Body, Dancing Mind by Chungliang Al Huang. It is a sports psychology book based on Tao teachings. It's a very unique adaptation of the Tao. I was fortunate enough to select it from a bookstore for reading when I was

15 years old. At the time, it greatly complemented my tae kwon do training. I still to this day pick that book up for random readings.

What purchase of $100 or less has most positively impacted your life in the last six months (or in recent memory)?

An electric single burner. I use the Aroma Housewares AHP-303/CHP-303 Single Hot Plate. It costs less than $20 and is great for keeping a cup of coffee (or three) hot!

How has a failure, or apparent failure, set you up for later success? Do you have a "favorite failure" of yours?

I sprained my ankle practicing acrobatics in March 2012. It was a grade II sprain. I wasn't able to practice my acrobatic moves correctly for seven months. It was a slow recovery, but here's the fun part: during the time my ankle was sprained, I decided to train gymnastic rings like a madman. I was doing very hard ring workouts every other day for about half a year. Putting muscle mass on with rings isn't as easy as putting it on with free weights, but I put on 15 pounds! The really high volume of gymnastic rings training inevitably had some crazy carryover to my acrobatic moves when my ankle was near full recovery. The ankle sprain triggered a huge transformation that has kept going to this day. Had I not sprained my ankle, I might never have diversified my skill set and become more than a skinny kid who did acrobatic moves in parks by himself.

If you could have a gigantic billboard anywhere with anything on it, what would it say and why?

"If you can't laugh at it, you lose."

I just made that one up this year—I choose to live by that quote more than any other. The great thing about the quote is that the exceptions to the quote suggest a powerful lesson. You wouldn't laugh when people die, especially someone you love, but that's because you can't always win in life. Sometimes we do lose! But we better be able to distinguish between real loss and weakness of character. Getting a scratch on your car or forgetting to take the trash down to the curb before the weekly pickup are annoying things you should probably get to laughing about sooner rather than later.

The sooner you can laugh about something, the sooner you can get on with your life. The sooner you can laugh at yourself, the sooner you will really be living life, truly.

What is an unusual habit or an absurd thing that you love?

Smelling salts! Smelling salts are what powerlifters smell before stepping up to the platform to move maximum weight. Smelling salts are chemically stuffed compounds (usually stuffed with ammonia) used to regain an alert state of mind and/or enhance performance.

Smelling salts come in many forms, but ampules store better and have consistent quality per use. One option is First Aid Only H5041-AMP Ammonia Inhalant Ampoules. I love watching someone smell them for the first time—it hurts! Most people just use them for heavy lifts, but I've taken them to another level. Have bad inertia from sitting too much? *Sniff some smelling salts!* Falling asleep while driving? *Sniff some smelling salts!* Can't get your mind off sex and have no way to release? *Sniff some smelling salts!*

In the last five years, what new belief, behavior, or habit has most improved your life?

Trying to grow my social media. There's a difference between consuming social media and creating for social media. Creating for social media instead of consuming will get you a lot of positive attention, but I created with the intention for growth in mind. Social media works best when you provide massive value. I paid attention to analytics (likes, dislikes, views, etc.) and curbed my postings to fit what was trending (what was most valuable). I'll never post something I don't want to do or don't like to do, but I'll always post something that is really "me" that maximally entertains or amuses others. Since focusing on growing my social media, I've been able to make a career out of doing the things I would be doing anyway. Essentially, I make a living "being me," and it's a magical experience. It's all because I focused on growing my social media.

What are bad recommendations you hear in your profession or area of expertise?

For flexibility training, most people think holding a stretch for longer periods of time is the way to get flexible. I think that's a bad recommendation. The real magic happens when you break that time stretching into sets with rest periods. Rest is very important for flexibility training. Even if you're not out of breath or tired, your body needs time to adjust to the stretch response. You'll get much better results performing a stretch for one minute with three minutes of rest, repeated three times, rather than doing the same stretch for three minutes all at once. If you're going to do it, you might as well do it right. Otherwise, you're wasting your time. To do it right, you need to do sets with rest.

In the last five years, what have you become better at saying no to?

I've gotten better at telling my brain "no" when it wants to relate to conversation with a "bigger" story. What I mean is, somebody might be telling me a story about an experience they had, while I have a related story that sounds even bigger or more dramatic than theirs. Rather than wait for a moment to jump in with mine, I'll just let that desire go and ask them more questions about their experience. What I've discovered is incredible: the loss of the opportunity to possibly impress someone is far outweighed by what I learn when I ask more questions. There is always something else to their story that will amaze you. Don't expect that what they start with is as exciting as it will get. Ask and encourage them to say more!

When you feel overwhelmed or unfocused, what do you do?

When I feel overwhelmed or unfocused, I call my mom or my dad. They've been married for over 40 years, and they're the most grounded people I have in my life. They still live in the house I grew up in, too! When I call them, I get that feeling of being at ease as a young boy in the house. I may talk about what's overwhelming me with my parents, but it makes me feel better to hear about the things my dad is building in the backyard, or how the family dog is doing, or whatever else has nothing to do with what I'm going through. I'm lucky I can still call home.

QUOTES I'M PONDERING

(Tim Ferriss: Feb. 3–Feb. 24, 2017)

"Life is either a daring adventure or nothing at all."

—HELEN KELLER
First deaf-blind person to earn a BA,
the inspiration for the film *The Miracle Worker*

"It had long since come to my attention that people of
accomplishment rarely sat back and let things happen to them.
They went out and happened to things."

—LEONARDO DA VINCI
Italian Renaissance polymath,
painter of the *Mona Lisa* and *The Last Supper*

"Don't think being at the bottom of the totem pole is a bad thing.... You have nowhere to go but up."

DARA TORRES
TW: @DaraTorres
IG: @swimdara
daratorres.com

DARA TORRES is arguably the fastest female swimmer in America. She entered her first international swimming competition at age 14 and competed in her first Olympic Games a few years later, in 1984. At Beijing in 2008, Dara became the oldest swimmer to compete in the Olympic Games at age 41. She took home three silver medals — including one for the infamous 50-meter freestyle race where she missed the gold by 1/100th of a second. Dara has competed in five Olympic Games and has won 12 medals in her Olympic career. She was the first female athlete to be featured in the *Sports Illustrated* Swimsuit Issue, and in 2009, she won the ESPY award for "Best Comeback." Dara was also named one of the "Top Female Athletes of the Decade" by *Sports Illustrated* magazine. She is the author of *Age Is Just a Number: Achieve Your Dreams at Any Stage in Your Life.*

What advice would you give to a smart, driven college student about to enter the "real world"? What advice should they ignore?

Many people have started from the bottom and have worked their way up, so don't think being at the bottom of the totem pole is a bad thing in the work world. You have nowhere to go but up. Ignore hearsay and rumors until you know it as fact.

What purchase of $100 or less has most positively impacted your life in the last six months (or in recent memory)?

Crepe Erase body products for my sun-damaged skin.

What is an unusual habit or an absurd thing that you love?

Eating raw Top Ramen when I've had an upset stomach.

When you feel overwhelmed or unfocused, what do you do?

I either get on a spin bike, swim, box, or do barre method to get the stress out and get more focused.

If you could have a gigantic billboard anywhere with anything on it, what would it say and why? Are there any quotes you think of often or live your life by?

"The future belongs to those who believe in the beauty of their dreams." —often attributed to Eleanor Roosevelt

"I love to sweat. It's like a cleansing process for me. I don't like to perspire but I like to *sweat*."

DAN GABLE
TW: @dannygable
FB: /DanGableWrestler
dangable.com

DAN GABLE is one of the most legendary figures in wrestling history. On the mat in high school and college, Dan compiled an unbelievable record of 181–1. He was also a two-time NCAA National Wrestling Champion, three-time all-American, and three-time Big Eight champion. Following his single loss in college, Dan was driven to train seven hours a day, seven days a week, which culminated in a gold medal at the 1972 Olympics without surrendering a single point. As a coach, he was the University of Iowa's all-time winningest coach from 1976 to 1997, where he won 15 NCAA National Wrestling Team titles. Dan was listed as one of the top coaches of the 20th century by ESPN, and during the 2012 Olympics, he was inducted into the FILA Hall of Fame Legends of the Sport category, making him the third person in the world to receive this honor. Dan has been named to several Halls of Fame, including the National Wrestling Hall of Fame and the U.S. Olympic Hall of Fame. He is the author of several books, including the best-selling *A Wrestling Life*.

What is the book (or books) you've given most as a gift, and why? Or what are one to three books that have greatly influenced your life?

The Heart of a Champion by Bob Richards was very important, because it answers all the questions. It just happened to come at the right time in my life. Bob was an Olympic pole vault champion back in the 1950s, and he was also on the front of Wheaties boxes. He was that spokesman for a long time.

I've always suggested that book, and, in fact, I wrote the foreword of his latest edition. . . . Number two is probably a book on saunas because I'm kind of a sauna fanatic. It takes away a lot of stress, and just reading about it helps me a lot.

What purchase of $100 or less has most positively impacted your life in the last six months (or in recent memory)?

As a kid and even now, when I move into a new house or I have a bedroom, I need something on the doorway . . . it's a simple chinning bar. It's less than $100, but you need a good bracket on it so you don't fall. I use it now more as a stretch bar, just to make sure all the kinks are out. I spend a few minutes on that every day as a warmup or when I get up. If I feel really good, I might hit a few chins.

If you could have a gigantic billboard anywhere with anything on it, what would it say and why?

I would have a big billboard saying, "Wrestling isn't for everybody, but it should be." Because you can use the discipline you have mastered through wrestling not just in wrestling but also in life. All the things you have to learn to be a good wrestler—nutrition, life skills, competition—make you a better performer in life.

What is an unusual habit or an absurd thing that you love?

Maybe in Finland it's not unusual, but for a lot of people it's unusual: I love to sweat. It's like a cleansing process for me. I don't like to perspire but I like to *sweat*. You can also do that through exercise, but I have saunas in a lot of my places that I go. For me it's every day, and when I don't [sweat every day], I actually get the shakes.

What advice would you give to a smart, driven college student about to enter the "real world"?

Don't plan on "winning the lottery" right away, because it usually doesn't happen. Doing a good job and building your assets is like winning the lottery, but over time. You gotta work hard every day, make progress every day, and make money every day. Over time, you'll be in good shape. If you do win it in the first year, hey, I'll be the first to congratulate you—but don't count on it.

"This may be ridiculous, but I have this belief that as long as we peer at the night sky, feel small, see the universe and say, 'Oh, wow, all that mystery,' then we'll drop some of our nearsighted hubris."

CAROLINE PAUL
TW: @carowriter
carolinepaul.com

CAROLINE PAUL is the author of four published books. Her latest is the *New York Times* bestseller *The Gutsy Girl: Escapades for Your Life of Epic Adventure*. Once a young scaredy-cat, Caroline decided that fear got in the way of the life she wanted. She has since competed on the U.S. National Luge Team in Olympic trials and fought fires as one of the first female firefighters in San Francisco, where she was part of the Rescue 2 group. Rescue 2 members not only fight fires; they are also called upon for scuba dive searches (i.e., for bodies), rope and rappelling rescues, hazardous material calls, and the most severe car and train accidents.

What is the book (or books) you've given most as a gift, and why? Or what are one to three books that have greatly influenced your life?

The Stars by H. A. Rey. I've always loved the night sky, but those old constellation charts made no sense to me as a kid. They were just a bunch of unintelligible squiggles labeled Ursa Major, Leo, Orion. But Rey redraws the lines between the stars so that Leo actually looks like a lion and Ursa Major like a big bear. Giving out this book is my small way of encouraging people to look up, make sense of the sky, and along the way experience an existential jolt. This may be ridiculous, but I have this belief that as long as we peer at the night sky, feel small, see the universe and say, "Oh, wow, all that mystery," then we'll drop some of our nearsighted hubris. Maybe even save the planet before it's too late. Is that too much to ask of a book? I think *The Stars* is up to the task.

What is one of the best or most worthwhile investments you've ever made?

Writers can write at a kitchen table for free, or in a cafe for the price of a coffee. But after my first published book, I decided it was worth it to pay rent at an office space called the San Francisco Writers Grotto, just to be among other committed writers. There is no substitute for the support of people who are doing what you are: sweating, crying, tearing their hair out for this thing called a book. Now I have four more published books and I've kept my sanity, none of which would have happened if I'd decided to write in isolation.

What is an unusual habit or an absurd thing that you love?

I love detangling necklaces. I used to be a paraglider pilot, where the lines to the wing would always seem to be irretrievably knotted when you first took the gear out of the bag. But you also knew that since they were all attached to a point on both ends, it would just take patience to figure out which line was over what. Wendy [MacNaughton, her partner, page 151] is always dropping her necklaces into drawers or pockets, then pulling them back out a complete mess. I love the feeling that despite the utter chaos I've been handed, with patience and faith, I can make sense of it again.

In the last five years, what new belief, behavior, or habit has most improved your life?

I used to hate walking, because I had bad knees and I also found it boring. But three years ago, Wendy and I adopted a shelter dog and, of course, dogs have to be walked. Lo and behold, I now *love* walking. It's an opportunity to be outside and to be nowhere else but exactly there with the doggie. I'm not on the phone (something frowned upon at dog parks, who knew) and I'm not trying to get somewhere quickly. The funny thing is that my knees have actually improved from the walking. I look forward to that hour of just putting one foot in front of the other, looking around, breathing. It's meditation, with a stop now and then for poop.

"Originality only happens on the edges of reality."

DARREN ARONOFSKY
TW/IG: @darrenaronofsky
darrenaronofsky.com

DARREN ARONOFSKY is the award-winning filmmaker behind cult classic films such as *Pi*, *Requiem for a Dream*, and *The Wrestler*. His first film, 1998's *Pi*, won him early plaudits and a Best Director award at the Sundance Film Festival. He is perhaps best known for *Black Swan*, which was nominated for five Academy Awards including Best Picture and Best Director. His biblically inspired epic *Noah* opened at #1 at the box office and grossed more than $362 million worldwide. His latest movie is *mother!*, a psychological horror-thriller film starring Jennifer Lawrence and Javier Bardem.

What is the book (or books) you've given most as a gift, and why? Or what are one to three books that have greatly influenced your life?

I was a terrified freshman walking through the library my first year at university, when I saw the word *Brooklyn* out of the corner of my eye. Being from

Brooklyn and for the first extended time away from my hometown, I was immediately interested. I slipped Hubert Selby Jr.'s *Last Exit to Brooklyn* off the shelf and devoured it in a single night. I had never seen anyone attack the page like he did. He deeply inspired me to write, which eventually led me to my form of storytelling. Eventually I would make another one of his books, *Requiem for a Dream*, into a film and even get pretty close to him as a dear friend.

How has a failure, or apparent failure, set you up for later success? Do you have a "favorite failure" of yours?

Every single film I have ever made was at first met with a chorus of "no"s. It led my producer at the time to even come up with the quote, "When everyone is saying no, you know you're doing something right." So I think all success starts with tremendous rejection, and being able to look past those attacks is key.

What purchase of $100 or less has most positively impacted your life in the last six months (or in recent memory)?

I bought a really good spatula. It's amazing what the right tool can do to your breakfast. [**Note from Tim:** I got a photo of Darren's spatula, and it looks like the very well-reviewed and <$10 Winco TN719 Blade Hamburger Turner.]

What advice would you give to a smart, driven college student about to enter the "real world"?

Most of the game is about persistence. It is the most important trait. Sure, when you get an opportunity, you have to perform and you have to exceed beyond all expectations, but getting that chance is the hardest part. So keep the vision clear in your head and every day refuse all obstacles to get to the goal.

When you feel overwhelmed or unfocused, what do you do?

I was blessed with parents who always said to me when I left them to go off to work, "have fun" and "don't work too hard." It gave me permission to excuse myself when it's just not happening. I think procrastination is a major part of the creative path. If you think you are just wasting time in general, even though you may not know it, your mind and body are solving problems you can't face head on. So it's okay to take a walk, get lost in a bookshop, watch a movie, or go for a swim (just don't get lost on your phone).

What are bad recommendations you hear in your profession or area of expertise?

If you put ten people in a room and they have to choose an ice cream flavor, they're gonna arrive at vanilla. There is always constant pressure to conform. But originality only happens on the edges of reality. And working on that line is always dangerous because it's only a short step to disconnected insanity. So resist temptations and advice to play to the middle. The best work always comes from pushing the edge.

"Some of the most successful deals are those you don't do."

EVAN WILLIAMS
TW/Medium: @ev
medium.com

EVAN WILLIAMS is the co-founder of Blogger, Twitter, and Medium. In January 1999, Evan co-founded Pyra Labs, which created the blog-publishing service Blogger (and coined the term "blogger"), which was acquired by Google in early 2003. He then co-founded Odeo and Obvious Corporation, which gave birth to Twitter in 2006. Evan was Twitter's co-founder and lead investor, and is its former CEO. He is currently CEO of Medium, the online publishing platform. Evan grew up on a farm in Clarks, Nebraska.

How has a failure, or apparent failure, set you up for later success? Do you have a "favorite failure" of yours?

At Blogger, it was after the dot-bust, and we were out of money (like lots of others) and looking around for a soft landing. We had a meager acquisition offer from another private company for all stock. I wasn't excited about it, but my team wanted to do it (understandably, as it meant they still had jobs and, in theory, we could continue working on our product). I would have acquiesced, but we failed to close the deal, because their board didn't approve it. I did have to lay off the team, but we scraped by and two years later sold Blogger to Google. The other potential acquirer went out of business. From then on, I realized that some of the most successful deals are those you don't do.

In the last five years, what new belief, behavior, or habit has most improved your life?
Mindfulness meditation, which I started doing regularly about five years ago, has changed my life more than any other behavior. I feel like it rewired my brain (probably because it did). At first, I felt the effects very powerfully. After a few years, it feels less dramatic but necessary. If I go more than a couple days without sitting, I feel off. Wish I had started many years before.

What advice would you give to a smart, driven college student about to enter the "real world"?
Be in a hurry to learn, not in a hurry to get validation. In a team environment, you will make a much better impression if it seems like you're not at all worried about yourself. It's okay to actually be worried about yourself —everyone is—just don't seem like it. If you resist asking for too much, you will often get more.

QUOTES I'M PONDERING

(Tim Ferriss: March 10—March 24, 2017)

"Kuei-shan asked Yun-yen,
'What is the seat of enlightenment?'
 Yun-yen said,
'Freedom from artificiality.'"

—KUEI-SHAN (771–854)
Chinese Ch'an monk and the founder of
the Kuei-Yang lineage, one of the "Five Houses" of Ch'an

"To dare is to lose one's footing momentarily. Not to dare is to
lose oneself."

—SØREN KIERKEGAARD
Prolific Danish writer, considered the first existentialist philosopher

"To be prepared against surprise is to be trained. To be prepared
for surprise is to be educated."

—JAMES P. CARSE
Professor emeritus of history and literature of religion at New York University,
author of *Finite and Infinite Games*

"Avoid sugar. Especially soda and juice. All other diet advice is noise."

BRAM COHEN
TW: @bramcohen
FB: /bram.cohen
Medium: @bramcohen

BRAM COHEN is the inventor of BitTorrent, the peer-to-peer (P2P) file-sharing protocol, and founder of BitTorrent, Inc. In 2005, *MIT Technology Review* named Bram one of the top 35 innovators in the world under the age of 35.

How has a failure, or apparent failure, set you up for later success? Do you have a "favorite failure" of yours?

Before working on BitTorrent, I was on an ill-fated project called Mojo Nation, which had a massive list of very cool features it was supposed to have, but due to lack of focus, it didn't deliver well on any of them. After that experience (and being part of similar software project failures earlier) I decided to make a project that did only one thing and did it well, with the goal instead of succeeding being to not fail. Anything is better than never shipping. The result was BitTorrent. These days the term of art is "minimum viable product," which is an overly clinical term for the ethos of forgetting about succeeding massively and instead focusing all your efforts on desperately trying to not fail. Abject failure is the result of most software development projects.

If you could have a gigantic billboard anywhere with anything on it, what would it say?

"Avoid sugar. Especially soda and juice. All other diet advice is noise."

What is an unusual habit or an absurd thing that you love?

I'm a published inventor of mechanical puzzles. The latest one is widely available in toy stores and is called the Fidgitz. Hopefully these sorts of puzzle toys are intellectually engaging and make people smarter for playing with them, and if not, then hopefully they're at least entertaining.

In the last five years, what have you become better at saying no to?

One life lesson I've grudgingly come to accept is that it's important not to work with crazy people. It's good to be open-minded and accepting about who you're friends with, but in a professional setting, where you're relying on someone, their overall mental health issues usually become a major problem.

There are some blazingly obvious things that are taboo to even talk about. If someone believes that all taxation is theft, or that a strictly vegan diet is healthier, they're demonstrating such a serious lack of judgment that you should be very leery of trusting them to make major decisions. It's laudable to maintain personal and professional relationships with people with a diversity of political opinions and life outlooks, and I try to do that myself, but at some point an opinion crosses from "extreme" to "crazy" and the difference is important.

In an interview situation, the thing you can look out for is flagrant narcissism. If a candidate tells you that you don't need the position they're interviewing for but a higher one, and you should hire them for that, or says that if you don't hire them then you're screwed, or harangues you about the business as if they're an investor doing due diligence, then they're playing obnoxious political games before they've even set foot in the door, and you should give them an immediate no. That sort of behavior only gets worse once someone is on the job, and telling them that that behavior isn't acceptable in advance won't result in them doing anything differently.

In the last five years, what new belief, behavior, or habit has most improved your life?

I've recently started taking my lactose intolerance a lot more seriously, which has resulted in a significant improvement in my quality of life. My case is much more serious than most, but lactose intolerance affects a large fraction of people in the U.S., and many of them aren't diagnosed or don't do anything about it. When I'm even a little bit not careful, I wind up having chronic pain from bloating, and a few basic steps are a huge improvement. Things I do are: 1) Try as much as possible to avoid lactose, including cheese and butter (and unfortunately almost all chocolate. If a label says, "may contain traces of milk," that means it does). 2) Take lactase pills twice a day, even if I'm not aware of having eaten anything with lactose in it, because when eating out you never know what's slipped in there. 3) Take simethicone (Gas-X) twice a day, because that directly helps with getting the gas out. And don't be afraid to burp, because any gas that is in there is going to have to get out one way or the other, and there are only two exits. It's better to let it out the front than to force it through the back.

It's frustrating how there's a fad of people mostly falsely thinking they're gluten sensitive, while lactose intolerance isn't even brought up. Especially because lacto-fermentation costs very little, and could even be done before the milk is used to make butter or cheese. Lactose-free should be the default. Most of the black and Asian people in the U.S. are lactose intolerant, and they're served food that they're incapable of digesting as a central part of every one of their school lunches.

What advice would you give to a smart, driven college student about to enter the "real world"?

Pick your early jobs based on what gets you the most valuable experience. If you want to be an entrepreneur, don't dive directly into doing your venture but go get work at an early-stage startup to learn the ropes and get paid to make your early mistakes. Only after getting the necessary experience and knowledge should you strike out on your own. This is what I did, and although the startups I worked at were mostly failures, I don't think I could have succeeded at my own thing without that experience.

"It's often the case that people want to help you or work with you. But they can't if you insist on holding on to tight control."

CHRIS ANDERSON
TW: @TEDChris
ted.com

CHRIS ANDERSON became the curator of the TED Conference in 2002 and has developed it into a global platform for disseminating ideas worth spreading. Chris was born in rural Pakistan, and grew up in India, Pakistan, Afghanistan, and England. He graduated from Oxford University with a degree in philosophy and politics, and then entered journalism. In 1985, he formed a startup to launch a computer magazine. Its success led to more launches, and his company Future Publishing grew rapidly under the slogan "media with passion." Chris expanded to the United States in 1994, where he built Imagine Media, publisher of *Business 2.0* magazine, and creator of the popular games website IGN. The combined companies eventually spawned more than 100 monthly magazines, employing 2,000 people. In 2001, Chris's nonprofit foundation, the Sapling Foundation, acquired the TED Conference, and Chris left his businesses to focus on growing TED.

Under his stewardship, TED has broadened its scope to include not only technology, entertainment, and design but also science, politics, business, the arts, and global issues. In 2006, TED began free distribution of its talks on the web and more than 2,500 talks are now available.

What is the book (or books) you've given most as a gift, and why? Or what are one to three books that have greatly influenced your life?

David Deutsch's *The Beginning of Infinity*. It's a remarkable argument for the power of knowledge—as not just a human capability but as a force that shapes the universe.

Steven Pinker (page 475): anything. He's one of the clearest thinkers and communicators of our time. Among many other things, he convinced me that I could never understand myself without understanding how humans evolved.

C. S. Lewis, the Narnia series. As a child, they exploded my imagination.

If you could have a gigantic billboard anywhere with anything on it, what would it say and why?

"Live for something that's bigger than you are." Weirdly, that's one of the keys to a more satisfying life, albeit not necessarily an easier one.

In the last five years, what new belief, behavior, or habit has most improved your life?

The realization that the best way to get things done is to let go. Here's the thing. . . . It's often the case that people want to help you or work with you. But they can't if you insist on holding on to tight control. The more you let go, the more people will surprise you. We've seen this vividly at TED over recent years. By giving away our content online, enthusiastic learners have spread the content across the Internet, vastly increasing TED's reach. By giving away our brand in the form of free TEDx licenses, thousands of volunteers have held TEDx events all around the world—ten every day. They have come up with ideas we would never have dreamed of. In this brave new connected age, the rules about what you hold on to and what you should let go of have changed forever. By adopting a generosity strategy, your reputation will spread, and you may be amazed at what you get back in return.

What advice would you give to a smart, driven college student about to enter the "real world"? What advice should they ignore?

Many of us have bought into the cliché "pursue your passion." For many, that is terrible advice. In your 20s, you may not really know what your best skills and opportunities are. It's much better to pursue learning, personal discipline, growth. And to seek out connections with people across the planet. For a while, it's just fine to follow and support someone else's dream. In so doing, you will be building valuable relationships, valuable knowledge. And at some point your passion will come and whisper in your ear, "I'm ready."

"Stop doing whatever else I am doing because it isn't actually work, and go and write something."

NEIL GAIMAN
TW/IG: @neilhimself
FB: /neilgaiman
neilgaiman.com

NEIL GAIMAN is listed in the *Dictionary of Literary Biography* as one of the top ten living postmodern writers. He is a prolific creator of prose, poetry, film, journalism, comics, song lyrics, and drama. His fiction has received the Newbery, Carnegie, Hugo, Nebula, World Fantasy, and Eisner awards. I first became fascinated by his imagination with the *Sandman* graphic novels in the '90s, followed by *Neverwhere* and *American Gods*. His other bestsellers include *The View from the Cheap Seats: Selected Nonfiction*, *The Ocean at the End of the Lane*, *The Graveyard Book* (my favorite audiobook of all time), *Coraline*, and others. Neil's commencement speech, "Make Good Art," is mandatory listening for anyone who hopes to be creatively successful over the long haul.

When you feel overwhelmed or unfocused, what do you do? What questions do you ask yourself?

- Have I had enough sleep?
- Have I eaten?
- Would it be a good idea to go for a short walk?

And once those have been answered, or fixed, if there's an actual situation that's overwhelming:

- Is there anything I can do to fix this?
- Is there anyone who actually has information or advice about this I can call and talk to?

If it's not actually a situation, just me being sad and moody and unfocused:

- How long has it been since I actually wrote something?
- Stop doing whatever else I am doing because it isn't actually work, and go and write something.

What purchase of $100 or less has most positively impacted your life in the last six months (or in recent memory)?

Probably the purchases I've made that have made me the happiest would be the Paco books, from France [by Magali Le Huche]: *Paco and the Orchestra*, *Paco and Jazz*, *Paco and Rock*, *Paco and Vivaldi*, *Paco and Mozart*. . . . When you press down on an indicated spot in the books, a sound effect or music plays. My small son Ash loves them, and when nothing else will soothe him, he will happily listen to/read a Paco book, and the strains of a short piece of music will make everything good. . . . It makes my life good because it makes his good.

In the last five years, what new belief, behavior, or habit has most improved your life?

The discovery that you can have private yoga sessions, where someone will come give you one-on-one yoga lessons. As soon as the baby turned up, the possibility that both Amanda [Palmer, his wife] and I would go to yoga together dropped immeasurably, and the probability that local yoga would actually fit in the time I had to do it was small. But I know how much I regret it if I do not bend and stretch and, eventually, relax.

"Every day is an opportunity to create a living masterpiece."

MICHAEL GERVAIS
TW/IG: @michaelgervais
findingmastery.net

DR. MICHAEL GERVAIS is a high-performance psychologist who has worked directly with Olympic gold medalists, world-record setters, and the Super Bowl-winning Seattle Seahawks, where he helped integrate meditation and mindfulness techniques. He is also the co-founder of Compete to Create (alongside Coach Pete Carroll), whose mission is to help people become the best they can be. A published author in peer-reviewed journals and recognized speaker on optimal human performance, Michael has been featured by media worldwide and is the host of the *Finding Mastery* podcast, where he interviews world-class performers and deconstructs paths to mastery.

What is the book (or books) you've given most as a gift, and why? Or what are one to three books that have greatly influenced your life?

Man's Search for Meaning by Viktor E. Frankl. He introduces the insights that he learned from surviving imprisonment in a Nazi concentration camp. He outlines methods to discover deep meaning and purpose in life.

The Tao Te Ching by Lao Tzu. His 81 Zen teachings are the foundation for the religion of Taoism, aimed at understanding "the way of virtues." Lao Tzu's depth of teachings are complicated to decode and provide foundations for wisdom.

Mind Gym by Gary Mack is a book that strips down the esoteric nature of applied sport psychology. Gary introduces a variety of mindset training principles and makes them extremely easy to understand and practice.

What purchase of $100 or less has most positively impacted your life in the last six months (or in recent memory)?

A book for my son: *Inch and Miles*, written by coach John Wooden. We read it together on a regular basis. The joy that I get from hearing him understand Coach Wooden's insights is fantastically rewarding.

How has a failure, or apparent failure, set you up for later success? Do you have a "favorite failure" of yours?

My first job as a sport psychologist in professional sports. I was introduced to the team's general manager by a mutual friend. We had a great conversation about his vision for the future of the team, and he offered me a job. Eagerly, and not knowing better, I accepted. What I failed to fully realize is that there were many other stakeholders who influence the culture and performance of the team, like the head coach (duh). Without ever sitting down with the coach, I had no idea what I was walking into. Little did I know that the coach had very little interest in sport psychology. In fact, he saw it as a potential threat to his coaching style.

Needless to say, the first meeting with the coach was challenging in nature —him challenging me. At this point, I was completely green, he knew it, and he carefully designed my first meeting with the athletes.

The following day, he held an extra-long practice that was physically intense and demanding. Immediately after practice, he asked the athletes to go to the locker room and stay in their practice gear. He then asked to speak with me for a few minutes in his office, just long enough for the athletes to become cold and agitated from their sweat-drenched clothing.

With a quick nod, as if the coach's internal monitor of agitation went off in his head, he said, "Okay. Whattya' say you introduce yourself to the team?"

He walked me into the locker room and said, "All right, guys. This is Mike Gervais, sport psychologist. If you're screwed up in the head, go to talk to him." Then he quickly left the locker room.

I love this experience because it led me to develop a deeper understanding of the people involved in an organization before making a decision about mutual commitment. "Know before you go."

If you could have a gigantic billboard anywhere with anything on it, what would it say and why?

"Every day is an opportunity to create a living masterpiece."

We have far more control in our lives than many embrace. We create or co-create our experiences in life, and each day is a new opportunity to be fully engaged in the present moment. It's the present moment where glimpses of our potential are revealed and expressed. A living masterpiece is not drawn on a canvas or etched in stone or inked by pen. It's the pursuit and expression of applied insight and wisdom.

What is one of the best or most worthwhile investments you've ever made?

Investing in others' growth.

When we make eye contact (sometimes literally and sometimes conceptually, seeing into the center of what is), we become connected. That connection can be so intense that we find ourselves occupying our time with distractions and busyness: the modern addiction to numb the discomfort of getting on the razor's edge of emotional intensity. It is through the relationships we have that we are able to experience what is true, beautiful, and good. It is through those relationships that high performance is expressed and our potential, meaning, and purpose are revealed.

What are bad recommendations you hear in your profession or area of expertise?

"You can do anything you put your mind to." Ah, no, that's not accurate, and it reveals the advice-giver's naiveté about human experiences.

In the last five years, what have you become better at saying no to?

"I'd love to pick your brain, can we set up a phone meeting or meet over a cup of coffee?" No. "I have an idea that I'd like to run by you, can we meet?" No. "I think I fit your criteria to be on your *Finding Mastery* podcast, can we set up a call to discuss?" No.

Saying no to tap water at restaurants.

Saying no to cable and network TV.

Saying no to phone calls that don't take place outside my car (calls happen best when I'm driving).

Saying no to new projects and business ideas.

Saying no to media interviews that don't have meaningful impact.

Saying no to partnerships (and potential clients) who aren't aligned in vision and appetite to work hard, work with passion, and adjust to the unknown.

Saying no to food that's made in a plant, not made from a plant.

When you feel overwhelmed or unfocused, what do you do?

Deep breathing when my arousal (internal activation) level has kicked into high gear.

Music and movement (walking outside) when my attention span is fatigued.

Turning off my email when I get overwhelmed with "keeping up" versus producing meaningful work.

"Obstacles are those frightful things you see when you take your eyes off the goal."
— Henry Ford

TEMPLE GRANDIN
IG: @templegrandinschool
FB: /drtemplegrandin
grandin.com

TEMPLE GRANDIN is an author and speaker on both autism and animal behavior. She is a professor of animal science at Colorado State University and also has a successful career consulting on animal welfare and livestock-handling equipment design. She has been featured on the BBC special *The Woman Who Thinks Like a Cow,* and her 2010 TED Talk, "The World Needs All Kinds of Minds," now has nearly five million views. Articles about her have appeared in *Time* magazine, *The New York Times, Discover* magazine, *Forbes,* and *USA Today*. HBO made an Emmy Award-winning movie about her life starring Claire Danes, and she was inducted into the American Academy of Arts and Sciences in 2016.

How has a failure, or apparent failure, set you up for later success? Do you have a "favorite failure" of yours?

When I first started my career designing facilities for handling livestock, I mistakenly believed that there was an engineering fix for every problem.

With the right design and engineering, all problems associated with moving animals could be solved. A big failure of one of my projects taught me that the root causes of problems have to be addressed. In 1980, I was hired to design a conveyor system that would move hogs to the third floor of an old meatpacking plant in Cincinnati. The hogs were having difficulty walking up the long ramps. With much enthusiasm, I took this job and designed a conveyorized chute. It was a total failure. The pigs sat down and flipped over backward. Further observations indicated that most of the hogs that had difficulty climbing the ramp came from a single farm. Fixing the problems at this farm would have been much easier and cheaper than the big conveyor mess I had created. A change in pig genetics would have solved most of the problems.

What I learned from this design disaster was that I had attempted to treat the symptom of a problem instead of its cause. From that point forward in my career, I was careful to differentiate between problems that can be fixed with new equipment and problems that should be fixed by other means. Later in my career, I have observed that people want the magic new thing more than they want improved management to fix problems. Managers need to carefully determine the areas in their business where new technology is the right choice and other areas where a back-to-basics management approach may be more effective.

When you feel overwhelmed or unfocused, what do you do?

When I was in my 20s, somebody had written on the wall of the university art building "Obstacles are those terrible things you see when you take your eyes off the goal." I have since learned that this was a quote from Henry Ford and the actual wording was "frightful" instead of "terrible." Throughout my career, I have designed many livestock handling systems for many of the major meat companies. During these projects, I have worked with both the very best plant managers and the worst. To deal with this, I developed the concept of "project loyalty." My job is to do a good job and make the project work. A bad plant manager is an obstacle that I have to work around. The concept of project loyalty has helped keep me going and successfully complete my projects.

QUOTES I'M PONDERING

(Tim Ferriss: March 31–April 21, 2017)

"The true soldier fights not because he hates what is in front of him, but because he loves what is behind him."

–G. K. CHESTERTON
English philosopher known as the "prince of paradox"

"All happiness depends on a leisurely breakfast."

–JOHN GUNTHER
American journalist, author of *Death Be Not Proud*

"The acquisition of riches has been for many men, not an end, but a change, of troubles."

–EPICURUS
Ancient Greek philosopher, founder of the school of Epicureanism

"To handle yourself, use your head; to handle others, use your heart."

–ELEANOR ROOSEVELT
Longest-serving First Lady of the United States, diplomat, and activist

"Think for yourself. Everyone has a unique picture of how things work and function, and yours is as valuable as anyone's."

KELLY SLATER
IG/FB/TW: @kellyslater
kswaveco.com

KELLY SLATER has been called "the world's best and best-known surfer" by *Businessweek*. He has been crowned World Surf League champion a record 11 times, including five consecutive titles from 1994 to 1998. He is the youngest (at age 20) and the oldest (at age 39) to win the title. Kelly has also won 54 World Championship Tour victories. His company, the Kelly Slater Wave Company, produces the longest man-made, high-performance open-barrel waves for surf training.

What is the book (or books) you've given most as a gift, and why? Or what are one to three books that have greatly influenced your life?
The Tao of Health, Sex, and Longevity by Daniel Reid. It's a wealth of knowledge, almost like a personal health bible, about real-life things that

you can put into practice to improve your physical, mental, and emotional health. *The Prophet* by Kahlil Gibran was one of the first "spiritual" books I read as a teenager, which gave me plenty of seeds for thought from short, but to-the-point, topics. Some books can overwhelm with details, which you can easily forget. *The Prophet* made me think about my point of view, and it filters a lot of subjects that I maybe didn't previously see the whole picture around.

How has a failure, or apparent failure, set you up for later success? Do you have a "favorite failure" of yours?

I narrowly lost a world title in surfing in 2003 after basically having locked it in the month prior. The loss felt horrible at the time, but it drove me to clear up a lot of things in my head and life that were holding me back . . . around love and truth and family and work, which ultimately helped me to win five more world titles.

What advice would you give to a smart, driven college student about to enter the "real world"?

Think for yourself. Everyone has a unique picture of how things work and function, and yours is as valuable as anyone's. It's sometimes the belief in yourself, open-mindedness toward others, and your delivery that allows things to be heard by others.

What is one of the best or most worthwhile investments you've ever made?

Investing in friends is important. My group of about 50 friends all have a house we grew up in, and we decided to pool our money and help make over the house, which needed some love. Not everyone had the abundance to help out, and getting something like that done can be like herding cats. One friend and I shouldered the bulk of the funds to make it happen because it was ultimately our idea. I found that the more freely I was willing and able to share, the faster it was made back through other areas of work. I definitely connected the joy and rewards I got from freeing myself up to help in that way with the good fortunes that came my way in other avenues shortly after.

"I have found that my absolute best is the best possible outcome. That is a 'win.'"

KATRÍN TANJA DAVÍÐSDÓTTIR
IG: @katrintanja
FB: /katrindavidsdottir

KATRÍN TANJA DAVÍÐSDÓTTIR is an Icelandic CrossFit athlete. She is the 2015 and 2016 CrossFit Games women's champion, which christened her "Fittest Woman on Earth." Katrín is the second woman to repeat as champion, following in the footsteps of her countrywoman, Annie Þórisdóttir (page 305).

What is the book (or books) you've given most as a gift, and why? Or what are one to three books that have greatly influenced your life?

Wooden: A Lifetime of Observations and Reflections On and Off the Court by John Wooden is one of my absolute favorites. My grandpa was a basketball player back in the day, and he gave me this book a couple years ago. Wooden's approach to training resonates a lot with me and my coach, Ben Bergeron. Reading the book, I found myself constantly nodding in agreement. His philosophies don't only apply in the gym or on the competition floor but to life in general. I always feel like sports are a microscopic view of life. The same principles and lessons apply, but they are more apparent in sports. My favorite part about this book, though, might be the foreword from one of Wooden's former players, Bill Walsh. The way he talks about their relationship and what he learned from his coach is absolutely beautiful and still sits with me.

The other book is *The Champion's Mind: How Champions Think, Train, and Thrive* by Jim Afremow. This was the first sports psychology book I ever picked up, and it was the exact right moment for me. It was the summer of 2014, right after I failed to qualify for the '14 [CrossFit] Games. That summer, I could have easily fallen into a mindset of "I don't belong, I am not good enough, I failed . . ." but the book gave me a better perspective. I wasn't a failure. I had just failed at a certain event. Past tense. What could I do in this exact moment to get better? It got me focusing on giving *my* absolute best in any given situation without the pressure of constantly stacking myself up to others. The same time I started reading this book, I started working with my coach, Ben, and he really focuses on all of the same things. He would talk to me before training, after workouts, sometimes during, and all of it started coming together. The new mindset allowed me to truly fall in love with the process.

What is a favorite exercise (or a valuable one) that most CrossFitters or athletes neglect?

Definitely the mind. It is so easy to get caught up in the physical, to get a faster mile time or a bigger squat number, faster thrusters or better pull-ups . . . but at the elite level, where everyone is fit and strong, it will be the mind that separates.

If you are asking about an exercise, I would say it is basic "fitness." It is hanging out around your lactic threshold for an extended period of time —it's hard. But that's where the magic happens. It's not going guns blazing through a workout and it's not "talking pace." It's hanging out right where you might start dropping off soon but you *can* hold on. Once your general fitness is higher, your recovery is better between lifts and between events; it translates into so many other things.

How has a failure, or apparent failure, set you up for later success? Do you have a "favorite failure" of yours?

When I started CrossFit, I became "good" right away. Not great, and not one of the best, but good enough to make the CrossFit Games. I made the Games in both 2012 and 2013 and I was very happy with being a CrossFit Games athlete and almost defined myself as just that. I was a full-time student and coach at the same time that I was training for the Games. I have always been a hard worker, but looking back at my training then, it was more of a go-through-the-motions and check-the-boxes approach. Getting the work done for the sole sake of getting the work done.

At the time, I honestly didn't know what I wanted to do in school, and I didn't love coaching. Both were things I felt like I *should* be doing. The CrossFit Games was the only thing I really *wanted* to be doing, and I failed to qualify in 2014. It was seemingly the biggest failure of my life. It was devastating, but it ended up being the best thing that ever happened to me.

Not making it that year showed me how much I truly wanted to be there . . . and how hard I was willing to work for it. I took the summer off, started reading sports psychology, and when I was ready to get back to it, I was really *ready*. I asked Ben to become my full-time coach, and I later made the decision to put school on hold, stop coaching, and move from Iceland to Boston so I could truly put everything I had into CrossFit alongside my coach. I *loved* it. This was at the beginning of 2015. We ended up winning the 2015 CrossFit Games that July.

Failing to make the 2014 CrossFit Games was the best thing that ever could have happened to me and a life-altering event.

What is one of the best or most worthwhile investments you've ever made?

My plane ticket from Iceland to Boston in early 2014 to attend a training camp with Ben at CFNE. It was almost all the money I had at the time, but I just wanted so much to work with Ben and his athletes. He wasn't my coach at the time, but going there for that training camp ultimately led to him becoming my full-time coach, and led to some of my closest relationships.

When you feel overwhelmed or unfocused, what do you do?

Sometimes, things aren't easy, or fun, and times get hard. Those are the moments that I tell myself really count! Anyone can go to the gym and work very hard when they want to. But who does it even when they don't feel like it? Even when they are tired?

In these situations, my "why" helps me. My "why" is my grandma and her light. She was my biggest supporter and best friend. When I moved from Iceland to Boston to train there full-time, we told each other we would still always be together. She passed away in April of 2015, and I still feel and know we will always be together. When things get tough, I know she is right there with me.

In the last five years, what new belief, behavior, or habit has most improved your life?

The belief that my best is enough. It is so easy to get caught up in the thought that to "win" a competition, a training day, or whatever the task, you must do something extraordinary.

I have found that *my* absolute best is the best possible outcome. That is a "win." To do your best may sound easy, but it is anything but. It requires everything you've got . . . and no less. The beauty of it is that it is totally within your control. You can always give your absolute best effort regardless of physical state or circumstances. That, to me, is always a win.

> **"If you want to get better in the sport, you need to work on *your* specific weaknesses, not those of someone who is successful."**

MATHEW FRASER
IG: @mathewfras

MATHEW FRASER won first place at the 2016 and 2017 Reebok CrossFit Games, earning him the title of "Fittest Man on Earth." He won the Rookie of the Year award at his first CrossFit Games in 2014 and placed second in 2014 and 2015. He's been a CrossFit athlete since 2012, after retiring from a career in weightlifting during which he was an Olympic hopeful.

What purchase of $100 or less has most positively impacted your life in the last six months (or in recent memory)?

Without a doubt, I would say my dawn simulator [Philips Wake-Up Light]. It is an alarm clock that wakes you up with light instead of sound. Because of this change, you feel as if you are waking up on your own and aren't groggy.

How has a failure, or apparent failure, set you up for later success? Do you have a "favorite failure" of yours?

My biggest failure has become one of the things that I am most well known for: taking second place at the CrossFit games two years in a row. The first year, I was a rookie and had zero expectations, so placing second felt like a victory. The next year, the reigning champ had retired, and I rested on my laurels, figuring I was a shoo-in for the title. I took second again, and it was a devastating loss. Because of that failure, I worked harder than I ever had in my life the following year, and the results led to the largest margin of victory ever at the CrossFit games in 2016. I never want to change my 2015 season, because it was a lesson I will reflect on the rest of my life.

In the last five years, what new belief, behavior, or habit has most improved your life?

I have realized that I value the results of a process more when I truly apply myself and, more important to me, make myself proud.

[For example], when I am struggling to get through some rowing intervals during my training, when my posterior chain is on fire every time I pull on the handle, when I can feel the blisters forming on my fingers, and when the top of my head is tingling because my body is trying to tell me to stop, I tell myself in between pulls, "Keep going. You are going to be so proud of yourself if you keep pushing." When I finish a workout like that, I am so happy the rest of the day because I know I did everything I could do to better myself.

What are bad recommendations you hear in your profession or area of expertise?

I hear constantly, "If you want to be the best, you need to do what the best are doing." In the sport of CrossFit, this couldn't be further from the truth. I see so many people mimicking the training of some of the top-ranked competitors. If you want to get better in the sport, you need to work on *your* specific weaknesses, not those of someone who is successful.

When you feel overwhelmed or unfocused, what do you do?

Whenever I feel overwhelmed, I make lists. It may seem simple and silly, but it works for me, and I now am rarely more than arm's reach from a notepad. I find I get overwhelmed when I am thinking about something that has too many steps, moving parts, or variables to keep straight in my head. So what's the solution? Writing them down. Sometimes it's starting at the desired solution and thinking backward in baby steps for how I can get there. Sometimes it's just making to-do lists to keep my day organized.

I usually make a list every morning while I'm drinking my coffee. I have a terrible habit of forgetting smaller things during the day, so I like to put them on paper before the day gets started and I become distracted. Having the list helps keep me calm and productive during the day.

A more unusual list I made in the past was after the 2015 CrossFit games. It was a terrible competition for me, and I ended up losing by 36 points out of a possible 1,200. Throughout the 13 events, I did fantastically in some, and I finished almost dead last in others. When the competition was over, I looked at my event finishes and made lists of how to improve on them for the next year.

One event that I did poorly in was the "soccer chipper." This event involved flipping the "pig" (essentially a 600-pound refrigerator) down a soccer field 12 times, and then completing four legless rope climbs up a 20-foot rope. To say my pig flips were bad is an understatement. So I had to figure out *why*. Was it too heavy? Did I not know the proper technique? Was my body not prepared for the stimulus? Once I figured out why, I had to figure out how to fix it. This then involved me working backward from the desired result (me being proficient in the movement) to where I currently was (being absolute shit in the movement). I set myself a few micro goals in between the two, wrote them down, and started working toward them, one at a time. This allowed me to only look at the next small, seemingly achievable goal, instead of at one large, very down-the-road, daunting goal that didn't seem obtainable.

"Ignore the concept of 'being yourself.' Of course this is literally true by definition, but it is a way to avoid self-improvement."

ADAM FISHER

ADAM FISHER is the head of macro and real estate at Soros Fund Management as of September 2017, before which he co-founded CommonWealth Opportunity Capital, a global macro hedge fund with assets under management of approximately $2.2 billion. Adam formed CommonWealth in 2008 and acted as its chief investment officer, building on his extensive experience investing in and managing public and private companies around the globe. Prior to CommonWealth, he co-founded Orient Property Group in 2006, focusing on investments throughout the Asia Pacific region.

What is the book (or books) you've given most as a gift, and why? Or what are one to three books that have greatly influenced your life?

The Rise of Superman by Steven Kotler. The book is inspirational, of course, and an easy read, but it was the first time the connection between physiology and performance became so real for me. It opened my eyes to the need to synthesize how I literally feel as a performer and to use training to replicate the best physiology I can.

For me, the ideal training regarding my physiology is maintaining my routine. This includes a great night's sleep, heart rate variability (HRV) training, meditation, and a number of deep work sessions per day, as well as some exercise. When I get all of these into my day, I flow well.

What advice would you give to a smart, driven college student about to enter the "real world"? What advice should they ignore?

Be humble and self-aware. Ignore the concept of "being yourself." Of course this is literally true by definition, but it is a way to avoid self-improvement. Pursuing your passion is fine.

How has a failure, or apparent failure, set you up for later success? Do you have a "favorite failure" of yours?

I was engaged in real estate investing before I became a macro trader. I always loved, even when I invested in real estate, to think in a top-down fashion and, when done well, I had my best insights by far.

Top down (macro thinking) means I consider the big-picture issues before the small when making decisions, and these [big-picture] issues dominate my preferences. It does *not* mean I ignore the small issues, as they are necessary but *not* dominant. For example, I invest in real estate where smart people want to live. While I could make money in other areas of the country, over the long term, this rule will be quite lucrative. There are other factors, of course, but this one is a requirement.

The real estate endeavor had some failures at the end, and many of them were the result of not getting buy-in from my whole team to this way of thinking. For me, the global financial crisis (or the risk of it) seemed fairly straightforward, but to my team, it was not as obvious. Decision-making would have been very different had we concurred on this.

In my current life, I've made sure that the platform and the people on it are comfortable with this philosophy. Had I not been in that previous predicament, I would not have appreciated the importance of having like-minded investment philosophies.

In the last five years, what new belief, behavior, or habit has most improved your life?

No question: meditation. I can't write down all the benefits, but they are legion. I almost feel like by not meditating before, my brain was sitting on the couch. I practice meditation in the morning after my HRV breathing. I use the same quiet space in my house every day of the week. I practice for at least ten minutes and do single-point meditation.

What is one of the best or most worthwhile investments you've ever made?

The best investment I have made over the last year is a performance coach. I always believed in the concept of a coach, but I was slow to embrace it as part of my life for whatever reason.

I strongly believe world-class performers need coaching. I suppose mentors function in this role for many, but coaches, in my opinion, are different.

[Coaches] focus on you first. Mentors rightly focus on themselves first and you second. Lastly, a good coach builds regimens designed to make you better, [versus simply] providing advice, as a mentor would.

What are bad recommendations you hear in your profession or area of expertise?

"Find an area of expertise." It's so weird when I hear this. Just learn how to learn. Then you can always figure out the next thing that you will need to know.

In the last five years, what have you become better at saying no to? What new realizations and/or approaches helped?

For me, it has been calendar architecture. I am a lion about it and expect everyone around me to respect it and help me with it. "Calendar architecture" is designing and implementing a repeatable schedule every day. As an introvert, this requires a lot of alone time, and everyone around me protects this in my day. It is also designed to keep my day from being filled up with "gristle."

When you feel overwhelmed or unfocused, what do you do?

I do HRV training. Ten good breaths get me to home. Ten good Buddha breaths seeking a quiet mind (no talk).

"You cannot do anything great without aggressively courting your own limits."

AISHA TYLER
TW/FB: @aishatyler
courageandstone.com

AISHA TYLER is an actor, comedian, director, author, and activist. Aisha is best known as a co-host of the Emmy Award-winning daytime show *The Talk*, the voice of Lana Kane in the hit series *Archer*, portraying Dr. Tara Lewis in *Criminal Minds*, and her recurring roles in *CSI: Crime Scene Investigation*, *Talk Soup*, and *Friends*. Aisha is also the host of the comedy show *Whose Line Is It Anyway?* and the author of *Self-Inflicted Wounds: Heartwarming Tales of Epic Humiliation*.

If you could have a gigantic billboard anywhere with anything on it, what would it say and why? Are there any quotes you think of often or live your life by?

I love that Jack Canfield quote, "Everything you want is on the other side of fear." If something terrifies me, I typically sprint flat-out toward it, and that has served me well, both professionally and personally. But everyone gets scared, and I sometimes have to remind myself to remain brave when I've taken enough steps toward a goal that I can't turn back, and feel like the floor has fallen out from underneath me.

I try to live in a space of bravery in every aspect of my life: creative, professional, familial, and in my friendships. Being brave means being present and willing to give of yourself regardless of result. I often write "be brave" in books when I sign them for fans—it's an admonishment for them and for myself. Remaining brave has helped me push toward those goals through paralyzing crises of confidence.

How has a failure, or apparent failure, set you up for later success? Do you have a "favorite failure" of yours?

My first short film was a pretty uniform disaster. It was years ago. I had never spent meaningful time on a real single-camera set before, and while I was long on ambition, I was very short on experience. I got a lot of friends to chip in, both in front of and behind the camera, and while I was enthusiastic, I had no idea how to run a set. The result was a sprawling hodgepodge of images that never cut together properly into a cohesive narrative, and I was never able to complete the film. I wasn't discouraged, though. What I realized was that I needed to learn more—about writing, production, preparation, planning, everything. I spent the next decade visiting every set I could, shadowing every director I knew, and several I didn't know, to learn about the craft I was so deeply passionate about. And every short I've done since then has been an extraordinary experience. Several of my shorts won awards, all of it culminating in my first feature, which has also won awards. My first feature was the most galvanizing and fulfilling creative experience of my career so far, and it lit the path forward toward the next phase of my creative life.

There are no radical creative choices that do not carry with them an inherent risk of equally radical failure. You cannot do anything great without aggressively courting your own limits and the limits of your ideas. So many things I've done haven't worked—but they led to me learning what did work, what not to repeat, and what to do better. So many times I thought, "If this doesn't work, I'm going to be devastated." But occasionally they didn't work, and I got up the next day and kept creating. There is nothing more powerful than failure to reveal to you what you are truly capable of.

Avoiding risk of failure means avoiding transcendent creative leaps forward. You can't have one without the other.

What is one of the best or most worthwhile investments you've ever made?

My Concept II rowing machine. I bought it in 2001 and it is still operating like new. I have a hard time finding time to make it to a gym or scheduling sessions with a trainer, but I can row at home any time, day or night. It's low-impact, total-body, and the results are insane.

My rowing workout varies. I was a competitive runner for many years, so my workout plans mirror a typical running weekly schedule: mid-distance 5K rows punctuated by short-distance 2K HIIT sprints, with a 10K long-distance row once or twice a week. Plus I can binge-watch shows when I row, which is the only time I'm able to watch television.

[For shows], I just jammed through the last season of *Homeland*, and my go-to shows are *The Walking Dead*, *Fear the Walking Dead*, *Game of Thrones*, *The Handmaid's Tale*, and *House of Cards*. Strangely, despite my background in comedy, I watch dramas almost exclusively. It's hard to laugh out loud and still maintain a 1:55/500 m pace on the rower.

What is an unusual habit or an absurd thing that you love?

I love organizing. But I wouldn't call it a habit. It's more of a compulsion. For example, I'll get home from a long trip abroad and start cleaning out my refrigerator. Not always the best use of time, especially when I get home late and have an early call time the next day. But it soothes me completely. Nothing I like better than a perfectly organized space. It gives me an illogical amount of joy, which more than compensates for the time wasted turning all the labels in my fridge to face forward.

In the last five years, what new belief, behavior, or habit has most improved your life?

Cutting out sugar. It's so Hollywood, I know, but I had a real sugar addiction for many years, and it affected everything from the quality of my sleep to how effective I was throughout the day. I was like a drug addict. I had to have sugar at certain times of the day just to function. When I cut it out of my diet, my blood sugar stabilized, my energy leveled out, my workouts got better, my mental acuity improved—literally everything got better when I stopped eating sugar. It was probably the hardest adjustment I've ever made in my diet but completely worth it. Now when I eat sugar, I get physically ill, which makes it easier to push away from the table at the end of a meal.

I wish I had a "trick" for cutting out sugar. It was a long, slow path that started at least 15 years ago. In my 20s I would eat a half-pint of frozen yogurt every night after dinner (sometimes more). I was powerless—if I started eating sweets, I could not stop until it was gone or I was sick to my stomach. I definitely didn't go cold turkey. I slowly started eliminating things from my diet—first substituting dark chocolate for the frozen yogurt, then cutting that back. Substituting iced coffee for sugar in the afternoon, then eliminating the sweetener from that until I was finally drinking it black. I stopped using sugar substitutes because they still trigger sugar cravings. One strategy that really helped was increasing the protein in my diet, which stabilized my blood sugar throughout the day. Another was to grab a Greek yogurt or baked sweet potato when I was dying for something sweet. I focus on high-protein, high-healthy fat meals now, which keeps me off the sugary crack. But I still eat a bit of dark chocolate when I am jonesing for a fix. I mean, I'm not a robot.

In the last five years, what have you become better at saying no to?

Almost everything. In the last few years I've tried to take on an approach of saying no to everything that doesn't energize me personally or creatively. It's incredibly hard to do, as I am typically someone who wants to help others, and in my business there is always one more fundraiser or cause to support. But over time, those commitments cannibalize my creative time and keep me from reaching my personal goals. I'm doing better but by no means have I perfected saying no. I'm always asking everyone around me to help me be more cold-hearted, but then of course, my resolve crumbles at the last minute. So I apply the Marie Kondo method: "Discard [say no to] everything that does not spark joy." This includes personal obligations. I'm working on it.

When you feel overwhelmed or unfocused, what do you do?

I stop everything and take a long walk alone. Long contemplative hikes, where I get ample time to daydream and think—with no opportunity to sprint to my desk and obsess over minute work obligations—allow solutions to bubble to the top of my mind. Not particularly a radical idea, but it always works for me. I have to take a device on my walks to take notes, because the ideas come so fast and furious that I'll typically forget them if I don't write them all down. And the solitariness is always wonderfully reinforcing. It's amazing how little time one gets to be truly alone during the day. That solitude is exquisite.

QUOTES I'M PONDERING

(Tim Ferriss: April 28–May 12, 2017)

"Strategy without tactics is the slowest route to victory. Tactics without strategy is the noise before defeat."

—SUN TZU
Chinese military strategist and author of *The Art of War*

"Let the first impulse pass. Wait for the second."

—BALTASAR GRACIÁN
Spanish Jesuit and baroque prose writer
lauded by Schopenhauer and Nietzsche

"Emptiness is the fasting of the mind."

—ZHUANG ZHOU
4th century B.C. Chinese philosopher and
author of *Zhuangzi*, a foundational text of Taoism

"Don't spend time chasing a right answer or a right path, but instead spend time defining how you are going to approach whatever path you choose."

LAURA R. WALKER
TW: @lwalker
wnyc.org

LAURA R. WALKER is president and CEO of New York Public Radio, the largest public radio station group in the nation. Under her leadership, New York Public Radio has increased its monthly audience from 1 million to over 26 million, has raised more than $100 million in long-term investment, and has been described by *Nieman Lab*'s Ken Doctor as being on "innovation overdrive." Laura was honored with an Edward R. Murrow Award from the Corporation for Public Broadcasting, the industry's highest honor. She was named one of New York City's "Most Powerful Women" by *Crain's New York Business*, was chosen for the *Crain's New York Business* special feature on "The 100 Most Influential Women in NYC Business," and was one of *Moves* magazine's "Power Women." She holds an MBA from the Yale School of Management and a BA in history from Wesleyan University, where she was an Olin Scholar.

What is the book (or books) you've given most as a gift, and why? Or what are one to three books that have greatly influenced your life?

When I give a book, I always try to find something that I loved, and most important, speaks to the person's dreams, yearnings, or challenges they are facing. For friends who have faced or are facing cancer, I often give them *The Emperor of All Maladies: A Biography of Cancer* by Siddhartha Mukherjee, because this beautifully written book weaves together science and story so elegantly, and helped me understand cancer—the history, causes, and innovative treatment—when my son had cancer.

For new cooks I give Mark Bittman's *How to Cook Everything* because it delivers exactly what it promises!

For New York City geeks—and I know a lot of them—I gave *Nonstop Metropolis* by Rebecca Solnit.

For a great novel that I have read three times, *Anna Karenina* by Leo Tolstoy.

For young women, I get *The Second Sex* by Simone de Beauvoir, which I read when I was studying in Paris. "One is not born, but rather becomes, a woman."

And for those who struggle with productivity and taking control of their lives, *The 4-Hour Workweek*, of course!

What purchase of $100 or less has most positively impacted your life in the last six months (or in recent memory)?

I'm a bit of a pen geek. I recently found an erasable pen—the FriXion by Pilot in blue. It writes so smoothly, and being able to erase it gives me a sense of power and delight. I often use the pen with a "smart" notebook (like the Rocketbook Everlast smart notebook) that can be reused.

In the last five years, what have you become better at saying no to?

Ever since my son got cancer several years ago, when I cleared my plate of almost all obligations but being with him and work, I have become better at saying no to invitations, especially those that don't involve my family.

When you feel overwhelmed or unfocused, what do you do?

In a tough situation, I try to remind myself that stress can make me stronger

—*if* I believe it can. I breathe deeply and visualize, focusing that feeling of stress and being overwhelmed into positive, loving action. I was inspired to do this after reading some research by Kelly McGonigal of Stanford.

What advice would you give to a smart, driven college student about to enter the "real world"?

Get out of your comfort zone when you graduate. Ask yourself what you are genuinely curious about and explore it. Embrace the ambiguity and contradictions that life invariably will bring, and develop habits—exercise, talking with friends, writing—that help you do so. Don't spend time chasing a right answer or a right path, but instead spend time defining how you are going to approach whatever path you choose. What values most define you? What questions do you want to pursue?

"Life is not designed to hand us success or satisfaction, but rather to present us with challenges that make us grow."

TERRY LAUGHLIN
TW: @TISWIM
FB: Total Immersion Swimming
totalimmersion.net

TERRY LAUGHLIN is the founder of Total Immersion, an innovative swimming method focused on teaching students to swim in a highly efficient manner. Between 1973 and 1988, Terry coached three college and two USA Swimming club teams, improving each team dramatically and developing 24 national champions. In 1989, Terry founded Total Immersion and turned his focus from working with young, accomplished swimmers to adults with little experience or skill. He is the author of *Total Immersion: The Revolutionary Way to Swim Better, Faster, and Easier,* which I recommend reading after watching the videos titled *Freestyle: Made Easy.* I was introduced to Terry and Total Immersion by billionaire investor Chris Sacca, and it single-handedly taught me how to swim in my 30s. In less than ten days of solo training, I went from a two-length maximum (of a 25-yard pool) to swimming more than 40 lengths per workout in sets of two and four. It blew my mind, and now I swim for fun. It changed my life.

What is the book (or books) you've given most as a gift, and why? Or what are one to three books that have greatly influenced your life?

Mastery by George Leonard. I first read this book 20 years ago, after reading Leonard's *Esquire* article, the seed from which the book grew. Leonard wrote the book to share lessons from becoming an Aikido master teacher, despite starting practice at the advanced age of 47.

I raced through its 170-plus pages in a state of almost feverish excitement, so strongly did it affirm our swimming method. The book helped me see swimming as an ideal vehicle for teaching the mastery habits and behaviors closely interwoven with our instruction in the physical techniques of swimming. I love this book because it is as good a guide as I've ever seen to a life well lived.

A brief summary: Life is not designed to hand us success or satisfaction, but rather to present us with challenges that make us grow. Mastery is the mysterious process by which those challenges become progressively easier and more satisfying through practice. The key to that satisfaction is to reach the nirvana in which love of practice for its own sake (intrinsic) replaces the original goal (extrinsic) as our grail. The antithesis of mastery is the pursuit of quick fixes.

My five steps to mastery:

1. Choose a worthy and meaningful challenge.

2. Seek a sensei or master teacher (like George Leonard) to help you establish the right path and priorities.

3. Practice diligently, always striving to hone key skills and to progress incrementally toward new levels of competence.

4. Love the plateau. All worthwhile progress occurs through brief, thrilling leaps forward followed by long stretches during which you feel you're going nowhere. Though it seems as if we're making no progress, we are turning new behaviors into habits. Learning continues at the cellular level . . . if you follow good practice principles.

5. Mastery is a journey, not a destination. True masters never believe they have attained mastery. There is always more to be learned and greater skill to be developed.

How has a failure, or apparent failure, set you up for later success? Do you have a "favorite failure" of yours?

I began my coaching career in 1972 and had immediate and unbroken success. Between 1975 and 1983, I coached 24 national club and college champions and tremendously transformed every team I coached, from middling to high-performing. However, in 1983 I suffered a discouraging setback, losing a coaching job in a power struggle with a control-oriented parent board immediately after my young team won a Junior National championship.

The disappointment of having a promising team taken away from me after investing five years in their development put me into a state I didn't recognize at the time: the stages of grief. Over the next four years, I went through three head coaching positions, experiencing success in the pool in each, yet never feeling happy or satisfied.

In 1987, I finally recognized that unresolved grief was keeping me from enjoying my work, and that only a hiatus from coaching could resolve it. As well, I had nothing in the bank to show for 16 years of employment and was looking at college tuition payments for three daughters, starting just five years later.

With reluctance, I left coaching—uncertain if I would return—to see whether my native intelligence and abilities would prove more remunerative in another field. For two years, I worked in marketing communications, first at a technology company, then in a hospital. I earned enough to pay the bills, but I still wasn't able to put anything away for the future. More important, I was unable to summon any enthusiasm for my work.

I easily understood the problem. As a head coach for all those years, I had been essential and instrumental in anything significant that occurred. The success or failure of the entire enterprise was due mainly to my efforts and abilities. In the corporate world, I felt like a cog: It didn't much matter if I even came to work or not, and I simply could not endure that feeling.

In the spring of 1989, I left the hospital job and began planning two one-week summer camps for Masters swimmers—the first Total Immersion programs. In the summer of 1990, I held four such sessions and in 1991, six, plus a few clinics for Masters teams. These didn't support our family—I did that with freelance magazine and marketing writing.

I had no long-term vision for where this might go, but I was making a real impact on those who attended and loved being self-employed with my job security dependent only on the quality of my efforts. Yet, from that modest beginning, I've gone on to undreamt-of success with Total Immersion, which has grown to a network of more than 300 coaches in 30 countries. It's recognized as the gold standard in effective swimming technique.

My earlier failure, and brief sojourn outside coaching, taught me that I was born to coach and teach swimming, but also that I was not cut out to be someone else's employee and needed to be in charge of my own destiny.

In the last five years, what have you become better at saying no to? What new realizations and/or approaches helped?

My lifetime goal was to be the best swimming coach possible. It was never to run a company. Yet with the growth of Total Immersion, I found myself —by default—in the position of CEO. I don't mind admitting that I was a pretty crap CEO. This occurred, in part, because whenever I was given the choice to perform an executive or coaching task, I would always opt to perform the coaching task. Far more of my energy went into developing coaching skills than company leadership skills. My failings as an executive often had greater adverse effect on Total Immersion's growth than my strengths as a coach had a positive effect.

Two years ago, I was given a diagnosis of incurable, stage IV prostate cancer. Realizing that treatment would take up time and sap my energy, and that I did not have limitless time to accomplish important undone work, I delegated most of my executive responsibilities to a pair of associates, both of whom are a generation younger and who have impressive loyalty and intelligence, and bring a boundless sense of caring to their work. Since that decision, Total Immersion has undergone a striking turnaround and is now far better positioned for business success—and to endure for the long term—than was previously the case.

Just as important, I'm now in my most productive period ever in the aspects of TI to which I add the greatest value—creating our educational and coaching content and curriculum and developing our coaching cadre. Finally, I'm more excited, energized, and satisfied than ever by my work and contributions. The positive energy this generates is doing a great deal to keep me healthy and help me respond in a more salutary way to my treatments.

What advice would you give to a smart, driven college student about to enter the "real world"? What advice should they ignore?

I would ask a smart, driven college student to examine what is it they are driven to do. Are you driven to achieve an intrinsic or extrinsic goal? Several years ago, I read an op-ed in *The New York Times* that described a study of 10,000 West Point cadets who were followed for up to 14 years. They were asked as first-year cadets to describe their career goals.

Those who cited goals intrinsic to being an outstanding officer—developing excellence as a leader and communicator, earning the respect of the troops under their command—went on at much higher rates to earn commissions as officers, extend their service beyond the five-year minimum, gain early promotion to higher ranks, and report a high degree of satisfaction with their Army service.

Those who cited extrinsic goals—earning promotions and gaining status—were less likely to earn commissions and early promotions, or report a high level of satisfaction, leading them to terminate their service after the minimum five-year period at higher rates.

The same will apply in any field of endeavor. If your highest goal is incremental, patient, continual learning and development in critical skills and core competencies—and you allow recognition, promotions, and financial rewards to be a natural result of the excellence you attain at core competencies—you will be far more likely to experience success and satisfaction, and perhaps even attain eminence, in your field. As a swimming coach, from my earliest days 40-plus years ago, these were my basic motivations:

- To continually deepen my understanding of technique and performance. I've never been satisfied that I had the last word, always felt certain there were further insights and nuances to be learned;

- To have a life-changing positive impact on those I coached; and

- To leave an enduring mark on the field of swim coaching, to leave the profession better off than I found it. At 66, I'm just as passionate and curious as I was at 21, if not more so, and I have no plans to retire. I can't imagine anything else I might have done which would have brought greater fulfillment.

> ## "After starting my first job at Oracle ... I ended up in Larry Ellison's old office, which he didn't entirely clean out, leaving behind some 40 copies of *The Mythical Man-Month*."

MARC BENIOFF
TW: @Benioff
salesforce.com

MARC BENIOFF is a philanthropist and chairman and CEO of Salesforce. A pioneer of cloud computing, Marc founded the company in 1999 with a vision to create an enterprise software company with a new technology model based in the cloud, a new pay-as-you-go business model, and a new integrated corporate philanthropy model. Under his leadership, Salesforce has grown from an idea into a Fortune 500 company, the fastest-growing top five software company in the world, and the global leader in CRM. He has been named one of the "World's 50 Greatest Leaders" by *Fortune,* "50 Most Influential People" by *Bloomberg Businessweek,* one of the top 20 "Best-Performing CEOs" by *Harvard Business Review,* one of the "Best CEOs in the World" by *Barron's*, and "Innovator of the Decade" by *Forbes* magazine and he received *The Economist's* Innovation Award. Marc is also a member of the World Economic Forum Board of Trustees. Marc is the author of three books, including the national bestseller *Behind the Cloud*, which details how he grew Salesforce from zero to $1 billion in annual sales. Currently, he is one of only four entrepreneurs in history to have built an enterprise software company with more than $10 billion in annual revenue (the other three being Bill Gates of Microsoft, Larry Ellison of Oracle, and Hasso Plattner of SAP).

What is the book (or books) you've given most as a gift, and why? Or what are one to three books that have greatly influenced your life?

One of the most powerful books in business I ever read was *Managing*, by the former head of ITT, Harold Geneen. It changed my life and my whole approach to business. He's old school, and his book is a chronicle of his regime at ITT. A lot of the things we do at Salesforce are based on his techniques, such as our quarterly operations reviews, which we're religious about.

The Mythical Man-Month by Frederick P. Brooks, Jr. is another book that had a huge impact on me. After starting my first job at Oracle, I was promoted in 1990 to be the youngest vice president. I ended up in Larry Ellison's old office, which he didn't entirely clean out, leaving behind some 40 copies of *The Mythical Man-Month*.

Larry had given this book to every software executive whom he met within the company. This short book says that to write great software, do it in small teams; having 100 or 1,000 or 2,000 developers won't make it happen. Ironically, when we first started Salesforce and started to have some success, I remember that Oracle, now a competitor, had 2,000 CRM developers and asked, in essence, "How would Salesforce ever beat us?" I would say it's because of *The Mythical Man-Month*. Small teams will always outperform large teams in software. It was serendipitous that I found the book in Larry's drawer.

A third influential book is *The Good Heart* by the Dalai Lama. It was a very important book to me because, at the time I read it, I was looking at all of the different religions in the world. I was taken aback by this book, subtitled "A Buddhist Perspective on the Teachings of Jesus." I really, really, really loved the book. What I liked the most was the Dalai Lama's guidance on converting to Buddhism. He wrote that if you are part of another religion, please do not convert to Buddhism. Your fastest path to enlightenment and peace of mind and your own good heart is in the religion that you are in. I started to change my spiritual philosophy based on that book. I kind of rebooted my religion of origin. I became more committed to Judaism and to exploring that as my primary path.

What purchase of $100 or less has most positively impacted your life in the last six months (or in recent memory)?

I really like this shirt that I bought from Under Armour, which displays one of basketball star Stephen Curry's mottos: "I can do all things." When you first see it, you think that it's actually a kind of ego statement. What you don't realize is that Curry, the MVP of the Golden State Warriors, is a religious person. He took this quote from Philippians 4:13 in the Bible, which says: "I can do all things through Christ who strengthens me." Curry says this verse before he takes a shot on the court.

It's become one of his major mottos—it's on his shoes and on this shirt. It's a motivational and powerful motto that orients you, not only to something within yourself, but also to something greater.

I think most people might look at his "I can do all things" motto and think it's all about him, but it's really about his faith. I bought several of them, and I really like them.

How has a failure, or apparent failure, set you up for later success?

I look at every failure as a learning experience and try to spend time with my failures. I stew on them for a while until I pick out some nugget from them that I can take forward.

For example, a few years ago, we were running out of space in our office in Japan and, coincidentally, I had a Tokyo meeting with the head of Japan Post around the same time. He brought me to his new building rising out of the original Japan Post office, next to the Imperial Palace and Tokyo Central Station in a very special part of Japan called Marunouchi.

He told me that he loved Salesforce and wanted us in this tower, and he offered us a naming opportunity. Honored and flattered, I went up and down the elevator with the architect to see all the floors. I didn't like the top floor, because after a recent earthquake, I worried that our employees would be too upset to work there. Also, I liked the human scale of the middle floors. I selected four middle floors. Yet, after moving in, I realized the top floor was actually absolutely the coolest floor, with a deck, which I could have chosen along with other lower floors. And I had declined putting our name on the tower.

I stewed on this for a couple years. Later we became anchor tenants in office buildings all over the world—in London, New York, San Francisco, Munich, and Paris. Each of these buildings is not only named Salesforce Tower, but we also took the top floor along with some lower floors. I learned from that experience in Japan to leverage a real estate strategy for Salesforce. It's an example of how I learned that if I'm upset about something, I should spend time asking myself, "What could I learn?" Because another opportunity is probably going to come in the future, and I will be better able to re-execute it.

We are keeping the top floors of the Salesforce Towers open space—we call them "Ohana" floors. *Ohana* is the Hawaiian word for "family," and for us, this includes employees, customers, partners, and the community. The Ohana floors will be used for meetings, events, and collaboration during the day. All employees are welcome to use the space. When the company is not using the Ohana floor, its use will be offered to NGOs and nonprofits. The top of Salesforce Tower San Francisco will be the highest floor in the city. It's a sight to see!

In the last five years, what new belief, behavior, or habit has most improved your life?

I've gotten my diet under control, adopting a low-sugar diet—what Tim Ferriss calls a slow-carb diet, which I completely agree with. Also, I try to take a day off a week and not eat at all. That has really helped me.

I have a friend, magician David Blaine, who fasted for 44 days over the city of London in a Plexiglas box. That's when I decided I could take at least one day a week and just not eat.

What is an unusual habit or an absurd thing that you love?

I love my Peloton cycle. I love being able to get on it to ride for 45 minutes, to get a good workout and have a social experience with people all over the world who are riding at the same time. My favorite instructor is Cody Rigsby. I try to stay in the top 10 percent of the class if I'm doing an active workout.

I'm getting very good, high-intensity interval training, all while having an entertainment experience with the music and with the instructor. I'm learning about my body and reducing my stress—all very important to me.

If you could have a gigantic billboard anywhere with anything on it, what would it say and why?

"Adopt a K-12 school." Nothing is more important than our children's education. If kids don't have a K-12 education, they won't have a chance in the future, especially for jobs that require competencies in core subjects like mathematics and writing. I've adopted my local school, Presidio Middle School, in San Francisco. It was fortuitous that I adopted the school my mother went to, even though I didn't know it at the time. It was almost like I felt directed there in some strange way.

By adopting a school, we can do relatively small amounts of work that have a huge and lasting impact. Today, schools are often isolated from their communities, including local businesses. Making a difference is as simple as knocking on the door of your neighborhood school and asking the principal how you can help. You'd be surprised by how this simple act can help change the lives of young students for the better. It's great to focus on parochial schools, charter schools, and other schools, but they are not the vast majority of schools in the United States. The 3.5 million public school teachers in the U.S., who make an average of $38,000 a year, need our help and our support to prepare our children for the future. They're only going to get that if every one of us pitches in and adopts a school.

Since 2013, Salesforce has partnered with Bay Area school districts to improve computer science education. To date, Salesforce.org has donated $22.5 million to the San Francisco and Oakland school districts and also provided technology and infrastructure. The most important thing isn't the money, but the time that our employees have spent in these schools, mentoring and tutoring kids, learning what they need, and understanding their challenges. So far, our employees have volunteered 20,000 hours in the schools.

What is one of the best or most worthwhile investments you've ever made?

One of the best investments I ever made is in my meditation practice. I typically pray and meditate every morning for 30 to 60 minutes. I have also expanded my practice to teaching meditation at my synagogue. I've been meditating for more than 25 years, and I view it as a critical part of my success.

It's a skill that I have used when things have gone wrong in my life. When there are life challenges—whether it was my father's death, health challenges with family members, extreme stress in Salesforce, or worry about the state of the world—I could always find refuge and strength in my meditation and prayer practice. This is an investment that has paid off over and over again.

I've been especially influenced by Thich Nhat Hanh, a Zen master who lives in Plum Village, a monastery in southwestern France. [**Note from Tim:** Thich Nhat Hanh's book, *Peace Is Every Step*, also had a huge impact on my life.]

After Thich Nhat Hanh suffered a stroke in 2014, he moved in with me (and also brought his top 30 monastics with him) for six months of stroke rehab, and, more than reading any book, it was profoundly moving for me to experience their lifestyle.

A few things that stuck with me were that they were committed to practicing every day, they had very strong adherence to their precepts, and they only traveled in groups and always stuck together.25

"Show up in every moment like you're meant to be there, because your energy precedes anything you could possibly say."

MARIE FORLEO
TW/IG: @marieforleo
marieforleo.com

MARIE FORLEO has been called "a thought leader for the next generation" by Oprah Winfrey. She is the creator of the award-winning show *MarieTV* and the founder of B-School, and *Forbes* has included her website on its list of "100 Best Websites for Entrepreneurs." Marie has mentored young business owners at Richard Branson's Centre of Entrepreneurship, and she is the author of *Make Every Man Want You: How to Be So Irresistible You'll Barely Keep from Dating Yourself!*, which has been published in 16 languages.

What is the book (or books) you've given most as a gift, and why? Or what are one to three books that have greatly influenced your life?

Hands down, *The War of Art* by Steven Pressfield (page 5). This book has a magical, activating quality to it. It's the essential no-bullshit guide for anyone who battles self-doubt or struggles to bring any important project to life. I reread it in full at least once a year. But it's also the kind of book that you can flip to any page, read the passage, and find the exact jolt of inspiration you need to move ahead.

If you could have a gigantic billboard anywhere with anything on it, what would it say and why?

My billboard would say, "Everything is figure-out-able." I learned this as a kid from my mom, and it's fueled every aspect of my career and life. It still does to this day.

The meaning is simple: No matter what challenge or obstacle you face, whether it's personal, professional, or global, there's a path ahead. It's all figure-out-able. You'll find a way or make a way, if you're willing to be relentless, stay nimble, and keep taking action. It's especially useful to remember when things go wrong, because rather than wasting time or energy on the problem, you shift immediately to brainstorming solutions. I honestly believe it's one of the most practical and powerful beliefs you can adopt.

What is one of the best or most worthwhile investments you've ever made?

A three-dollar yellow legal pad. When I was 25, I taught hip-hop classes and tended bar to pay the bills while slowly building my online business. Every time I taught a class or poured drinks, I brought that yellow legal pad with me. Because inevitably, people would ask, "So, what else do you do when you're not teaching/bartending?" I'd tell them about my online business, hand them a pen and my yellow legal pad, and ask them to subscribe to my email list.

That yellow legal pad and a long-term focus on nurturing my subscriber list is the foundation of my entire career. It's helped me set and exceed major life goals, build a global business, and generate more than $75 million in revenue for my company.

What is an unusual habit or an absurd thing that you love?

I love grocery shopping alone, especially when there's no time pressure. I like pushing the cart, cruising up and down each aisle, and crossing things off of my paper list.

In the last five years, what new belief, behavior, or habit has most improved your life?

Learning and using a relationship communication tool called the Imago Dialogue, created by Dr. Harville Hendrix and Dr. Helen LaKelly Hunt. It's a structured way to talk with your spouse or significant other, especially when you're fighting. At first, it all feels a bit hokey and totally unnatural. But when you learn how it works and use it earnestly, it's nothing short of miraculous for your intimate relationships.

What advice would you give to a smart, driven college student about to enter the "real world"? What advice should they ignore?

[My advice:] Pursue every project, idea, or industry that genuinely lights you up, regardless of how unrelated each idea is, or how unrealistic a long-term career in that field might now seem. You'll connect the dots later. Work your fucking ass off and develop a reputation for going above and beyond in all situations. Do whatever it takes to earn enough money, so that you can go all in on experiences or learning opportunities that put you in close proximity to people you admire, because proximity is power. Show up in every moment like you're meant to be there, because your energy precedes anything you could possibly say.

Ignore the advice to specialize in one thing, unless you're certain that's how you want to roll. Ignore giving a shit about what other people think about your career choices or what you do for a living—especially if what you do for a living funds your career choices. Ignore the impulse to dial down your enthusiasm for fear it'll be perceived as unprofessional. And especially for women, ignore societal and familial pressures to get married and have kids.

What are bad recommendations you hear in your profession or area of expertise?

When it comes to building an online audience, a big mistake people make is trying to be everywhere at once. They're scrambling to generate a ton of mediocre content to fill up a seemingly endless number of social feeds and online platforms, which leads to dismal results.

Trying to crush it on every platform, especially if you're a one-person show, is not a wise or sustainable use of your time, talent, or energy. Even if you have a team, I still recommend choosing one platform to focus on at first. Before committing to another content channel or social platform, ask yourself, why exactly do you want to be on this platform? What are the specific business reasons you're going to commit time, energy, and resources to regularly creating and engaging in that space? Does this really make sense given your other time commitments and big-picture goals?

One thing business owners don't realize is that every social media platform you're active on becomes an open channel for customer service. People will ask questions there and, yes, they'll complain there, too. Think that through. Have a process in place for someone on your team to sweep social channels on a regular basis so you don't create a customer service nightmare for yourself. Just because you can be active on a platform doesn't mean you should.

When you feel overwhelmed or unfocused, what do you do?

Whenever I feel unfocused or stuck on a particular issue, I do some kind of intense physical workout. Could be a spin class or a circuit training series with great, loud music. The goal is full sensory immersion, which does a few key things. First, it clears my mental and emotional cache. But more important, it opens up what I can best describe as a channel of inner intelligence that I rarely, if ever, access through focused thinking. Without fail, I get some spontaneous download that leads to a clear plan of action to move ahead. For me, creativity lives in the body, not the mind.

"Over the last few years, I've found myself looking at all my important relationships through the Enneagram lens. . . . I wish I had discovered it much earlier."

DREW HOUSTON
TW: @drewhouston
FB: /houston
dropbox.com

DREW HOUSTON is CEO and co-founder of Dropbox. After graduating from MIT in 2006, he turned his frustration with carrying USB drives and emailing files to himself into a demo for what became Dropbox. In early 2007, he and co-founder Arash Ferdowsi applied to tech accelerator Y Combinator. Dropbox went on to become one of the fastest-growing startups in YC history. Dropbox now has more than 500 million registered users and employs more than 1,500 people in 13 global offices.

What is the book (or books) you've given most as a gift, and why? Or what are one to three books that have greatly influenced your life?

I've always admired Warren Buffett and Charlie Munger's clarity of thought and how they manage to explain complex topics in simple terms. *Poor Charlie's Almanack* by Charlie Munger is one of my favorite examples.

As the CEO of a company, and in life in general, you find yourself making a dizzying variety of decisions in areas where you don't have a lot of expertise, and your environment is constantly changing. How do you navigate this? How do you cultivate judgment and wisdom without waiting for a lifetime of experience?

Poor Charlie's Almanack is a good start. It describes how to make good decisions in any situation with a relatively limited mental toolkit: the big, enduring ideas of the fundamental academic disciplines. Virtually everyone is exposed to these concepts by high school, but few people truly master them or apply them in everyday life. In my experience, it's this kind of essential, first-principles thinking that enables the unusual level of insight and conviction that sets the great founders apart from the merely good ones.

In the last five years, what new belief, behavior, or habit has most improved your life?

I've found the Enneagram to be incredibly helpful. At first glance it's a personality typing tool like Myers-Briggs. There are nine Enneagram "types" and every person has one dominant type. But I've found it to be much more useful and predictive of how people actually behave.

At first I was skeptical, but after reading the description for my type I found it spookily accurate in pinpointing what makes me tick: what motivates me, what my natural strengths are, what my blind spots tend to be, and so on. It's helped me tailor my role and leadership style to my strengths.

It's even better with a team—all of our senior leaders have typed themselves and we encourage everyone at Dropbox to learn about it. You can easily find (free) online tests and resources.

Over the last few years, I've found myself looking at all my important relationships through the Enneagram lens. It's a great way to build deeper empathy for the people in your life and better understand why they are the way they are. I wish I had discovered it much earlier.

What advice would you give to a smart, driven college student about to enter the "real world"? What advice should they ignore?

I thought about this a lot when I gave the commencement address at MIT back in 2013. I said that if I had a cheat sheet I could give myself at 22, it would have three things on it: a tennis ball, a circle, and the number 30,000.

The tennis ball is about finding something that you can become obsessed with, like my childhood dog who would go crazy whenever anyone threw a ball for her. The most successful people I know are all obsessed with solving a problem that really matters to them.

The circle refers to the idea that you're the average of your five closest friends. Make sure to put yourself in an environment that pulls the best out of you.

And the last is the number 30,000. When I was 24, I came across a website that says most people live for about 30,000 days—and I was shocked to find that I was already 8,000 days down. So you have to make every day count.

I'd give the same advice today, but I would clarify that it's not just about passion or following your dreams. Make sure the problem you become obsessed with is one that needs solving and is one where your contribution can make a difference. As Y Combinator says, "Make something people want."

In the last five years, what have you become better at saying no to? What new realizations and/or approaches helped?

This was a hard thing for me to learn; I like helping people. But realizing a couple things made a big difference: You have a lot less time than you think, and you're not spending your time the way you think you are.

I've found this analogy useful. Think of your time like a jar, your priorities as "rocks," and everything else as pebbles or sand. What's the best way to fill your jar?

Doesn't seem like rocket science. Ask anyone and they'll be utterly convinced they already start with the rocks, then fill in the pebbles, then the sand. I was, too. The first time I did this exercise (when reading *The Effective Executive* by Peter Drucker, one of my all-time favorite management books) I was convinced that the majority of my time went into recruiting and working on our product [the "rocks"].

But once I actually created an hour-by-hour log of where my time was spent over a couple of weeks, I was shocked (along with everyone else who has ever done this exercise) that 1) my jar was mostly filled with sand and 2) really important rocks were falling on the ground.

That helped me put outside requests into perspective. My jar isn't very big to begin with; am I going to fill it with my rocks or am I going to let other people fill it with theirs? I actually have an email label called "OPP" to remind myself that those requests are "other people's priorities" and to think carefully before putting unsolicited requests for favors ahead of all my teammates and customers, who are quietly counting on me to do my actual job. Note that this doesn't mean "never help people." Just be conscious of your choices.

A couple more tips: Schedule specific blocks of time in advance for your rocks so you don't have to think about them. Don't rely on wishful thinking (e.g., "I'll get that workout in when I have some downtime"); if you can't see your rocks on your calendar, they might as well not exist. This is doubly important for things like sleep and exercise. If you don't put those in first, no one will.

As far as actually saying no, I've learned you don't owe anyone lengthy explanations, and you don't have to respond to every email (particularly anything unsolicited). Brief, one-line responses like "I can't make it but thank you for the invitation" or "Thanks for thinking of me — unfortunately my hands are full with [my company] so I can't meet right now" are more than adequate.

"Great opportunities never have 'great opportunity' in the subject line."

SCOTT BELSKY
TW/IG: @scottbelsky
scottbelsky.com

SCOTT BELSKY is an entrepreneur, author, and investor. He is a venture partner at Benchmark, a venture capital firm based in San Francisco. Scott co-founded Behance in 2006 and served as CEO until Adobe acquired Behance in 2012. Millions of people use Behance to display their portfolios, as well as track and find top talent across the creative industries. He is an early investor and advisor in Pinterest, Uber, and Periscope, among many other fast-growing startups.

If you could have a gigantic billboard anywhere with anything on it, what would it say and why?

The billboard would say, "Great opportunities never have 'great opportunity' in the subject line."

Whether you're looking for the best new job, client, partner, or new business opportunity, it is unlikely to lure you when you first see it. In fact, the best opportunities may not even catch your attention at first. More often than not, great opportunities look unattractive on the surface. What makes an opportunity great is upside. If the potential upside were explicitly clear, the opportunity would have already been taken.

Don't call yourself a visionary, or aspire to make a disproportionate impact, if you anchor all your decisions with what you see and know now. I am always surprised by how lazy people are when making serious decisions about their careers. Join a team not for what it is, but for what you think you can help it become. Be a "founder" in the sense that you're willing to make something rather than just join something.

You must seize opportunities when they present themselves, not when they are convenient or obvious. The only way to cultivate your own luck is to be more flexible (you'll need to give up something for the right opportunity), humble (timing is out of your control), and gracious (when you see it, seize it!). Life's greatest opportunities run on their own schedule, not yours.

What is an unusual habit or an absurd thing that you love?

As my life has gotten busier and more demanding, I have chosen certain songs and snacks that I love and preserved them for when I am doing certain kinds of work. For example, there is a "writing" playlist of music on my computer that I only allow myself to listen to while writing, because time for writing can be particularly painful to plan and adhere to. In some ways, I have otherwise cut out things I like and take for granted and turned them into highly coveted rewards. My playlist reserved for writing/deep work periods includes:

- "Everyday" by Carly Comando
- "The Aviators" by Helen Jane Long
- "Divenire" by Ludovico Einaudi
- "Mad World" by Michael Andrews and Gary Jules
- "Festival" by Sigur Rós

Snacks that I keep for extended writing and work periods (though less important than the sacred playlist) include:

- Parmesan crisps from Eli Zabar in NYC
- White chocolate-covered pretzels

I don't enjoy these snacks at the beginning—only when it has clearly become a legitimate deep work period. Other than that hurdle, there are no other rules. "Deep work" for me means no interruptions or jumping around casually between tasks. Deep work is the three-plus-hour focus-on-one-problem stuff that I find especially hard to do in the constantly connected era we live in . . . hence the rewards and incentives I reserve for such work.

What advice would you give to a smart, driven college student about to enter the "real world"? What advice should they ignore?

Don't hold out for the perfect job or title. Don't optimize for the slightly higher salary. Instead, focus on the only two things that actually matter.

Number one: Every step in your early career must get you incrementally closer to whatever genuinely interests you. The most promising path to success is pursuing genuine interests and setting yourself up for the circumstantial relationships, collaborations, and experiences that will make all the difference in your life. A labor of love always pays off, just not how and when you expect. Set yourself up to succeed by taking new jobs and roles that get you closer to your interests.

Number two: The greatest lessons you learn in the beginning of a career are about people—how to work with people, be managed by people, manage expectations with people, and lead other people. As such, the team you choose to join, and your boss, are huge factors in the value of a professional experience early in your career. Choose opportunities based on the quality of people you will get to work with.

What are bad recommendations you hear in your profession or area of expertise?

"Industries are led by experts."

While we idolize the experts in our industry, we often forget that industries are often transformed by neophytes. The boldest transformations, like Uber disrupting transportation or Airbnb disrupting hospitality, are led by outsiders. Perhaps the playbook to change an industry is to be naive enough at the start to question basic assumptions and then stay alive long enough to employ skills that are unique and advantageous in the space you seek to change. Perhaps naive excitement and pragmatic expertise are equally important traits at different times.

"Customers know best."

The only focus group I ever ran at Behance was in the very beginning, in 2007, when we were debating a number of different approaches toward our mission "to organize the creative world." We presented the focus group participants with five or six different ideas and then asked them to complete a survey. Universally, participants said the last thing they wanted was "yet another social network to connect with creative peers." They figured Myspace was sufficient for this purpose. But when they were asked about their greatest struggles, participants talked about the expense and inefficiencies of maintaining an online portfolio and how difficult it was to get attribution for the creative work they had made.

We were faced with a classic example of "don't ask customers what they want, figure out what they need." We ultimately built a social network for creative professionals that is now the world's leading creative professional community, with more than 12 million members, and was, six years later, acquired by Adobe.

When you feel overwhelmed or unfocused, what do you do?

I whisper to myself, "Scott, do your fucking job." With all the drama around us and inside of us, it is too easy to get distracted or overthink a situation. It is too easy to rationalize why you're too busy, or why you should wait to do something that just needs to get done. I opt for the no-bullshit approach. When I need to do something mundane, or when I need to do something especially difficult like deliver bad news or fire an employee, I just tell myself to stop screwing around and "do your fucking job." I find that self-directive hard to argue with.

QUOTES I'M PONDERING

(Tim Ferriss: May 19–June 2, 2017)

"You can do so much in ten minutes' time. Ten minutes, once gone, are gone for good. Divide your life into ten-minute units and sacrifice as few of them as possible in meaningless activity."

—INGVAR KAMPRAD
Swedish business magnate, founder of IKEA

"There will come a time when you believe everything is finished. That will be the beginning."

—LOUIS L'AMOUR
Widely popular American Western novelist and short-story writer, author of more than 100 works

"All good things are wild and free."

—HENRY DAVID THOREAU
American essayist and philosopher, author of *Walden*

"We all should reassess what we think and believe constantly—in politics, in life, and in our thinking. Otherwise, we get too rigid."

TIM McGRAW
TW/IG: @TheTimMcGraw
FB: /TimMcGraw
timmcgraw.com

TIM McGRAW has sold more than 50 million records and dominated the charts with 43 worldwide #1 singles. He's won three Grammy Awards, 16 Academy of Country Music Awards, 14 Country Music Association Awards, 11 American Music Awards, three People's Choice Awards, and numerous other honors. His iconic career achievements include being named BDS Radio's "Most Played Artist of the Decade" for all music genres and having the "Most Played Song of the Decade" for all music genres. He is the most played country artist since his debut in 1992, with two singles spending more than ten weeks at #1. His career-long tour successes include the record-setting Soul2Soul: The World Tour with his wife, Faith Hill. He starred in and narrated the hit movie *The Shack,* and other film credits include *Friday Night Lights* and *The Blind Side.*

What is the book (or books) you've given most as a gift, and why? Or what are one to three books that have greatly influenced your life?

I give *Jayber Crowe* (by Wendell Berry) as a gift all the time. It's a killer book! It's calming and thought-provoking at the same time. It gives you a perspective on life that you [might not have otherwise]. . . . Great art makes you reassess. We all should reassess what we think and believe constantly —in politics, in life, and in our thinking. Otherwise, we get too rigid.

When you feel overwhelmed or unfocused, what do you do?

One of the questions I'm asked a lot is "What's the single thing that most prevents success?" And to me, the answer is always focus [or lack of focus]. I believe focus is the key to everything. So, figuring out how to find focus or get back to my focus is something I ponder a lot. My gym is how I get refocused. When I start a workout, I can tell if my focus is off, and by the end of my workout I see a change. The physical activity clears my mind and allows me to draw back into focusing on what I need to do next to get to where I want to go. It changes everything for me—my outlook on the day, my mental stability, and how I set myself up for the rest of the things I'll do that day.

In the last five years, what new belief, behavior, or habit has most improved your life?

Fitness has changed my life. I believe it's directly led to prolonged success in my business, for a lot of reasons. I'm certainly in a business where aesthetics are important. But more than that, it's back to the topic of focus. It's given me a place to draw focus from. It's easy to make it seem like a trivial thing: being physically fit and keeping yourself healthy. But in the long run, that's really what you want more than anything else. Plus, it's a small step that teaches you discipline in other areas. But you can't let yourself get overwhelmed thinking of the long term when you start. When I started getting into being more fit, I didn't think, "I gotta do this for a year." I thought, "I'm going do this for an hour today." Then today leads to tomorrow, tomorrow leads to the next day, and you look up and it's been a year.

I prefer to work out first thing in the morning because it just starts my day off better. It gives me more energy, and I don't dread it for the rest of the day.

If you could only pick two to five workouts for the next six months, which would you pick?

First, I would do something called the "bar complex." It's 12 barbell exercises done in a sequence. I do five rounds of the 12 exercises, starting with just the bar (45 pounds) and ten reps of each exercise. Each time I finish the circuit, I add five pounds to the bar and do two reps fewer than the round before it, so it looks like this:

10 reps x barbell (for each of the 12 exercises; same for the below)
8 reps x barbell + 5 lbs
6 reps x barbell + 10 lbs
4 reps x barbell + 15 lbs
and (at heaviest) 2 reps x barbell + 20 lbs

Then I reverse the whole process and come back down over five rounds, removing five pounds and adding two reps each round, finishing where I started: barbell x ten reps for each of the 12 exercises.

The second workout I would do is a pool workout that my trainer, Roger, taught me, which is a series of different, repetitive martial arts-based movements done in the water.

What is an unusual habit or an absurd thing that you love?

I love spearfishing, even though a lot of people have never even heard of it. Or they think of scuba tanks and the spear gun, but that's not how we do it. We free dive with what they call a Hawaiian or Bahamian sling. It's like a sling shot with a spear. I love it because, when I'm doing it, I feel completely at ease and confident. It's totally quiet, except you can hear the sound of your heart beating or the sound of breathing and blood rushing in your head. It tunes you into yourself in a weird way . . . and it's dangerous. I like that!

If you could have a gigantic billboard anywhere with anything on it, what would it say and why?

If I had a billboard, it would say "DAD." We often expect things from Mom: Mom will make it work, Mom can take care of this or that. But especially as a dad of daughters, how I talk to them and treat them is crucial to how they see themselves. Reminding myself that I'm a dad makes me want to be the best parent I can be for my kids. I don't do it well all the time—believe me. I think I'm terrible at it most of the time! But simply "DAD" on a billboard would be great to remind us all of how important it is to be a dad.

"When I'm old, how much would I be willing to pay to travel back in time and relive the moment that I'm experiencing right now?"

MUNEEB ALI
TW: @muneeb
muneebali.com

MUNEEB ALI is the co-founder of Blockstack, a new decentralized Internet where users control their data, and apps run without remote servers. Muneeb received his PhD in computer science from Princeton University, specializing in distributed systems. He went through Y Combinator—considered the Harvard/SEAL Team Six of startup incubators—and has worked in the systems research group at Princeton and PlanetLab, the world's first and largest cloud computing test bed. Muneeb was awarded a J. William Fulbright fellowship and gives guest lectures on cloud computing at Princeton. He has built a broad range of production systems and published research papers with more than 900 citations.

What is one of the best or most worthwhile investments you've ever made?

I took a loan of around $1,000 USD (in Pakistani rupees) to self-fund a three-month unpaid researcher gig in Sweden. There were no high-quality research opportunities in Pakistan, and I had to get out of the country and work with top researchers in my field in Europe or the U.S. to make progress toward my goals. The money wasn't enough to survive in Sweden for three months, but I made it work by eating once a day and living on the free coffee and snacks available at the office. That investment opened the door to my PhD admission at Princeton, which opened the door to my current startup, which has raised $5.1 million in venture funding so far.

In the last five years, what new belief, behavior, or habit has most improved your life?

Asking myself the question, "When I'm old, how much would I be willing to pay to travel back in time and relive the moment that I'm experiencing right now?"

If that moment is something like rocking my six-month-old daughter to sleep while she hugs me, then the answer is anything: I'd literally pay all the money I'd have in the bank at, say, age 70 to get a chance to relive that moment. This simple question just puts things in perspective and makes you grateful for the experience you're having right now versus being lost in thoughts about the past or the future.

In the last five years, what have you become better at saying no to? What new realizations and/or approaches helped?

For me, the realization was that I can add more value by going deep on a few things rather than engaging with a broad set of activities. I'm a startup founder, and there is always something or other to do. Here are some approaches that have helped:

- I started saying no to all external meeting requests as a rule of thumb. External meetings should be initiated by me (doesn't happen that often) and not initiated by others.

- Saying no to all involvements outside of my startup, such as being an advisor to some other startup or project, investing in or trading some cryptocurrency where I have domain expertise, etc. There is only one job/role that I can think about. No exceptions.

- Letting other people on my team deal with external invitations, calls, meetings, events, etc. Build strong connections with your team and stay updated on things through them. In other words, the team members are a filter for all the invitations and distractions. Important stuff has a way of bubbling up and you won't miss out.

HOW TO SAY
NO

NEAL STEPHENSON
TW: @nealstephenson
FB: /TheNealStephenson
nealstephenson.com

NEAL STEPHENSON is an author known for his speculative fiction works, variously categorized as science fiction, historical fiction, maximalism, and cyberpunk. His bestsellers include, among others, *The Diamond Age, Cryptonomicon, The Baroque Cycle,* and *Snow Crash,* which was named one of *Time* magazine's "Top 100 All-Time Best English-language Novels." He also writes nonfiction articles about technology in publications such as *Wired* magazine and has worked part-time as an adviser for Blue Origin, a company developing a manned suborbital launch system.

Note from Tim: By now, you know what this is: the type of email that makes me cry and smile at the same time. Herewith a lovely *hasta la próxima* from one of my idols, writer Neal Stephenson.

Hey there, Tim,

Sorry for the slow response and thanks for thinking of me in this context.

It has become pretty obvious of late that I'm trying to do too much, and so I started an experiment of not adding anything whatsoever to my "to-do" list, so that it wouldn't get any longer.

The result is that the items that were ALREADY on my "to-do" list only spawned more items as I crossed them off, and so it's a little like fighting a hydra. I am hoping that if I am ruthlessly efficient, I can one day get to the point where the list actually gets shorter instead of longer.

In the meantime, unfortunately, the "ruthlessly efficient" part of this plan means that I am turning down things like this just as a blanket policy.

Again, thanks for thinking of me and good luck with the project!

"Effective communication matters. Good works usually require an accurate perception thereof."

CRAIG NEWMARK
TW/FB: @craignewmark
craigconnects.org

CRAIG NEWMARK is a web pioneer, philanthropist, and leading advocate on behalf of trustworthy journalism, veterans and military families, and other civic and social justice causes. In 1995, Craig started curating a list of San Francisco arts and technology events he emailed to friends and colleagues. People were soon calling it "Craig's List," and when Craig turned it into a company, he monetized minimally, opting for a business model that prioritized "doing well by doing good." In 2016, he created the Craig Newmark Foundation to promote investment in organizations that effectively serve their communities and drive broad civic engagement at the grassroots level. In 2017, he became a founding funder and executive committee member of the News Integrity Initiative, administered by the CUNY Graduate School of Journalism, which seeks to advance news literacy and increase trust in journalism.

What is the book (or books) you've given most as a gift, and why? Or what are one to three books that have greatly influenced your life?

I feel my rabbi is Leonard Cohen, even though when I met him I was too tongue-tied to say anything. Anyway, I've given away a number of copies of his *Book of Longing*, since it articulates a sense of the compassionate and spiritual that I've found nowhere else. His work brings me closer to sensing the divine, and apparently that's also true for millions across the globe.

It might be more accurate to say that his collected poetry and music constitute a book, in the Biblical sense. I've probably given away more Cohen CD collections than the physical books, prior to widespread streaming.

He uses the hummingbird as a metaphor for spiritual freedom, and as I write this, there's an Anna's hummingbird feeding maybe ten feet in front of me.

How has a failure, or apparent failure, set you up for later success? Do you have a "favorite failure" of yours?

Throughout my career, my failure to recognize the need for effective communications has done me a lot of damage. In the first 20 years, at IBM and Charles Schwab, poor communications reinforced the perception that I'd be a poor team member. I've learned that inept communications or lack of communication can cause harm, sometimes the hard way.

However, in the last several years, I've come to understand how effective communication matters. Good works usually require an accurate perception thereof; without that, the means to continue those works might be withdrawn. Or worse, bad actors will interfere with that work, sometimes pointlessly prolonging human suffering.

Nowadays, I'm involved with a lot of nonprofits in areas that include women in tech, veterans and their families, and trustworthy, good-faith journalism. My help and grant-making require recipients to get smart about their own communications so that they can learn from my mistakes.

That's my idea of the successful use of my own failure.

If you could have a gigantic billboard anywhere with anything on it, what would it say and why?

Seems like all religions recognize the precept that you should "treat others as you want to be treated." However, people normally kind of forget that early in their youth. In my work, I'm finding that a simple reminder helps people act in a more benevolent way. So, repetition, via literal or metaphorical billboard, no matter how naive seeming, can matter.

What is an unusual habit or an absurd thing that you love?

I've grown to love seeing birds visit my house, and to attract them, I've put out birdbaths and feeders. The deal is that my wife and I do this, then the birds visit and pose for us. That's to say that I can do all my birdwatching from inside.

[For someone who wants to try this] I'd recommend The Nuttery NT065 Classic Seed Feeder, Extra Large. It's been really effective for attracting a range of small birds, like juncoes, chickadees, nuthatches, and finches. Some smarter larger birds like scrub jays (a kind of blue jay) and even an ambitious pigeon, can feed from it. It discourages squirrels.

At this point, the birds have trained us to feed them. In particular, a Western scrub jay has trained Mrs. Newmark to feed it suet, which is a big treat for them.

Now, when I walk to the train, a couple of ravens have started training me to feed them dog treats. (They seem to want to bring messages to Winterfell.)

Oh, that's right, I love treating the neighbors' dogs.

Also, I love playing with babies, mostly staring at each other and smiling. Drooling is also involved, and sometimes it's the baby.

"If it's already common knowledge, it's probably too late to make a major contribution. If you're the only one excited, you may be deluding yourself."

STEVEN PINKER
TW: @sapinker
FB: /Stevenpinkerpage
stevenpinker.com

STEVEN PINKER is a Johnstone Family Professor in the Department of Psychology at Harvard University. He conducts research on language and cognition, writes for publications such as *The New York Times* and *The Atlantic,* and is the author of ten books, including *The Language Instinct, How the Mind Works, The Blank Slate, The Better Angels of Our Nature,* and most recently, *The Sense of Style: The Thinking Person's Guide to Writing in the 21st Century.* He has been named "Humanist of the Year" by the American Humanist Association and is one of *Prospect* magazine's "Top 100 Public Intellectuals," *Foreign Policy*'s "100 Global Thinkers," and *Time* magazine's "100 Most Influential People in the World Today."

What purchase of $100 or less has most positively impacted your life in the last six months (or in recent memory)?

The X1 Search program: instant, precision searching by independent criteria (not just Google-style search string goulash) to pinpoint my files and emails going back to the 1980s. As info explodes, and my memory doesn't get better, it's a godsend.

If you could have a gigantic billboard anywhere with anything on it, what would it say? Are there any quotes you think of often or live your life by?

"If I am not for myself, who will be for me? But if I am only for myself, what am I? And if not now, when?" –Rabbi Hillel

What advice would you give to a smart, driven college student about to enter the "real world"? What advice should they ignore?

1. Find a new topic or area or concern that has a small number of people you respect behind it, but which has not become a culture-wide fad or conventional wisdom. If it's already common knowledge, it's probably too late to make a major contribution. If you're the only one excited, you may be deluding yourself.

2. Ignore advice to simply follow your intuition or gut without thinking through whether the course of action is likely to be fruitful and rewarding.

3. Focus on effectiveness—what your actions will actually accomplish—and not self-actualization or other ways of trying to feel good about yourself.

4. Don't think that the arts and verbal professions are the only respectable occupations (a common mindset of grandchildren of workers). The elites sneer at commerce as tawdry, but it's what gives people what they want and need, and pays for everything else, including the luxury of art.

5. Think about what you will add to the world. Some lucrative professions (e.g., ultra-high-tech finance) are dubious applications of human brainpower.

Besides your own, what is the book (or books) you've given most as a gift, and why? Or what are one to three books that have greatly influenced your life?

36 Arguments for the Existence of God: A Work of Fiction by Rebecca Newberger Goldstein (full disclosure: I am married to her, but that puts me even more firmly on the hook, because my judgment would be even more discredited if this turned out to be an unworthy recommendation). It's the best examination of the arguments about God's existence, laid out as a nonfiction Appendix written by the protagonist, a psychologist of religion. It's also funny, moving, and a dead-on satire of the foibles of academic and intellectual life today.

Among the books that have influenced my thinking: no single (or even three) *Aha!* books—my mind doesn't work like that. But here are some important ones:

> *The Strategy of Conflict* by Thomas C. Schelling
> *The Science of Words* by George A. Miller
> *Retreat from Doomsday* by John Mueller
> *The Nurture Assumption* by Judith Rich Harris
> *The Evolution of Human Sexuality* by Donald Symons
> *Knowledge and Decisions* by Thomas Sowell
> *Clear and Simple as the Truth* by Francis Noël-Thomas and
>   Mark Turner

In the last five years, what new belief, behavior, or habit has most improved your life?

A boring, clichéd, but essential behavior: keeping all of my articles, and all new books except those I read for pleasure, in electronic form. I used to swim in a vortex of paper, and since I live in several places and travel a lot, I always missed what I needed. Not only are electronic versions searchable, but—since we may have reached "peak stuff"—I'm participating in the great dematerialization of life, which will help the environment rebound.

In the last five years, what have you become better at saying no to?

Email from strangers or distant acquaintances seeking time-consuming favors, often ways of leveraging what they think is my (in fact dubious) influence and power. It's said that rich people and beautiful women never know who their friends really are. That can also be true of people with a reputation in professional circles.

When you feel overwhelmed or unfocused, what do you do?

The superficial, but temporarily useful, stratagem is to follow Oscar Wilde's advice, "The only way to get rid of a temptation is to yield to it" (assuming it's not destructive to oneself or others). Sometimes I'll let myself peruse nerdy discussion groups for camera equipment, or watch YouTube videos of 1960s rock music. The deeper stratagem is to think, "What will matter to me in six months, a year, five years? What is essential, and what is optional, in my life priorities?"

"I'm in three book groups where we discuss children's literature (no actual children attend), and I have a room in my apartment where I showcase my collection of beloved books."

GRETCHEN RUBIN
TW/FB: @gretchenrubin
gretchenrubin.com

GRETCHEN RUBIN is the author of several books, including the *New York Times* bestsellers *Better Than Before*, *The Happiness Project*, and *Happier at Home*. Her books have sold nearly three million copies worldwide in more than 30 languages. On her popular podcast, *Happier with Gretchen Rubin*, she discusses good habits and happiness with her sister Elizabeth Craft (they've been called "the Click and Clack of podcasters"). Her podcast was named one of iTunes' "Best Podcasts of 2015" and the Academy of Podcasters "Best Podcasts of 2016." *Fast Company* named Gretchen to its list of "Most Creative People in Business," and she's a member of Oprah's "SuperSoul 100."

What is the book (or books) you've given most as a gift, and why? Or what are one to three books that have greatly influenced your life?

I frequently give the book *A Pattern Language* by Christopher Alexander. I'm not a visual person, but this book taught me to see the world around me in an entirely new way. It's a brilliant way of analyzing experience and information. It's haunting.

What is one of the best or most worthwhile investments you've ever made?

I invested in three desktop computer monitors. I was afraid that having more than one monitor would make me feel overwhelmed and scattered, but in fact, having three monitors has dramatically increased my focus and efficiency while processing information. I can easily look something up while I'm writing, or copy information from the Internet into a piece I'm writing, or answer an email when referring to a document.

In the last five years, what new belief, behavior, or habit has most improved your life?

I'm now a zealous low-carb eater. I quit sugar as well as high-carb foods like flour, rice, and starchy vegetables. At last, my sweet tooth has vanished —such a relief! Changing that habit made an enormous difference in my health and also in my sense of well-being.

I was persuaded to adopt a low-carb approach to eating when I read Gary Taubes' book *Why We Get Fat*. I read that book, and overnight, I changed just about everything about the way I eat. For instance, these days, my daily breakfast is three scrambled eggs (with the yolks) and some form of meat (bacon, turkey, whatever's in the fridge).

What is an unusual habit or an absurd thing that you love?

I'm a giant raving fan of children's literature and young-adult literature. I'm in three book groups where we discuss children's literature (no actual children attend), and I have a room in my apartment where I showcase my collection of beloved books.

I made a list of my 81 favorite works of children's literature—what a joy it was to make that list! If I had to list just three books, I would cheat and list the names of three authors who've each written many books that I love: the Little House books by Laura Ingalls Wilder; the Narnia books by C. S. Lewis; and the His Dark Materials books by Philip Pullman.

"Most likely, the problem won't be around in a year, but my reputation of how I dealt with it will."

WHITNEY CUMMINGS
TW/IG: @whitneycummings
whitneycummings.com

WHITNEY CUMMINGS is a Los Angeles-based comedian, actor, writer, and producer. Whitney is the executive producer and, along with Michael Patrick King, co-creator of the Emmy-nominated CBS comedy *2 Broke Girls*. She has headlined with comics including Sarah Silverman, Louis C.K., Amy Schumer, Aziz Ansari, and others. Her first one-hour standup special, *Money Shot*, premiered on Comedy Central in 2010 and was nominated for an American Comedy Award. Her second standup special, *I Love You*, debuted on Comedy Central in 2014, and her latest special, *I'm Your Girlfriend*, premiered on HBO in 2016. Whitney is the author of *I'm Fine . . . And Other Lies*.

What is the book (or books) you've given most as a gift, and why? Or what are one to three books that have greatly influenced your life?

Getting the Love You Want by Harville Hendrix. Love the book, hate the title. It's a very illuminating exploration of how we're attracted to people who have the negative qualities of our primary caretakers. It was very eye-opening given who I was gravitating to in my work and personal life. It's helped me to make better relationship and hiring decisions, which ultimately saved me a lot of time and helped me to be way more efficient with my time. It's been a game changer for my self-awareness and made me a better picker of employees and co-workers.

The Fantasy Bond by Robert W. Firestone. This book helped me to understand how psychological defenses work, which gave me the power to disarm mine and move into a more honest, productive way to handle conflict. It helps stop your childhood from getting in the way of your adulthood.

The Female Brain by Louann Brizendine. I was so into this book that I made a movie about it, because I think everyone should be required to understand how their neurochemical engine works, and how we can be a puppet of our primordial brain at times. It helped me to master a basic understanding of chemistry, hormones, and the amygdala, which has given me patience with myself and others. This is invaluable when I'm dealing with difficult decisions or conflict. It also gives me a huge sense of freedom to be able to delineate between a neurochemical reaction and a legitimate feeling.

What purchase of $100 or less has most positively impacted your life in the last six months (or in recent memory)?

A weighted blanket. I am not an expert on the science of why it works, but the "deep touch pressure" helps the body release more serotonin. When I'm anxious, stressed, or can't sleep, I use it and I instantly feel calmer.

[One model that Whitney likes is the large weighted blanket from Weighted Blankets Plus LLC.]

If you could have a gigantic billboard anywhere with anything on it, what would it say and why?

"Fly high." In any given situation, I can't control anything except my reaction and my contribution, so this mantra helps me to not deplete myself with lowbrow responses to problems. Most likely, the problem won't be around in a year, but my reputation of how I dealt with it will. As long as I can handle a situation with grace, I usually come out having won and don't waste valuable time and energy feeling guilty or replaying it in my head. In my creative work, "fly high" is a reminder to always strive for an A-plus no matter how tired I am or how late it is. If you run out of time, ask for more. Never settle for "good enough."

What is one of the best or most worthwhile investments you've ever made?

I rescued a horse and three dogs. After years of experimenting with antidepressants, meditation, hypnosis, and various forms of therapy, I realized that for me, animals are the easiest way to help me to feel calm, centered, and present. They've also taught me countless priceless lessons about boundaries, consistency, and discipline that I apply to my work and relationships every day. They are the best performance-enhancing drug I've come across, by far.

What is an unusual habit or an absurd thing that you love?

Lying down in dirt. I do this a lot with my horse and with my dogs. There's something very liberating about being dirty, because then you don't have to worry about getting dirty.

In the last five years, what new belief, behavior, or habit has most improved your life?

Equine therapy and dog training are high up there, but I'm gonna have to go with gratitude lists. Every morning I make myself write a gratitude list, regardless of how busy I am, or how much I don't want to. It can feel silly and redundant at times, but it's atrophied my negative thinking. It's built up the muscle that focuses on what's going well and how fortunate I am, which helps me be more productive, creative, and focused. It yields a type of mental freedom that's hard to explain. Negativity used to consume and exhaust me, so now I literally have more energy. It's so easy for perfectionists to focus on what's wrong, and finding flaws is a big part of my job, but in terms of the big picture, negative thinking was a serious obstacle to creativity. Also, white tattoos! I have little messages tattooed on my arms, but nobody can see them except me.

What advice would you give to a smart, driven college student about to enter the "real world"? What advice should they ignore?

My advice would be to figure out some kind of charitable element to whatever endeavor you undertake, whether it's a benevolent motive or a literal profit donation à la Blake Mycoskie. Chances are, if you're reading books like this, you will succeed, but I've found that it all feels pretty meaningless if you're not in some way helping people or improving humanity in some way. Instead of striving to be a CEO or an entrepreneur, strive to be a hero. We need more of those.

What are bad recommendations you hear in your profession or area of expertise?

"Network." In creative fields, I think networking actually hurts you in most cases. Don't waste your time socializing with people who you think can help you. Just get better, and opportunities will naturally present themselves once you deserve them. Only focus on things within your control. And if you don't know what those things are, find someone who can tell you. Don't network, just work.

In the last five years, what have you become better at saying no to?

I say no to almost everything these days, thanks to going into therapy for a condition called codependence, which is a neural wiring issue that tricks me into being unable to tolerate the discomfort, or perceived discomfort, of others. I've rewired my brain for the most part, and, as a result, I no longer do anything out of guilt, pressure, or obligation. I've also worked through releasing the shame around not being "fun" and my "fear of missing out" complex, which was a big energy drain. It compelled me to go to events I simply didn't have time for, and that did not serve me.

An obvious corollary to this is social media minimization. I use the Freedom app to cut down on social media time. Not only is it very unhealthy and addictive, but it was also giving my lizard brain the sense that I was somehow being left behind or left out, which triggered deep fears. And fear is obviously annoying and exhausting. Speaking of annoying and exhausting, I also unfollowed a lot of close friends and coworkers on social media, which actually made our relationships much stronger and more productive, respectively.

When you feel overwhelmed or unfocused, what do you do?

In my photos on my phone, I made an album called "calm." I have photos and videos of my animals, funny pictures, memes, inspiring quotes, articles about neurology, gratitude lists, all sorts of things that make me smile and reconnect to my source. It's like my own personal digital Zen museum. Honestly, I think I'd be way more embarrassed if hackers released this album than any nude photos in my phone, but it's worth the risk. When I'm adrenalized, distracted, emotional, or anxious, I go into the album and it always grounds me; it reminds me of what's important and what's temporary. It's super helpful at work, because I can do it around people, while traveling, and at times when I don't have the luxury of a quiet room or a walk. Oh, and I put my phone in airplane mode first, so I'm not getting texts and emails while trying to find sanity away from texts and emails.

QUOTES I'M PONDERING

(Tim Ferriss: June 9–June 16, 2017)

"When your sparring partner scratches or head-butts you, you don't then make a show of it, or protest, or view him with suspicion or as plotting against you. And yet you keep an eye on him, not as an enemy or with suspicion, but with a healthy avoidance. . . . You should act this way with all things in life. We should give a pass to many things with our fellow trainees. For, as I've said, it's possible to avoid without suspicion or hate."

–MARCUS AURELIUS
Emperor of Rome and Stoic philosopher, author of *Meditations*

"Boxing is a sport of self-control. You must understand fear so you can manipulate it. Fear is like fire. You can make it work for you: it can warm you in the winter, cook your food when you're hungry, give you light when you are in the dark, and produce energy. Let it go out of control and it can hurt you, even kill you. . . . **Fear is a friend of exceptional people.**"

–CUS D'AMATO
Legendary American boxing trainer and manager
(Mike Tyson, Floyd Patterson, José Torres, etc.)

"Free yourself to try anything. The best ideas are revolutionary."

RICK RUBIN

RICK RUBIN has been called "the most important [music] producer of the last 20 years" by MTV. Rick's résumé includes everyone from Johnny Cash to Jay-Z. His metal artists include groups like Black Sabbath, Slayer, System of a Down, Metallica, and Rage Against the Machine. He's worked with pop artists like Shakira, Adele, Sheryl Crow, Lana Del Rey, and Lady Gaga. He's also been credited with helping to popularize hip-hop with artists like LL Cool J, the Beastie Boys, Eminem, Jay-Z, and Kanye West. Believe it or not, that's just the tip of the iceberg.

What is the book (or books) you've given most as a gift, and why?

The book I've gifted most is Stephen Mitchell's translation of the *Tao Te Ching*: ancient Taoist wisdom applicable to anything. It can be read at different times in your life, and every time it's revisited, it takes on entirely new meanings.

The wisdom in it is timeless: how to be a good leader, a good person, a good parent, a good artist—how to be good at anything. It's a beautiful read that awakens aspects of the brain in a really nice way.

Another one is Jon Kabat-Zinn's *Wherever You Go, There You Are*. It's a wonderful book from 1994. The beauty of it is that it can spark the desire in a nonmeditator to take up the practice. [At the same time] you could be a lifelong meditator, read it, and still learn a tremendous amount. Thinking about it now inspires me to read it again.

A third book is Robb Wolf's *The Paleo Solution*. I continue to give it to friends because it really helped me know what was healthy to eat and how our bodies process different foods. There is a plethora of misinformation on diet out there. I became vegan for two decades because of that information. This book makes it easy to make good choices by teaching the dangers of so many foods that are widely available and often touted as healthy. It's very clear and fun to read, and my experience is that it inspires a healthy life.

What purchase of $100 or less has most positively impacted your life in the last six months (or in recent memory)?

The Nasaline nasal irrigator. It's a big plastic syringe, like a turkey baster. It gets filled with saline solution. I usually use it in the tub or shower. You squirt water up one nostril and it comes out the other nostril, and then repeat back and forth. Typically, you use one cup of water and one spoon of this solution, but I do two cups. It not only clears out all the mucus, but if you do it every day, or a couple of times a day, it shrinks the inner lining of your sinuses so that you have more space and a better capacity to breathe.

I used to have trouble flying and equalizing to counter the pressure changes, and hyperbaric chambers would hurt my ears. But since using this sinus cleaner, I haven't had those problems.

Warning: If you forget to put in the salt, it's horribly painful.

Another item, probably a little more than $100, is the HumanCharger. The HumanCharger shoots light in your ears to help alleviate jet lag (other devices shine bright lights into your eyes, which can be uncomfortable and damaging to the eyes). The HumanCharger can also be used for other things like meditation. If you have to be alert for a meeting, appointment, or training session, you can wear it on the way.

How has a failure, or apparent failure, set you up for later success? Do you have a "favorite failure" of yours?

The first one that comes to mind is this: The first few albums I made were very, very successful. So, based on those early successes and being young,

I assumed that's what happened every time. Then the first time I had an album that was less successful, it was really traumatic.

It took a few more successful albums, and some unsuccessful ones, to understand that the success of a project very often has nothing to do with the quality of a project. Sometimes really good projects fail commercially. And sometimes projects that might not have artistically hit the mark as I would have liked have had great commercial success.

There are so many elements that go into making something successful —all of which are out of your control. You're in control of making your project the best it can possibly be *for you,* but you are powerless over most of what happens after that. Even if you do your best in terms of marketing and promotion, you have no control over how people react to it.

Seeing an album that I felt was really good not do well commercially taught me the reality of the ups and the downs of honest work, and that has served me since.

If you could have a gigantic billboard anywhere, what would it say?

"Choose peace."

What is one of the best or most worthwhile investments you've ever made?

When I was 14 years old, my neck hurt, and my pediatrician suggested Transcendental Meditation. The time spent meditating since then has been my most worthwhile investment.

Building up that reservoir at an age when time was much freer in my life significantly changed me for the better. It plays a big role in who I am and everything that I do.

Some of the more specific effects it's had on my life include the ability to focus—to be one-pointed. It's also a way to get yourself out of the way and see things for what they are, without the narrative that we put on them.

When I was in college, I stopped meditating, then restarted soon after I moved to California. That was the moment when I realized how much of an impact meditation had on me. When I started up again, it was so familiar to me. I was like a plant that didn't know it needed water, but when watered, just sucks in the nourishment. It felt so right and integral in my life. And it was really luck that I started meditating in the first place.

What is an unusual habit or an absurd thing that you love?

I've been a pro wrestling fan my whole life and continue to be. It's an absurd performance art, not dissimilar from Steve Martin, Andy Kaufman, and Monty Python. It uses the trappings of a sporting event to make a bigger commentary about existence and the human heart.

In the last five years, what new belief, behavior, or habit has most improved your life?

It's been a little more than five years, but movement and exercise have most improved my life. I was a sedentary person before that. But then I started standup paddling, weight training, exercising on the beach, pool training, doing sauna and ice contrast training, and having different physical experiences. Prior to all that, I never had any physical experiences. It's helped me be in my body instead of just in my head. [**Note from Tim:** Rick has lost more than 100 pounds since his peak weight. He often works out in the same group as Neil Strauss (page 96).]

What advice would you give to a smart, driven college student about to enter the "real world"? What advice should they ignore?

I would ignore most anything you learn in school and ignore all accepted standards. Free yourself to try anything. The best ideas are revolutionary.

If you're searching for wisdom, try to find it from people who've done it more than from people who teach it. Ask a lot of questions.

In addition, focus on something you love, because you have a far greater chance of succeeding by doing something you love, and regardless of whether you succeed or not, your life will be better. So you can't really lose by dedicating yourself to what you love.

Also, work tirelessly. I feel very lucky and blessed in my life, and I know this is because I totally submerged myself in what I was doing. I spent my every waking hour, every day, enjoying it when I was doing it and truly living it. In a sense, it wasn't a job because it was my whole life. In retrospect, I probably missed a lot of life because of it, but that's the give and take.

As I think about it, that might be what it takes to start something, but not necessarily to sustain it. So when you start something new, it's okay to do it in an unsustainable way. Once you achieve it, then you can devote your time to figuring out how to sustain it. They're two different playbooks.

What are bad recommendations you hear in your profession or area of expertise?

Anything having to do with commercial success. Anything having to do with testing things, doing polls, or getting public opinion on your work so you can change it. Anything suggesting a safe path and anything suggesting a stable situation, especially in the beginning.

When you start out doing something, you're likely charting uncharted territory, and it's good to ask a lot of questions from people in the industry and to learn from them. Remember, though, when people give you advice, they're giving you advice based on their particular skills, experiences, and perspectives. So know that when you get expert advice, it's often people telling you about their journey, and every journey is different.

This doesn't mean to not listen to the wisdom of others, but to really try it on for size and ask yourself, "Does this fit me mentally and physically?" Some people go through abusive situations to get what they think they want and can lose their souls in the process.

Every person who goes on these journeys takes a different path. It's not, "Well, when you get to the corner, make a left." In fact, if you're on the exact same path, something's wrong. It's not meant to be the same path. You need to tune in to yourself to know what works for you.

In the last five years, what have you become better at saying no to?

I don't know if I can answer this one. I'm probably not so good at saying no.

When you feel overwhelmed or unfocused, what do you do?

I try to take a break. I'll go for a walk or do something to clear my head. It could be doing deep breathing, alternate nostril breathing, meditating, or something physical. I don't always remember to do these things, but when I do, it really works.

I think probably the most important thing for me to remember when I get overwhelmed is to not feel the need to continue on and push through. It doesn't necessarily benefit whatever it is I'm working on. It's almost always better to take a break.

"Be present."

RYAN SHEA
TW: @ryaneshea
shea.io

RYAN SHEA co-created Blockstack, a new decentralized Internet where users control their data, and apps run without remote servers. With his co-founder Muneeb Ali (page 468), Blockstack has raised funding from top investors like Union Square Ventures and Naval Ravikant (page 31). Ryan majored in mechanical and aerospace engineering at Princeton with a minor in computer science. After graduation, Ryan started working on tech startups, was named to the *Forbes* "30 Under 30" list, went through Y Combinator, and authored several popular open source libraries in cryptography and blockchain technology.

What is the book (or books) you've given most as a gift, and why? Or what are books that have greatly influenced your life?

Sapiens by Yuval Noah Harari (page 554)
The Alchemist by Paulo Coelho
Snow Crash by Neal Stephenson (page 470)
The Sovereign Individual by James Dale Davidson and Lord William
    Rees-Mogg

If you could have a gigantic billboard anywhere with anything on it, what would it say and why?

"Be present." It's very hard for almost all of us, and sometimes we need a reminder. The act of being present versus being preoccupied with the past or the future can have a massive impact on our happiness.

When you feel overwhelmed or unfocused, what do you do?

I lift hard, go for a run, get a massage, read a book, or watch a movie.

My workouts typically have three phases: First, I will do three or four sets of either bench press, squats, or deadlifts. For each set, I aim for six to ten reps ranging from 70 to 85 percent of my one-rep max. Then, I'll do three or four supersets of either (a) 15 to 20 reps of pull-ups and dips, (b) ten reps of bicep curls and tricep extensions, or (c) ten reps of shoulder presses, lateral raises, and front raises. Last, I'll do my core workout, which includes either (a) four sets of one-minute planks alternated with four sets of sit-ups, leg raises, suitcases, and bicycles or (b) one set each of sit-ups, planks, side planks, and ball knee tucks followed by three sets of side bends.

What is one of the best or most worthwhile investments you've ever made?

In 2016, I started doing New Month Resolutions [as opposed to New Year Resolutions]. Here's some of what I did:

July: Daily reading
August: No TV or movies
September: No dairy
October: No gluten
November: Daily meditation
December: No news or social media feeds

As you can see, a few of the months were elimination months and a few were daily behavior months. The elimination months were interesting because I learned that I came away less dependent on the thing I eliminated. I now watch less TV and fewer movies, I eat less bread and gluten, and I still block the news and my social media feeds. The only thing I reinstated was dairy, choosing to continue to consume it.

The daily behavior months were interesting because they gave me an on-ramp to maintaining certain behaviors. I still meditate daily, and while I don't read daily, I read at a frequency close to that.

So far, my favorite experiments have been no news or social media feeds, workouts every day, no TV or movies, reading every day, and waking up at 7:30 every morning.

"I try to be a realistic optimist: I'm very clinical about where we are today, but extremely optimistic about what we're going to get done in the future."

BEN SILBERMANN
PI/TW: @8en
pinterest.com

BEN SILBERMANN helps millions of people collect things they love as co-founder and CEO of Pinterest. Ben grew up in Iowa, where he spent a lot of time collecting bugs, so this makes sense. Prior to Pinterest, which launched in March 2010, Ben worked at Google in the online advertising group. He graduated from Yale in 2003 with a degree in political science. He lives in Palo Alto, California, with his wife and son.

What is an unusual habit, or an absurd thing, that you love?
Have you ever seen the blog *Wait But Why*? [written by Tim Urban, page 40] They have a chart of the weeks of your life.

I have a wall chart of boxes representing every year of my life: ten years across and nine rows down. Then things are plotted on it, like average life expectancy in the U.S. I always thought it was kind of cool, because it puts time into a visual format, and I'm a visual person. Even at the company, every week I show employees the current week within the year visually, just to remind them that every week matters. I didn't think my own chart was weird, but in January, I showed it to my team, thinking they'd find it really inspiring and motivating. But people respond to mortality in very different ways. It was the worst meeting I've ever run.

I don't think they knew what I was trying to convey. Some people see that as, "Hey, every year is really exciting and valuable," and some people react with, "Oh wow, I'm gonna die." It didn't go over well, so I don't share that chart anymore.

Experiment failed.

How has a failure, or apparent failure, set you up for later success?

I'll say the following, and it's not exactly an answer to your question, but it does shape the way I think. Both of my parents, both of my sisters, and a lot of my friends are doctors. One thing that always struck me was how it takes a minimum of 12 years to become a doctor, and then you're a low-level doctor. One thing that is different about where I live now [Silicon Valley] is that people tend to measure everything in very short time frames, like one or two years. A lot of professions assume that you're going to take eight to ten years just to achieve the minimum level of competence necessary to start to practice.

That's been a good grounding force when doing projects, because a lot of things go wrong here and there, but if you just assume that anything worthwhile is going to take five to ten years, they don't feel as severe.

For instance, I left Google in 2008 to start a company, and the first two or three things didn't work out. Pinterest launched in 2010. It didn't really start growing quickly for another year or two, and it really took off around 2012. That's a four-year period where things *weren't* going awesome. But, I thought: "That's not that long. That's like med school before you go into residency."

What is the book (or books) you've given most as a gift, and why? Or what are one to three books that have greatly influenced your life?

The Better Angels of Our Nature by Steven Pinker (page 475). Most news is about things that are going wrong. It can be discouraging and makes people feel powerless. This book takes a long view and shows the long-term decline in violence that has occurred.

Salt, Fat, Acid, Heat: Mastering the Elements of Good Cooking by Samin Nosrat (page 1). I enjoy cooking, and this book taught me a lot of the basics of flavor and cooking technique. It helped me feel more confident going off-recipe.

What is one of the best or most worthwhile investments you've ever made?

I had never been to the gym until around two years ago. This was partially laziness and partially intimidation.

I don't think there was a single breakthrough moment. I just had this realization: "Am I going be the kind of guy who doesn't exercise *ever*? Or not? And if the answer is 'not,' then why not right now?" That was the reasoning, but I didn't have a medical crisis or anything. It's one of the things that I always felt I was putting off. Then I went to the gym and realized I had no idea what to do. That's why I got a trainer and invested in them for a year. I just went to the gym and asked, "Do you have any trainers?" I didn't put a lot of thought into the person, but the benefit was that, once it was scheduled and I was paying for it, it became harder to not go than to go.

It was a sunk cost, and there was a person who I'd have to text and say, "I'm not going to show up," which is a different type of accountability. That helped me to get over the initial hump of starting an exercise routine. If regular exercise could be bottled, it would be a miracle drug. Basically, everything in your life gets better if you find time to exercise regularly.

I feel like a lot of people in Silicon Valley serialize their lives. They think, "First I'll do college. Then I'll do a startup. Then I'll make money. Then I'll do X." There's some truth in that [approach], but most of the most important stuff has to be parallel-processed, like your relationships and your health, because you can't make up the time by doing more of it later. You can't neglect your wife for four years and then say, "Okay, now it's my wife years." Relationships don't work that way, and neither does your health or your fitness. . . . Figuring out a system, so that the stuff you need to do all the time happens, even while you might be placing disproportionate focus on one thing, is pretty important. Otherwise, you'll be setting yourself up to be lonely and unhealthy in your future.

What purchase of $100 or less has most positively impacted your life in the last six months (or in recent memory)?

It's not very original, but I like Apple AirPods headphones a lot. They're wireless and they stay charged. I really like them a lot more than I expected.

What are bad recommendations that you hear in your profession or area of expertise?

I think this idea that you learn the most from failures is wrong. It's a good thing to say so that people feel better, but whenever you want to learn how to do something well, you start by studying people who are really good. You don't study all the failed sprinters to learn how to run fast; you study the person who's really fast. There are a lot of reasons things can go wrong, but your job is to make things work.

I'm not saying it's either/or. Obviously, when something goes wrong, you should make the most of it and think about what you could have done better. Because of the way people process failure, those lessons will have a longer emotional carry. Most people have a pretty heavy emotional aversion to failing.

I think it's great to make people feel safe to take risks, but it's become distorted into believing that you should take all of your lessons from things that don't work, versus studying the people who are doing really well.

[This overfocus on failure] seeps into everything. I have to tell my managers: You need to spend time with your best performers, not just with all of your problems.

In the last five years, what have you become better at saying no to? What new realizations and/or approaches helped?

I'm still not very good at it, but I know time really is zero-sum, and it's the one thing that no one's making more of.

I don't have special go-to language. I try to tell people the truth, and people are surprisingly understanding. I might say something like "I really wish that I could, but I'm really trying to focus on [XYZ project] right now, and I hope you understand. I genuinely hope that we'll connect in the future." Maybe they're just not telling me [they're upset], but people are more understanding than I imagine. In my head, I have this image of them doing something like slamming their computer down with "That asshole!" but I think people kind of get it.

When you feel overwhelmed or unfocused, what do you do?

One, I usually go for a walk, and two, I try to write down everything that's going on, so I can get it out of my head and look at it. Sometimes your brain gets caught in little loops, and it's not making any progress. For me, it's helpful to write everything down and visually reflect on what's important.

It isn't super structured. I might write down, "Here's what's on my mind . . ." and put it on paper. Then I try to step back and ask, "Okay, what's going on here, and which stuff matters?" There's something to be learned from the way that companies set goals on different time resolutions: what matters this week, this month, this year, in ten years. . . . I think people usually end up losing it when they let short-term things crowd out what they want to take care of in the medium or long term.

Over the longer term, what really matters to you? If you answer that, you can reverse-engineer toward that end.

In the last five years, what new belief, behavior, or habit has most improved your life?

It sounds kind of cheesy, but I started to keep a gratitude journal. If you [have a habit of writing] things down that you're grateful for, then some part of your brain is constantly looking for those things, and you feel happier. It's absurd in its simplicity.

I find the time during the day and write down one thing. Sometimes I miss a day; I'm not perfect about it. I always tell my team that I try to be a realistic optimist: I'm very clinical about where we are today, but I'm extremely optimistic about what we're going to get done in the future. I feel that optimism is important to communicate to the team, instead of solely focusing on problems. Someone once told me, "If you only engage with people about problems, pretty soon, you'll become the problem for them," and I agree with that. I now try to make space and time for saying, "This is what's going really well . . ." whereas, when I first managed people, the approach was more, "What do we need to fix today?"

I use a little notebook I got at Office Depot or somewhere. It's not super cool, and it's more about the habit. But I do want to get that culty Japanese journal that all the designers use, a Hobonichi Techo. It's the kind of thing you see in Japan: a notebook turned into a high art. Maybe next year. . . .

"No one is qualified to tell you how you experience the world."

VLAD ZAMFIR
TW: @VladZamfir
Medium: @vlad_zamfir
vladzamfir.com

VLAD ZAMFIR is a blockchain architect and researcher at Ethereum, working on blockchain efficiency and scaling. Vlad is interested in governance and privacy solutions, and he was also the first person to introduce me to absurdism. He is a frequent contributor on Medium and lives in Antarctica (or so he wants us to believe).

What is the book (or books) you've given most as a gift, and why? Or what are one to three books that have greatly influenced your life?

Introduction to Mathematical Philosophy by Bertrand Russell
Complexity and Chaos by Dr. Roger White
The Lily: Evolution, Play, and the Power of a Free Society
    by Daniel Cloud

If you could have a gigantic billboard anywhere with anything on it, what would it say and why?
"No one is qualified to tell you how you experience the world." I find this helps people think for themselves more than anything else I've come

across. I'm not really sure why. I should credit my friend Tom for the quote.

What is an unusual habit or an absurd thing that you love?

I love being very pedantic about the use of the word "absurd." You meant absurd as in "ridiculous," not as in "self-defeating" or "futile," for example. I usually reserve the term for use in the second "futile" sense, and I have an "unusual" habit of pointing this out whenever anyone uses the word informally.

How has a failure, or apparent failure, set you up for later success? Do you have a "favorite failure" of yours?

My "favorite failure" actually led me to discover absurdism. I made the mistake of taking things too seriously, and I ended up hurting someone I cared about as a result.

I should maybe mention that "absurdness" and "reasonableness" are not binary questions, nor are they quantities. Instead, there is a precise reality of which behaviors and intentions are reasonable or absurd in any given context. Thinking of them in a binary or quantitative way is still very useful.

Absurdism provides a clear philosophy of failure: either the intention was absurd, the strategy was not reasonable, or it was reasonable but was not executed correctly.

It's often hard to tell whether I'm trying to do the impossible, or whether there are reasonable behaviors that I haven't yet thought of trying, or if I'm trying the right behavior but without enough skill.

If I become confident that my intention is absurd, then I give up. Deliberately, if I have to. If I think it's not absurd, I'll continue trying strategies I think might be reasonable, and I will practice the strategies I highly suspect are reasonable, if I really care about bearing out my intention.

Absurdism is not just a tool for helping people be reasonable. It is also a critique of rationalism. It says that there are contexts where having intentions is absurd. That sometimes rationality is absurd, and should therefore be abandoned. In these contexts, it doesn't make sense to decide what to do or how to spend your time, if by that you mean "pick a goal that you want to achieve."

In the last five years, what new belief, behavior, or habit has most improved your life?
Absurdism! There is no comparison.

I have found absurdism to be unreasonably effective for doing mathematics, maintaining relationships, dealing with ignorance, reasoning about ethics, dealing with depression, and living a happier life. Whenever I don't know what to do, I defer to absurdism for guidance.

And by "unreasonably effective," I mean something quite specific: Something is unreasonably effective if it seems to be useful outside the scope of its assumptions, outside the scope of the context in/for which it was developed.

Mathematics is unreasonably effective because it applies to lots of fields that have nothing to do with mathematics or the context in which that math is developed.

Economics is unreasonably effective because it is useful even though the assumptions made are often obviously false: assumptions like rationality, quadratic utility, efficiency, and prices following Brownian motion.

Statistics is unreasonably effective because it seems to be useful even when we make obviously false assumptions, like when we assume that things are normally distributed even when they aren't. But also because it seems it works well even when we blatantly disrespect best practices (like by changing our methods or hypothesis after observing data, then doing hypothesis tests).

Using unreasonably effective theories is very defensible (in my opinion) when we don't have better strategies. There are lots of ways this can happen, including lack of information, lack of computational power, or lack of compatibility with other ideas, or just out of simple convenience or interest.

Absurdism is unreasonably effective because it apparently has very little to do with any setting in particular, but still (I claim) ends up useful in practice in lots of settings. This is especially noticeable to me when I am at a loss for what to do.

Take depression, for example. I find that my depression is usually born from intentions that I have, but for some reason cannot (or do not, perhaps for lack of motivation) bear them out. And when I'm struggling in the absurd, I do my best to give up.

I often decide to do something, or a whole pile of somethings, then beat myself up for not doing it. It turns out that I often beat myself up to the point of depression for not doing it. I get depressed just because I am not doing what I think I should be doing.

I've learned that it really helps just to give up on everything I've decided to do, if only temporarily (when it's possible to identify my intentions, and possible to give them up, and it isn't always). After I give up, and decide that I'm not going to do any of the things I previously decided to do, I almost always immediately am relieved of depression. Sometimes this is all I need to start working on the things I previously decided to do. Sometimes it isn't, and I need to spend time doing other stuff before I'm ready. Often, I end up realizing that those things aren't important and I just forget about them forever.

What is one of the best or most worthwhile investments you've ever made?

Lots of time spent doing math and philosophy has paid off and will continue to pay off, I have (almost) no doubt.

Questioning the foundation of Bayesian statistics has been a very valuable process.

Reworking definitions and impossibility results from consensus literature has been equally valuable.

What purchase of $100 or less has most positively impacted your life in the last six months (or in recent memory)?

An audio lecture series on institutional economics called "International Economic Institutions: Globalism vs. Nationalism." It was interesting/important to me because it was the first information about institutional design that I've ever really internalized. I feel like I have a much better idea about "how society works" now that I understand something about the nature of institutions. Not that I can claim to understand much! I tried to "crystallize" some of my understandings, but I didn't do a great job.

In practical terms, though, I am now able to think much more clearly about blockchain governance. I can see that we already have a handful of nascent blockchain governance institutions! I can understand what it means for an institution to be more or less formal, and more or less tacit/ad hoc. I am now completely open to the possibility that institutionalization can be a reasonable process, rather than one that is inevitably powered by hubris.

When you feel overwhelmed or unfocused, what do you do?

I nap a lot. I try not to eat carbohydrates.

I try to take three to four hours to myself every day. It's not always possible. I try to work offline. I meditate sometimes.

I try to make plans that allow me to be more relaxed and focus my time on more important things. I try not to make my life more complicated than it needs to be. This often means turning down engagements, but it's worth it.

I'm still getting better at all of this!

"Several years ago, following the example of my then wife, Amber O'Hearn, I eliminated all plants from my diet. . . ."

ZOOKO WILCOX
TW: @zooko
z.cash
ketotic.org

ZOOKO WILCOX is the founder and CEO of Zcash, a cryptocurrency that offers privacy and selective transparency of transactions. Zooko has more than 20 years of experience in open, decentralized systems, cryptography and information security, and startups. He is recognized for his work on DigiCash, Mojo Nation, ZRTP, "Zooko's Triangle," Tahoe-LAFS, BLAKE2, and SPHINCS. He is also the founder of Least Authority, which offers an affordable, ethical, usable, and lasting data storage solution.

What is the book (or books) you've given most as a gift, and why? Or what are one to three books that have greatly influenced your life?

Good Calories, Bad Calories by Gary Taubes. When it came out ten years ago, it was the definitive study of the history and science of human nutrition in the 20th century. As well as exploring history, it became part of history itself, since a subsequent generation of nutrition researchers have been forced to take sides for or against the thesis of this book.

Unfortunately, most of the people I've given copies to didn't get much from it! They were not historians or researchers; they were just people who needed to decide what to eat every day, and a dense tome of facts and scientific arguments wasn't what they needed. I learned that in order to communicate with people, you have to meet them where they live.

How has a failure, or apparent failure, set you up for later success? Do you have a "favorite failure" of yours?

I failed at undergraduate university studies. I was disorganized, distracted, depressed, and my grades were barely passing, at best. I procrastinated and skipped class. I had an irregular sleep schedule, no exercise, and a terrible diet.

But there was a new technology that I loved. It was being invented by a startup, and whenever I was focused enough to do anything, I read about that technology and worked on coding projects of my own related to it.

I learned very little from my courses, and I was eventually expelled from university for failing too many of them. I begged for another chance and the dean reluctantly readmitted me. In retrospect, it would've been better for me if he had said no!

Nonetheless, I felt like it was an important goal—almost a duty—to get my degree, so I persevered. When I got an opportunity to try out for a junior coding job at that very same startup, the company that I was so excited about, I ruefully told them I couldn't because I had to finish college first.

Then I called my best friend and excitedly told him that this company had offered me a job interview. "What did you say?" he asked.

"Oh," I said sadly, "I told them I had to finish college first."

"I just have one question for you," he said. "Is this exactly the kind of opportunity you've been waiting for?"

"You're right," I said. I hung up on him and called them back.

Dropping out of college was one of the best decisions of my life. Not only did it set me on the career path that led directly to my most important successes today, but, more important, when I started succeeding at my new job, I gained self-respect.

The technology and startup was DigiCash, a predecessor of modern digital money technologies like Bitcoin and Zcash. Joining that startup led directly (over a 20-year path) to Zcash.

In the last five years, what new belief, behavior, or habit has most improved your life?

Several years ago, following the example of my then wife, Amber O'Hearn, I eliminated all plants from my diet. I had previously tried low-carb dieting in various forms, but I had never been able to practice it with consistency. I was addicted to carbs, and had never, in years of trying low carb, managed to kick the addiction. I was also beset with a series of health problems that were mysterious and worsening. The 30 pounds—and growing—of excess flab hanging over my belt was only the most visible of my numerous ailments.

The big breakthrough was when I tried, not to practice "everything in moderation," but instead to completely eliminate not only all carbohydrates, but all plant food in general from my diet. Like Amber had done before me, I started eating nothing but fatty meat (fatty prime rib, ground beef, pork chops, juicy salmon, etc.). The first four days were a torment of "carb withdrawal" and cravings, but on the fifth day, I woke up with a strange new sensation: a sensation of complete freedom from cravings.

For the first time, I gained control over my eating. The excess fat rapidly disappeared, effortlessly, and all of my other health problems likewise disappeared over the next few months. My energy levels, mood, and mental acuity improved.

This marked the beginning of the most productive and successful period of my life thus far, and also the beginning of Amber's and my research into the science of human nutrition and evolution.

In the last five years, what have you become better at saying no to?

I have gotten better at saying no to requests, such as requests for jobs at my company, offers to take advisory roles in other people's businesses, invitations to events, and even requests to begin conversations, such as strangers writing an email or a social media message saying, "Hey, can I talk to you about such-and-such?" The realization that helped me was that the kindest and best thing that I can do for people in a case like that is to give them a "no" explicitly, quickly, and firmly.

Whenever I feel myself pulled to reluctantly give a "yes" (which is often), or to put off deciding, I remind myself that giving in to those temptations is unkind to the asker.

"Everything you want is on the other side of fear."

STEPHANIE McMAHON
TW: @StephMcMahon
FB: /stephmcmahonWWE
corporate.wwe.com

STEPHANIE McMAHON is the chief brand officer of World Wrestling Entertainment, Inc. (WWE) and is the organization's global brand ambassador. She is the primary spokesperson for WWE's corporate social responsibility initiatives, including the Special Olympics, Susan G. Komen for the Cure, and Be a STAR, WWE's anti-bullying program. In 2014, Stephanie and her husband, Paul "Triple H" Levesque, established Connor's Cure, a fund dedicated to fighting pediatric cancer. Stephanie appears regularly on WWE's flagship programming as a personality. She has been recognized as one of the "Most Powerful Women in Cable" for the past five years by *CableFAX* magazine. *Adweek* has included Stephanie in their list of the "Most Powerful Women in Sports" for the past two years. Most recently, Stephanie received the Stuart Scott ENSPIRE Award at the 2017 ESPN Sports Humanitarian of the Year Awards.

What purchase of $100 or less has most positively impacted your life in the last six months (or in recent memory)?

My Bucky neck pillow. I travel all the time, and I don't get much rest on the road, so it's important for me to be able to sleep when I can. The Bucky neck pillow is rectangular in shape and fits perfectly behind my head when sitting on an airplane. I can't stand the U-shaped pillows because I have a pea-size head (Irish people either have giant heads or tiny heads; I'm of the tiny variety) and they slide up too much. The Bucky pillow stays perfectly in place, giving me all I need for a comfortable flight.

If you could have a gigantic billboard anywhere with anything on it, what would it say and why? Are there any quotes you think of often or live your life by?

"Do something you're afraid of every day."—often attributed to Eleanor Roosevelt.

I live my life by this quote, and I've heard various incarnations of it over the years, most recently, "Everything you want is on the other side of fear." Not long ago, I was at WrestleMania (WWE's Super Bowl) about to walk out in front of a record-breaking crowd of more than 100,000 people at AT&T Stadium. It was the event my father created, as a part of my husband's entrance on the 20th anniversary of his career, with my children and nephews sitting ringside. John Cena and The Rock were leaving the ring and the arena went black. I was supposed to ascend to the top of my throne, which seemed suspended in mid-air, and recite the dialogue that would set the stage for Triple H's villainous entrance. Together, we were known as "The Authority," and everyone needed to bow down to our omnipotent presence.

Only, in that moment, in the darkness that was enveloping me, I froze. I forgot every word I was supposed to say. I could hear my heart pounding in my ears and my throat squeezed tight. I felt like I was going to implode. Then I thought about that Eleanor Roosevelt quote. If I didn't go out there, I would regret it for the rest of my life. How many people would ever get an opportunity to do what I was about to do? And there it was, right in front of me. I took a deep breath and let it all in, all the emotion and all the energy of all of those people. I owned that moment. It was the highlight of my career as a performer.

My youngest daughter is seven years old, and just yesterday, she conquered her fear of going off the big swing at a climbing facility near our house. She had been up there before, all ready to go, and backed out at the last moment. But this time, she said she was ready. She psyched herself up listening to "Am I Evil" by Metallica (I'm not kidding, she found the song on her daddy's playlist and listened to it on replay the entire 20-minute ride) and climbed all the way up to the swing, which was a good 30 feet in the air. She got clipped in, and she moved her tiny body to the end of the platform. Then she had her own moment of doubt and started to back up . . . but something came over her; she hummed a few bars of the song and moved herself forward again. This time the countdown began "3-2-1" and off she went! When it was over she yelled, "I want to do it again, Mommy!" and "I did it! I conquered my fear!" I hope she remembers that feeling forever.

What is the book (or books) you've given most as a gift, and why? Or what are one to three books that have greatly influenced your life?

Tools of Titans by Tim Ferriss.

What is an unusual habit or an absurd thing that you love?

I chug water bottles; it's the only way I stay hydrated! Who enjoys sipping water? I'll sip coffee all day (Starbucks venti Cold Brew with two shots of espresso and two stevia packets, if anyone is interested), but if I feel the least bit thirsty, I'll grab a bottle of water and chug the entire bottle without stopping.

What is one of the best or most worthwhile investments you've ever made?

Most recently, spending time with my grandmother. My grandmother is a remarkable person. She's a 90-year-old North Carolinian who was a budget analyst in the 1940s, loves to drink her vodka tonics and smoke cigarettes, and has absolutely no filter on what she says. She broke her hip over Christmas and made a full recovery, had discs fused in her neck a few months later, and just found out today that her lung cancer (which she had beaten before) has come back. In spite of all of this, when I went to visit her, she sat with her back straight and had a fire burning in her beautiful blue-green eyes. I've been visiting her more since her neck surgery, going to see her after dropping the girls at school instead of doing my morning cardio routine, and I couldn't be more grateful for this time. She always reinforces what's most important in life (the people you love), and constantly reminds me not to let anyone walk over me. "You got to stand up for yourself, Steph," she says. "No one told me how to do it, but I did it anyway, and it's served me well. And you teach those girls (my daughters) to do the same."

In the last five years, what new belief, behavior, or habit has most improved your life?

I'm not as religious as I want to be, but before I go to bed, I try to think of three things that made me *happy* during the day. It's an evolution of thinking of three things that I'm *grateful* for before bed. I found that I would feel guilty if I didn't say certain things I was grateful for, and I wound up saying the same things over and over. Thinking of things that made me *happy* helps me put aside all the baggage I've packed throughout the day, and it helps me focus on what's really important, like jumping in Lake Winnipesaukee with my three girls or getting a random text from my husband telling me I'm beautiful. A colleague gave me the idea and said she had heard it from Sheryl Sandberg. I know I'm supposed to write these things down (and writing them down is an important exercise), but I have three kids, aged 11, 9, and 7, and I train at midnight, so I do the best I can.

In the last five years, what have you become better at saying no to? What new realizations and/or approaches helped?

I actually had a hard time learning to say no at all. The culture at WWE is a "can do" or "yes" environment. There is no such thing as no. There can be "Yes, we can do that, but here are the challenges if we do . . ." but I really can't imagine saying, "No, Vince (Vince McMahon, chairman and CEO of WWE, who also happens to be my father), sorry, that's impossible."

I did learn, however, that saying no in the right situation can actually be empowering. A couple of years ago, I was pushing myself a little too hard. On top of traveling every week as a performer for our live television shows, I was also traveling in my executive role as chief brand officer. I was finally about to get a few days at home with my girls, when I was informed of a speaking "opportunity" that would be good for the company. Someone on my team was looking out for me, and said, "You know what, Steph, this would be a good opportunity for WWE, but is it really a 'need to have' or is it a 'nice to have'?" I realized it was the latter and actually said no. The result was a couple of very needed days of downtime with my family that actually helped fuel my performance when I returned.

QUOTES I'M PONDERING

(Tim Ferriss: June 23–July 7, 2017)

"He suffers more than necessary, who suffers before it is necessary."

—SENECA
Roman Stoic philosopher, famed playwright

"We try more to profit from always remembering the obvious than from grasping the esoteric. It is remarkable how much long-term advantage people like us have gotten by trying to be consistently not stupid, instead of trying to be very intelligent."

—CHARLIE MUNGER
Investing partner of Warren Buffett, vice chairman of Berkshire Hathaway

"One whose mind is
one with the sky-void steps
into a spring mist
and thinks to herself she might
in fact step out of this world."*

—SAIGYŌ (1118–1190)
Famous Japanese poet of the late Heian and early Kamakura period

* This very odd quote might make more sense if you read the psychedelic discussion in the James Fadiman chapter of *Tools of Titans*.

"When you stop caring about being right in the eyes of everyone . . . it's amazing how little you care to waste energy trying to convince people of your view."

PETER ATTIA
TW/IG: @PeterAttiaMD
peterattiamd.com

DR. PETER ATTIA is a former ultraendurance athlete (e.g., swimming races of 25 miles), a compulsive self-experimenter, and one of the most fascinating human beings I know. He is one of my go-to doctors for anything performance- or longevity-related. Peter earned his MD from Stanford University and holds a BS in mechanical engineering and applied mathematics from Queen's University in Kingston, Ontario. He did his residency in general surgery at the Johns Hopkins Hospital, and conducted research at the National Cancer Institute under Dr. Steven Rosenberg, where Peter focused on the role of regulatory T cells in cancer regression and other immune-based therapies for cancer.

What is the book (or books) you've given most as a gift, and why? Or what are one to three books that have greatly influenced your life?

Books that influenced me the most:

> *The Transformed Cell* by Steven A. Rosenberg
> *Mistakes Were Made (but Not by Me)* by Carol Tavris and
>   Elliot Aronson
> *Surely You're Joking, Mr. Feynman!* by Richard P. Feynman

If you could have a gigantic billboard anywhere with anything on it, what would it say? Are there any quotes you think of often or live your life by?

Well, assuming it's a big billboard, I'd lobby for the following:

> "The fundamental cause of the trouble is that in the modern world
> the stupid are cocksure while the intelligent are full of doubt."
> —Bertrand Russell

> "For the great enemy of truth is very often not the lie—deliberate,
> contrived and dishonest—but the myth—persistent, persuasive, and
> unrealistic. Too often we hold fast to the clichés of our forebears.
> We subject all facts to a prefabricated set of interpretations. We
> enjoy the comfort of opinion without the discomfort of thought."
> —John F. Kennedy

> "No problem can be solved from the same level of consciousness
> that created it."—Albert Einstein

> "If you set a goal, it should meet these two conditions: 1) It matters;
> 2) You can influence the outcome."—Peter Attia

In the last five years, what new belief, behavior, or habit has most improved your life?

My understanding of hormone replacement therapy (HRT) for both men and women has evolved by leaps and bounds. That JFK billboard quote really spanked me. I had long taken on face value that HRT was "bad" because, well, that's what I learned in school and heard a bunch of seemingly smart talking heads saying. I'm not suggesting that my view today is that everyone should take hormones—the endocrine system is upsettingly complex and I can't even comprehend blanket statements—but that I was unwilling to even consider this therapy without actually going back and poring over the literature is upsetting. It also makes me wonder how I'll answer this question five years from now. . . .

What is one of the best or most worthwhile investments you've ever made?

Probably learning to box, though I have mixed feelings about it, since I'm almost assuredly 10 to 20 IQ points lighter as a result of the concussions. I spent many years boxing, as I wanted to be a professional boxer. It became the foundation for the work ethic and discipline that would define my life once I decided, at age 18, to pursue mathematics and engineering. It also gave me great confidence that, oddly, still remains (though I can't fight my way out of a proverbial wet paper bag today). Back in the day, I recall being so confident that I could defend myself, or any person, that I didn't feel the need to look for trouble, and I was actually happy to let someone (i.e., a pseudo tough guy) think I was afraid of him. It was not the case, but the point is that I realized ability alone was sufficient; I did not need to demonstrate it.

What is an unusual habit or an absurd thing that you love?

Egg boxing, though I'm convinced if the world knew about it, it would become a worldwide sport and eventually an Olympic sport and therefore cease to be absurd. [**Note from Tim:** Egg boxing arguably deserves its own chapter, but it's beyond the scope of this book. For a video of Peter demonstrating egg boxing, please visit tim.blog/eggboxing]

What advice would you give to a smart, driven college student about to enter the "real world"? What advice should they ignore?

My advice: Be as genuine as you can. Don't fake it. In my view, better to be a cold stiff than fake that you care. If you are genuinely interested in a subset of other people, even if that number is small, you will foster relationships that really matter. As we age, I believe, frivolous relationships in business and our personal life become less and less bearable, so only put energy into completely genuine interactions with other people.

A second piece of advice would be to seek out mentors constantly and without shame (and mentor others). This requires adhering to the above point, of course, but it highlights a vulnerability and asymmetry. Always be a student and always be a teacher.

As for advice to ignore: Too often, I hear people effectively given advice that is consistent with sunk cost fallacies. I certainly heard it a lot. "You've spent X years learning Y, you can't just up and leave and now do Z," they say. I think this is flawed advice because it weighs too heavily the time behind you, which can't be changed, and largely discounts the time in front of you, which is completely malleable.

For example, when I decided to go to college, I wanted to specialize in aerospace engineering, so I entered a program where I could study mechanical engineering and applied math concurrently as an undergrad and planned to do my PhD in aerospace with an emphasis on control theory (hence, all the math). Unrelated to this aspiration, during my undergrad also, I spent quite a bit of time volunteering with kids who had been sexually abused and, separately, with kids who were going though cancer treatment. By my senior year, I felt really conflicted about doing my PhD in engineering. I felt a real tug to do something completely different with my life, but I didn't know exactly what. After much agony and soul searching, I realized medicine was a better fit for me, despite all the reasons I should have stuck with engineering (e.g., lots of scholarships to the best PhD programs in the country). People I respected—professors, family, friends—thought I was crazy. I had worked so hard to get where I was. But I took an extra year, did a post-baccalaureate program, and applied to med school.

Ten years later, I again found myself at a point where I was contemplating the unimaginable—after a decade of medical training, I left medicine altogether to join a consulting firm and work on modeling credit risk. The next decade would bring two more seismic career shifts. Perhaps I'm just rationalizing my own behavior, but I've never looked back at my winding path to here and either (a) regretted the time I spent trying to master previous domains (e.g., engineering, surgery) or (b) regretted a career change, even when on the other side of the proverbial fence.

What are bad recommendations you hear in your profession or area of expertise?

In my specific area of longevity, I hear too much emphasis on how people look (sort of important) and feel (important, to be sure), but very little on the actual task of delaying the onset of chronic disease, which is almost the mathematical equivalent of delaying death and improving quality of life. I'm consistently amazed how little the experts in this space advocate for approaches to delay the onset of cardiovascular disease, cancer, neurodegenerative disease, and accidental deaths.

In the last five years, what have you become better at saying no to?

Saying no to always having to be right, feeling the need to argue every point, and responding to every criticism. If anything, the pendulum has probably swung too far in the other direction, at times approaching apathy. When you stop caring about being right in the eyes of everyone — versus being right in your own eyes and the eyes of those who matter to you — it's amazing how little you care to waste energy trying to convince people of your view.

"I've realized that instead of following the trends, you want to identify the trends but not follow them."

STEVE AOKI
IG/FB: @steveaoki
steveaoki.com

STEVE AOKI is a two-time Grammy nominated producer/DJ, entrepreneur, founder of Dim Mak Records, and designer of the contemporary menswear line Dim Mak Collection. Since launching in 1996, Dim Mak Records has become a springboard for acts such as The Chainsmokers, Bloc Party, The Bloody Beetroots, and Gossip. As a solo artist, Steve lives on the road, averaging more than 250 tour dates per year. His 2016 Netflix Original documentary *I'll Sleep When I'm Dead* was nominated for a Grammy. Known for his genre-bending productions, Steve has collaborated with Linkin Park, Snoop Dogg, Fall Out Boy, and more. His hits "Just Hold On" with One Direction's Louis Tomlinson and "Delirious (Boneless)" with Kid Ink are both certified Gold. His latest album, *Kolony*, debuted at #1 on the Electronic Album charts. Marking his first full turn into rap music, *Kolony* features Lil Yachty, Migos, 2 Chainz, Gucci Mane, T-Pain, and more.

What purchase of $100 or less has most positively impacted your life in the last six months (or in recent memory)?

The iMask Sleep Eye Mask is an absolute blessing to have on tour; I carry it with me wherever I go. Because we travel and our schedules are so stressful, I need to be able to sleep any time there is quiet. That time isn't necessarily the traditional time that people sleep. For me, it's when I have finished DJing or I'm in a car. It is then that I put on my iMask and get those 15 minutes of sleep. When you're tackling a strenuous work weekend—something like five countries in two days, which is something that we do in the summer —you have to sleep in any situation. This could be in the car, on the plane, going from hotel to the venue, or from the venue to the airplane. I carry the iMask with me and stick it on to sleep or practice my Transcendental Meditation, which sometimes allows me to fall asleep. I like the iMask because it shuts everything out. It's absolutely one of the necessities on the road that helps me get my z's.

If you could have a gigantic billboard anywhere with anything on it, what would it say and why? Are there any quotes you think of often or live your life by?

The quote I live by is "By any means necessary." It's from Malcolm X. When I was in college, I read *The Autobiography of Malcolm X* and was blown away by the determination and commitment that Malcolm X had to his people and to fight against a system that was not designed to support or help him or his people. He really made strides in bringing civil rights to the forefront of the American people. It was a very moving book, and I remember reading it a few times.

As I started my label, I wanted to create a slogan with this concept, and I wanted to use this idea of "by any means necessary" as a way of life. When we started [my label] Dim Mak back in 1996, I didn't have any money to launch the label, as I only had $400 to my name. So I would find any way possible to make sure these records came out. I did whatever I could with the tools in front of me with no excuses and no complaining. You gotta find a way to get your project done; you gotta think outside the box.

My team also lives and works by the mantra of "by any means necessary," and because of that, we can get things done that others might not. I feel lucky to have such a great team that will share this way of life with me.

How has a failure, or apparent failure, set you up for later success? Do you have a "favorite failure" of yours?

There was a period when I was drinking at every show, and I was DJing a lot, maybe four nights a week, playing local shows in Los Angeles. I had a couple of Dim Mak parties, and we were on top of the world! We had cornered the market with our sound and culture, and I was just getting booked left and right. I was the ambassador of this new culture that was burgeoning in electronic music called "electro," and my ego was flexing a bit. I was drinking and having fun. It was a great feeling, but then you forget about the most important things in life because you're in that fog of self-indulgence.

My mom was coming to visit me, and she never flies in. This was one of the few times she had. I was supposed to pick her up in the morning. I had a big night the night before—we had a party, I drank, and I stayed out super late. The next morning my mom landed around 7 A.M., and I slept through it. I woke up at 10 A.M., or something awful like three hours later. I saw a text message from my mom—she barely even knew how to text! I don't know why, but she waited at the airport for three hours, sitting outside on a bench. My poor mom.

Once I got to the airport an hour later—making it four hours she had been there—she was just innocently sitting on this bench, and I broke down. She was still so sweet about it. It was at that moment that I felt like this whole life of partying and drinking was all bullshit, especially if you can't maintain your priorities of valuing and taking care of your family.

That was one fail I will never forget. After that, I stopped being caught up in that Hollywood bubble where everyone parties and drinks every single night. You can live in that bubble and forget about the realities of your family and relationships outside the bubble. But those relationships are vital to who you are and are important in your life. Eventually, I quit drinking, which I am happy about, partly because of this major fail.

What is an interesting routine that you do on the road?

Being on the road, you deal with lots of traveling that can bog you down, and a lot of bad food options, which means you can't control all the variables around you. At home, you would have your juice spot, your gym, and your market where you can shop every day, so you can eat the right foods and keep your life in balance.

One thing that I do on the road is "Aoki Bootcamp," which utilizes accountability between the people I travel with to meet a certain goal every single day. We set a certain number of repetitions to complete each day, such as push-ups, sit-ups, etc., and even have a WhatsApp group chat to show evidence that we did the workouts. Beyond exercise, it also crosses into food, because it is not just about the workout you do but also about your diet. We have a list of foods that we can't eat, and if you eat them, then you have to add 15 more repetitions to your workout to account for it. So, each day, we do our best to eat properly and exercise and meet these goals. That's the underlying philosophy of Aoki Bootcamp: to use group accountability to meet these goals for food, nutrition, and workouts.

If you don't meet the goals by a particular time, by midnight, then you get financially penalized, and [the money] goes toward brain research non-profits through the Aoki Foundation.

What is the book (or books) you've given most as a gift, and why? Or what are one to three books that have greatly influenced your life?

Fast-forward through college, to after my father passed away. I got into studying cancer so I could understand what killed my dad. It was eye-opening. It got me looking into the future at how science is finding cures for other diseases. It all pointed to *The Singularity Is Near* by Ray Kurzweil. It opened me up to the idea of science fiction becoming science fact. I grew up reading comic books, and I loved sci-fi and anime. *Ghost in the Shell* was my favorite anime. I also really liked *Armitage III*, which dealt with the issues of self-aware robots.

I read Ray's other books, which feature radical future science concepts, and it showed me how some of these ideas are actually attainable. Not just feasible in the distant future but in our lifetimes! It is incredible to think that some of these imaginative ideas, such as living forever or turning into a robot, could actually happen. [For example,] in the book *Ending Aging*, Dr. Aubrey de Grey talks about his research into how we can stop the degeneration of cells, essentially finding ways to extend life.

Ray Kurzweil talks about the law of accelerating returns, which states that fundamental measures of information technology follow predictable and exponential trajectories. For instance, in the '70s, we had a computer that was the size of a room and cost $250,000, and now we have a computer the size of my hand that is much more powerful. In the end, it's not just about rich people having technology; it's about scaling it so that everyone can be a part of it.

You never know what can happen, but this book made me feel that there is a neon futurist hope, a hopeful utopian future where we use technology to better our lives, enhance our creativity, and live longer, happier, and healthier lives that are not plagued with disease, and where we use our resources in a way that doesn't destroy the planet. I hope for that future. *The Singularity Is Near* informed my music—I named an album after it, and I wrote a song called "Singularity" in 2012. I even got Ray Kurzweil in the music video.

I then decided to create a concept album series called *Neon Future*. I wanted to not just fuse all my collaborative musical efforts into this concept but to also do songs with a scientist. Ray Kurzweil agreed to join me. I interviewed him in his apartment in San Francisco and also interviewed different people who inspired me.

In *Neon Future II,* I continued that conversation with different people and non-scientists like J. J. Abrams and Kip Thorne. The project is ongoing with *Neon Future III*, so we still have more to go, and it's had a huge influence on my life.

In the last five years, what new belief, behavior, or habit has most improved your life?

The one thing I learned in music and collaboration is that music is a cyclical trend and entertainment in general is always in a cyclical trend. I've realized that instead of following the trends, you want to identify the trends but not follow them. It's good to recognize trends, but if you follow them, you get sucked into them, and then you also fall with the trend.

It is a testament to my label, an independent record label that I've been running for 20 years now, that it has survived the bullets that were supposed to take us out when we were forging our own path, creating new movements with sound and artists. We created and were part of certain trends, but we survived past the death of those trends. What I've learned is that people can position me in certain trends, and somehow I've been able to reemerge when the trend has passed. I can continue to hover above the up-and-down cycle.

I focus on the energy of my music, not the trend. The energy itself doesn't have a name. It doesn't exist in that space of being cool or not, and at the end of the day, the feeling itself is the most important thing to recognize, because the energy that my music will give off and attract is a very human feeling.

Essentially, music is our tool to engage with our feelings. I want to make sure I always stay in a zone where whoever I work with and however I make my music, I take the cultural cue of what is inspiring me at the time. This may be associated with trends, but I will always make sure that the energy of the music is at the forefront, and make that the loudest voice in the mix. I will always think about not riding that roller coaster. I know the roller coaster exists, but I am not going to put all my eggs in one basket and stick it on the roller coaster. Stay away from the trend! Identify, recognize, but stay away.

When you feel overwhelmed or unfocused, what do you do?

When I'm in the studio and I get in a state where I can't get my ideas across, and I'm banging my head against the computer, I have to leave the space. The same goes if I'm trying to finish a project and I'm just hitting a wall. You have to leave the space so you can reset.

Generally, the first thing I do is meditate so I can reset everything—reset my brain and reset my energy. I believe in the ability to find flow, and when you are in that state of flow, you are capable of finishing projects really fast. To give an example, The Clash finished one of the best albums in rock history, *London Calling*, in three weeks. They finished that entire album so fast, in my opinion, because they were in a state of flow. In times like that, you are extremely productive and creative.

When I'm in that state of flow, I stay there as long as I possibly can, because once you're out, it's hard to get back in. If you're hitting that wall or getting upset with yourself and can't get back to finding inspiration and creativity, you have to reset and go back to the basics. That's why some of my favorite artists to work with, whenever I go in the studio with them, say, "We don't want to work in a big studio"—they want to go back to the basics and work in the small, kind-of-shithole studio. By doing this, you go back to the soul of why you do what you do. And most important, it's not about how much money you can put into a project; it's not about how many people you can put into the project; it's about the gut feeling that you find in the center of why you did it in the first place.

You just gotta get back to that place, and if it makes you happy, then ride that happiness into a state of flow, and the rest is history!

"In a real sense, to grow in life, I must be a seeker of stress."

JIM LOEHR
corporateathlete.com

DR. JIM LOEHR is a world-renowned performance psychologist and cofounder of The Johnson & Johnson Human Performance Institute. He is the author of 16 books including his most recent, *The Only Way to Win: How Building Character Drives Higher Achievement and Greater Fulfillment in Business and Life*. Jim has worked with hundreds of world-class performers from the elite ranks of sports, law enforcement, military, and business, including gold medalists, FBI hostage rescue teams, military Special Forces, and Fortune 100 executives. Sports clients include golfers Mark O'Meara and Justin Rose; tennis players Jim Courier, Monica Seles, and Arantxa Sánchez Vicario; boxer Ray Mancini; hockey players Eric Lindros and Mike Richter; and Olympic gold medal speed skater Dan Jansen. Jim's science-based energy management training system has achieved worldwide recognition and has been featured in the *Harvard Business Review, Fortune, Time, U.S. News & World Report, Success,* and *Fast Company,* among many other media outlets.

What is the book (or books) you've given most as a gift, and why? Or what are one to three books that have greatly influenced your life?

The book that I have gifted most, and one that I continue to read and reread myself, is Viktor Frankl's *Man's Search for Meaning*. His brilliant articulation of the importance and power of purpose in life resonates deeply within me. I continue to be struck by his seemingly boundless capacity to feel deep compassion and love for his fellow concentration camp prisoners as well as the cruel prison guards who enabled the horror, and he was able to experience this even as he inched closer to death himself.

What purchase of $100 or less has most positively impacted your life in the last six months (or in recent memory)?

For less than $100, a case of Collins Stretch Tape from Collins Sports Medicine is the best buy ever for active athletes. I go through several cases a year just for myself. Our athletes immediately fall in love with this product. It's self-adhesive and elastic, making it a perfect performance combination for the support and protection of feet, hands, arms, and legs. It's the best!

How has a failure, or apparent failure, set you up for later success? Do you have a "favorite failure" of yours?

Three times across the course of my professional life, I have had people whom I have trusted—deeply trusted—take money and intellectual property from me. Twice this happened at the very beginning of my entrepreneurial life, when money was an incredibly scarce resource. I felt and continue to feel these occurrences were serious failures in my judgment of the character of others. I also felt that I had failed to properly vet the "investment" (although, in one case, I actually had a Federal Reserve chairman vouch for one of the individuals involved in the project). And of course, I was so deeply hurt by these individuals that I considered not trusting anyone. I viewed it as a failure of the goodness of mankind and, for a while, it made me bitter.

I've learned from years of working with highly diverse populations that nearly everyone experiences this during their lifetime. The only way to make certain this never happens is to build a wall so high and so thick that no one can get close to you. The lifetime cost of emotional isolation far exceeds the pain of occasional betrayal. The truth is that the pain of broken trust and betrayed friendship is simply the cost of caring and deeply connecting to others. My healing occurred through writing about it and by exploring ways I could convert my pain into something positive and constructive. For me, it was leveraging the betrayal to build more resilience and discernment in judging character . . . and learning forgiveness.

Resilience has been a powerful force in my writing more than a dozen books (many setbacks, long nights, and long days) while simultaneously growing and developing the Human Performance Institute. Without learning how to overcome my initial failures, I do not know that I would have had the courage and resolve to assume the risks necessary to build this business. And, of course, forgiveness is a double gift. I've learned how to forgive myself, to let go of beating myself up for the mistakes in judgment I had made. Forgiveness has enabled me to let go of the unproductive anger and to replace it with gratitude and hope. I eventually realized that the pain I endured never once created discomfort for those *other* individuals who betrayed my trust!

Here is what I know now after many years of living: Failure will happen, and failure is an opportunity to build resilience, to practice forgiveness of self and of others, and to gain wisdom.

If you could have a gigantic billboard anywhere with anything on it, what would it say and why?

"PRACTICE KINDNESS."

It takes courage to be truly kind. I have met Navy SEAL commanders who can do pull-ups all day long and navigate the coldest, most treacherous waters on dangerous missions, and the most remarkable thing that I walk away with after meeting these men—who appear molded of steel—is the power and authenticity of their kindness and humility. I've also witnessed incredible athletes achieve inspirational wins that bestow millions of dollars of prize money on them, and when they take their group of coaches and friends out to dinner to celebrate they refuse to pay for anything . . . even for their own meal. The key insight for me is not that these individuals are winners . . . it is that their self-absorption, inability to feel grateful, and utter lack of kindness toward others can never be justified for any reason, most certainly not because they are champions or are famous.

One of my favorite quotes is by Ralph Waldo Emerson: "To laugh often and much; to win the respect of intelligent people and the affection of children . . . to leave the world a bit better . . . to know even one life has breathed easier because you have lived; this is to have succeeded."

In the last five years, what new belief, behavior, or habit has most improved your life?

The practice of daily journaling has been a remarkable tool in helping me navigate the storms of life and be my best self through it all. The daily ritual of self-reflected writing has produced priceless personal insights in my life. For me, daily writing heightens my personal awareness in a nearly magical way. I see, feel, and experience things so much more vividly as a consequence of the writing. The hectic pace of life becomes more balanced and manageable when I intentionally set aside time for self-reflection. I am able to be more in the present in everything I do and, for whatever reason, more accepting of my flaws.

Journal writing can be used for catharsis and healing or for growing and expanding capacity. Entries can be as short as a minute or as long as time permits. It typically takes two to four weeks before one can see and feel positive results. For the best outcomes, entries to one's journal should be made by hand rather than on a computer.

My experiences with journaling began in my early work with athletes. Every athlete was required to keep a detailed training journal on a daily basis. An important insight gained over several years was that anything that was quantified and tracked on a regular basis would invariably show improvement (sleep times, liquid intake, stretching frequency, nutritional habits, etc.). Quantifying behavior raises awareness and, as a consequence, habit acquisition times are typically accelerated. Eventually, we applied this understanding to mental and emotional training. Using daily journal entries to quantify the frequency of positive versus negative thinking, giving 100 percent effort in practice, engagement levels, the tone and content of one's private voice, anger management, etc., produced similarly exciting results. Because of these insights, I decided to take up daily journaling myself. After only a few weeks, the only regret I had was that I hadn't started the process much earlier in my life.

What are bad recommendations you hear in your profession or area of expertise?

"Be your authentic self."

I understand the intent of this statement, but it can be used as a lethal weapon to hurt others. In many cases, people use the statement "I'm just being authentic" as cover for treating others badly. You see people being dismissive or rude in a discussion and they brush off any personal accountability by stating, "Hey, I just have to be myself." The truth I have discovered after working with incredible athletes, leaders, and individuals from across the globe is that our humanity is expressed most fully in our treatment of others—when we are respectful, humble, caring, honest, and grateful despite our struggles, disappointments, and failures. It represents the heart and soul of who we are at our best.

Think of the tennis player who, in the middle of a match, blows up at the umpire and begins yelling and screaming at her. Is he being truly authentic because he is a frustrated and angry person? Or is there more to consider, such as, where on his scale of importance is his treatment of others? Consider another tennis player who is certain that a linesperson has made an incorrect call. She appeals the call to the chair umpire and the umpire does not overturn it. That player immediately feels cheated and angry. Reflecting on her core values of respect and patience for others, she takes a deep breath and proceeds calmly forward in the match. Which example is more representative of true authenticity?

For me, when the statement "I just have to be myself" is used to justify bad, unethical behavior, the argument is nothing but a ruse.

Another piece of bad advice: "Protect yourself from stress and your life will be better."

Protection from stress serves only to erode my capacity [to handle it]. Stress exposure is the stimulus for all growth, and growth actually occurs during episodes of recovery. Avoiding stress, I have learned, will never provide the capacity that life demands of me.

For me, balancing episodes of stress with equivalent doses of recovery is the answer. Playing tennis, working out, meditation, and journaling provide rich mental and emotional recovery. Adhering to my optimal sleep, nutritional, and exercise routines during stressful times is critical. Seeking stress in one dimension of my life surprisingly brings recovery in another. Avoiding stress simply takes me out of the game and makes me weaker.

In a real sense, to grow in life, I must be a seeker of stress.

When you feel overwhelmed or unfocused, what do you do?

I immediately begin by recalling all the things I am grateful for in my life. I start with each of my three sons, my brother, sister, and on to my mother and father. I then allow my thoughts of gratitude to go wherever they go, from the smallest things to the largest. Literally within minutes, the perspective I have about what's happening in this stressful moment takes a dramatic shift. I become calmer, less panicked, and more measured in my feelings and thinking. I then pull forward the thought of my best self and who I most want to be in the storms of life. Connecting with my deepest values and purpose in life strengthens my resolve to respond to the crisis according to my highest ethical and moral character.

"To avoid criticism, say nothing, do nothing, be nothing."
—Elbert Hubbard

DANIEL NEGREANU
TW: @RealKidPoker
YT: /user/DNegreanu

DANIEL NEGREANU is a Canadian professional poker player who has won six World Series of Poker (WSOP) bracelets and two World Poker Tour (WPT) championship titles. In 2014, the independent poker ranking service Global Poker Index (GPI) recognized Daniel as the best poker player of the decade. Since his second-place finish in the Big One for One Drop tournament in 2014, he is considered the biggest live tournament poker winner of all time, having accumulated more than $33 million in prize money. He was named the WSOP Player of the Year in 2004 and again in 2013, making him the first (and only) player in WSOP history to win the accolade more than once. He was also the 2004–05 WPT Player of the Year. He is the first player to make a final table at each of the three WSOP bracelet-awarding locations (Las Vegas, Europe, and Asia-Pacific) and the first to win a bracelet at each. In 2014, he was inducted into the Poker Hall of Fame.

What is the book (or books) you've given most as a gift, and why? Or what are one to three books that have greatly influenced your life?

The Four Agreements by Don Miguel Ruiz. It is a quick read, just 140 pages or so, and it's the simplicity that makes the book so powerful. Anytime I have a friend who wants to embark on the journey of introspection, that's always where I start.

How has a failure, or apparent failure, set you up for later success? Do you have a "favorite failure" of yours?

I still distinctly remember the time I lost my whole bankroll on one of my first trips to Las Vegas from my hometown of Toronto. It was about 4 A.M. and I was playing at a table of eight people. I lost my last $5 chip and went to the bathroom. When I got out of the bathroom, I looked over at the table I was just playing at and noticed everyone had left! For the first time in my life, I realized I was the sucker. They were playing because of me. I was their tourist for the evening.

I remembered every one of their faces and was determined to never let that happen to me again. I worked harder on my game in Toronto with the goal of going back to Las Vegas and beating each of the players I lost to that night.

Turns out, one of those players, a guy everyone called Hawaiian Bill, became somewhat of a mentor to me. I hated him that first night, but I grew to understand what it takes to be a professional from watching how he works.

If you could have a gigantic billboard anywhere with anything on it, what would it say and why? Are there any quotes you think of often or live your life by?

"To avoid criticism, say nothing, do nothing, be nothing." — Elbert Hubbard

This quote has deep meaning to me, much like [Theodore Roosevelt's] "man in the arena" quote. It's a reminder that when you challenge the norms, when you make your voice heard, you are guaranteed to receive criticism, but in the end, it's all worth it. The alternative is being invisible, and that's not how I live my life.

What is one of the best or most worthwhile investments you've ever made?

I've invested in people I trust. My manager, Brian Balsbaugh, has become a great friend and confidant over the years, and it's been invaluable to have him as a sounding board for ideas. In addition to Brian, having a personal assistant who I overpay has allowed me to make better use of my free time.

In the last five years, what new belief, behavior, or habit has most improved your life?

The realization that all events are neutral, and I can choose how to react to them. I can choose to be a victim to my circumstances, or I can choose to stand responsible for how I handle my circumstances. The latter approach is a powerful place to come from, while being a victim is a helpless place to come from and is rarely productive.

What are bad recommendations you hear in your profession or area of expertise?

In poker, the "poker face" is romanticized. It gives you the impression that, to succeed in the game, you need to be stonefaced and emotionless. That all that matters are the numbers and the math. That emotion plays no role at the poker tables.

It's just not true. If we were robots, this approach would be optimal, but it's not realistic. A better approach is to acknowledge the emotions you are feeling as you either win or lose and just be present to them. Stuffing away emotion or frustration at the poker tables isn't the way to go.

In the last five years, what have you become better at saying no to?

In the past, if someone asked me for something, I may have given them a, "Sounds good, man. I'll check my schedule and we'll figure something out." The hope was that it would just go away, but the result was me being pestered for a meeting I didn't want to take. I'd have to come up with new excuses as to why I was too busy. Why would anyone do something like that? Well, I naively figured this approach would keep me from hurting people's feelings, but I ultimately realized the opposite was true. I was out of integrity and wasting their time.

So, I've learned to be honest and respectful at the same time: "Thanks so much for thinking of me for this. I really appreciate it. Unfortunately, it's not something I want to take on, but I wish you the best of luck with the project." They may be disappointed in the moment, but it's a much better way to deal with it.

When you feel overwhelmed or unfocused, what do you do?

I go through an exercise that helps me to get present to the reality of the situation. I tell my story to myself from the perspective of a victim, then I tell the exact same story from a place of 100 percent responsibility.

Victim: "I was late to an important event because my girlfriend took too long to get ready. It's not my fault."

Responsible: "I acknowledge my breakdown in being late. In the future I am committed to making sure that I do everything I can to ensure that I'm on time."

Telling myself the victim story allows me to vent briefly. Once I'm over it, then I realize that if this meeting was so important to me, I should have made it clear to my girlfriend that I couldn't be late, and let her know that if she was running late, I'd have to leave without her.

"Discipline equals freedom."

JOCKO WILLINK
TW: @jockowillink
FB: Jocko Willink
jockopodcast.com

JOCKO WILLINK is one of the scariest human beings imaginable. He is a lean 230 pounds and a Brazilian jiujitsu black belt who used to tap out 20 Navy SEALs per workout. He is a legend in the special operations world, and his viral podcast interview with me was the first public interview he ever did. Jocko spent 20 years in the U.S. Navy and commanded SEAL Team Three's Task Unit Bruiser, the most highly decorated special operations unit from the Iraq War. Upon returning to the United States, Jocko served as the officer-in-charge of training for all West Coast SEAL Teams, designing and implementing some of the most challenging and realistic combat training in the world. After retiring from the Navy, he co-founded Echelon Front, a leadership and management consulting company, and co-authored the #1 *New York Times* bestseller *Extreme Ownership: How U.S. Navy SEALs Lead and Win.* He has since authored a best-selling children's book, *Way of the Warrior Kid,* and his latest, *Discipline Equals Freedom: Field Manual,* which details his unique mental and physical "operating system." Jocko also discusses human nature through the lens of war, leadership, and business on his top-rated podcast, *Jocko Podcast.* Last, but not least, Jocko is a husband, an avid surfer, and the father of four "highly motivated" children.

What is the book (or books) you've given most as a gift, and why? Or what are one to three books that have greatly influenced your life?

At some point about halfway through my 20-year career in the SEAL Teams, I read *About Face* by Colonel David H. Hackworth. I haven't stopped reading it since. Hackworth came up through the ranks and served as an infantry officer in the Korean and Vietnam wars. He was revered by his men and respected by all who worked with him. While the stories of combat are incredible and there is much to be learned about battlefield tactics in the book, the real lessons for me are about leadership. I adapted many of his leadership principles over the years and still continue to learn from his experiences. Thanks for everything, Colonel Hackworth.

How has a failure, or apparent failure, set you up for later success? Do you have a "favorite failure" of yours?

During my second tour in Iraq, I was commander of SEAL Team Three, Task Unit Bruiser. We were deployed to the war-torn city of Ramadi, the epicenter of the insurgency at the time. Only a few weeks into the deployment, we conducted a large operation in conjunction with U.S. Army soldiers, U.S. Marines, and friendly Iraqi Army soldiers. There were multiple elements on the battlefield, all engaged in heavy enemy contact. In the fog of war, mistakes were made. Bad luck emerged. Things went wrong. There ended up being a vicious firefight between one of my SEAL elements and a friendly Iraqi unit. An Iraqi soldier was killed and several others were wounded, including one of my SEALs. It was a nightmare.

While there was plenty of blame to go around, and plenty of people who had made mistakes, I realized there was only one person to blame: me. I was the commander. I was the senior man on the battlefield, and I was responsible for everything that happened. Everything.

As a leader, there is no one else to blame. Don't make excuses. If I don't take ownership of problems, I can't solve them. That's what a leader has to do: take ownership of the problems, the mistakes, and the shortfalls, and take ownership of creating and implementing solutions to get those problems solved.

Take ownership.

If you could have a gigantic billboard anywhere with anything on it, what would it say and why?

"Discipline equals freedom." Everyone wants freedom. We want to be physically free and mentally free. We want to be financially free and we want more free time. But where does that freedom come from? How do we get it? The answer is the opposite of freedom. The answer is discipline. You want more free time? Follow a more disciplined time-management system. You want financial freedom? Implement long-term financial discipline in your life. Do you want to be physically free to move how you want, and to be free from many health issues caused by poor lifestyle choices? Then you have to have the discipline to eat healthy food and consistently work out. We all want freedom. Discipline is the only way to get it.

What is one of the best or most worthwhile investments you've ever made?

Ever since I have had a home with a garage, I have had a gym in my garage. It is one of the most important factors in allowing me to work out every day regardless of the chaos and mayhem life delivers. The convenience of being able to work out any time, without packing a gym bag, driving, parking, changing, then waiting for equipment . . .

The home gym is there for you. No driving. No parking. No little locker to cram your gear into. In your home gym, you never wait for equipment. It is waiting for you. Always.

And, perhaps most important: You can listen to whatever music you want, as loud as you want.

GET SOME.

In the last five years, what new belief, behavior, or habit has most improved your life?

Reading and writing every day. FREE YOUR MIND.

What advice would you give to a smart, driven college student about to enter the "real world"?

Work harder than everyone else. Of course, that is easy when you love your job. But you might not love your first, or second, or even third job. That doesn't matter. Work harder than everyone else. In order to get the job you love or start the company you want, you have to build your résumé, your reputation, and your bank account. The best way to do that: Outwork them all.

When you feel overwhelmed or unfocused, what do you do?

Prioritize and execute. I learned this in combat. When things are going wrong, when multiple problems are occurring all at once, when things get overwhelming, you have to prioritize and execute.

Take a step back.

Detach from the mayhem.

Look at the situation and assess the multitude of problems, tasks, or issues. Choose the one that is going to have the biggest impact and execute on that.

If you try to solve every problem or complete every task simultaneously, you will fail at all of them. Pick the biggest problem or the issue that will provide the most positive impact. Then focus your resources on that and attack it. Get it taken care of. Once you have done that, you can move on to the next problem or issue, then the one after that. Continue doing that until you have stabilized the situation. Prioritize and execute.

QUOTES I'M PONDERING

(Tim Ferriss: July 14–July 27, 2017)

"I happen to be in a very tough business where there are no alibis. It is good or it is bad, and the thousand reasons that interfere with a book being as good as possible are no excuses if it is not. . . . Taking refuge in domestic successes, being good to your broke friends, etc., is merely a form of quitting."

—ERNEST HEMINGWAY
Renowned American novelist, short-story writer, and journalist

"Poets do not 'fit' into society, not because a place is denied them but because they do not take their 'places' seriously. They openly see its roles as theatrical, its styles as poses, its clothing costumes, its rules conventional, its crises arranged, its conflicts performed, and its metaphysics ideological."

—JAMES P. CARSE
Professor emeritus of history and literature of religion at New York University, author of *Finite and Infinite Games*

"Be the silence that listens."

—TARA BRACH
Teacher of meditation and emotional healing, author of *Radical Acceptance*

"Our brains, our fear, our sense of what's possible, and the reality of 'only' 24 hours in a day give us preconceived notions of what is humanly possible."

ROBERT RODRIGUEZ
TW/IG: @rodriguez
elreynetwork.com

ROBERT RODRIGUEZ is a director, screenwriter, producer, cinematographer, editor, and musician. He is also the founder and chairman of El Rey Network, a new genre-busting cable network. There, he hosts one of my favorite interview-format shows, *The Director's Chair*. While a student at the University of Texas at Austin, Robert wrote the script for his first feature film while he was a paid subject in a clinical experiment at a drug research facility. That paycheck covered the cost of shooting over two weeks. The film, *El Mariachi*, went on to win the Audience Award at the Sundance Film Festival and became the lowest-budget movie ever released by a major studio. He went on to write, produce, and direct many successful films, including *Desperado*, *From Dusk Till Dawn*, the *Spy Kids* franchise, *Once Upon a Time in Mexico*, *Frank Miller's Sin City*, *Machete*, and others.

In the last five years, what new belief, behavior, or habit has most improved your life?

I finally found a strategy that really helps me stay focused while doing a major task that I'm not very enthused to do. It's not just that I'd put it off; it's that whenever I tried to do it, ten other more enjoyable and often equally worthwhile distractions would pop into my head that would send me off track. That was the biggest challenge. Those distractions were just as important as my major task, so I'd be justified in running off and doing those first. But my major task would remain untouched, turning itself into a chore to even think about. Now what I'll do is sort of a more efficient method, similar to a Premack [a motivational system where a more-preferred activity can be used to reinforce a less-preferred activity] or a rewards system, but with a more concrete strategy.

I'll have two notepads by my side, while sitting in the most comfortable place I can find. (You'll have to read my upcoming book to hear what that is!)

I'll write my list of two or three least desirable major tasks on one pad, with the word "Tasks" written on top. And I'll keep the second pad ready with the heading "Distractions" on top.

I'll then set my phone timer for 20 minutes.

I'll tackle one of my undesirable major tasks for a full 20 minutes. No straying from that. During that time, like clockwork, I'll always have several distractions: tasks and ideas that inevitably pop up in my head. These thoughts and temptations would normally send me off and running to accomplish whatever they were while they were burning in my head: an idea for music, a drawing or plan that was a eureka moment on a totally different project, answers to a problem I'd been trying to solve elsewhere, etc. Because when you're engaged mentally on a task, creativity fires off more ideas. But that becomes a problem when those ideas distract from your major less-desirable task.

That's what always threw me. These things weren't frivolous activities I was allowing myself to be distracted by. They were totally legit things to be done, and if I ignored them, I'd stress that I'd forget them or lose the mojo that was firing at that moment.

So how to keep myself from doing that? During my 20 minutes, I'll just physically write down any incoming missile of a thought on my "Distractions" pad, and I immediately go back to my major undesirable task. Now I don't have to worry I'll forget it. I'm not trying to disregard it and ignore the thought. I'm just keeping track of it by writing it down and deferring it, even if it's an extremely productive thing, because anything that takes away from my main task is technically a distraction. Once it's written down, I can go back to my main task until the 20 minutes is up.

If I'm on a roll on my main task, I'll add another 10 minutes to the timer and go as far as 30 minutes. But that's the limit. I find that if I don't reward myself often enough, my brain will mutiny.

I then take a 10- to 15-minute "reward break." I get up after 30 minutes and walk around. I take my distraction pad (which by now probably already has several things listed) and I'll get to go do one of those things for 10 to 15 minutes only. You must set a timer for this, too.

I try and do the ones that take less time, so I'm not an hour away from my main task. I don't have to complete the distraction in one sitting. If it's going to take longer than 10 or 15 minutes, then I'll just chip away at it and save the rest of it for the next break. I then come back and reset the 20-minute timer and start again on my main task.

I usually write any kind of to-do list in my phone, but there's a visual satisfaction to scratching out a tedious task by hand once it's complete, and having a handwritten distractions list. That's why I use the notepads. Writing out the distractions list was a real game changer and what finally made the concept of a Premack work for me. Makes it all so *fácil*.

If you could have a gigantic billboard anywhere with anything on it, what would it say and why?

"FÁCIL!" It's one of my favorite words! I don't even remember when I started using it in an empowering way; it might have been after starting my television network. I was already a pretty busy guy, so the idea of taking on a 24-hour television network that would need to be filled with content gave me some pause. But in usual Rodriguez naive fashion, I took it on anyway!

When the reality of the sheer amount of content we'd need to conjure up hit me, I'd try and wrangle collaborators together to accomplish the tall task of making shows for the network. [In simply managing the] network itself, there was a mind-boggling amount of work to do. I knew I'd need a whole new strategy to instill confidence in the troops and myself. This was different than movies, which were projects few and far between. Here I was attempting something impossible. Most new networks take years, if not decades, to even put on their first original TV series. In year one of the El Rey Network, I was launching four new shows. I could see people's eyes widen and look overwhelmed just by hearing me rattle off the list of things we all needed to do.

I started adding the Spanish word *"FÁCIL!"* to the end of my lists of tasks, and they'd laugh and give a bewildered look. (*Fácil* means "easy," but has a nicer ring to it in Spanish and also comes off as "No big deal!") They'd wonder, "Why does he keep saying that? How is any of that *easy*?" But then you'd see that it would actually put them at ease. If their leader has no fear, why should they?

That word became very empowering for us all. In practice it would sound like this: "We have such and such and such and such and such and such *plus* such and such to do by next Wednesday. *FÁCIL!*" You'd see them start off at first being shocked and stressed, but by the end of the sentence, they're laughing . . . . And we would get it done! When that task, or show, or creating something out of thin air was done, I'd be quick to return to them and point it out. "See? It was *FÁCIL!*"

I actually had no idea how we'd pull it all off either, but I knew stressing about it wasn't going to help at all. Basically, we're all capable of doing a lot more than we think. Our brains, our fear, our sense of what's possible and the reality of "only" 24 hours in a day give us preconceived notions of what is humanly possible.

I like the idea of setting impossible challenges and, with one word, making it sound doable, because then it suddenly is. So I'd choose *FÁCIL!* for my billboard. It's a good reminder that anything can be done, with relative ease and less stress, if you have the right mindset. If you go in saying, "This is impossible, there's just physically not enough time in the day to do all these things," then you're breaking your right leg and chopping off your left foot before you've even left the starting line. But if, in your mind, it's *fácil*, then you'll breeze through it and ideas will flow. Attitude comes first.

I sometimes forget to whom I've even told that concept, and I will get emails or texts from people I haven't spoken to in years, and they'll tag their message with *FÁCIL!* I realize it's become part of their language and way of thinking.

So, here's hoping it becomes part of yours. Because there's a lot of life we can experience in this world. It's all out there, ripe for the making, and it all starts in your head. What we tell ourselves is of utmost importance. We can conjure up new worlds with our imaginations and our creativity. And there's 24 entire hours in a day and seven whole days to a week and it can all be so very *FÁCIL!*

When you feel overwhelmed or unfocused, what do you do?

The distractions list I talked about earlier is the biggest help for me. I like being busy and having a lot of tasks to accomplish in different arenas. I find the solutions you discover in one area help you solve equally perplexing challenges in another area. But then there are times when everything hits at once.

There are times when everything just collides, and you have to try not to get overwhelmed. There's no time for the usual meditations or strategies and your head feels like it's full of cotton.

I remember one time I had to be out the door in two minutes, because I was already late for a meeting. I had a plate of food, and I also had to go use the bathroom. There was literally only time to do one or the other. I had to choose. Should I eat? Or should I use the restroom? So I did both! I sat on the toilet while eating my food. The whole time thinking, "I'm officially *too* busy today."

When I got a five-minute break later, I listened to a guided meditation that I made myself. It's five minutes long. Part of the meditation reminds me that bottlenecks occur, and they only help clarify what's important and what's not. And that there is a natural sifting that takes place.

If everything hits at once, it's a rarity. Life tends to shift events around so that everything you want to accomplish can be accomplished. On their own! You're triple-booked for the afternoon? Guess what, someone will end up canceling, or pushing, and the other thing will suddenly no longer be relevant.

That's why I keep piling it on. I'm rarely *too* busy, if you can keep the right attitude about it, which is, "I can definitely say I am living my life to the fullest."

I'll then clarify which items are causing the most stress and why. It's usually because you haven't done something you should have taken care of. So out come the two notepads, and you have to begin immediately on chipping away at a stressor. *FÁCIL!*

"Never let a good crisis go to waste. It's the universe challenging you to learn something new and rise to the next level of your potential."

KRISTEN ULMER
FB: /ulmer.kristen
kristenulmer.com

KRISTEN ULMER is a master facilitator who challenges norms around the subject of fear. She was a mogul specialist on the U.S. Ski Team and later became recognized as the best female big-mountain extreme skier in the world, a status she held for 12 years. Known for enormous cliff jumps and you-fall-you-die descents, she was sponsored by Red Bull, Ralph Lauren, and Nikon. Her work on fear has been featured on NPR and in *The Wall Street Journal*, *The New York Times*, *Outside* magazine, and others. Kristen is the author of *The Art of Fear: Why Conquering Fear Won't Work and What to Do Instead*.

What purchase of $100 or less has most positively impacted your life in the last six months (or in recent memory)?

[As background], my mom was the youngest of nine kids. Her dad was a raging alcoholic and the family had a simple existence as tenant farmers. She grew up with severe money issues. They are so solidified that, at age 83, she still washes and reuses Ziploc bags and eats around moldy food. And . . . I am my mother's daughter. I am frugal as hell, which is okay—it helped me become a self-made millionaire—but I think it holds me back from going to the next level financially at this point.

So, whenever I feel bad, I make a point to do something nice for other people. Either I stand outside the movie theater looking for someone who seems like they could use a break and I pay for their movie tickets, or I leave a $50 tip on a takeout burrito. Not only does it make other people feel good, it makes me feel good, and it also impacts my life in one other way that's not so obvious. Spending money like this is my subtle attempt to break free from my lineage and resolve my inherited money issues.

How has a failure, or apparent failure, set you up for later success? Do you have a "favorite failure" of yours?

As for a favorite failure, my time on the U.S. Ski Team was a biggie. Here's why:

My goal had never been to get on the national team. I'd only been competing in moguls to take cool road trips with friends. So when I found myself wearing the jacket, representing my country in World Cup competitions, I was in shock, and terrified.

Thousands of screaming people were now watching me ski, hundreds of cameras documented my every move, and I had no idea what to do with fear except take the bad advice of well-meaning coaches, friends, and family who told me to—you know the language—control, overcome, or rationalize away the fear. Think positive thoughts. Take deep breaths. Let it go. All that.

Alas, while I couldn't see it at the time, I've since realized we can control fear about as much as we can control our breathing. Not very well, and not for long.

I could become stoic enough to get in the gate and push off, so it seemed to "work," but I also skied terribly. I was not in flow with fear, thus I was not in flow with my life, and thus not in the flow state necessary for world-class performance. Not only that, but I unconsciously wanted off that team so badly that (of course) I got injured later that season. I was even relieved by my injury, which is crazy. I blamed fear as the problem for all of this, when I should have blamed myself for trying to control something that ultimately proves uncontrollable.

What I realize now is that you can't conquer fear. The only thing you can do is block it out temporarily by pushing it down into what I call "the basement," otherwise known as your body. You then have to hold so much tension to keep it pressed down that 1) you will become very stiff and prone to injury and 2) your body, not meant to be a dumping ground for repressed emotion, will rebel.

Injury is just one of the problems you'll face. That undealt-with fear will not be denied. Any time your guard is dropped, it will come out of the basement stronger than ever, showing up in ways that feel like fear (persistent or irrational anxiety, insomnia, etc.) or in distorted, covert ways (anger, depression, PTSD, insecurity, underperforming, burnout, blame, defensiveness, etc.). This makes you want to work harder to push it down even further, until that effort, over time, takes over your whole world.

How I dealt with fear back then was a colossal failure. What I should have done instead was realize that fear is not a sign of personal weakness, but rather a natural state of discomfort that occurs whenever you're out of your comfort zone. It's there not to sabotage you, but to help you come alive, be more focused, and put you into the present moment and a heightened state of excitement and awareness. If you push the fear away, the only version of fear available to you will be its crazy, irrational, or contorted version. If you're willing to feel it, and merge with it, its energy and wisdom will appear.

What is one of the best or most worthwhile investments you've ever made?

I went on an immersive nine-day retreat 14 years ago when I was *not* in crisis. It was called Nine Gates Mystery School. It still exists today and I hear it's better than ever. (By the way, I recommend going to one awareness retreat per year.) Nine Gates took my still half-baked idea, injected it with both certainty and energy, and raised my awareness from an ego to a global-centric perspective, which is why I credit this event with provoking much of my success today.

Nine Gates is an 18-day intensive retreat broken into two nine-day sessions. If you're drawn to a silent Vipassana retreat but hesitate because it sounds like torture (it does to me), consider Nine Gates instead. I suspect it gives you a similar awakening experience without the inactivity.

People tend to only do personal work when they're trying to crawl out of a hole, and I was no different. I'd signed up for the event when going through a bad breakup, which is fine. Often crisis is what drives evolution, and little else does.

By the time the retreat happened, though, I felt great again, and I went anyway and—wow. Just wow. Instead of spending the week getting the mud out of my eyes, it took my already clear vision to the top of a personal high mountain, where I could clearly see what I wanted to happen next in my life. I left the event and started my mindset-only ski camps—which (according to *USA Today*) were the only mindset training camps in the world, in any sport.

On one hand, never let a good crisis go to waste. It's the universe challenging you to learn something new and rise to the next level of your potential.

On the other hand, when not in crisis, I consider "my life is great" as a cop-out, a stuck place, where learning is no longer available to us. Which is why you shouldn't wait for crisis to happen before you take steps to go beyond what you're capable of seeing on your own. Go to marriage counseling when your marriage is going great. What then becomes possible? Hire a fitness coach when you're already in the best shape of your life. Bring in a marketing expert when your marketing department is already kicking ass. And watch next-level magic happen.

What is the book (or books) you've given most as a gift, and why? Or what are one to three books that have greatly influenced your life?

My two favorite books are:

The Wisdom of the Enneagram by Don Richard Riso and Russ Hudson. This book offers you a blueprint of your personality. This is important. Let's say you learn you're a tiger. You now know not to waste time trying to get rid of your stripes, but instead to develop your innate strengths. Or if you're a lamb, which is no better or worse than a tiger, you'd learn not to waste your life trying to be something that you're not, and how to instead be the best lamb possible.

I love this book so much, in fact, that I wouldn't date or certainly hire anyone unless I knew what their enneagram type was. It's like being armed with their operating manual, which prevents any confusion or potential conflict down the road.

The Power of Now by Eckhart Tolle. I was encouraged to read this book by four different people in one week, so I bought it and dove in. But . . . snoozefest! I stored it on the bookshelf. A year later, I dusted it off, and again . . . nothing. Back to the bookshelf. This happened four years in a row until, in the fifth year, I started yet again and it was so good, I suddenly devoured it like a starving person devours a buffet.

It was so powerful because it outlines non-dual states—a.k.a something bigger than my own personal, limited view of the world. Tolle calls it the "Now," I call it "Connected Self" or "the Infinite." In sports, we call this reality "The Zone." In Zen, it's called enlightenment. Every spiritual tradition has a name for this place.

I judge the quality of my life based on how often I access this higher state of awareness. Being into Zen, I don't see it as sustainable, which is different from what Tolle suggests, but it's so important to for us to go find it in our lifetimes. It's that state when your lights really come on and you can see, if only for a moment, who and what you are, and the nature of what's really going on beyond our own individual mind. It's also the place where your greatest ideas can be discovered. But this state is not going to find you; you have to go find it. This book helps you do that.

What are bad recommendations you hear in your profession or area of expertise?

Talk therapy. Talking and thinking about your fear is great—who doesn't like to talk about themselves for an hour? But it will keep you in the loop of your thinking mind, often for decades. Emotional problems need to be dealt with emotionally, not intellectually.

In the last five years, what have you become better at saying no to? What new realizations and/or approaches helped?

Past age 40, it seems that we really start to filter who we hang out with. For decades, I had several friends whom I picked in my 20s, when I was drawn to crazy, eccentric people. But in my 40s, they weren't my style anymore.

Some of them were even abusive to themselves and thus also to me. So, what to do? Stay close out of habit, history, and a desire not to hurt them, or finally say no to these toxic friendships and walk away?

I decided to walk away. One by one—and mind you this was not easy to do—I ended it with five best friends and ultimately hundreds of acquaintances. It set me free from my past self and made me able to explore what parts of my personality I wanted to nurture next. It has been a bit lonely, sure. I have yet to find a new best girlfriend even though I've been hunting for eight years, and I don't go to as many parties as before. But the ones I do go to, and the people I meet there, are always fascinating, energizing new experiences.

Friendships are supposed to support your growth, not hold you back. End the ones that hold you back, and be curious about what kind of people you're drawn to next. I find whomever you're attracted to today possesses whatever qualities in yourself you're ready to nurture.

[Note from Tim: I asked Kristen how she broke up with her friends, exactly, and she sent a detailed four-page blueprint. Find it for free at tim. blog/kristen]

When you feel overwhelmed or unfocused, what do you do?

I honor those states by walking away from work and instead doing what seems like "nothing," which is of course something (take a walk, stretch my body, watch a movie). I do these things for as long as it takes, whether a few hours or even a few days, until my motivation comes back.

If I have a tight deadline, though, I take just five minutes to do that "nothing." But during these five minutes, I go *alllll* the way. I become fully present to my unfocused or overwhelmed state. Maybe I'll take a hot shower and just stand there and let water luxuriously rain down my neck while groaning about how overwhelmed I feel. It's lovely. Or I'll find the cat and bury my unfocused mind into his soft belly and just enjoy how spacey and stupid I am at the moment.

Not only is it a relief to submit like that to my present reality, but—*surprise!*—these actions also have the great ability to allow another reality to enter, without my having to force anything. I usually come back after those five minutes, organically energized and ready for another big push.

Honor your moods not by forcing a different reality, but by just letting them be. It's very Zen. When you're sad, just be sad. When you're afraid, just be afraid. When you're overwhelmed, just be overwhelmed. When you're unfocused, can you find a way to let it be and simply enjoy that state?

This is how—like water through a hose—these states will come into, through, and out of your life. Do this and that reality will always run its course, and there will be space right behind it for something else to enter.

In the last five years, what new belief, behavior, or habit has most improved your life?

Because my belief is that your relationship with fear is the most important relationship in your life, I now spend at least two minutes a day engaged in what I call a fear practice.

Especially first thing in the morning before I get out of bed, I do a body scan to assess my mood. I'm particularly interested in how much I feel fear (it's always there, whether we're willing to admit it or not), and where in my body it's located.

Fear is a sense of discomfort in our bodies. It may show up in obvious ways as fear, stress, or anxiety (which are all pretty much the same thing), or maybe it will feel more like anger or sadness (which can be tied to fear, if fear is in the basement). If it seems like it's in our minds, that's because we're not dealing with it emotionally but rather intellectually, which is never a good idea. I locate the feeling in my body—sometimes it's in my jaw or shoulders, sometimes my forehead. Then I have a one- to two-minute, three-step process:

1. I spend about 15 to 30 seconds affirming that it's natural to feel this discomfort. I may have a big talk coming up or a deadline. You are supposed to be scared when you're doing big things—okay? Acknowledging this can be life-changing.

2. I spend the next 15 to 30 seconds being curious about what my current relationship is with that discomfort. If the anxiety seems out of proportion to the situation, or if it seems irrational in any way, that means I've been ignoring fear and thus it's starting to speak louder or act out. If this is the case, I give it my full attention then, and ask what it's been trying to say to me that I haven't acknowledged (e.g., "Write

a new speech; the one you have sucks." Or, "You forgot to call your mother"). Being such a great advisor, I use this time with fear to juice its knowledge like you would juice an orange.

3. Then, I spend as long as it takes to feel it. Now, this is important: I don't try to get rid of it. That is not what this is about, because that would be disrespectful to fear. The key is to feel the feeling by spending some time with it, like you would with your dog, friend, or lover. I usually do this for about 30 to 60 seconds. After which, fear, feeling acknowledged and heard, often dissipates.

Then for the rest of the day, any time I feel anxious or upset, I do it again. My clients have a fear practice too, and the results are quite profound. After about a week, not only does their fear and anxiety calm way down, but many other problems like insomnia, depression, PTSD, and anger become resolved. Keep doing it past that week, and you'll start to notice the percolation, energy, and heightened states this practice offers.

I don't have a gratitude, peace, or forgiveness practice, which are super popular in America right now. I see this as turning away from a truth that is trying to get your attention, and forcing a lie. My analogy is that this is like putting a Band-Aid over a wound so you don't have to look at it. Which is a problem because that wound, if you continue to not deal with it, will ultimately start to fester.

Instead, I turn toward my discomfort and try to have an honest relationship with it by engaging in this fear practice. I focus on my discomfort, fear, sadness, anger, or anything else that seems unpleasant—all of it—and that effort not only affords me insights but, even though you'd never expect it, also thoroughly and amazingly sets me free.

"It is likely that most of what you currently learn at school will be irrelevant by the time you are 40.... My best advice is to focus on personal resilience and emotional intelligence."

YUVAL NOAH HARARI
TW: @harari_yuval
FB: tim.blog/harari-facebook (redirect)
ynharari.com

YUVAL NOAH HARARI is the author of the international bestsellers *Sapiens: A Brief History of Humankind* and *Homo Deus: A Brief History of Tomorrow.* He received his PhD from the University of Oxford in 2002 and is now a lecturer in the Department of History at the Hebrew University of Jerusalem. Yuval has twice won the Polonsky Prize for Creativity and Originality, in 2009 and 2012. He has published numerous articles, including "Armchairs, Coffee, and Authority: Eye-witnesses and Flesh-witnesses Speak About War, 1100–2000," for which he won the Society for Military History's Moncado Award. His current research focuses on macro-historical questions: What is the relation between history and biology? What is the essential difference between Homo sapiens and other animals? Is there justice in history? Does history have a direction? Did people become happier as history unfolded?

What is the book (or books) you've given most as a gift, and why? Or what are one to three books that have greatly influenced your life?

Aldous Huxley's *Brave New World*. I think it is the most prophetic book of the 20th century, and the most profound discussion of happiness in modern Western philosophy. It had a deep impact on my thinking about politics and happiness. And since, for me, the relationship between power and happiness is the most important question in history, *Brave New World* has also reshaped my understanding of history.

Huxley wrote the book in 1931, with Communism and Fascism entrenched in Russia and Italy, Nazism on the rise in Germany, militaristic Japan embarking on its war of conquest in China, and the entire world gripped by the Great Depression. Yet Huxley managed to see through all these dark clouds and envision a future society without wars, famines, and plagues, enjoying uninterrupted peace, abundance, and health. It is a consumerist world, which gives completely free rein to sex, drugs, and rock-and-roll, and whose supreme value is happiness. It uses advanced biotechnology and social engineering to make sure that everyone is always content and no one has any reason to rebel. There is no need of a secret police, concentration camps, or a Ministry of Love à la Orwell's *1984*. Indeed, Huxley's genius consists in showing that you could control people far more securely through love and pleasure than through violence and fear.

When people read George Orwell's *1984*, it is clear that he is describing a frightening nightmare world, and the only question left open is "How do we avoid reaching such a terrible state?" Reading *Brave New World* is a far more disconcerting experience, because it is obvious that there must be something dreadfully wrong, but you are hard pressed to put your finger on it. The world is peaceful and prosperous, and everyone is supremely satisfied all the time. What could possibly be wrong with that?

The truly amazing thing is that when Huxley wrote *Brave New World* back in 1931, both he and his readers knew perfectly well that he was describing a dangerous dystopia. Yet many readers today might easily mistake it for a utopia. Our consumerist society is actually geared to realizing Huxley's vision. Today, happiness has become the supreme value, and we increasingly use biotechnology and social engineering to ensure maximum satisfaction to all citizen-customers. You want to know what could be wrong with that? Read the dialogue between Mustapha Mond, the World Controller for Western Europe, and John the Savage, who lived all his life on a native reservation in New Mexico, and who is the only man in London who still knows anything about Shakespeare or God.

What is an unusual habit or an absurd thing that you love?
When going on an elevator or escalator, trying to stand on the tips of my toes.

How has a failure, or apparent failure, set you up for later success? Do you have a "favorite failure" of yours?
After I published *Sapiens* in Hebrew and it became a bestseller in Israel, I thought it would be easy to publish an English translation of it. I translated it and sent it to various publishers, but all rejected it out of hand. I still preserve a particularly humiliating rejection letter I got from one very prominent publishing house. So, I then tried to self-publish it on Amazon. The quality was quite dreadful, and it sold just a couple of hundred copies. I was very frustrated for some time.

Then I realized that the DIY method just doesn't work, and that instead of looking for shortcuts, I needed to do it the hard and long way and rely on professional help. My husband, Itzik, who is a far better businessman than me, took over. He found us a wonderful literary agent, Deborah Harris, whose advice led us to hire an outstanding editor, Haim Watzman, who helped me rewrite and polish the text. With their assistance, we got a contract from Harvill Secker (a division of Random House). My editor there, Michal Shavit, turned the text into a real gem, and hired the best independent PR agency in the UK book market—Riot Communications—to do the PR campaign. I make a point of mentioning their names because it was only thanks to the professional work of all these experts that *Sapiens* became an international bestseller. Without them, it would have remained an unknown rough diamond, like so many other excellent books that nobody has heard about. From the initial failure, I learned the limits of my own abilities, and the importance of going to the experts instead of looking for shortcuts.

What advice would you give to a smart, driven college student about to enter the "real world"? What advice should they ignore?

Nobody really knows what the world and the job market will look like in 2040, hence nobody knows what to teach young people today. Consequently, it is likely that most of what you currently learn at school will be irrelevant by the time you are 40.

So what should you focus on? My best advice is to focus on personal resilience and emotional intelligence. Traditionally, life has been divided into two main parts: a period of learning followed by a period of working. In the first part of life you built a stable identity and acquired personal and professional skills; in the second part of life you relied on your identity and skills to navigate the world, earn a living, and contribute to society. By 2040, this traditional model will become obsolete, and the only way for humans to stay in the game will be to keep learning throughout their lives and to reinvent themselves again and again. The world of 2040 will be a very different world from today, and an extremely hectic world. The pace of change is likely to accelerate even further. So people will need the ability to learn all the time and to reinvent themselves repeatedly—even at age 60.

Yet change is usually stressful, and after a certain age, most people don't like to change. When you are 16, your entire life is change, whether you like it or not. Your body is changing, your mind is changing, your relationships are changing—everything is in flux. You are busy inventing yourself. By the time you are 40, you don't want change. You want stability. But in the twenty-first century, you won't be able to enjoy that luxury. If you try to hold on to some stable identity, some stable job, some stable worldview, you will be left behind, and the world will fly by you. So people will need to be extremely resilient and emotionally balanced to sail through this never-ending storm, and to deal with very high levels of stress.

The problem is that it is very hard to teach emotional intelligence and resilience. It is not something you can learn by reading a book or listening to a lecture. The current educational model, devised during the 19th century

Industrial Revolution, is bankrupt. But so far we haven't created a viable alternative.

So don't trust the adults too much. In the past, it was a safe bet to trust adults, because they knew the world quite well, and the world changed slowly. But the 21st century is going to be different. Whatever the adults have learned about economics, politics, or relationships may be outdated. Similarly, don't trust technology too much. You must make technology serve you, instead of you serving it. If you aren't careful, technology will start dictating your aims and enslaving you to its agenda.

So you have no choice but to really get to know yourself better. Know who you are and what you really want from life. This is, of course, the oldest advice in the book: know thyself. But this advice has never been more urgent than in the 21st century. Because now you have competition. Google, Facebook, Amazon, and the government are all relying on big data and machine learning to get to know you better and better. We are not living in the era of hacking computers—we are living in the era of hacking humans. Once the corporations and governments know you better than you know yourself, they could control and manipulate you and you won't even realize it. So if you want to stay in the game, you have to run faster than Google. Good luck!

In the last five years, what have you become better at saying no to? What new realizations and/or approaches helped?

I have become much better at saying no to invitations. Which is a matter of survival, because I get dozens of invitations a week. To tell the truth, though, I'm still quite lousy at refusing. I feel so bad saying no. So I outsourced it. My husband, who is much better not only at business but also at refusing, does most of the hard work for me. And now we hired an assistant, who spends hours every day just refusing people.

What is one of the best or most worthwhile investments you've ever made?

By far, the best investment of time I ever made was to do a ten-day Vipassana meditation (www.dhamma.org) retreat. As a teenager and later as a student, I was a very troubled and restless person. The world made no sense to me, and I got no answers to the big questions I had about life. In particular, I didn't understand why there was so much suffering in the world and in my own life, and what could be done about it. All I got from the people around me and from the books I read were elaborate fictions: religious myths about gods and heavens, nationalist myths about the motherland and its historical mission, romantic myths about love and adventure, or capitalist myths about economic growth and how buying and consuming stuff will make me happy. I had enough sense to realize that these were probably all fictions, but I had no idea how to find the truth.

While I was doing my doctorate at Oxford, a good friend nagged me for a year to try a Vipassana meditation course. I thought it was some New Age mumbo jumbo, and since I had no interest in hearing yet another mythology, I declined to go. But after a year of patient nudging, he got me to give it a chance.

Previously I knew very little about meditation, and presumed it must involve all kinds of complicated mystical theories. I was therefore amazed by how practical the teaching turned out to be. The teacher at the course, S. N. Goenka, instructed the students to sit with crossed legs and closed eyes, and to focus all their attention on the breath coming in and out of their nostrils. "Don't do anything," he kept saying. "Don't try to control the breath or to breathe in any particular way. Just observe the reality of the present moment, whatever it may be. When the breath comes in, you just know: Now the breath is coming in. When the breath goes out, you just know: Now the breath is going out. And when you lose your focus and your mind starts wandering in memories and fantasies, you just know: Now my mind has wandered away from the breath." It was the most important thing anybody has ever told me.

The first thing I learned by observing my breath was that notwithstanding all the books I had read and all the classes I had attended at university, I knew almost nothing about my mind, and I had very little control over it. Despite my best efforts, I couldn't observe the reality of my breath coming in and out of my nostrils for more than ten seconds before the mind wandered away! For years I lived under the impression that I was the master of my life and the CEO of my own personal brand. But a few hours of meditation were enough to show me that I hardly had any control of myself. I was not the CEO—I was barely the gatekeeper. I was asked to stand at the gateway of my body—the nostrils—and just observe whatever comes in or goes out. Yet after a few moments I lost my focus and abandoned my post. It was a humbling and eye-opening experience.

As the course progressed, students were taught to observe not just their breath, but sensations throughout their body: heat, pressure, pain, and so forth. The technique of Vipassana is based on the insight that the flow of mind is closely interlinked with bodily sensations. Between me and the world, there are always bodily sensations. I never react to events in the outside world. I always react to the sensations in my own body. When the sensation is unpleasant, I react with aversion. When the sensation is pleasant, I react with craving for more. Even when we think we react to what another person had done, or to a distant childhood memory, or to the global financial crisis, the truth is we always react to a tension in the shoulder or a spasm in the pit of the stomach.

You want to know what anger is? Well, just observe the sensations that arise and pass in your body while you are angry. I was 24 years old at the time I went to this retreat, and had probably experienced anger 10,000 times previously, yet I never bothered to observe how anger actually felt. Whenever I was angry, I focused on the object of my anger—something somebody else did or said—rather than on the physical reality of the anger.

I think I learned more about myself and about humans in general by observing my sensations for those ten days than I learned in my whole life before. And to do so, I didn't have to accept any story, theory, or mythology. I just had to observe reality as it is. The most important thing I realized was that the deep source of my suffering is in the patterns of my own mind. When I want something and it doesn't happen, my mind reacts by generating suffering. Suffering is not an objective condition in the outside world. It is a mental reaction generated by my own mind.

Since that first course in 2000, I began practicing Vipassana for two hours every day, and each year I take a long meditation retreat for a month or two. It is not an escape from reality. It is getting in touch with reality. At least for two hours a day, I actually observe reality as it is, while for the other 22 hours I get overwhelmed by emails and tweets and funny cat videos. Without the focus and clarity provided by this practice, I could not have written *Sapiens* and *Homo Deus*.

When you feel overwhelmed or unfocused, what do you do?
I observe my breath for a few seconds or minutes.

SOME CLOSING THOUGHTS

"Don't aim at success. The more you aim at it and make it a target, the more you are going to miss it. For success, like happiness, cannot be pursued. . . . Happiness must happen, and the same holds for success: you have to let it happen by not caring about it. I want you to listen to what your conscience commands you to do and go on to carry it out to the best of your knowledge. Then you will live to see that in the long-run — in the long-run, I say! — success will follow you precisely because you had forgotten to think about it."

— **VIKTOR E. FRANKL,** *MAN'S SEARCH FOR MEANING*

ICE BATH EPIPHANIES

"No, I don't know *why* he needs four laundry bags full of ice."

The concierge was shrugging her shoulders in exasperation as she spoke to housekeeping. She repeated the instructions. It was 8 P.M., and everyone at the front desk was confused.

I, on the other hand, was a dead man walking. My batteries had hit empty hours before. Cringing with low-back pain, I used a garbage bag of sweaty clothes as a pillow and rested my head on the countertop. The bellboy moved a few feet further away.

After what seemed like an eternity, the riddle of the ice was solved. I shuffled to my room and face planted.

Twenty minutes later, I awoke to a knock on the door and had my 40 pounds of ice. Into the tub it went, and—after taking off my elbow brace, unwrapping blistered toes, and popping anti-inflammatories—I eased into the freezing water. As I lost my breath and the adrenaline hit, an old phrase came to mind:

"LOVE THE PAIN."

My senior year of high school, I read a book called *Mental Toughness Training for Sports* by Dr. Jim Loehr. My best competitive season of sports—then or since—followed. Throughout that entire period, I wrote one thing at the top of my journal before every wrestling practice: "LOVE THE PAIN."

Now, I found myself in Orlando, Florida, the same phrase running through my mind.

Months earlier, someone from the Johnson & Johnson Human Performance Institute had reached out to ask me a simple question: "Would you like to learn how to play tennis?" Then they added, "Dr. Jim Loehr would also enjoy spending some time with you."

I learned that Jim was retiring the following year. He'd worked with Jim Courier, Monica Seles, and dozens of other legends. If I traveled to Florida, I'd have a pro tennis coach for the technical game and Jim for the mental game. Jim himself! And tennis had been on my list for decades. How could I not jump at the chance? So I did.

Now, slumped in an ice bath, there was no jumping.

I'd just finished my first day of a planned five days. Each day included six hours of training, and I already felt broken. My long-standing elbow tendinosis had flared up with a vengeance, making it agonizing to pick up a water glass. Brushing my teeth or shaking someone's hand was out of the question. Not to mention the low back and everything else.

This is when my mind started running:

Maybe this is just what 40 feels like? Everyone tells me that's what happens. Maybe I should cut my losses and get back to other projects? And let's be real: I'm fucking terrible at this, and I'm in pain. Besides, it'll be hard to get to the courts in San Francisco regularly. No one would blame me if I had to leave early. In fact, no one would really even know . . .

I shook my head. Then I slapped the back of my neck to snap out of it.

No, you can suck it up, Ferriss. This is ridiculous. You've barely even started, and this is what you've always wanted. You're going to come all the way to Florida to turn around after one day? C'mon.

Think. Maybe I could play left-handed? Or toss balls to mimic the game, and work on footwork? Worst case, I suppose I could cancel ball work altogether and focus on my mental game?

I let out a long exhale and shut my eyes for a few deep breaths. Then I reached over the side of the tub. Books are my go-to distraction when submerged in ice baths for a testicle-punishing 10 to 15 minutes. That night, the flavor *du jour* was *The Inner Game of Tennis* by W. Timothy Gallwey.

One passage stopped me in my tracks a few pages in:

> The player of the inner game comes to value the art of relaxed concentration above all other skills; he discovers the true basis for self-confidence; and he learns that the secret to winning any game lies in not trying too hard.

The secret to winning any game lies in not trying too hard?

It was with that thought that I dragged myself out of the ice bath and to bed, where I fell soundly asleep.

THE POINT OF IMPACT

I walked into the training center the next morning and was greeted by Lorenzo Beltrame, my incredibly talented and affable tennis coach.

Jim was around the corner with his huge smile, size 15 shoes, and usual good advice: "Today, do everything more softly: grip more softly, hit more softly . . . Let your shoulders and hips hit the ball."

The three of us knew today would decide whether we forged ahead, attempted left-handed play, or threw in the towel altogether. Jim didn't want me destroying myself, and he didn't want optimism bleeding into masochism.

Out to the courts we walked.

Two hours into practice, Lorenzo stood a broom up in the middle of the net and put a towel on top. My job was to aim for the towel.

I proceeded to hit a seemingly endless streak of balls into the net. There was zero accuracy and constant shooting pain in my arm.

Lorenzo stopped the action and walked around the net. He spoke quietly: "When I was a young player in Italy, nine or ten years old," he said, "my coach gave me a rule: I could make mistakes, but I couldn't make the same mistake twice. If I was hitting balls into the net, he would say, 'I don't care if you hit balls over the fence or anywhere else, but you're not allowed to hit any more balls into the net. That's the only rule.'"

Lorenzo then changed the focus of the drill entirely. Instead of compulsively looking at my target, the towel, I would only focus on what was directly in front of me:

The point of impact.

The point of impact is where the ball makes contact with the racket. It's the split second in which your intention collides with the outside world. If you look at freeze-frames of top professional players in this critical moment, you will most often see their eyes on the ball as it smashes into their strings.

"Ready?" he asked.

"Ready."

He fed me the first ball and . . . it worked like magic.

As soon as I stopped fixating on the destination—where I wanted to hit the ball—and instead focused on what was in front of me—the point of impact—everything began to work. 10, 15, 20 balls later, they were all going where I wanted them to go, and I wasn't thinking about where I wanted them to go.

Lorenzo smiled, made a twirling hand motion like a bow, and kept feeding me balls. He yelled over to the sidelines, where Jim had just returned from the offices, "Doc, you have to watch this!"

A gigantic grin spread across Jim's face. "Well, look at that!"

It flowed, and it kept flowing. The more I focused on the point of impact, the more the rallies and games took care of themselves. My elbow somehow hurt less, and I made it through the entire five days of training.

It was glorious.

THE DANGER OF BIG QUESTIONS

Most of the time, "What should I do with my life?" is a terrible question.

"What should I do with this tennis serve?" "What should I do with this line at Starbucks?" "What should I do with this traffic jam?" "How should I respond to the anger I feel welling up in my chest?" These are better questions.

Excellence is the next five minutes, improvement is the next five minutes, happiness is the next five minutes.

This doesn't mean you ignore planning. I encourage you to make huge, ambitious plans. Just remember that the big-beyond-belief things are accomplished when you deconstruct them into the smallest possible pieces and focus on each "moment of impact," one step at a time.

I've had a life full of doubts . . . mostly for no good reason.

Broadly speaking, as good as it feels to have a plan, it's even more freeing to realize that nearly no misstep can destroy you. This gives you the courage to improvise and experiment. As Patton Oswalt put it, "My favorite failure is every time I ever ate it onstage as a comedian. Because I woke up the next day and the world hadn't ended."

And if it seems like the world has ended, perhaps it's just the world forcing you to look through a different, better door. As Brandon Stanton put it, "Sometimes you need to allow life to save you from what you want."

What you *want* may be that towel in the middle of the tennis court, the compulsive goal that's preventing you from getting what you *need*.

Keep your eye on the ball, feel what you need to feel, and adapt as you go. Then the game of life will take care of itself.

THE POWER BROKER

During my second lunch in Orlando, Jim told me the story of Dan Jansen.

Dan Jansen was born in Wisconsin, the youngest of nine kids. Inspired by his sister, Jane, he started speed skating and, by age 16, he had set a junior world record in the 500-meter race. He decided to dedicate his life to the sport.

Dan earned his way to the top but was plagued by tragedy at every Olympic Games. His pain peaked at the 1988 Winter Olympics. Hours before his 500-meter race, Dan found out that Jane had lost her battle against leukemia. He fell in the 500, crashing into the barriers, and did the same several days later during the 1,000. He had arrived in Calgary as the favorite for two gold medals, and he instead went home with a death in the family and no medals.

Dan came to expect bad luck, and he began working with Jim Loehr in 1991 to correct course.

At the time, many people thought it was impossible to break the 36-second barrier in the 500. This "impossible" had seeped into Dan's head, and he started writing "35:99" at the top of his journal pages to counteract the doubt.

The 1,000-meter race was also a problem . . . or so it seemed. It gave him too much time to think, too much time to create self-defeating loops in his own mind.

So, every day for two years, Jim had Dan add another reminder next to "35:99" in his journal:

"I LOVE THE 1,000."

On December 4, 1993, Dan finished the 500 meters with 35:92, breaking the 36-second barrier and setting a world record. He broke it again on January 30, 1994. Dan landed at the 1994 Winter Olympics in Lillehammer, Norway, in the best shape of his life. He had one final chance at an Olympic medal.

In "his event" of the 500, he took eighth place. It was a devastating loss. The curse of the Olympics seemed intact.

Then came the 1,000 meters, his nemesis. It would be his last race at his last Olympics. He did not fall. He stunned everyone by blowing away the competition, setting a world record, and winning a gold medal in the process.

Dan had learned to love the 1,000, and he became a national hero.

It's one hell of a story, right?

Now, you might say, "That's inspiring and all, sure, but what if you don't have access to Jim Loehr?"

At age 17, I didn't either. I read *Mental Toughness Training for Sports* in a bunk bed, and it changed my life. To learn from the best, you don't need to meet them, you just need to absorb them. This can be through books, audio, or a single powerful quote.

Feeding your mind is how you become your own best coach.

To paraphrase Jim: The power broker in your life is the voice that no one ever hears. How well you revisit the tone and content of your private voice is what determines the quality of your life. It is the master storyteller, and the stories we tell ourselves are our reality.

For instance, how do you speak to yourself when you make a mistake that upsets you? Would you speak that way to a dear friend when they've made a mistake? If not, you have work to do. Trust me, we *all* have work to do.

This is where I should explain my old friend "LOVE THE PAIN."

"LOVE THE PAIN" isn't about self-flagellation. It's a simple reminder that nearly all growth requires discomfort. Sometimes the discomfort is mild, like an uphill bike ride or swallowing your ego to listen more attentively. Other times, it's far more painful, like lactic-threshold training or the emotional equivalent of having a bone reset. None of these stressors are lethal, and it's the rare person who pursues them. The benefits or lack thereof depend on how you talk to yourself.

Hence, "LOVE THE PAIN."

Earlier in this book, Brian Koppelman mentioned that he considers Haruki Murakami the world's best writer of fiction. To boot, Murakami is an excellent long-distance runner. Here is what Murakami has to say about running, which can be applied to anything:

> Pain is inevitable. Suffering is optional. Say you're running
> and you think, "Man, this hurts, I can't take it anymore." The
> "hurt" part is an unavoidable reality, but whether or not you
> can stand anymore is up to the runner himself.

If you want to have more, do more, and be more, it all begins with the voice that no one else hears.

FORKING PATHS UPON FORKING PATHS

Several weeks ago, I came across this poem by Portia Nelson:

Autobiography in Five Short Chapters

Chapter One
    I walk down the street.
        There is a deep hole in the sidewalk.
    I fall in.
    I am lost . . . I am helpless.
        It isn't my fault.
    It takes forever to find a way out.

Chapter Two
    I walk down the same street.
        There is a deep hole in the sidewalk.
    I pretend I don't see it.
    I fall in again.
    I can't believe I am in this same place.
        But it isn't my fault.
    It still takes a long time to get out.

Chapter Three
    I walk down the same street.
        There is a deep hole in the sidewalk.
    I see it is there.
    I still fall in . . . it's a habit . . . but,
        my eyes are open.
        I know where I am.
    It is my fault.
    I get out immediately.

Chapter Four
I walk down the same street.
There is a deep hole in the sidewalk.
I walk around it.

Chapter Five
I walk down another street.

To feel more at peace and more successful, you don't need genius-level brain power, access to some secret society, or to hit a moving target of "just" an additional X dollars. Those are all distractions.

Based on everything I've seen, a simple recipe can work: focus on what's in front of you, design great days to create a great life, and try not to make the same mistake twice. That's it. Stop hitting net balls and try something else, perhaps even the opposite. If you *really* want extra credit, try not to be a dick, and you'll be a Voltron-level superstar.

The secret to winning any game lies in not trying too hard.

Feeling as though you are *trying* too hard indicates that your priorities, technique, focus, or mindfulness is off. Take it as a cue to reset, not to double down. And take comfort in the fact that, whenever in doubt, the answer is probably hidden in plain sight.

What would this look like if it were easy?

In a world where nobody really knows anything, you have the incredible freedom to continually reinvent yourself and forge new paths, no matter how strange. Embrace your weird self.

There is no one right answer . . . only better questions.

Take it easy, ya azizi,
Tim

Breathe . . .

RECOMMENDED RESOURCES

The following resources are all free and complement lessons in this book. Many of them provide jumping-off points to tools I now use on a daily or weekly basis.

Links to all "most gifted" and "most recommended" books in
Tribe of Mentors — tim.blog/booklist

Links to all the "best under $100 purchase" answers from *Tribe of Mentors* — tim.blog/under100

5-Bullet Friday — tim.blog/friday
5-Bullet Friday is one of the most popular newsletters in the world. I met roughly 30 percent of the people in this book because they subscribe to 5-Bullet Friday. It's a short email I send out each Friday that lists five cool things I've discovered or enjoyed that week, including gadgets, articles, startups, books, experimental supplements, new hacks or tricks, and all sorts of weird stuff. The content is not published anywhere else.

The Tao of Seneca — tim.blog/seneca
The Tao of Seneca is an introduction to Stoic philosophy through the words of Seneca, complete with illustrations, profiles of modern Stoic figures, interviews, and much more. If you were to ask me what my "most gifted" book is, it would be this.

I've read Seneca's letters hundreds of times and recommended them thousands more.

Stoicism is a no-nonsense philosophical system designed to produce real-world results. Think of it as an operating system for thriving in high-stress environments. Thomas Jefferson kept Seneca's writing on his bedside table. George Washington, thought leaders in Silicon Valley, and NFL coaches and players alike (e.g., Patriots, Seahawks) have embraced Stoicism because it makes them better competitors. *The Tao of Seneca* covers all of the fundamentals.

TED Talk on "Fear-Setting" — tim.blog/ted

In this talk (3M+ views) I describe the most important exercise that I do at least once a month. My best investment and business decisions can be traced to "fear-setting," but it's even more valuable for avoiding self-destruction.

Experiments in Lifestyle Design Blog — tim.blog

This blog is what put me on the map before the podcast and other shenanigans. It features experts, experiments, and real-world case studies of all types, including fat loss, investing, language learning, psychedelics, and much more. My top-10 most popular (and recommended) posts can be found at tim.blog/top10

The Solution to The Riddle — tim.blog/spin

Thank me later.

THE TOP 25 EPISODES OF
THE TIM FERRISS SHOW

The Tim Ferriss Show is the first business-interview podcast to pass 200 million downloads, and it has been selected for "Best of iTunes" by Apple three years running.

My top-25 most popular episodes, as of September 1, 2017, are listed on the following page.

But *achtung*! I didn't rank episodes in descending order of total downloads. Due to rapid growth, there would be a misleading recency bias—in other words, a newer *decent* episode could be "more popular" than an older *blockbuster* episode that was 3x the average at the time. To correct for this, we used a better methodology, and I owe special thanks to my brother for the help.*

All 250+ episodes to date can be found at tim.blog/podcast and itunes.com/timferriss

---

* Explanation from my statistician brother: "I first modeled the growth of the podcast over time. I used a linear regression model after a logarithmic transformation. (A logarithmic transform, which implies that the downloads have been growing exponentially, was the near optimal box-cox transformation.) I calculated the standard error at each point using the 95 percent prediction bands. For each podcast episode, I then calculated the residual (the difference between the observed downloads and the regression line) and then standardized this difference by the standard error. I then ranked episodes according to this metric, by how many standard deviations they exceeded the mean trend line."

1. Jamie Foxx on Workout Routines, Success Habits, and Untold Hollywood Stories (#124)—tim.blog/jamie

2. The Scariest Navy SEAL I've Ever Met . . . and What He Taught Me (#107)—tim.blog/jocko

3. Arnold Schwarzenegger on Psychological Warfare (and Much More) (#60)—tim.blog/arnold

4. Dom D'Agostino on Fasting, Ketosis, and the End of Cancer (#117)—tim.blog/dom2

5. Tony Robbins on Morning Routines, Peak Performance, and Mastering Money (#37)—tim.blog/tony

6. How to Design a Life—Debbie Millman (#214)—tim.blog/debbie

7. Tony Robbins—On Achievement Versus Fulfillment (#178)—tim.blog/tony2

8. Kevin Rose (#1)—tim.blog/kevinrose [If you want to hear how bad a first episode can be, this delivers. Drunkenness didn't help matters.]

9. Charles Poliquin on Strength Training, Shredding Body Fat, and Increasing Testosterone and Sex Drive (#91)—tim.blog/charles

10. Mr. Money Mustache—Living Beautifully on $25–27K Per Year (#221)—tim.blog/mustache

11. Lessons from Warren Buffett, Bobby Fischer, and Other Outliers (#219)—tim.blog/buffett

12. Exploring Smart Drugs, Fasting, and Fat Loss—Dr. Rhonda Patrick (#237)—tim.blog/rhonda

13. 5 Morning Rituals That Help Me Win the Day (#105)—tim.blog/rituals

14. David Heinemeier Hansson: The Power of Being Outspoken (#195)—tim.blog/dhh

EXTENDED CONVERSATIONS

I've recorded extended interviews with many of the people in this book.

These wide-ranging conversations cover everything from their morning routines to the best advice they've ever received. In most cases, there is almost *zero* overlap with what's in this book, so it's all extra tools, tactics, and habits that you can use.

I hope you enjoy them as much as I did! All are free.

In alphabetical order by first name, here they are:

Adam Robinson—tim.blog/robinson

Amelia Boone—tim.blog/amelia

Brené Brown—tim.blog/brene

Brian Koppelman—tim.blog/koppelman

Caroline Paul—tim.blog/caroline

Darren Aronofsky—tim.blog/darren

Debbie Millman—tim.blog/debbie

Eric Ripert—tim.blog/eric

Esther Perel—tim.blog/esther

Kevin Kelly—tim.blog/kevin

Kyle Maynard—tim.blog/kyle

Jerzy Gregorek—tim.blog/jerzy

Jocko Willink—tim.blog/jocko

Josh Waitzkin—tim.blog/josh

Larry King—tim.blog/larry

Maria Sharapova—tim.blog/sharapova

Mark Bell—tim.blog/markbell

Michael Gervais—tim.blog/gervais

Mr. Money Mustache—tim.blog/mustache

Naval Ravikant—tim.blog/naval

Neil Strauss—tim.blog/strauss

Nick Szabo—tim.blog/crypto

Peter Attia—tim.blog/attia

Ray Dalio—tim.blog/dalio

Rick Rubin—tim.blog/rubin

Robert Rodriguez—tim.blog/robert

Sam Harris—tim.blog/harris

Soman Chainani—tim.blog/soman

Stewart Brand—tim.blog/stewart

Terry Laughlin—tim.blog/terry (points to a TV show we did together)

Tim O'Reilly—tim.blog/oreilly

Whitney Cummings—tim.blog/whitney

MENTOR INDEX

QUESTION INDEX

What is the book (or books) you've given most as a gift, and why? Or what are one to three books that have greatly influenced your life?

482; Rick Rubin, 487; Ryan Shea, 492; Ben Silbermann, 497; Vlad Zamfir, 501; Zooko Wilcox, 506; Stephanie McMahon, 511; Peter Attia, 515; Steve Aoki, 522; Jim Loehr, 527; Daniel Negreanu, 533; Jocko Willink, 537; Kristen Ulmer, 549; Yuval Noah Harari, 555

What purchase of $100 or less has most positively impacted your life in the last six months (or in recent memory)?

Samin Nosrat, 1; Steven Pressfield, 7; Debbie Millman, 25; Matt Ridley, 36; Tim Urban, 42; Graham Duncan, 59; Soman Chainani, 72; Dita Von Teese, 77; Dustin Moscovitz, 83; Richa Chadha, 86; Neil Strauss, 97; Veronica Belmont, 101; Patton Oswalt, 105; Jerzy Gregorek, 114; Aniela Gregorek, 124; Amelia Boone, 128; Joel McHale, 133; Ben Stiller, 137; Andrew Ross Sorkin, 145; Vitalik Buterin, 154; Rabbi Lord Jonathan Sacks, 158; Turia Pitt, 168; Adam Robinson, 190; Josh Waitzkin, 196; Arianna Huffington, 213; Gary Vaynerchuk, 215; Tom Peters, 227; Brené Brown, 233; Leo Babauta, 236; Kevin Kelly, 248; Jérôme Jarre, 258; Fedor Holz, 266; Eric Ripert, 269; Liv Boeree, 301; Anníe Mist Þórisdóttir, 306; Mark Bell, 311; Ed Coan, 319; Ray Dalio, 322; Brian Koppelman, 330; Sarah Elizabeth Lewis, 337; Gabor Maté, 341; Sam Harris, 366; David Lynch, 380; Nick Szabo, 383; Jon Call, 386; Dara Torres, 391; Dan Gable, 393; Darren Aronofsky, 399; Neil Gaiman, 411; Michael Gervais, 413; Mathew Fraser, 426; Laura Walker, 438; Marc Benioff, 447; Steven Pinker, 476; Whitney Cummings, 483; Rick Rubin, 488; Ben Silbermann, 498; Vlad Zamfir, 504; Stephanie McMahon, 509; Steve Aoki, 520; Jim Loehr, 527; Kristen Ulmer, 547

How has a failure, or apparent failure, set you up for later success? Do you have a "favorite failure" of yours?

Samin Nosrat, 2; Steven Pressfield, 8; Susan Cain, 11; Kyle Maynard, 15; Terry Crews, 20; Debbie Millman, 25; Naval Ravikant, 32; Tim Urban, 43; Janna Levin, 51; Graham Duncan, 59; Mike Maples Jr., 65; Soman Chainani, 71; Dita Von Teese, 76; Richa Chadha, 86; Neil Strauss, 97; Veronica Belmont, 102; Patton Oswalt, 105; Lewis Cantley, 108; Jerzy Gregorek, 115; Aniela Gregorek, 122; Ben Stiller, 137; Anna Holmes, 142; Joseph Gordon-Levitt, 148; Rabbi Lord Jonathan Sacks, 158; Turia Pitt, 168; Annie Duke, 173; Maria Sharapova, 183; Josh Waitzkin, 196; Ann Miura-Ko, 200; Jason Fried, 204; Arianna

Huffington, 212; Gary Vaynerchuk, 215; Bear Grylls, 230; Brené Brown, 234; Leo Babauta, 237; Mike D, 240; Esther Dyson, 244; Ashton Kutcher, 251; Brandon Stanton, 255; Jérôme Jarre, 258; Fedor Holz, 266; Eric Ripert, 269; Sharon Salzberg, 272; Franklin Leonard, 277; Peter Guber, 281; Daniel Ek, 288; Strauss Zelnick, 290; Tony Hawk, 298; Anníe Mist Þórisdóttir, 306; Mark Bell, 311; Ray Dalio, 322; Jacqueline Novogratz, 325; Brian Koppelman, 330; Sarah Elizabeth Lewis, 337; Gabor Maté, 342; Linda Rottenberg, 350; Tommy Vietor, 354; Maurice Ashley, 369; David Lynch, 380; Nick Szabo, 384; Jon Call, 386; Darren Aronofsky, 399; Evan Williams, 402; Bram Cohen, 404; Michael Gervais, 413; Temple Grandin, 416; Kelly Slater, 420; Katrín Tanja Davíðsdóttir, 423; Mathew Fraser, 426; Adam Fisher, 429; Aisha Tyler, 432; Terry Laughlin, 442; Marc Benioff, 447; Craig Newmark, 473; Rick Rubin, 488; Ben Silbermann, 496; Vlad Zamfir, 502; Zooko Wilcox, 507; Steve Aoki, 521; Jim Loehr, 527; Daniel Negreanu, 533; Jocko Willink, 537; Kristen Ulmer, 547; Yuval Noah Harari, 556

If you could have a gigantic billboard anywhere with anything on it, what would it say?

Steven Pressfield, 8; Kyle Maynard, 15; Terry Crews, 21; Debbie Millman, 26; Naval Ravikant, 32; Bozoma Saint John, 38; Tim Urban, 44; Ayaan Hirsi Ali, 54; Graham Duncan, 57; Mike Maples Jr., 65; Soman Chainani, 72; Dita Von Teese, 75; Richa Chadha, 87; Max Levchin, 93; Neil Strauss, 98; Veronica Belmont, 102; Patton Oswalt, 105; Lewis Cantley, 110; Jerzy Gregorek, 116; Aniela Gregorek, 123; Amelia Boone, 128; Ben Stiller, 138; Anna Holmes, 142; Andrew Ross Sorkin, 145; Joseph Gordon-Levitt, 149; Rabbi Lord Jonathan Sacks, 160; Maria Sharapova, 183; Josh Waitzkin, 197; Jason Fried, 204; Arianna Huffington, 214; Tim O'Reilly, 221; Bear Grylls, 230; Brené Brown, 233; Leo Babauta, 237; Esther Dyson, 244; Ashton Kutcher, 251; Jérôme Jarre, 258; Fedor Holz, 266; Eric Ripert, 270; Sharon Salzberg, 273; Peter Guber, 281; Greg Norman, 284; Strauss Zelnick, 289; Steve Jurvetson, 296; Tony Hawk, 299; Liv Boeree, 302; Anníe Mist Þórisdóttir;, 306; Mark Bell, 310; Ed Coan, 318; Ray Dalio, 322; Jacqueline Novogratz, 326; Sarah Elizabeth Lewis, 338; Gabor Maté, 343; Linda Rottenberg, 350; Tommy Vietor, 355; Muna AbuSulayman, 363; Sam Harris, 366; Maurice Ashley, 370; David

Lynch, 381; Nick Szabo, 383; Jon Call, 386; Dara Torres, 391; Dan Gable, 393; Bram Cohen, 405; Chris Anderson, 408; Michael Gervais, 414; Aisha Tyler, 432; Marc Benioff, 449; Marie Forleo, 452; Scott Belsky, 459; Tim McGraw, 466; Craig Newmark, 473; Steven Pinker, 476; Whitney Cummings, 483; Rick Rubin, 489; Ryan Shea, 493; Vlad Zamfir, 502; Stephanie McMahon, 510; Peter Attia, 515; Steve Aoki, 520; Jim Loehr, 528; Daniel Negreanu, 533; Jocko Willink, 538; Robert Rodriguez, 543

What is one of the best or most worthwhile investments you've ever made?

Samin Nosrat, 3; Steven Pressfield, 8; Susan Cain, 11; Debbie Millman, 26; Naval Ravikant, 33; Tim Urban, 44; Janna Levin, 51; Graham Duncan, 60; Mike Maples Jr., 65; Soman Chainani, 73; Richa Chadha, 87; Neil Strauss, 98; Patton Oswalt, 105; Lewis Cantley, 109; Jerzy Gregorek, 116; Aniela Gregorek, 124; Amelia Boone, 128; Joseph Gordon-Levitt, 149; Rabbi Lord Jonathan Sacks, 160; Esther Perel, 180; Adam Robinson, 188; Jason Fried, 207; Arianna Huffington, 212; Tom Peters, 227; Brené Brown, 233; Kevin Kelly, 249; Jérôme Jarre, 259; Fedor Holz, 266; Eric Ripert, 270; Greg Norman, 284; Strauss Zelnick, 291; Liv Boeree, 301; Mark Bell, 311; Ray Dalio, 322; Sarah Elizabeth Lewis, 338; Gabor Maté, 343; Tommy Vietor, 354; Muna AbuSulayman, 364; David Lynch, 381; Nick Szabo, 384; Caroline Paul, 396; Michael Gervais, 414; Kelly Slater, 420; Katrín Tanja Davíðsdóttir, 423; Adam Fisher, 430; Aisha Tyler, 433; Marc Benioff, 450; Marie Forleo, 452; Muneeb Ali, 468; Gretchen Rubin, 480; Whitney Cummings, 483; Rick Rubin, 489; Ryan Shea, 493; Ben Silbermann, 497; Vlad Zamfir, 504; Stephanie McMahon, 511; Peter Attia, 516; Daniel Negreanu, 533; Jocko Willink, 538; Kristen Ulmer, 548; Yuval Noah Harari, 558

What is an unusual habit or an absurd thing that you love?

Samin Nosrat, 3; Steven Pressfield, 8; Susan Cain, 12; Kyle Maynard, 16; Debbie Millman, 28; Bozoma Saint John, 38; Tim Urban, 45; Graham Duncan, 57; Soman Chainani, 73; Dita Von Teese, 78; Richa Chadha, 87; Max Levchin, 94; Neil Strauss, 99; Veronica Belmont, 101; Patton Oswalt, 106; Lewis Cantley, 109; Jerzy Gregorek, 117; Aniela Gregorek, 125; Amelia Boone, 128; Ben Stiller, 136; Anna Holmes, 143; Joseph Gordon-Levitt, 149; Vitalik Buterin, 154; Rabbi

Lord Jonathan Sacks, 160; Maria Sharapova, 183; Adam Robinson, 193; Josh Waitzkin, 197; Ann Miura-Ko, 201; Tim O'Reilly, 222; Tom Peters, 227; Leo Babauta, 237; Esther Dyson, 244; Jérôme Jarre, 260; Fedor Holz, 267; Eric Ripert, 270; Franklin Leonard, 277; Greg Norman, 284; Steve Jurvetson, 296; Tony Hawk, 299; Liv Boeree, 302; Anníe Mist Þórisdóttir, 307; Mark Bell, 311; Ed Coan, 319; Ray Dalio, 322; Brian Koppelman, 330; Sarah Elizabeth Lewis, 338; Gabor Maté, 343; Linda Rottenberg, 351; Larry King, 361; Muna AbuSulayman, 363; Mr. Money Mustache, 377; David Lynch, 381; Nick Szabo, 384; Jon Call, 387; Dara Torres, 391; Dan Gable, 393; Caroline Paul, 397; Bram Cohen, 405; Aisha Tyler, 433; Marc Benioff, 449; Marie Forleo, 452; Scott Belsky, 460; Tim McGraw, 466; Craig Newmark, 474; Gretchen Rubin, 481; Whitney Cummings, 484; Rick Rubin, 490; Ben Silbermann, 495; Vlad Zamfir, 502; Stephanie McMahon, 511; Peter Attia, 516; Yuval Noah Harari, 556

In the last five years, what new belief, behavior, or habit has most improved your life?

Samin Nosrat, 3; Steven Pressfield, 8; Debbie Millman, 28; Naval Ravikant, 33; Matt Ridley, 36; Tim Urban, 45; Janna Levin, 52; Graham Duncan, 61; Mike Maples Jr., 66; Soman Chainani, 72; Dita Von Teese, 78; Jesse Williams, 80; Richa Chadha, 88; Max Levchin, 94; Neil Strauss, 98; Patton Oswalt, 106; Lewis Cantley, 110; Aniela Gregorek, 126; Amelia Boone, 130; Ben Stiller, 138; Anna Holmes, 143; Joseph Gordon-Levitt, 149; Vitalik Buterin, 154; Rabbi Lord Jonathan Sacks, 161; Julia Galef, 164; Turia Pitt, 169; Jimmy Fallon, 177; Adam Robinson, 187; Josh Waitzkin, 197; Jason Fried, 207; Arianna Huffington, 213; Gary Vaynerchuk, 217; Tim O'Reilly, 222; Bear Grylls, 231; Brené Brown, 233; Leo Babauta, 237; Mike D, 241; Esther Dyson, 245; Kevin Kelly, 249; Ashton Kutcher, 252; Brandon Stanton, 255; Jérôme Jarre, 261; Fedor Holz, 267; Eric Ripert, 270; Franklin Leonard, 278; Greg Norman, 285; Daniel Ek, 287; Strauss Zelnick, 290; Steve Jurvetson, 295; Tony Hawk, 299; Liv Boeree, 303; Anníe Mist Þórisdóttir, 307; Ed Coan, 319; Ray Dalio, 322; Stewart Brand, 333; Gabor Maté, 343; Sam Harris, 366; Maurice Ashley, 370; Mr. Money Mustache, 377; David Lynch, 381; Jon Call, 387; Caroline Paul, 397; Evan Williams, 402; Bram Cohen, 406; Chris Anderson, 408; Neil Gaiman, 411;

Katrín Tanja Davíðsdóttir, 424; Mathew Fraser, 426; Adam Fisher, 430; Aisha Tyler, 434; Marc Benioff, 448; Marie Forleo, 453; Drew Houston, 456; Tim McGraw, 465; Muneeb Ali, 469; Steven Pinker, 477; Gretchen Rubin, 480; Whitney Cummings, 484; Ben Silbermann, 499; Vlad Zamfir, 503; Zooko Wilcox, 508; Stephanie McMahon, 511; Peter Attia, 515; Steve Aoki, 523; Jim Loehr, 529; Daniel Negreanu, 534; Jocko Willink, 538; Robert Rodriguez, 542; Kristen Ulmer, 552

What advice would you give to a smart, driven college student about to enter the "real world"? What advice should they ignore?

Samin Nosrat, 4; Steven Pressfield, 6; Susan Cain, 12; Kyle Maynard, 16; Terry Crews, 22; Debbie Millman, 28; Naval Ravikant, 33; Matt Ridley, 36; Tim Urban, 46; Ayaan Hirsi Ali, 54; Graham Duncan, 62; Mike Maples Jr., 66; Soman Chainani, 73; Richa Chadha, 88; Max Levchin, 95; Veronica Belmont, 103; Patton Oswalt, 106; Lewis Cantley, 110; Jerzy Gregorek, 118; Amelia Boone, 130; Joel McHale, 133; Anna Holmes, 142; Andrew Ross Sorkin, 146; Joseph Gordon-Levitt, 149; Annie Duke, 172; Esther Perel, 180; Maria Sharapova, 184; Josh Waitzkin, 197; Ann Miura-Ko, 202; Jason Fried, 208; Arianna Huffington, 213; Gary Vaynerchuk, 216; Tim O'Reilly, 223; Tom Peters, 227; Leo Babauta, 238; Esther Dyson, 245; Kevin Kelly, 249; Ashton Kutcher, 252; Jérôme Jarre, 261; Franklin Leonard, 279; Peter Guber, 282; Strauss Zelnick, 291; Tony Hawk, 299; Mark Bell, 312; Ray Dalio, 323; Jacqueline Novogratz, 326; Stewart Brand, 334; Gabor Maté, 343; Steve Case, 346; Linda Rottenberg, 351; Tommy Vietor, 355; Sam Harris, 367; John Arnold, 374; Mr. Money Mustache, 377; David Lynch, 381; Nick Szabo, 383; Dara Torres, 391; Dan Gable, 394; Darren Aronofsky, 399; Evan Williams, 402; Bram Cohen, 406; Chris Anderson, 409; Kelly Slater, 420; Adam Fisher, 429; Laura Walker, 439; Terry Laughlin, 444; Marie Forleo, 453; Drew Houston, 457; Scott Belsky, 461; Steven Pinker, 476; Whitney Cummings, 484; Rick Rubin, 490; Peter Attia, 516; Jocko Willink, 538; Yuval Noah Harari, 557

What are bad recommendations you hear in your profession or area of expertise?

Steven Pressfield, 9; Kyle Maynard, 17; Terry Crews, 22; Debbie Millman, 29; Naval Ravikant, 34; Tim Urban, 47; Graham Duncan,

60; Mike Maples Jr., 66; Soman Chainani, 73; Richa Chadha, 88; Veronica Belmont, 103; Patton Oswalt, 106; Lewis Cantley, 111; Jerzy Gregorek, 119; Amelia Boone, 130; Ben Stiller, 139; Vitalik Buterin, 155; Rabbi Lord Jonathan Sacks, 162; Julia Galef, 164; Adam Robinson, 190; Josh Waitzkin, 197; Jason Fried, 208; Tim O'Reilly, 222; Tom Peters, 228; Brandon Stanton, 255; Jérôme Jarre, 262; Fedor Holz, 267; Eric Ripert, 271; Franklin Leonard, 278; Greg Norman, 285; Daniel Ek, 288; Liv Boeree, 303; Mark Bell, 312; Ed Coan, 320; Ray Dalio, 323; Jacqueline Novogratz, 327; Brian Koppelman, 331; Gabor Maté, 344; Steve Case, 347; David Lynch, 381; Nick Szabo, 383; Jon Call, 388; Darren Aronofsky, 400; Michael Gervais, 415; Mathew Fraser, 426; Adam Fisher, 430; Marie Forleo, 453; Scott Belsky, 461; Whitney Cummings, 484; Rick Rubin, 491; Ben Silbermann, 498; Peter Attia, 518; Jim Loehr, 530; Daniel Negreanu, 534; Kristen Ulmer, 550

In the last five years, what have you become better at saying no to?

Samin Nosrat, 4; Steven Pressfield, 8; Kyle Maynard, 17; Terry Crews, 23; Naval Ravikant, 34; Tim Urban, 48; Janna Levin, 52; Graham Duncan, 61; Soman Chainani, 74; Mike Maples Jr., 76; Dustin Moscovitz, 83; Richa Chadha, 89; Neil Strauss, 98; Veronica Belmont, 102; Patton Oswalt, 106; Jerzy Gregorek, 119; Aniela Gregorek, 124; Anna Holmes, 143; Rabbi Lord Jonathan Sacks, 161; Julia Galef, 165; Annie Duke, 173; Josh Waitzkin, 198; Jason Fried, 209; Gary Vaynerchuk, 217; Tim O'Reilly, 222; Esther Dyson, 245; Kevin Kelly, 249; Jérôme Jarre, 263; Eric Ripert, 271; Sharon Salzberg, 274; Liv Boeree, 303; Sarah Elizabeth Lewis, 339; Gabor Maté, 344; Sam Harris, 367; John Arnold, 374; David Lynch, 381; Jon Call, 388; Bram Cohen, 405; Michael Gervais, 415; Adam Fisher, 430; Aisha Tyler, 434; Laura Walker, 438; Terry Laughlin, 443; Drew Houston, 457; Muneeb Ali, 469; Steven Pinker, 478; Whitney Cummings, 485; Rick Rubin, 491; Ben Silbermann, 498; Zooko Wilcox, 508; Stephanie McMahon, 512; Peter Attia, 518; Daniel Negreanu, 534; Kristen Ulmer, 550; Yuval Noah Harari, 558

When you feel overwhelmed or unfocused, what do you do?

Samin Nosrat, 4; Steven Pressfield, 9; Susan Cain, 13; Debbie Millman, 30; Naval Ravikant, 34; Bozoma Saint John, 38; Graham

Duncan, 61; Soman Chainani, 74; Mike Maples Jr., 76; Jesse Williams, 81; Richa Chadha, 89; Neil Strauss, 99; Veronica Belmont, 103; Patton Oswalt, 106; Lewis Cantley, 111; Jerzy Gregorek, 120; Aniela Gregorek, 125; Amelia Boone, 130; Anna Holmes, 144; Andrew Ross Sorkin, 146; Joseph Gordon-Levitt, 150; Vitalik Buterin, 155; Rabbi Lord Jonathan Sacks, 162; Julia Galef, 165; Esther Perel, 181; Maria Sharapova, 184; Adam Robinson, 192; Josh Waitzkin, 198; Jason Fried, 209; Arianna Huffington, 214; Gary Vaynerchuk, 218; Tom Peters, 228; Bear Grylls, 231; Brené Brown, 233; Leo Babauta, 238; Mike D, 242; Esther Dyson, 245; Ashton Kutcher, 252; Jérôme Jarre, 264; Fedor Holz, 267; Eric Ripert, 270; Sharon Salzberg, 274; Franklin Leonard, 277; Greg Norman, 285; Strauss Zelnick, 291; Liv Boeree, 304; Anníe Mist Þórisdóttir, 307; Ed Coan, 318; Ray Dalio, 323; Jacqueline Novogratz, 327; Sarah Elizabeth Lewis, 339; Gabor Maté, 344; Linda Rottenberg, 351; Tommy Vietor, 355; Scott Belsky, 362; Muna AbuSulayman, 363; Sam Harris, 367; David Lynch, 381; Nick Szabo, 384; Jon Call, 388; Dara Torres, 391; Darren Aronofsky, 399; Neil Gaiman, 410; Michael Gervais, 415; Temple Grandin, 417; Katrín Tanja Davíðsdóttir, 424; Mathew Fraser, 427; Adam Fisher, 430; Aisha Tyler, 435; Laura Walker, 438; Marie Forleo, 454; Tim McGraw, 465; Steven Pinker, 478; Whitney Cummings, 485; Rick Rubin, 491; Ryan Shea, 493; Ben Silbermann, 499; Vlad Zamfir, 505; Steve Aoki, 524; Jim Loehr, 531; Daniel Negreanu, 535; Jocko Willink, 539; Robert Rodriguez, 545; Kristen Ulmer, 551; Yuval Noah Harari, 560

CREATE-YOUR-OWN INDEX

As an obsessive note-taker, I wanted to put together what I wish more books had: pages dedicated to synthesizing lessons and ideas.

Here, I invite you to jot down your favorite insights, quotes, or next steps, along with the relevant profiles and page numbers. By creating this index, you can refer to your favorite parts at a moment's notice.

For example, if you love Brené Brown's quote "Courage over comfort," you can add it to your index and, ideally, include a next step:

"Courage over comfort." Brené Brown, p. 232. Next step: On Tuesday, at 1 PM, try [INSERT SMALL NEXT STEP]?

Different things resonate with different people, of course. I'd love to know what you're taking away from this book! If you'd care to share, take a pic and share with me on Instagram (@timferriss) or Twitter (@tferriss). I see and reply to quite a bit. See you on the Interwebs.

Happy note-taking!
Tim

ACKNOWLEDGMENTS

First, I must thank the mentors whose advice, stories, and lessons are the essence of this book. Thank you for your time and generosity of spirit. May the good you share with the world be returned to you a hundredfold.

To Stephen Hanselman, my agent and friend, thank you. Here's to celebrating the little wins along the way. More margaritas soon.

To the entire team at Houghton Mifflin Harcourt, especially the superhuman Stephanie Fletcher and the amazing design and production team: Rebecca Springer, Katie Kimmerer, Marina Padakis Lowry, Jamie Selzer, Rachael DeShano, Beth Fuller, Jacqueline Hatch, Chloe Foster, Margaret Rosewitz, Kelly Dubeau Smydra, Chris Granniss, Jill Lazer, Rachel Newborn, Brian Moore, Melissa Lotfy, and Becky Saikia-Wilson—you helped tame this beast and pull off another miracle. Thank you for burning the midnight oil alongside me! To my publisher Bruce Nichols and his incredible team, including president Ellen Archer, Deb Brody, Lori Glazer, Debbie Engel, and all members of the dedicated marketing and sales team, thank you for believing in this book and moving mountains. It's going to help a whole lot of people.

To Donna and Adam, thank you for holding down the fort! The podcast wouldn't exist, and I wouldn't be able to do any of the rest, without you. You guys rock.

To Hristo, many thanks for the double-checking of details (spatulas!) and endless research. Would you like more Mediterranean wraps? To throw more tomato sauce on artwork? Round three next summer? By the way, I still don't understand why you like working in the dark . . .

To Amelia, you are the warrior princess of redlining. Words cannot express how much your help and support mean to me. Thank you, thank you, thank you. Just remember your bracelet, and payment in nut butters (#messybaby!) and mobility tools is in process.

Last but not least, this book is dedicated to my family, who have guided, encouraged, loved, and consoled me through it all. I love you more than words can express.